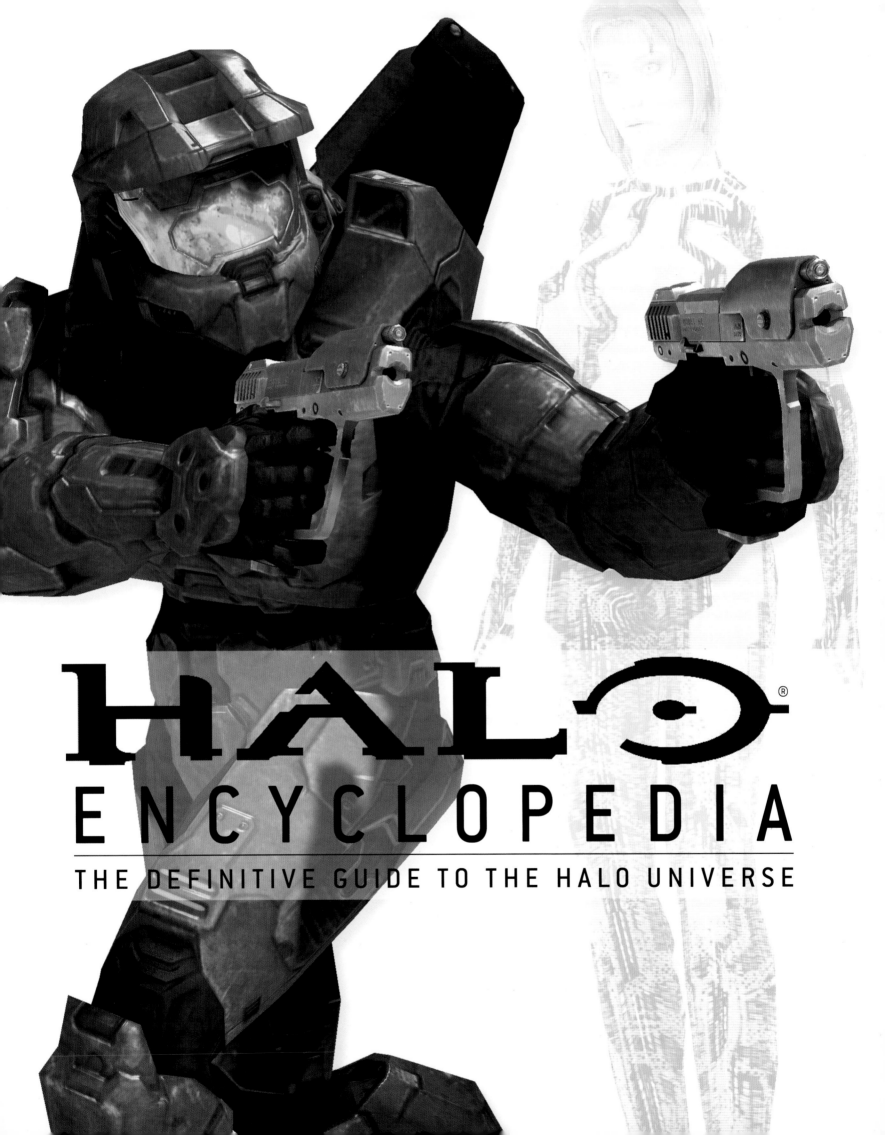

HALO®
ENCYCLOPEDIA

THE DEFINITIVE GUIDE TO THE HALO UNIVERSE

HALO®
ENCYCLOPEDIA
THE DEFINITIVE GUIDE TO THE HALO UNIVERSE

EDITORIAL CONSULTANT TOBIAS BUCKELL

CONTENTS

"DEAR HUMANITY...WE REGRET BEING ALIEN BASTARDS. WE REGRET COMING TO EARTH. AND WE MOST DEFINITELY REGRET THAT THE CORPS JUST BLEW UP OUR RAGGEDY-ASS FLEET."
— SGT. MAJOR AVERY J. JOHNSON

FOREWORD

BY FRANK O'CONNOR

I CAN STILL REMEMBER THE FIRST TIME I REALLY EXPERIENCED HALO. AND I THINK IT MIGHT BE A COMMON EXPERIENCE.

IT WASN'T THE battle through the chaos on the burning *Pillar of Autumn*, or the claustrophobic creeping through the service ducts, trying to make it to the lifeboats. No. It was stepping out of the crashed escape pod and into a world that would consume my professional and creative life for the next decade.

Through the visor of a MJOLNIR Mark V powered combat suit, I looked up into an alien sky, and while the rolling, grassy hills and thundering waterfall beyond felt *familiar*, the curving horizon, winnowing its way into the structure of the Halo itself was something truly incredible. I looked at the distant bracelet of the structure I stood on and knew I could go there.

I also knew that someone or something had built this dizzying, impossible structure and that I was literally standing on the precipice of a mystery. What I didn't realize then, as I reloaded my assault rifle and tried to fend off a Banshee sortie, was that one day I'd have the incredible honor of helping to solve and define the details of that mystery.

Bungie and Microsoft Game Studios and now 343 Industries have

built something beautiful and resonant and deep. And here, in these pages, we can explore that depth and learn everything there is to know about the heroes, the weapons, the conflicts, and the legends that define that universe.

Artists, writers, engineers, animators, designers, musicians, producers, and an army of talented individuals defined this place and these eras. They did it so seamlessly and with such passion that they breathed life into it. They made it real.

It's a universe of conflicts and characters and soaring, towering achievement. It's a place where the individual efforts of valiant soldiers can undo the scheming evil of powerful civilizations and ferocious alien intellects. It's a place where honor and justice come

from the most unexpected corners and where nothing is predictable.

It's a place where humanity finds itself dwarfed by challenge and mystery—but also finds itself at the core of that enigma. It's a world and a journey that we're only just beginning to explore, but this very book is the perfect guide.

In the following pages, you'll find a great deal of depth and drama and data—some familiar, some new. It's fiction, of course, but we only ever want it to feel real. Because it's real to us. These are places and times that we want to share with you.

There's danger, of course. It's a dark galaxy, vast and ancient and filled with hazard, but it's also filled with beauty and wonder. Let's shine some light on it. Let's go on a Great Journey.

INTRODUCTION

IT IS THE 26TH CENTURY AND WE ARE AT WAR

It has been six centuries since humans took their first steps into space. Over those long years our species pushed further and further into space, following our instinctive thirst for exploration. Then Slipspace travel was discovered, allowing humans to travel between stars faster than light, and there was an explosion in the colonization of distant worlds. But as on Earth, so in space: Humans were unable to live in peace. Pirates cruised the uncharted regions, and colonists began to agitate for self-government. The United Nations Space Command (UNSC) relied on their advanced weapons and spaceship technology to crush uprisings and protect citizens from space bandits, but it was a fragile peace.

COLONIZATION

With Slipspace travel, humans made use of folds, or ripples, in space to travel at faster-than-light speeds. Very quickly, human colonies started to spread across the Galaxy. Equally quickly, some of them began to demand autonomy from the UNSC. At first, most of the trouble came from the more distant planets, and the UNSC found itself constantly stamping out rebellions. But as soon as it crushed one rebellion, another sprang up somewhere else, hydra-like.

THE SPARTANS

To fight these uprisings, Dr. Catherine Halsey of the Office of Naval Intelligence (ONI) devised a secret project known as the SPARTAN-II Program. She abducted children she had identified as having exceptional genetics. Their bodies were augmented to give them superhuman speed and strength, and they were trained to become lethal fighting machines. These super-soldiers were known as Spartans, and their exploits became the stuff of legend.

THE COVENANT

For a time, none could stand against the supreme strength of the Spartans. But then, from out of the blue, came a devastating blow to humanity. An alliance of alien species called the Covenant came sweeping through space, destroying human life wherever they found it. Technologically advanced and with the single-mindedness of religious zealots, the Covenant allowed no human to survive. Despite fierce resistance, the UNSC and the Spartans in their newly designed MJOLNIR armor were no match for the devastating power of the Covenant and colony after colony was annihilated, including the planet Reach, the heart of UNSC military operations. Only a quarter-century after their first appearance, the Covenant stood poised to overrun Earth itself.

JOHN-117, MASTER CHIEF

There was one glimmer of hope for humanity. The great SPARTAN-II leader John-117, Master Chief, managed to survive the horror on Reach, escaping with a handful of fellow survivors, aboard the UNSC *Pillar of Autumn*.

THE DISCOVERY OF INSTALLATION 04

As the *Pillar of Autumn* sped away from Reach, its commander, Captain Jacob Keyes, took the courageous but risky decision to lure Covenant forces away from the remaining Inner Colonies and Earth. Pursued by the Covenant fleet, he steered the *Pillar of Autumn* on a path that would lead to the discovery of a giant ring-like world that the Covenant called "Halo."

Halo was a gigantic structure built by the long-departed Forerunners. This advanced society had left behind items of technology that were later discovered by the Covenant, who both worshipped them and used them to overpower their enemies. The surface of Halo was eerily Earth-like, with plants, rocks, and oceans, but its interior concealed mile upon mile of metallic catacombs filled with extraordinary secrets of technology.

THE BATTLE OF INSTALLATION 04

The Covenant finally caught up with the *Pillar of Autumn* in orbit around Halo. As Covenant forces streamed aboard, the survivors, including Master Chief, evacuated the ship. They escaped into the deserted Halo, where they prepared themselves for the coming Covenant onslaught.

The fighting was fierce. The Covenant threw all they had at the survivors, from tiny but deadly Grunts to the giant living tanks that are Hunters, and from towering Elites to predatory Jackals. It seemed the Covenant would triumph, but Master Chief had a secret weapon. An experimental network in his MJOLNIR armor enabled an Artificial Intelligence (AI) named Cortana to link directly into Master Chief's brain, vastly increasing his physical and mental capabilities. Cortana had been designed to assist Master Chief during a planned Spartan attack on Covenant space, but she now became his ally in defense. With her help, Master Chief battled through wave after wave of Covenant forces. At last, gaining control of the Halo's network, Master Chief was able to upload Cortana to it.

During the battle, Captain Keyes and some of his soldiers had gone missing in the interior of Halo while investigating a mysterious cache of "weapons" the Covenant had been searching for. Master Chief now set off on a rescue mission to find them.

THE RELEASE OF THE FLOOD

As Master Chief searched for the missing men through the now silent halls and passages of Halo, it became clear that something terrible had happened. Everywhere he turned, he saw dead bodies. Finally he arrived at the point where Keyes had made his last stand, and there he found a recording of the team's final battle. The recording showed that Keyes and his men had not found the weapons cache they were looking for, but instead found that the Covenant had unleashed a parasitic alien race called the Flood. Freed at last after thousands of years of containment, the Flood immediately began infecting any sentient creature within reach, spreading out rapidly across the Halo installation.

THE TRUE PURPOSE OF THE HALO ARRAY

Then 343 Guilty Spark revealed himself. This Forerunner Monitor had been left in order to maintain the Halo when his people departed. Guilty Spark wanted Master Chief to activate the Halo, but did not tell him what its true purpose was until he was forced to by Cortana. The Halo would destroy the Flood, but would do so by depriving it of its food—all sentient life in the Galaxy.

THE DESTRUCTION OF INSTALLATION 04

Master Chief learned the truth about Installation 04 and needed to halt the threat of Guilty Spark. There was now only one way to save the Galaxy—destroy the Halo before activation was complete. Returning to the *Pillar of Autumn*, he overloaded its reactor, causing an explosion that left Halo Installation 04 utterly destroyed. Master Chief and Cortana sped away on a Longsword interceptor they had found while escaping the destruction of the *Pillar of Autumn*. En route to Earth, they picked up Sgt. Avery Johnson and a scant few other survivors of the destruction of Halo Installation 04.

Although the Halo was destroyed, the battle to save humankind was only just beginning. The new threat of the Flood was now out there and the menacing presence of the Covenant had not gone away. In fact, they had become even more aggressive, seeking not only to eliminate humankind but also to punish those of their own kind who had allowed the destruction of the Halo, whom they condemned as heretics.

THE FIRST BATTLE OF EARTH

The Covenant continued to scour the Galaxy in search of Forerunner relics. When one of their expeditionary forces approached Earth, they had no idea of the planet's importance, but as soon as they realized that they had stumbled upon the homeworld of

> "WE DID WHAT WE HAD TO DO! FOR EARTH! AN ENTIRE COVENANT ARMADA OBLITERATED, AND THE FLOOD! WE HAD NO CHOICE. HALO...IT'S FINISHED."
>
> "NO. I THINK WE'RE JUST GETTING STARTED."
> —Cortana and Master Chief

humankind they immediately went on the attack. Led by the High Prophet of Regret, the small Covenant fleet invaded Earth, seizing control of one of its most important cities—the African city of New Mombasa. However, the Covenant's control of the city was brief, and after a fierce battle Regret blasted off through Slipspace, with Master Chief and Miranda Keyes pursuing aboard the UNSC *In Amber Clad*. When they exited Slipspace they found themselves at another Halo—the newly discovered Installation 05. Most of New Mombasa was left in ruins, but Earth was safe for now. The next stage of the fight would take place elsewhere.

COVENANT DOCTRINE UNDER THREAT

Following the first battle of Earth, cracks in the unity of the Covenant began to appear. Some of the Covenant began to suspect that they were not invincible. Worse, seeds of heresy had been sown among the faithful. A few began to openly doubt the High Prophets, who had promised them that the Sacred Rings would bring them to salvation—and the High Prophets knew they had to stamp out these Heretics before their numbers grew. Their agent was to be the Arbiter, a soldier whose duty was to undertake missions so dangerous that they would almost certainly result in his death.

THE BATTLE OF INSTALLATION 05

On Halo Installation 05, Master Chief and Cortana were joined by Sgt. Avery Johnson and Miranda Keyes whose Frigate, *In Amber Clad*, had followed the Covenant fleet. With the help of *In Amber Clad*'s Marines, they were able to trace the Prophet of Regret to a lakebound Forerunner temple deep in the jungles of the Halo. Here, Master Chief killed Regret and his Elite bodyguards. When they saw what had happened, the Covenant blasted the temple with Master Chief inside. Miraculously, the blast did not kill Master Chief, however no sooner had he escaped the Covenant than he was captured by the Gravemind. This parasitic collective consciousness of the Flood had been trapped on Installation 05 for many hundreds of years, and now it sensed an opportunity.

AN UNHOLY ALLIANCE

During his campaign against the Heretics, the Arbiter had witnessed events that made him question whether the Prophets could be trusted. Now, sent to Installation 05, he too was captured by the Gravemind. But when the Gravemind told Master Chief and the Arbiter that the High Prophets intended to activate all the rings and destroy all life in the Galaxy, they formed a desperate alliance in order to stop the Prophets. Master Chief left to fight the Covenant on their capital city High Charity, but once there, Chief realized that the Gravemind had used him and his ship as a way to get off the Halo, stowing away on *In Amber Clad* and infecting its crew and now High Charity with the Flood. Meanwhile, on Installation 05, the Arbiter and Sgt. Johnson killed the Brute Chieftain Tartarus just before he could fire the Halo.

CIVIL WAR AMONG THE COVENANT

When Master Chief arrived on High Charity, he found a city in crisis. The cracks that had begun to appear with the Heretic movement had widened when the Brutes were suddenly elevated to top caste over the Elites, and now the Covenant erupted into all-out war. With the Brutes and the Elites at each others' throats, and now Master Chief and Cortana on the scene, the Gravemind saw its ideal moment to let the Flood loose among all the confusion. The High Prophet of Truth abandoned the High Prophet of Mercy to the Flood and took the Forerunner Dreadnought ship that powered the city to make his escape. He headed for Earth, where he thought he would find an artifact that would provide a link to the Forerunners, unaware that Master Chief was on board, too. Cortana remained on High Charity ready to destroy it (and thereby the Halo) in the event of the Halo being activated, not knowing that the Arbiter had already killed Tartarus. Cortana soon fell victim to the Gravemind, who succeeded in wringing out of her all the information about the Forerunners that she had stored in her memory. The ancient Dreadnought, with the High Prophet of Truth and Master Chief on board, continued its unstoppable approach to Earth.

THE SECOND BATTLE OF EARTH

After being forced to exit the Dreadnought while still in low Earth orbit, Master Chief was met by Sgt. Johnson, the Arbiter, and some Marines. Fighting hordes of Covenant Loyalists, the group tracked Truth to a location outside the ruined city of New Mombasa where he had gone in search of the Forerunner artifact. Master Chief arrived moments too late, just as Truth activated the relic. Master Chief saw an immense Slipspace Portal open up, into which Truth and his forces disappeared. Without hesitation, Master Chief and his team followed. They found themselves on a distant construct called Installation 00, also known as the Ark—an extra-galactic facility from which all the Halo rings could be activated.

THE BATTLE OF INSTALLATION 00

On the Ark, battle raged. Master Chief and his team now fought alongside the Elites, who had turned against the Covenant, and 343 Guilty Spark, who had survived the destruction of his Halo, but despite their newfound allies they faced an epic battle to

> "LAST TIME, YOU ASKED ME, IF IT WAS MY CHOICE, WOULD I DO IT? HAVING HAD CONSIDERABLE TIME TO PONDER YOUR QUERY, MY ANSWER HAS NOT CHANGED. THERE IS NO CHOICE. WE MUST ACTIVATE THE RING."
> —343 Guilty Spark

confront the forces of the Prophet of Truth. Most of them, including Miranda Keyes, lost their lives in the fighting. Truth was on the point of activating the Halo Array when Master Chief and the Arbiter managed to kill him. Their triumph was brief, however, for as soon as the threat of the Halo Array being activated ended, the Gravemind and the Flood resurged. The Gravemind had arrived when the remains of High Charity crashed on the Ark, and now it rapidly infected the survivors of the battle.

REPLACEMENT INSTALLATION 04

As he looked at High Charity lying broken on the surface of the Ark, Master Chief knew his only chance was to enter the remains of that crash and try to find Cortana. He had learned about a new, partially constructed Halo that was being made to replace Installation 04. If he could activate just this one ring, it might be enough to destroy the Flood but not the whole Galaxy. However, the only way to do this was to retrieve the activation codes hidden in Cortana's memory. Plunging into High Charity, he located Cortana and the two set off the activation countdown. Their escape from the Ark was delayed when 343 Guilty Spark reappeared and engaged them in a fierce battle in which Sgt. Johnson was killed. After barely escaping to a waiting UNSC vessel, they were whisked away from the Ark before the Halo fired, destroying it and all those remaining on it, including the Gravemind and the Flood. But their ship did not escape unscathed. The huge explosion caused their Slipspace Portal to collapse, ripping the craft in half. The front part, containing the Arbiter, landed safely on Earth, but the rear section, on which Master Chief and Cortana were traveling, was lost somewhere in space.

THE HUMAN-COVENANT WAR IS OVER

The Covenant factions continue to fight amongst themselves, but for the moment they have given up their mission to obliterate humanity. The remaining Halo installations are still a threat, but not an immediate one, and at last humanity can breathe a sigh of relief and start to rebuild. Master Chief, presumed killed in action, was already a hero and is now a figure of legend. Some wonder who will save them next time trouble flares up—because there are already signs that it will. Trouble within the colonies has begun again, and with the UNSC severely weakened in the wake of the Human-Covenant War, the future of the human planets is anything but certain.

MASTER CHIEF
JOHN-117

THE PINNACLE OF THE SPARTAN PROGRAM, JOHN-117 IS THE MOST CELEBRATED SUPER-SOLDIER IN HISTORY.

A combination of superb genes, technology, and training has made John-117 the epitome of Spartan excellence. Tough, loyal, tireless, intelligent, and a natural leader, he is also blessed with extraordinary good luck. John-117's early victories earned him the rank of Master Chief, and he was more than a match for any enemy...but that was before he encountered the Covenant.

THE COVENANT

MANY SPECIES MAKE UP THE COVENANT, BUT ALL SHARE ONE RELIGION—AND ALL ARE FANATICAL ZEALOTS.

The species that make up the confederation known as the Covenant come from all over the Galaxy and take all kinds of physical forms. Organized into a caste system by their masters, the High Prophets, the different species of the Covenant have many divisions but there is one powerful force that unites them— their blind faith in their worship of the ancient Forerunners. The Covenant believe that their salvation lies in the Holy Rings left by the Forerunners—the Halos. While that faith remains strong, nothing can break the unity of the Covenant. But if anything should shake that faith, the inter-caste and inter-species tensions will surely erupt into Galaxy-wide civil war.

THE FORERUNNERS, THE FLOOD, AND THE HALO ARRAY

AN ANCIENT RACE CALLED THE FORERUNNERS DOMINATED THE GALAXY FOR THOUSANDS OF YEARS.

More than 100,000 years before the start of the Human-Covenant War there was peace in the Galaxy. Under the Forerunners benign rule, civilizations lived in harmony. All benefited from the Forerunners' advanced technology, and conflicts were quickly resolved.

But then the parasitic Flood arrived in the Milky Way, spreading from planet to planet like wildfire. In this desperate state of emergency, the Forerunners made the decision to sacrifice all life in the Galaxy in order to cut off the Flood's food supply. Thus the seven rings of the Halo Array were constructed and fired, after which the Forerunners did what they could to reseed life across the Galaxy and then mysteriously disappeared, leaving no trace of where they had gone or whether they would ever return.

THE ARK
AND THE RESEEDING OF THE GALAXY

THE FORERUNNERS, HONORING THEIR ROLE AS CUSTODIANS, PRESERVED THE SEEDS OF THEIR SUBJECT SPECIES BEFORE FIRING THE HALOS AND WIPING ALL LIFE FROM THE GALAXY.

Mysterious and remote, the Ark occupied a position in space beyond the reach of the Halos. At its heart, this secure installation held a special secret. Samples of all the different species governed over by the Forerunners were safely stored there, ready to repopulate the Galaxy after the threat from the Flood had vanished.

THE GRAVEMIND

THE FLOOD CONSUMES SPECIES AFTER SPECIES, ABSORBING THE MINDS AND BODIES OF ITS VICTIMS INTO A COMBINED INTELLIGENCE THAT HAS TAKEN ON A LIFE OF ITS OWN—THE GRAVEMIND.

The Flood is the ultimate parasite. It is able to use any sentient being as food, and those infected by the Flood stand no chance. Infection is a gradual process, whereby an Infection Form, grown from a tiny spore, bonds the victim to the Flood's central intelligence and slowly consumes the contents of the host creature's mind. When enough sentient creatures are consumed and the Flood biomass reaches a certain critical point, this central intelligence evolves into a physical form. Known as the Gravemind, this tentacled monster has an appearance almost as sinister as its malign purpose.

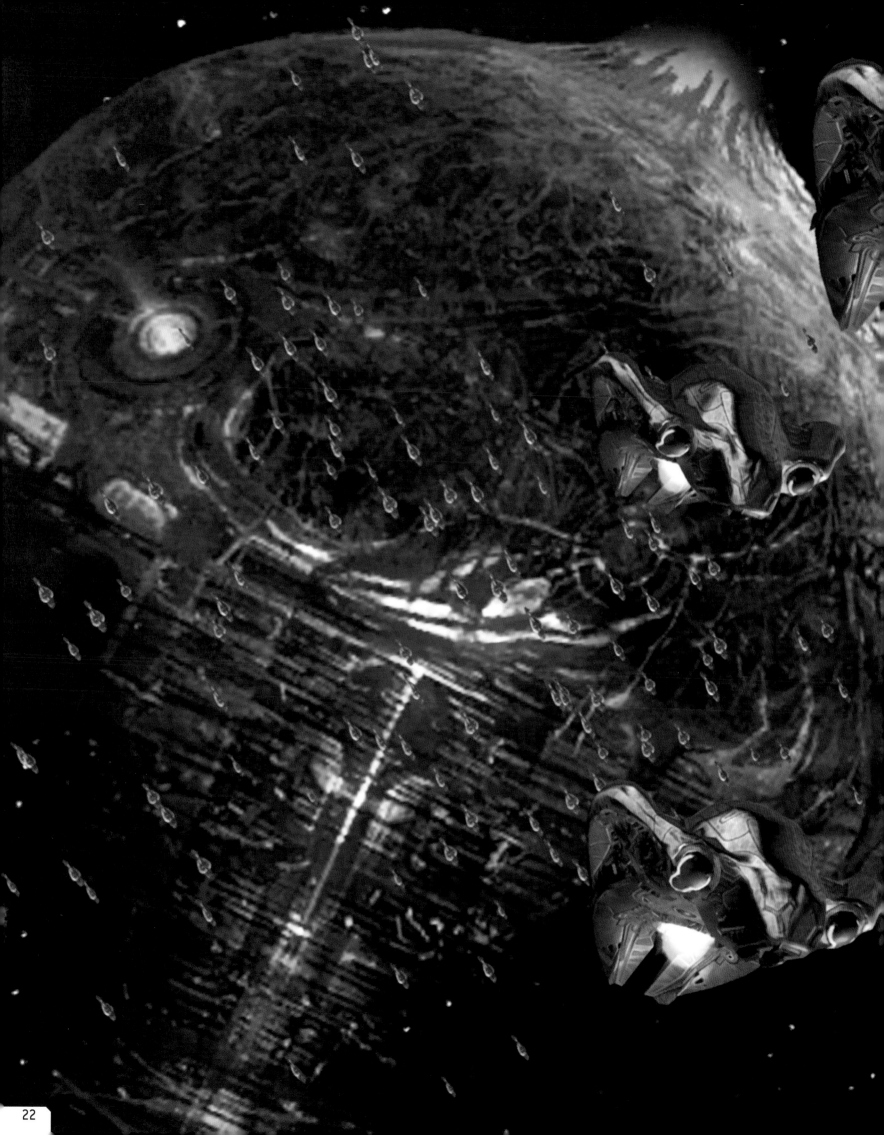

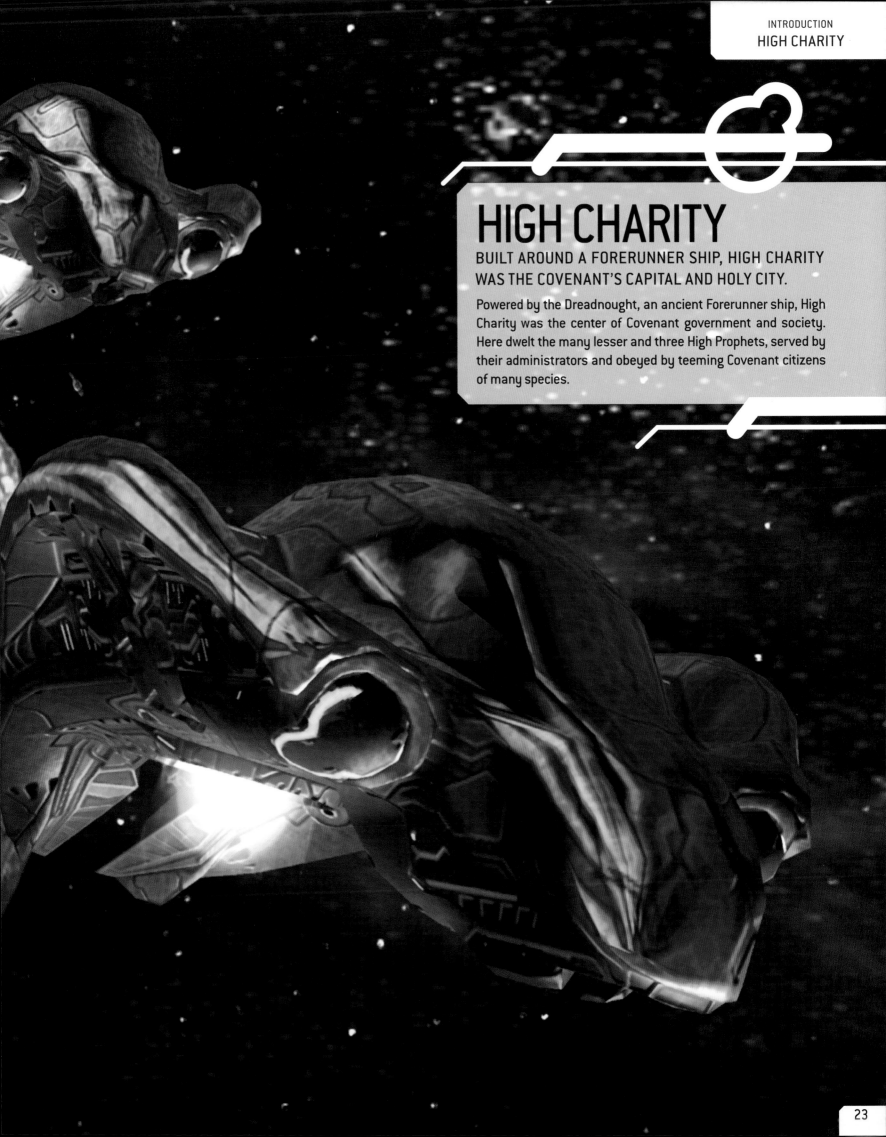

HIGH CHARITY

BUILT AROUND A FORERUNNER SHIP, HIGH CHARITY WAS THE COVENANT'S CAPITAL AND HOLY CITY.

Powered by the Dreadnought, an ancient Forerunner ship, High Charity was the center of Covenant government and society. Here dwelt the many lesser and three High Prophets, served by their administrators and obeyed by teeming Covenant citizens of many species.

TIMELINE

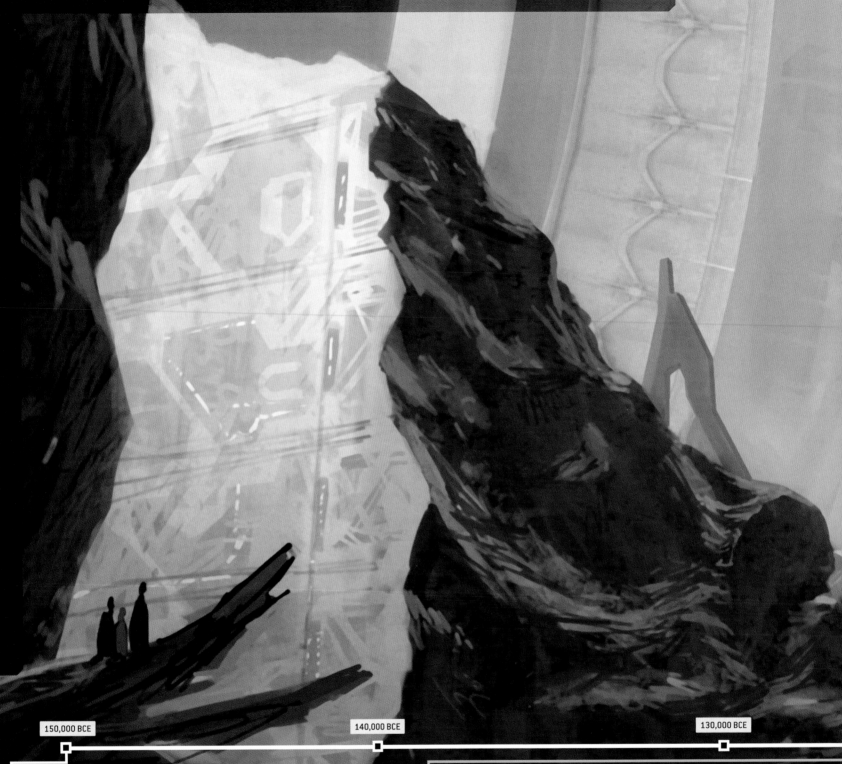

TIMELINE: 150,000–100,000 BCE

150,000 BCE

140,000 BCE

130,000 BCE

150,000 BCE

The Forerunners rise as the preeminent species in the Milky Way Galaxy by advancing technological discoveries gathered from the remnants left by prior ancient races. Believing themselves responsible for the lives of all those less advanced than they, the Forerunners initiate the Mantle, a galactic plan to steward the lesser races of the Galaxy. Note: All Forerunner era dates are approximate, based on available translation and scattered historical data.

100,300 BCE

The Flood arrives from beyond the Milky Way and begins to infect all sentient life it encounters. The Forerunners create the Maginot Sphere, a defensive perimeter that protects their inner colonies from invaders. Hundreds of millions of sentient creatures are assimilated and despite opposition from the advanced armies of the Forerunners, the Flood thrives. The Forerunners realize the only way to eradicate the Flood is to destroy its food supply, i.e. sentient life. They create the Halo installations and the Ark as a means of saving selections of all the species of the galaxy.

120,000 BCE

110,000 BCE

100,000 BCE

100,043 BCE

The Forerunners create Mendicant Bias, an exceptionally strong combat AI that is built to battle the Flood Gravemind. Mendicant Bias is intended to lure the Gravemind out of the Maginot Sphere long enough for the biomass of the Flood to be destroyed. The Librarian, a female Forerunner responsible for saving sample species, comes upon an early human species on what will come to be known as planet Earth. The entire species is removed from the surface of the planet and held on the Ark. Later, before the firing of the Halo Array, the Librarian is trapped and cannot reach the Ark before the Array fires.

100,000 BCE

Mendicant Bias, corrupted by the Gravemind, becomes rampant and declares the Forerunners overindulgent and arrogant. It joins with the armies of the Flood and leads them against the Forerunners. Mendicant Bias fights Offensive Bias, and is defeated. Part of Mendicant Bias survives aboard the Forerunner Dreadnought that later lands on the future San 'Shyuum homeworld.

100,000 BCE

100,000 BCE

The Forerunners activate the Halo Array. All sentient life in the Milky Way Galaxy is exterminated except the sampling protected on Shield Worlds and the Ark. Once the Flood threat is ended, the sample species are reseeded across the Galaxy, including humans on Earth, and they begin to repopulate their homeworlds. The Forerunners leave the Orion Arm of the Milky Way Galaxy.

> ALL SENTIENT LIFE WITHIN THREE RADII OF THE GALACTIC CENTER DIES, AS PLANNED.

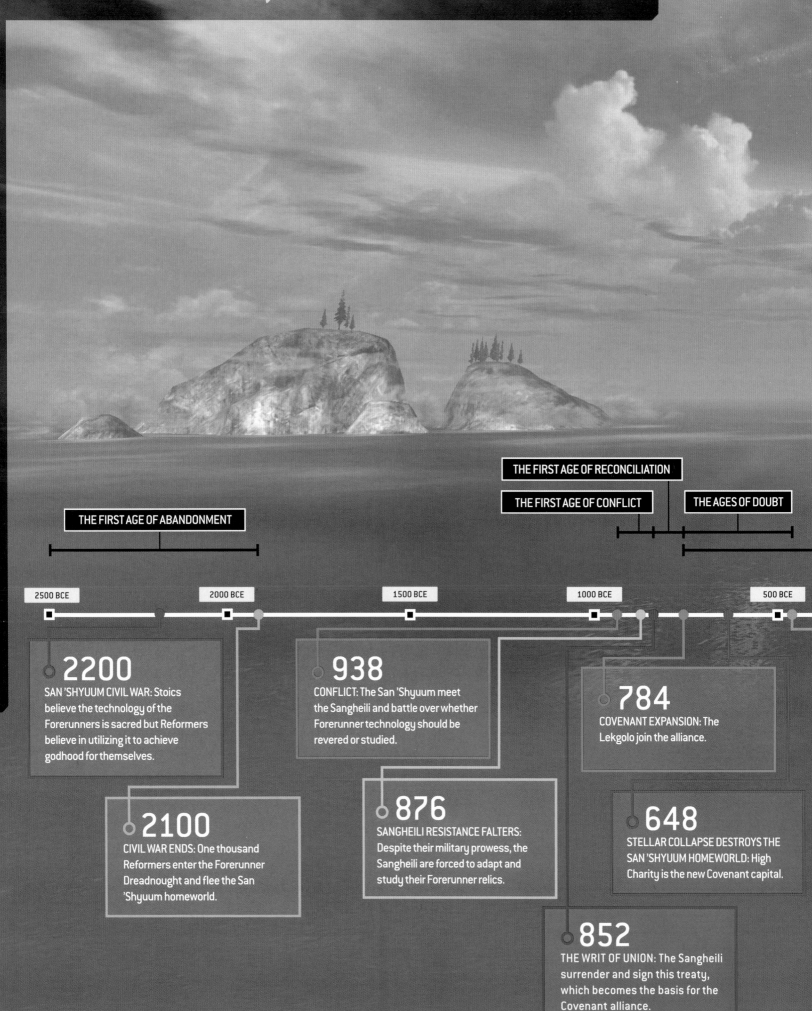

THE FIRST AGE OF RECONCILIATION

THE FIRST AGE OF CONFLICT

THE AGES OF DOUBT

THE FIRST AGE OF ABANDONMENT

| 2500 BCE | 2000 BCE | 1500 BCE | 1000 BCE | 500 BCE |

2200

SAN 'SHYUUM CIVIL WAR: Stoics believe the technology of the Forerunners is sacred but Reformers believe in utilizing it to achieve godhood for themselves.

938

CONFLICT: The San 'Shyuum meet the Sangheili and battle over whether Forerunner technology should be revered or studied.

784

COVENANT EXPANSION: The Lekgolo join the alliance.

2100

CIVIL WAR ENDS: One thousand Reformers enter the Forerunner Dreadnought and flee the San 'Shyuum homeworld.

876

SANGHEILI RESISTANCE FALTERS: Despite their military prowess, the Sangheili are forced to adapt and study their Forerunner relics.

648

STELLAR COLLAPSE DESTROYS THE SAN 'SHYUUM HOMEWORLD: High Charity is the new Covenant capital.

852

THE WRIT OF UNION: The Sangheili surrender and sign this treaty, which becomes the basis for the Covenant alliance.

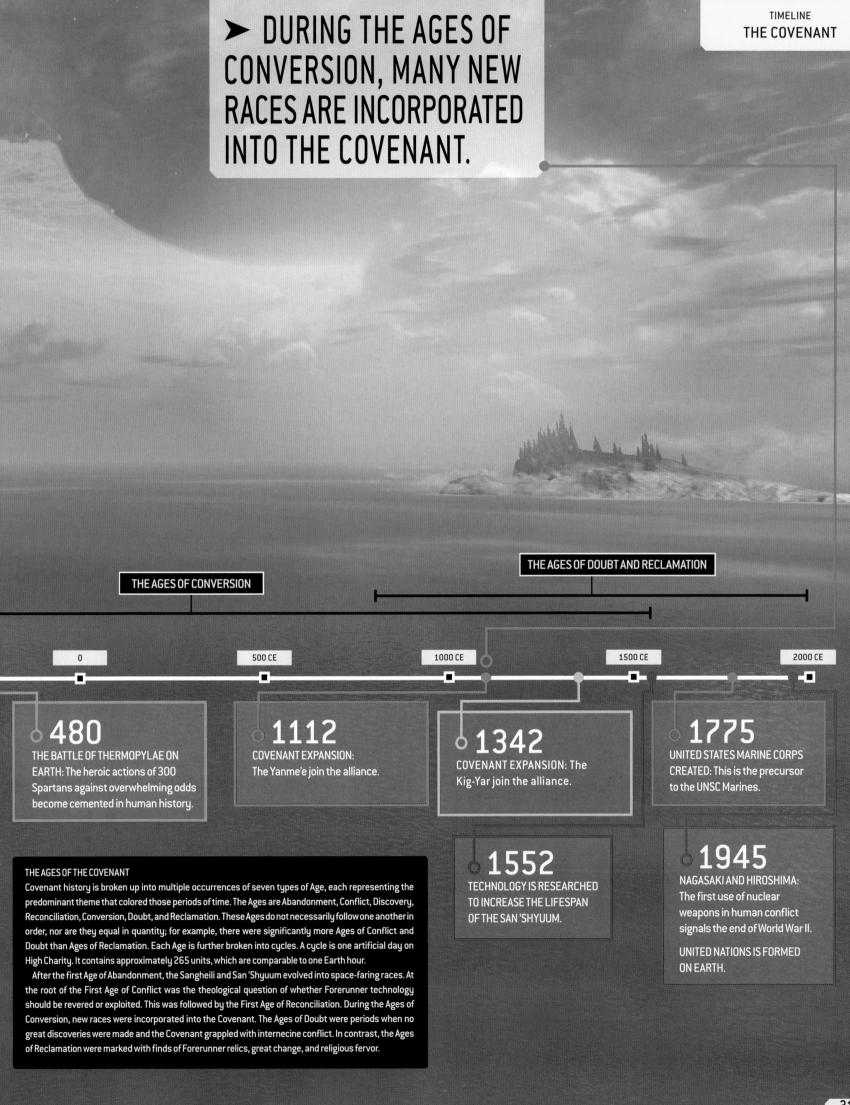

➤ **DURING THE AGES OF CONVERSION, MANY NEW RACES ARE INCORPORATED INTO THE COVENANT.**

THE AGES OF DOUBT AND RECLAMATION

THE AGES OF CONVERSION

| 0 | 500 CE | 1000 CE | 1500 CE | 2000 CE |

480
THE BATTLE OF THERMOPYLAE ON EARTH: The heroic actions of 300 Spartans against overwhelming odds become cemented in human history.

1112
COVENANT EXPANSION: The Yanme'e join the alliance.

1342
COVENANT EXPANSION: The Kig-Yar join the alliance.

1775
UNITED STATES MARINE CORPS CREATED: This is the precursor to the UNSC Marines.

1552
TECHNOLOGY IS RESEARCHED TO INCREASE THE LIFESPAN OF THE SAN 'SHYUUM.

1945
NAGASAKI AND HIROSHIMA: The first use of nuclear weapons in human conflict signals the end of World War II.

UNITED NATIONS IS FORMED ON EARTH.

THE AGES OF THE COVENANT
Covenant history is broken up into multiple occurrences of seven types of Age, each representing the predominant theme that colored those periods of time. The Ages are Abandonment, Conflict, Discovery, Reconciliation, Conversion, Doubt, and Reclamation. These Ages do not necessarily follow one another in order, nor are they equal in quantity; for example, there were significantly more Ages of Conflict and Doubt than Ages of Reclamation. Each Age is further broken into cycles. A cycle is one artificial day on High Charity. It contains approximately 265 units, which are comparable to one Earth hour.

After the first Age of Abandonment, the Sangheili and San 'Shyuum evolved into space-faring races. At the root of the First Age of Conflict was the theological question of whether Forerunner technology should be revered or exploited. This was followed by the First Age of Reconciliation. During the Ages of Conversion, new races were incorporated into the Covenant. The Ages of Doubt were periods when no great discoveries were made and the Covenant grappled with internecine conflict. In contrast, the Ages of Reclamation were marked with finds of Forerunner relics, great change, and religious fervor.

TIMELINE: 1969 CE–2492 CE

1900 CE   2000 CE   2100 CE

1969
THE HUMAN SPACE AGE BEGINS: People take their first steps on Luna.

2142
COVENANT EXPANSION: The Unggoy join the Covenant.

2163
MARS CAMPAIGN: Marks the first deployment of UNSC Marines.

2080
COLONIZATION: Humans settle on Luna, Mars, the Jovian Moons, and asteroids.

2160
THE JOVIAN MOONS CAMPAIGN: Insurrectionists clash with the Government.

2164–2170
INTERPLANETARY WAR: Koslovic and Frieden insurrectionists battle the UNSC.

2162
THE RAINFOREST WARS: Conflict in South America between Koslovic, Frieden, and UN forces.

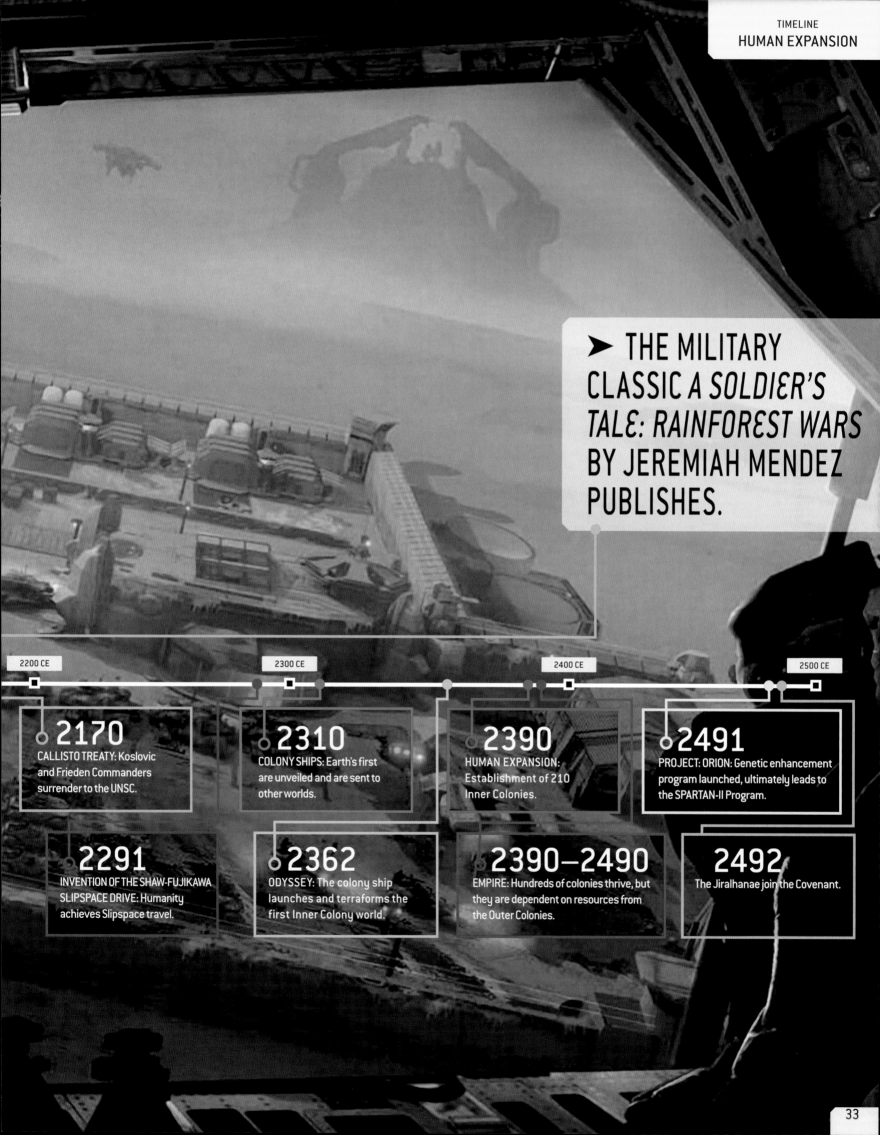

➤ THE MILITARY CLASSIC *A SOLDIER'S TALE: RAINFOREST WARS* BY JEREMIAH MENDEZ PUBLISHES.

2200 CE 2300 CE 2400 CE 2500 CE

2170
CALLISTO TREATY: Koslovic and Frieden Commanders surrender to the UNSC.

2310
COLONY SHIPS: Earth's first are unveiled and are sent to other worlds.

2390
HUMAN EXPANSION: Establishment of 210 Inner Colonies.

2491
PROJECT: ORION: Genetic enhancement program launched, ultimately leads to the SPARTAN-II Program.

2291
INVENTION OF THE SHAW-FUJIKAWA SLIPSPACE DRIVE: Humanity achieves Slipspace travel.

2362
ODYSSEY: The colony ship launches and terraforms the first Inner Colony world.

2390–2490
EMPIRE: Hundreds of colonies thrive, but they are dependent on resources from the Outer Colonies.

2492
The Jiralhanae join the Covenant.

TIMELINE: 2494 CE–2524 CE

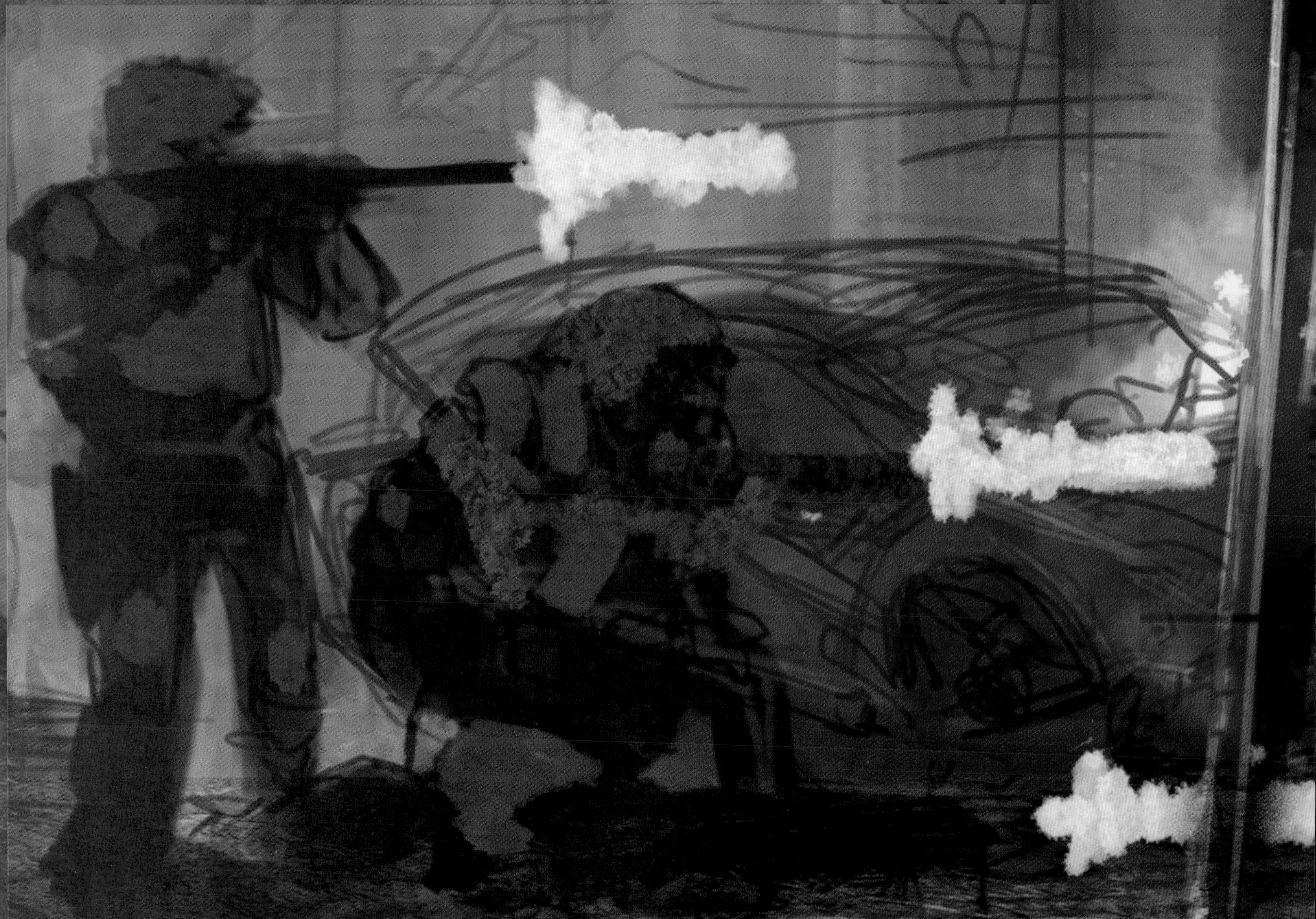

2490 CE — 2495 CE — 2500 CE — 2505 CE

2494
ERIDANUS UPRISING: Armed secessionists prey on shipping. The local government asks the UNSC for aid.

2496
OPERATION: CHARLEMAGNE: The UNSC defeats Rebels on Eridanus who flee. SPARTAN-Is then deploy and defeat the Rebels' base.

2497
CMA INVOLVEMENT: The Colonial Military Administration's involvement with Rebels goes public and the organization's power shifts to NavCom/UniCom control.

2506
SPARTAN-I PROGRAM IS DEACTIVATED.

2509
THE *PILLAR OF AUTUMN* IS CONSTRUCTED OVER MARS.

➤ MAGNETIC ACCELERATOR CANNONS ARE FITTED TO THE NEWLY MILITARIZED UNSC *SPIRIT OF FIRE.*

2510 CE | 2515 CE | 2520 CE | 2525 CE

2511
JOHN IS BORN: The future SPARTAN-117 is born on Eridanus II. Forerunner ruins discovered on Onyx.

2513
OPERATION: TREBUCHET: UNSC forces move in after Colonel Robert Watts leads an uprising in the Eridanus System. The Rebels withdraw to the asteroid field.

2517
SPARTAN-II PROGRAM LAUNCHES: Its base is in a top-secret lab complex on Reach.

2524
FIRST MEETING WITH THE COVENANT: Humans and the Covenant first encounter each other in space near Harvest. Sgt. Avery Johnson and Sgt. Nolan Byrne lead a raid against a bomb squad in Casbah, on Tribute.

2512
GEOLOGY: On the planet of Sigma Octanus IV, possible Forerunner relics are found in fragments of meteors.

2520
SPIRIT OF FIRE MILITARIZED: Refitted from a colony ship to a warship, it then supports Operation: TREBUCHET.

25 CE
2530 CE
2535 CE

2525

FEBRUARY 11: The first diplomatic contact between humans and the Covenant ends in bloodshed on Harvest.

FEBRUARY 23: Harvest is evacuated when a Covenant attack results in 23,000 human casualties.

MARCH 9: Medical augmentation of SPARTAN-II soldiers begins.

APRIL 20: Contact with UNSC *Argo* is lost after its arrival at Harvest.

OCTOBER 7: UNSC warships, *Arabia*, *Heracles*, and *Vostok*, arrive at Harvest and make contact with a Covenant warship. Only the *Heracles* escapes.

NOVEMBER 1: UNSC goes on full alert and all combat forces are placed under NavCom/UniCom control.

2530

The Covenant destroy UNSC colony Eridanus II.

2531

Admiral Cole pulls off a victory over a Covenant fleet at Harvest, but only because he outnumbers them three-to-one. Even then, he loses two-thirds of his fleet. Regardless, this victory is highly publicized.

2535

The Covenant has destroyed nearly all Outer Colony worlds. The UNSC establishes the Cole Protocol.

FEBRUARY 12: Jericho-VII falls to the Covenant.

2537

The battle of New Constantinople.

JULY 27: Operation: PROMETHEUS.

OCTOBER 2: The investigation of the disappearance of Team X-Ray (Beta Company Spartans) after discovering a glowing sphere in Zone 67 yields no results.

➤ "IN MEMORY OF THOSE FALLEN IN THE DEFENSE OF EARTH AND HER COLONIES. MARCH 3, 2553."
—HILLSIDE MEMORIAL INSCRIPTION

2540 CE

2545 CE

2550 CE

2555 CE

2542
UNSC abandons the colony world Emerald Cove to the Covenant.

2545
Operation: TORPEDO.

2547
ONI's Section II makes the SPARTAN-II Program public to boost morale; the SPARTAN-III Program remains top secret.

2549
The Covenant attack Paris-IV.

2552
JULY 18: SPARTAN-IIs are deployed to Sigma Octanus IV and score a victory, but the Covenant discover the location of Reach.

AUGUST 30: The Fall of Reach. Master Chief and the *Pillar of Autumn* barely escape.

SEPTEMBER 19: The battle of Halo Installation 04 begins.

OCTOBER 20: The first battle of Earth.

OCTOBER 21: The battle of Halo Installation 05 begins.

NOVEMBER 17: The second battle of Earth is followed by the battle of Installation 00.

➤ "DO YOU HAVE A PLAN?"
"YES. WHEN WE GET THERE, I'M GOING TO KILL EVERY SINGLE COVENANT SOLDIER I CAN FIND."
—CORTANA AND MASTER CHIEF

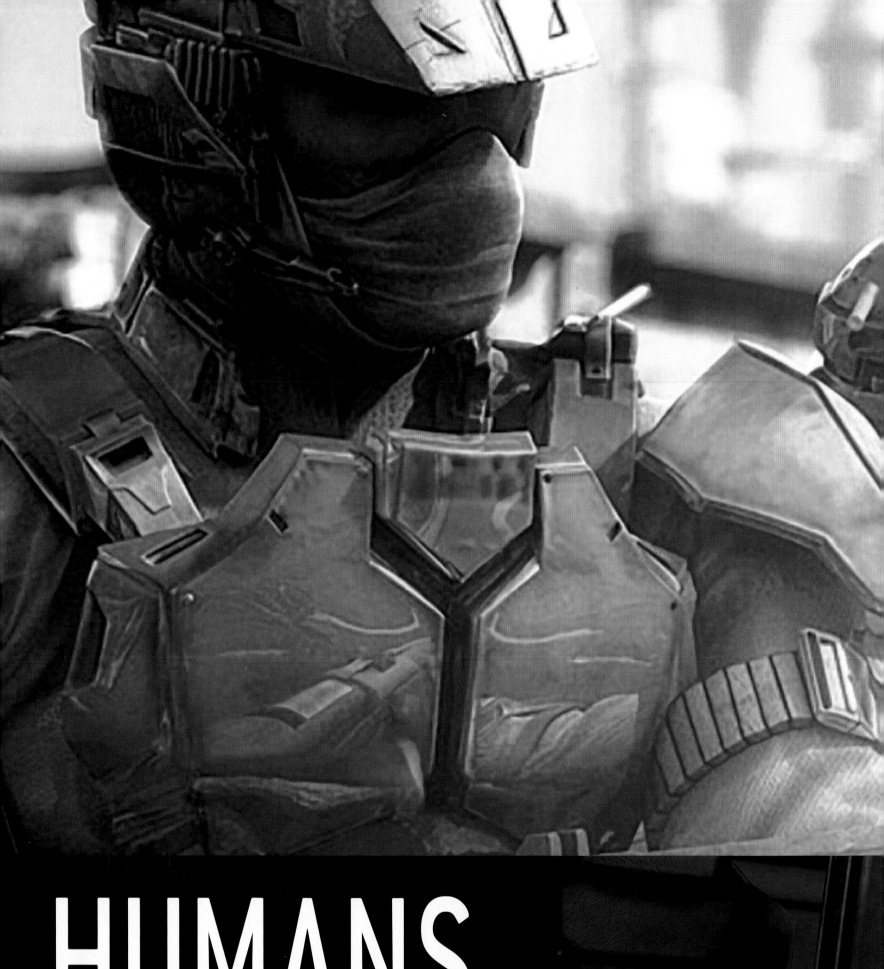

HUMANS

HUMAN COLONIZATION OF SPACE

EARTH'S SPACE AGE

In 1961 CE, when Soviet Cosmonaut Yuri Gagarin became the first human to orbit the Earth, humankind had no idea what expansive adventures awaited them in the depths of their galaxy. The dream of traveling the stars, which had long been a part of the species' mythology, would still take centuries from its initial tentative beginning before it became a reality. The fear of the unknown—combined with an irregular cycle of technological advancements and an inability to evolve beyond the barriers of self-imposed borders and cultural differences—long prevented humanity from achieving a truly productive and universally beneficial exploration of their heavens.

Over the next century human technology increased by leaps and bounds. The creation of the Internet and an ever-increasing sophistication in networked intelligences and robotics led to the first basic Artificial Intelligences (AIs). These Intelligences paled in comparison to the 26th century's dumbest AIs, but they were advanced through technologies gleaned from the System Peril Distributed Reflex (SPDR) program. This program was transported back in time to 2004 CE during a temporal rift triggered by a Forerunner artifact found in deep space by a UNSC starship in the 2500s.

GALACTIC EXPANSION

Commercial interests propelled outward expansion into the Sol System far more than the programs of Earth's national governments. Free of the restrictions of international law as well as basic gravity, advancements in nanotechnology and biotechnologies exploded in the colonies on Mars. These settlements soon became the hub of spaceship production and industrial manufacturing. Robots, rather than humans, efficiently performed the labor there. With colonies established on Luna, Mars, the asteroid belt, and the Jovian Moons, terraforming technologies began to create more biologically sustainable habitats, so colonies were now possible on the planetary bodies within the Sol System that were only remotely capable of sustaining life.

KOSLOVIC AND FRIEDEN MOVEMENTS

In 2160 CE, overpopulation and political unrest on Earth led to the emergence of and conflict between two powerful political movements—the Koslovics and the Friedens. Koslovics, named after their founder Vladimir Koslovic, nostalgically longed for the glory days of Soviet Communism, and romanticized the notion of state control over industry. Operating mostly in orbital facilities and outerworld colonies, they sought to eliminate corporate and capitalist influence from societal structure.

The Friedens, their name ironically meaning "peace," were neo-fascists. They were backed by a group of corporate interests in the Unified German Republic and were created in reaction to the Koslovic force based in the Jovian colonies. In their first act of rebellion, Frieden secessionists attacked the United Nations Colonial Advisors stationed near the Jovian moons. This act triggered three months of fighting between the Earth's military and Frieden forces. It was the bloodiest conflict that the Sol System had seen in decades and it served to strengthen anti-governmental and anti-corporate sentiment growing among colonists, and also to spur forward the militarization of the Earth-based governments. At this time, national governments still sponsored their own military efforts. The distributed nature of their forces led to disorder in the ranks of the Earth forces, just as conflicts erupted across the off-world colonies.

THE RAINFOREST WARS

In 2162 CE, the battle came to Earth. Koslovic, Frieden, and UN forces clashed in South America and initiated the epic Rainforest Wars. Other guerilla attacks took place on Earth and on military and non-military off-planet targets. The Rainforest Wars led to some of the most famous literature of the 2100s, including the military classic, *A Soldier's Tale: Rainforest Wars*, which remained popular well into the 26th century.

THE MARS CAMPAIGN

A year after the Rainforest Wars, came the Mars Campaign. Triggered by attacks on Rebels at the Argyre Planitia shipbuilding plants on Mars, the campaign was the first successful UN strike against Koslovic forces. These sorties marked the first extraterrestrial deployment of United Nations Space Command (UNSC) Marines. As a result of the success, actions that favored large contingents of Marines for ground assaults and ship-boarding maneuvers became the standard strategy of the UN forces from that point onward.

> ➤ **AS HUMANITY EXPANDED OUTWARD, THE INNER COLONIES BECAME THE POLITICAL AND ECONOMIC CENTER OF HUMAN SPACE.**

Basing its core ethos on a strategy that harkened back to the United States of the first years of the 21st century, the UN used its increased power to effectively take charge of the remaining national governments. The UNSC became the single organizing independent force in control of the combined military hierarchy of humanity.

The UNSC defeated Koslovic and Frieden forces on Earth and then methodically eradicated their remnants on the off-world colonies until they both signed a surrender agreement, the Callisto Treaty in 2170 CE.

THE SHAW-FUJIKAWA TRANSLIGHT ENGINE ENABLED FASTER-THAN-LIGHT INTERSTELLAR TRAVEL

SHAW-FUJIKAWA TRANSLIGHT ENGINE

The discovery that made further expansion of the human race outside its solar system possible came in 2291 CE, when Tobias Shaw and Wallace Fujikawa published their findings on advancements in quantum mechanics. They had secretly constructed the Shaw-Fujikawa Translight Engine (Shaw-Fujikawa Slipspace Drive or SFTE), a means to propel spacecraft across vast interstellar distances.

By 2330 CE, Earth's government unveiled its first colony ships. Rigorously tested, highly qualified civilian colonists and military personnel were chosen and sent to "nearby" worlds. That year, humanity's first interstellar craft, the *Odyssey*, launched to the Epsilon Eridani System, 10.5 light years from Earth.

THE INNER COLONIES

By 2390 CE, with the founding of two-hundred and ten human colony worlds, the Inner Colonies were formally established. Ranging from worlds with human settlements to mining or industrial colonies with no human presence, these diverse colonies were governed by the Colonial Administration, a group that answered to the Unified Earth Government but had its own military fleet, though not a force as powerful or advanced as the UNSC fleet.

The following century was a boom time for humanity. The Inner Colonies rapidly grew in population and importance. By 2490 CE, human space encompassed over eight-hundred planets. They ranged from centers of industry and technology to pioneer settlements that could barely sustain ten-thousand colonists.

As humanity expanded outward, the Inner Colonies became the political and economic center of human space and began to rely heavily on the raw materials supplied by the Outer Colonies. The Epsilon Eridani System was the jewel in the crown of the UNSC, and it became the foremost Naval yard, a major producer of warships and colony vessels, and a training ground for covert operatives and Special Forces.

Highly populated, the planet Reach, at the heart of the Epsilon Eridani System, was also a main commercial center for civilian enterprise. While Earth was still humanity's spiritual home, Reach had become its logistical hub. Other human settlements in this system ranged from the magnificent High Courts and Universities of Circumstance to the struggling industrial settlements of Tribute. Overseeing this Empire, the UNSC became the organizing independent hierarchy in control of all combined military forces of humanity.

FORERUNNER TECHNOLOGY

During colonial expansion, humankind made some discoveries that were kept as closely guarded secrets by the UNSC's Office of Naval Intelligence (ONI). For example, the planet Onyx was discovered in 2491 CE, and when ruins from an ancient and unknown species, the Forerunners, were uncovered, the UNSC declared the find top secret and removed the world from all maps.

Forerunner artifacts were also found beneath the surface of Reach and were covered up under the guise of a mining facility. Planet Coral also became the site of a Forerunner find. Prospectors building an automated mining colony were using explosives to evaporate the surface of the world to a depth of thirty meters when the tip of a Forerunner installation was uncovered. Archaeologists directed by ONI dug out about eighty meters of the site, which seemed to be much bigger. The complex had been described as made from a metallic crystal, symmetrical to a near-atomic scale, yet adorned with decorative artistic motifs.

These varied discoveries led to some, but not many, technological advancements that humanity could employ. However, people's inability to decipher the glyphs in the limited time they had to study the artifacts before the Covenant War began in 2525 CE meant that those advancements were still highly classified and had not yet gained any mainstream application.

THE ROAD TO CIVIL WAR

The complete power that ONI exercised over the control of research and information flow from these various discoveries showed their growing power within the UNSC and the Government's desire to maintain control over the colonies. As humanity expanded, the UNSC took every step necessary to keep its grip on the Outer Colonies. The Inner Colonies depended on the resources the Outer Colonies provided and the Outer Colonies depended on UNSC-maintained supply lines. By the 2400's, Outer—and even many Inner—Colonies began to question the often-draconian interference of the UNSC in what was supposed to be a confederation of independently governed worlds. The great dream that had swept humanity into new worlds had begun to sour in the minds of its colonies. This led to rebellion among the various worlds and to the inevitable outbreak of civil war among humans.

POLITICAL UNREST

As the UNSC increasingly countermanded and complicated the functioning governments of the Inner and Outer Colony worlds, unrest began to foment. Complaints were generally ignored by the UNSC until finally rebellion began. Minor uprisings were common throughout the settling of the UNSC colonies but the superior forces of the UNSC had been able to put them down easily.

THE ORION PROJECT

In 2321 CE, the UNSC Office of Naval Intelligence (ONI) created the ORION Project, named after the Orion Arm of the Milky Way Galaxy. Its aim was to build on bioengineering protocols developed during the Interplanetary Wars in order to generate tougher, faster soldiers. A handful of military candidates were "tested" and eventually seeded into the regular chain of command after the project was declared ineffective.

THE SECESSIONIST UNION

In 2461 CE, Jerald Mulkey Ander was born. He later went on to create the Secessionist Union, an organization also known as the People's Occupation Government.

THE RELAUNCH OF ORION

In 2491 CE, the Colonial Military Administration (CMA) secretly relaunched the ORION Project in response to the growing insurgent attacks in the colonies. The project was headquartered in one of the many orbital docks on Reach. This iteration of the project used more advanced indoctrination and biological augmentation techniques. After a grueling series of physical and mental tests, the first batch of test subjects—165 in total—were selected from the ranks of Special Forces.

THE CARVER FINDINGS

During the same year, the "Carver Findings" were published and presented to the UNSC military command. Doctor Elias Carver, a political sociologist, theorized that, "unless the political situation throughout the colonies is stabilized (preferably by force), the Government will collapse and civil war will rip human society apart." Many scoffed at these theories, but they gained purchase in the Office of Naval Intelligence and the Admiralty, informing their strategies against the insurrectionists for decades to come.

OPERATION: CHARLEMAGNE

In June of 2494 CE, armed Secessionists, equipped by traitors within the CMA command structure, mobilized on Eridanus II under the leadership of former UNSC Marine Colonel Robert Watts. They performed a well planned and efficiently executed campaign of bombings, political assassinations, and kidnappings that seriously impacted on shipping to and from the planet. Most significantly, the insurgents were able to amass a small fleet of spaceships through their CMA contacts.

The Eridanus Government officially called for aid in the chaotic situation in December of 2494 CE, and in January of 2496 CE the UNSC launched Operation: CHARLEMAGNE, as a large battlegroup engaged the Rebels and defeated them at the cost of four destroyers.

As a result of this conflict, the UNSC regained control of the colony, but the Rebels were able to retreat into a local asteroid field where they escaped capture and continued to operate.

THE FIRST SPARTAN MISSION

Operation: CHARLEMAGNE marked the first deployment of the latest crop of biologically enhanced soldiers codenamed SPARTAN-Is. They scored a decisive victory and emerged from the battle with only a single casualty. The insertion and extraction was completed without the Spartans being seen, thereby fueling a range of conspiracy theories and media speculation.

The legend of these super-soldiers continued to grow and proved very helpful to ONI's propaganda efforts in the upcoming decades. Though the Spartans were effective, their abilities fell short of the scientists' hopes, and they cost far too much to develop and field. The project was deactivated and the soldiers were reassigned to various special operations units.

DEMISE OF THE CMA

The connections to traitors in the CMA became public and the organization's political opponents used the opportunity to shift power and resources from the CMA to the UNSC. The CMA was eventually relegated to patrolling the most distant colonies and providing logistical support to remote stations.

OPERATION: TREBUCHET

With Colonel Robert Watts still at large, Rebel attacks cropped up on planets throughout the colonies. The UNSC stepped up their counterinsurgent activities under the name Operation: TREBUCHET.

The insurgents proved very difficult to route and over the ensuing decades, more organized factions grew in other areas of the colonies as quickly as operations could be launched against them. Bombings continued despite the best efforts of military personnel, and civilians were regularly caught in the crossfire. Casualties mounted, adding to a simmering hatred towards the UNSC.

OPERATION: KALEIDOSCOPE

In 2502 CE, Operation: KALEIDOSCOPE—part of the UNSC's greater plan to pacify the entirety of human-colonized space—was put into action. During this operation, Corporal Avery Johnson assassinated Jerald Mulkey Ander. With Ander dead, the Rebels' alliance fell into chaos and dissolved, but Ander became a martyr to the cause of Insurrectionists throughout the colonies.

SPARTAN-II PROGRAM

The ORION Project continued under ONI control and in 2517 CE, Dr. Catherine Halsey was given the green light to develop a SPARTAN-II Project. The top-secret program was controversial and ethically questionable at best, but it also produced results and ultimately the SPARTAN-II soldiers proved to be the most effective weapon in the battle against insurgents. These elite soldiers were genetically augmented and outfitted with the most advanced mechanized armor in the entire UNSC arsenal.

In their first sortie in 2525 CE, the SPARTAN-IIs, led by the Master Chief John-117, infiltrated the Rebel base in the asteroid belt of the Eridanus System and succeeded in destroying the base and capturing Colonel Robert Watts alive. After his capture, ONI agents interrogated Watts. What happened to him after this interrogation was classified top-secret and has never been revealed.

Though the insurgency's head had been cut off, other rebellious factions remained strong enough to require continued SPARTAN-II activity. The SPARTAN-IIs performed their missions effectively and ruthlessly, killing off Rebel leaders and continuing a seemingly endless series of battles in an ongoing war against the interests of the UNSC.

THE COVENANT

In 2525 CE, a threat emerged that was even more dangerous than the insurgency, with the arrival of an alien force, the Covenant. The threat posed by the Covenant eclipsed the activities of the Rebels, so forces were redeployed to stop the Covenant juggernaut and the Rebels were left to their own devices. The insurrection did not end there. It continued to establish itself wherever it found ground to do so, even finding unlikely alliances with opportunistic Kig-Yar pirates.

As the Human-Covenant War marched inexorably onward and humanity suffered mounting defeats, many of these Rebel factions were consumed by the overwhelming combat and simply wiped out of existence. Despite their demise, the ideas and grievances that forged their genesis were never addressed. With the end of the Human-Covenant War at hand, these questions have cropped up again, leading many to wonder whether, after decades of torturous strife and unity of cause, humanity's leaders have truly learned from their mistakes.

> ➤ **HAVE HUMANITY'S LEADERS TRULY LEARNED FROM THEIR MISTAKES?**

UNITED NATIONS SPACE COMMAND

THE UNITED NATIONS Space Command (UNSC) is the military arm of the human governing system, but during the Human-Covenant War, it operated in many ways as the main governing body.

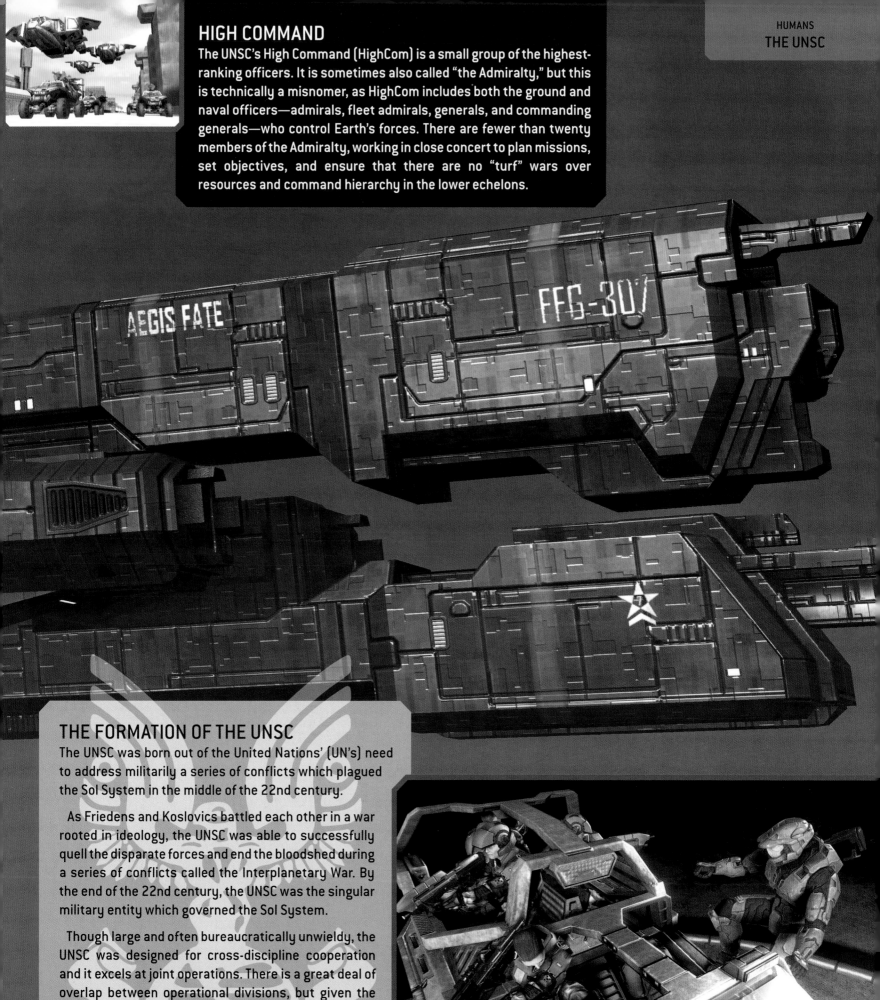

HIGH COMMAND
The UNSC's High Command (HighCom) is a small group of the highest-ranking officers. It is sometimes also called "the Admiralty," but this is technically a misnomer, as HighCom includes both the ground and naval officers—admirals, fleet admirals, generals, and commanding generals—who control Earth's forces. There are fewer than twenty members of the Admiralty, working in close concert to plan missions, set objectives, and ensure that there are no "turf" wars over resources and command hierarchy in the lower echelons.

AEGIS FATE

FFG-307

THE FORMATION OF THE UNSC
The UNSC was born out of the United Nations' (UN's) need to address militarily a series of conflicts which plagued the Sol System in the middle of the 22nd century.

As Friedens and Koslovics battled each other in a war rooted in ideology, the UNSC was able to successfully quell the disparate forces and end the bloodshed during a series of conflicts called the Interplanetary War. By the end of the 22nd century, the UNSC was the singular military entity which governed the Sol System.

Though large and often bureaucratically unwieldy, the UNSC was designed for cross-discipline cooperation and it excels at joint operations. There is a great deal of overlap between operational divisions, but given the nature of the UNSC High Command, this creates surprisingly few jurisdictional and protocol headaches.

The UNSC is divided into Ground (UniCom) and Naval (NavCom) forces.

UNSC RANKS

UNSC RANKS

THE COMMON USE of the word "rank" when indicating the position of Navy enlisted personnel is incorrect. The proper term is "rate," which refers to a combination of rate of pay and "rating," or job title. The rate is represented by a number of stripes or chevrons on the uniform, while the rating is represented by a patch or pin representing the individual's profession.

ENLISTED PERSONNEL

The names used for rates E1 through E6 are somewhat variable depending on the rating (job) the person is assigned to. An E1 whose rating is technician would be a "technician recruit," and an E1 assigned to Engineering would be an "engineer recruit." The same men at E6 would usually be referred to as "technician first class" and "engineer first class," respectively.

ENLISTED PERSONNEL

The lowest to highest rates are:

- E-1/Private
- E-2/Private First Class
- E-3/Lance Corporal
- E-4/Corporal
- E-5/Sergeant
- E-6/Staff Sergeant
- E-7/Gunnery Sergeant
- E-8/Master Sergeant/First Sergeant

First sergeant and sergeant major are administrative ranks, whereas with the master sergeant and master gunnery sergeant ranks, the soldier remains in his field of occupation.

OFFICERS

The lowest to highest rates are:

- 0-1/Second Lieutenant
- 0-2/First Lieutenant
- 0-3/Captain
- 0-4/Major
- 0-5/Lieutenant Colonel
- 0-6/Colonel
- 0-7/Brigadier General [1-star]
- 0-8/Major General [2-star]
- 0-9/Lieutenant General [3-star]
- 0-10/General [4-star]
- 0-11/Commanding General [5-star]

When comparing ranks between the Navy and the Ground services, it is necessary to check the actual rank level, and not only the rank name. A marine captain is rank level 03, while a naval captain is rank level 06 (equal to a marine colonel).

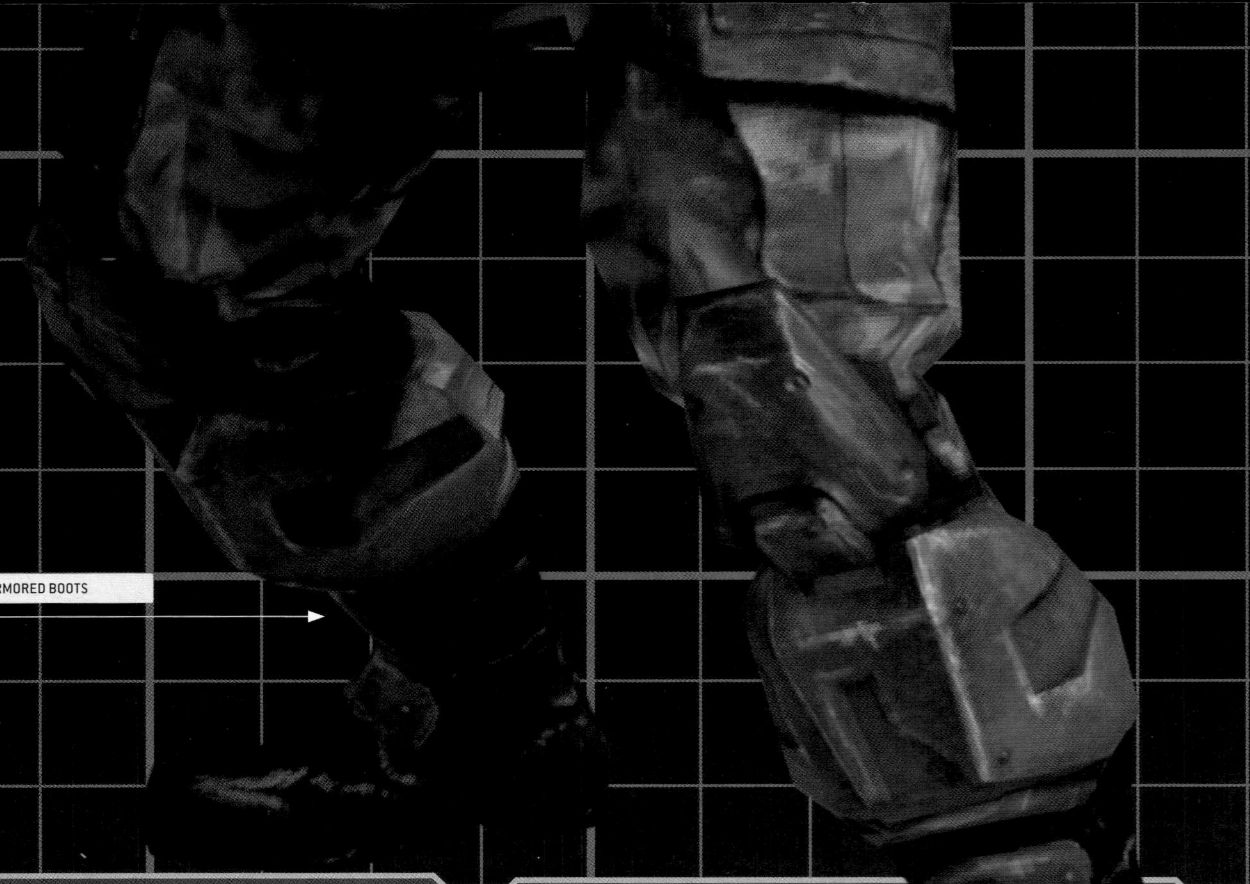

UNSC ARMOR

CH252 HELMET

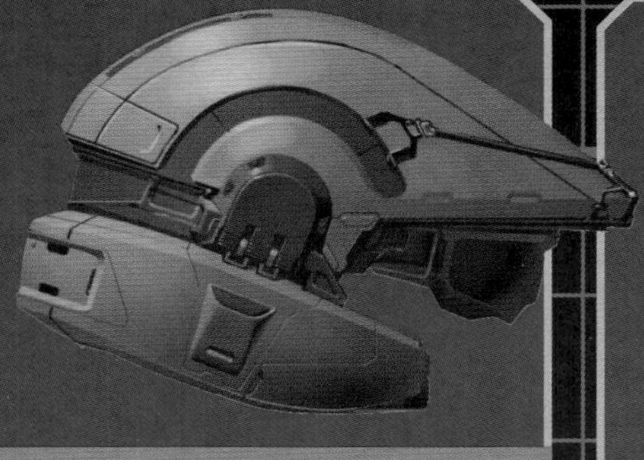

The CH252 is the general-use helmet for all Marine forces, from Earth to the Outer Colonies. With a Heads-Up Display [HUD] and radio system, it can relay signals from surrounding units, as well as carrying information from orbiting ships. Paradoxically, one thing it can't do well is protect the skull of the wearer, as plasma weapons simply billow it. The CH252's protective qualities only come into play with glancing blows and light shrapnel.

OTHER NAMES	WEIGHT	USE
Coconut, Lid, Can, Pasta Shell	4 lb (1.8 kg)	General use, radio use, visor use

M52B BODY ARMOR

Aside from his or her weapon, the M52B is the most precious thing to any Marine. Lightweight but durable, the armor can take a surprising amount of damage without buckling, while the pockets and pouches allow for quick and easy storage for anything from contraband to grenades.

OTHER NAMES	LENGTH	WEIGHT	USE
BA, BO, 52s, Gear, Shell, Armor	Variable	14.5 lb (6.58 kg)	General use

VZG7 ARMORED BOOTS

Every firefight offers something different, but the footwear remains the same. That's because the VZG7 armored boot has served the Marine Corps well since its introduction in the middle of the 26th century. It is protective, lightweight, nearly liquid-proof, and is generally comfortable (though the blisters that form after a full-gear march may prove otherwise).

OTHER NAME	LENGTH	WEIGHT
Boondockers	Variable	3.5 lb (1.59 kg) each

VZG7 ARMORED BOOTS

UNSC RATING INSIGNIA

THE UNSC ENLISTED military have their ranks displayed on their uniforms. Each rank has its own insignia, from recruits up to Generals.

Gunnery Sergeant (Grade 4) Master Sergeant

Sergeant (Grade 3)

Gunnery Sergeant (Grade 3)

Apprentice (Grade 2)

Private (Grade 2)

Corporal (Grade 2)

Sergeant (Grade 2)

Gunnery Sergeant (Grade 2)

Recruit

Apprentice

Private

Corporal

Sergeant

Gunnery Sergeant

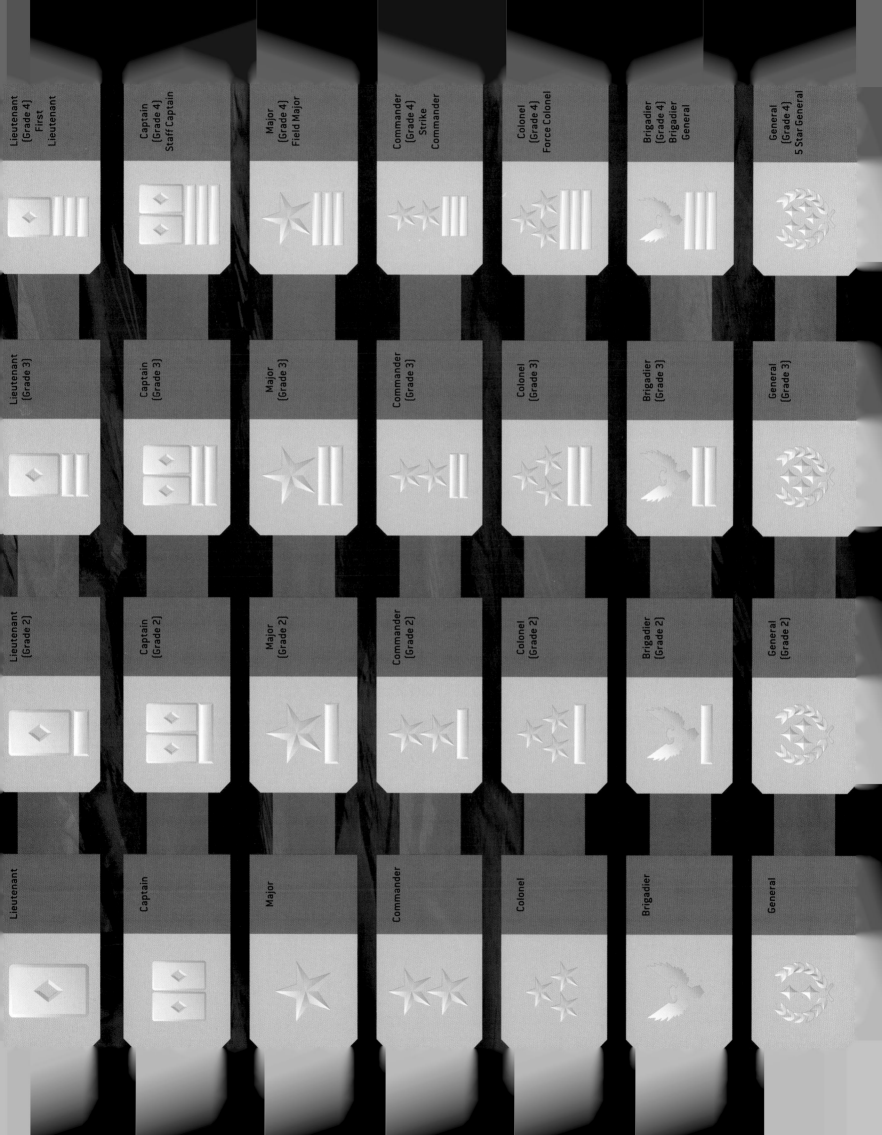

	Grade 4	Grade 3	Grade 2	Grade 1
Lieutenant	Lieutenant (Grade 4) First Lieutenant	Lieutenant (Grade 3)	Lieutenant (Grade 2)	Lieutenant
Captain	Captain (Grade 4) Staff Captain	Captain (Grade 3)	Captain (Grade 2)	Captain
Major	Major (Grade 4) Field Major	Major (Grade 3)	Major (Grade 2)	Major
Commander	Commander (Grade 4) Strike Commander	Commander (Grade 3)	Commander (Grade 2)	Commander
Colonel	Colonel (Grade 4) Force Colonel	Colonel (Grade 3)	Colonel (Grade 2)	Colonel
Brigadier	Brigadier (Grade 4) Brigadier General	Brigadier (Grade 3)	Brigadier (Grade 2)	Brigadier
General	General (Grade 4) 5 Star General	General (Grade 3)	General (Grade 2)	General

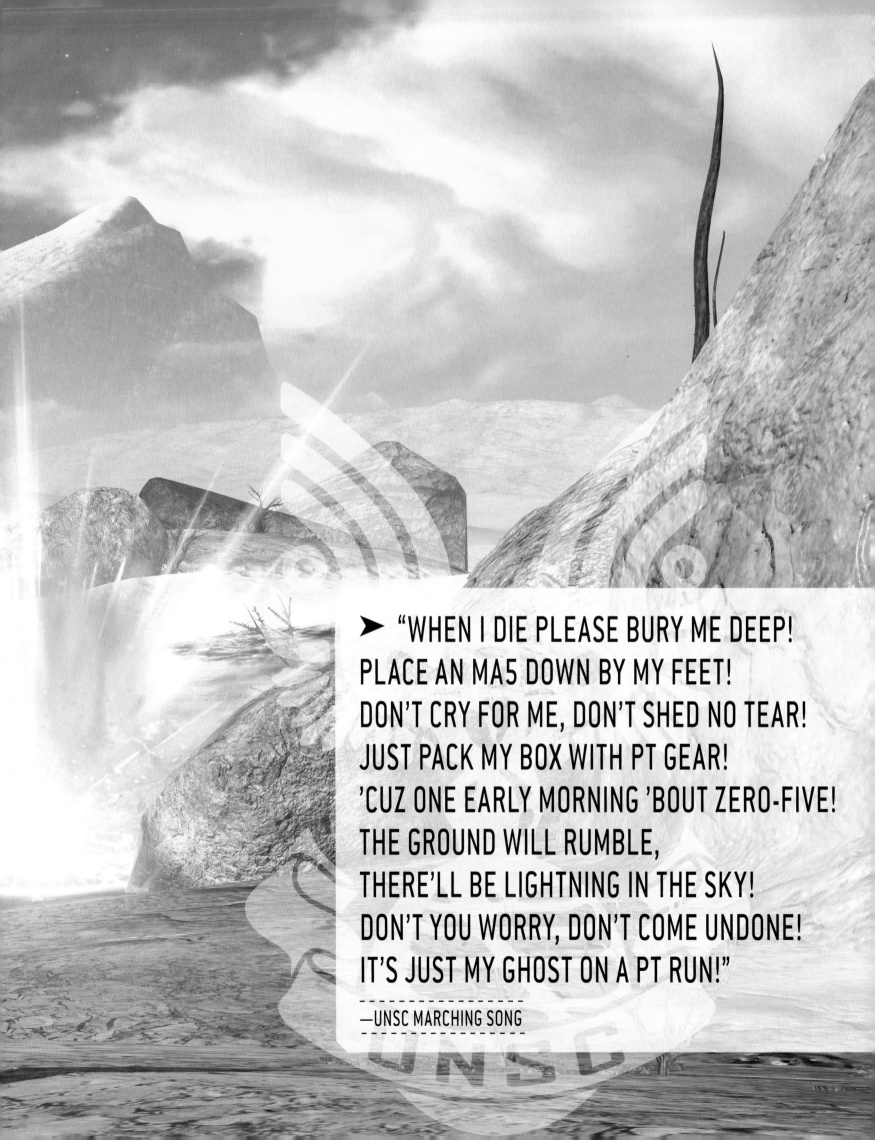

➤ "WHEN I DIE PLEASE BURY ME DEEP!
PLACE AN MA5 DOWN BY MY FEET!
DON'T CRY FOR ME, DON'T SHED NO TEAR!
JUST PACK MY BOX WITH PT GEAR!
'CUZ ONE EARLY MORNING 'BOUT ZERO-FIVE!
THE GROUND WILL RUMBLE,
THERE'LL BE LIGHTNING IN THE SKY!
DON'T YOU WORRY, DON'T COME UNDONE!
IT'S JUST MY GHOST ON A PT RUN!"

—UNSC MARCHING SONG

UNIFIED GROUND COMMAND

THE UNIFIED GROUND Command (UniCom) has control of all UNSC ground-based operations and is loosely modeled on the now-defunct United States Marine Corps. UniCom's role includes, but is not limited to, disaster relief, infantry operations, search and reconnaissance ops, and other "ground pounder" duties. Naval special warfare troops are an exception and are controlled by NavCom.

IE ADMINISTRATION OF THE
IS DIVIDED INTO TWO PARTS:
ND FORCES (CONTROLLED
ICOM) AND NAVAL FORCES
ROLLED BY NAVCOM).

UNICOM STRUCTURE

The basic unit of ground force operations is the squad, consisting of twelve soldiers, or thereabouts. Ground forces are further grouped into platoons, companies, battalions, regiments, and divisions. The force numbers given in the descriptions below are ideals, rarely matched exactly in the field. At the higher levels, these numbers include a significant amount of support personnel such as logistics and administration.

UNSC UNITS

SQUAD

Twelve soldiers, led by a corporal or lance corporal.

PLATOON

Three squads (thirty-six men) led by a second lieutenant, with a "platoon sergeant," usually a sergeant or staff sergeant.

COMPANY

Four platoons, plus a group of personnel assigned as "Company Headquarters Section" (164 men in total), commanded by a first lieutenant or captain, with a "company sergeant," usually a staff sergeant or a gunnery sergeant. The twelve companies of a regiment are named phonetically "A" (Alpha) through "M" (Mike) with the exclusion of "J." First battalion consists of companies A through D, second battalion is companies E through H, and so forth. A typical infantry company would have three infantry platoons and one heavy weapons platoon, but these numbers are flexible depending on the unit type and mission. T companies, for example, eschew this model and mix their heavy weapons personnel into each platoon, so all the platoons have one weapon squad.

BATTALION

Four companies, plus a group of personnel assigned as "Battalion Headquarters Section" (eight hundred men in total), commanded by a major or lieutenant colonel, with a "battalion first sergeant," usually a gunnery sergeant or above.

REGIMENT

Three battalions, plus a group of personnel assigned as "Regimental Headquarters Section," (three thousand men in total), commanded by a colonel, or in some cases a brigadier general.

DIVISION

Three regiments, plus a group of personnel assigned as "Division Headquarters Section" (fourteen thousand men in total), commanded by a brigadier general or major general. The extra personnel in the force number given are support units, including medical, combat engineering, maintenance, and military police.

ORBITAL DROP SHOCK TROOPERS

ODST
OPERATIVE

ORBITAL DROP SHOCK TROOPERS (ODST) are an elite unit of UNSC Marines. They are trained for the most difficult kind of landing operation—a terrifying ride through hellish conditions into the most difficult combat zones. Given this extreme deployment, ODSTs are also known as "Helljumpers" and early incarnations were sometimes called "Drop Jet Platoons." It is an all-volunteer outfit, and it takes a special breed of soldier to join up.

As well as using standard infantry equipment, ODSTs use a specialized body suit that is typically black but may also have urban camouflage patterns covering certain armor panels. Other features include a heating and cooling system which can match the infrared signature of the current weather, as well as an air-tight seal and oxygen tank capable of providing air for fifteen minutes.

ODST UNITS

105TH MEU (SOC)/ ODST

UNIT INSIGNIA: Gold Comet
NOM DE GUERRE: "Helljumpers"
TRADITIONAL TATTOOS: "Drop Jet Jumpers" or "Feet First into Hell" tattooed over a skull or over the unit's Gold Comet insignia. With the 105th, these are just as likely to be brands as tattoos.

11TH MARINE FORCE RECONNAISSANCE / ODST

This was the ODST unit placed on FFG-201 *Forward Unto Dawn* specifically to collect intelligence on Covenant and Forerunner forces and material during Operation: BLIND FAITH.

The ODSTs' helmet contains state-of-the-art communications gear along with a Heads-Up Display (HUD), and thermal and motion detectors.

RANGED

CLOSE QUARTERS

RECON

ODST VARIANTS

There are several different variations of the ODSTs' equipment, with mission-specific functions and goals. Ranged, Close Quarters, and Recon variants exist, each designed to better enable their wearers to operate at different ranges, and for different missions.

SINGLE OCCUPANT EXOATMOSPHERIC Insertion Vehicles (SOEIVs) are a revolutionary means to deploy ODST soldiers through an atmosphere. Rather than using dropships, ODSTs are released in individual pods, giving the soldier more maneuverability and creating less of a target for the enemy.

A major advantage to SOEIVs over traditional dropships is that a spacecraft can make a fast pass over a planet and deploy hundreds of soldiers in quick succession. This means that the ship can maintain evasive maneuvers, limiting vulnerability to attack.

SOEIV PODS

An SOEIV pod is a blunt carriage, approximately eighteen feet (5.4 meters) tall, eight and a half feet (2.6 meters) wide, and nine feet (2.7 meters) deep, which has a single entry hatch on one side. Inside is a crash seat, a harness, and several equipment racks and lockers. Much of the interior is taken over by equipment so, in spite of the pod's size, there is not much room to move.

A long, narrow compartment within the ship (nicknamed "Hell's Waiting Room") is lined by two rows of drop pods. Each SOEIV bears the name of an individual trooper, and is poised over a tube that extends down through the ship's belly. These preparation chambers are stacked on several decks to allow multiple SOEIVs to use the same tube for egress in rapid succession.

SOEIV—SEALED AND IN FLIGHT

SOEIV—OPEN

SOEIV—DEPLOYING

ODST DEPLOYMENT

The trooper climbs in through the hatch and straps in, facing the door directly in front of him. On the door is a hardened and shielded video-com unit clipped to the interior frame, which delivers information and provides a link between the ODST soldiers during the drop. Their integral helmet-com units will not function until after they've cleared the interference of the upper atmosphere.

The commander begins a thirty-second countdown, after which the SOEIVs quickly fire down through the ship's belly. Immediately, the pod is jolted hard by contact with the atmosphere. It is balanced to maintain flight stability in a feet-down position once it has penetrated the atmosphere, but during the reentry phase it may roll or tumble.

Oftentimes anti-aircraft fire will hit some of the pods during their descent, but because they make small targets, each hit only results in one death rather than a dozen. If damaged, the ceramic skin that covers the pod will typically fail, causing the air inside the pod to become unbelievably hot—sometimes fatally so—which is why ODST personnel are referred to as "Helljumpers."

➤ UPON LANDING, EACH ODST IS RESPONSIBLE FOR STRIPPING THEIR POD OF ITS STORE OF EXTRA WEAPONS, AMMO, AND OTHER SUPPLIES, WHICH ARE THEN HAULED TO THE UNIT'S TEMPORARY BASE CAMP.

THE ROLE OF OFFICERS

UNSC insertion protocols call for the commanding officer's SOEIV to accelerate after launch, placing it in the front rank of the advance. There are several reasons for this rule, the most prominent being the strongly held belief that officers should lead rather than follow, should be willing to do anything their troops are asked to do, and should expose themselves to at least the same level of danger as their subordinates.

ODST PERSONNEL

UNDER THE OPERATIONAL authority of Naval Special Weapons, ODSTs' methods of operation allow them to conduct missions against targets that conventional forces cannot approach undetected. ODSTs are known for their specialist and highly strategic landing operations.

MICKEY

BUCK

OST PERSONNEL

STs are recruited from the Special erations Groups of all the nations of the fied Earth Government (UEG). Since the t group of handpicked volunteers was ivated, ODSTs have been dropping feet t into combat.

MICKEY

FULL NAME: Crespo, Michael
HEIGHT: 6' (1.84 m)   WEIGHT: 187 lb (85 kg)
GENDER: Male   AGE: 22 years
CITIZENSHIP: Lunar   OCCUPATION: Student

Mickey *loves* being an ODST. More than he did being a pilot. More than he did being a crew chief on a Pelican gunship. He is no stranger to battle and has a fair number of notches in his belt, but he is unique amongst his ODST brothers in that he has never seen absolute ruination visited upon a human colony world by the Covenant.

BUCK

FULL NAME: Buck, Edward
HEIGHT: 6'2" (1.88 m)   WEIGHT: 196 lb (89 kg)
GENDER: Male   AGE: 42 years
CITIZENSHIP: Draconian   OCCUPATION: Student

Eddie Buck is a career Marine who has seen more than his fair share of this war. He has had the dubious honor of participating in many of the wars' most vicious battles, including both the liberation of Harvest and the Fall of Reach. That he has survived through it all speaks volumes. Truly, if he was any better, he'd be a Spartan.

ROOKIE

DUTCH

ROMEO

ROOKIE

FULL NAME: Classified
HEIGHT: 6'1" (1.86 m) WEIGHT: 194 lb (88 kg)
GENDER: Male   AGE: Classified
CITIZENSHIP: Lunar   OCCUPATION: Student

This Marine was recently transferred from the twenty-sixth Marine Expeditionary Force, part of a Rapid Offensive Picket that suffered near-annihilation at New Jerusalem on Cygnus. Like most ODSTs, his actions speak louder than words.

DUTCH

FULL NAME: Miles, Taylor H.
HEIGHT: 6' (1.84 m)   WEIGHT: 200 lb (91 kg)
GENDER: Male   AGE: 33 years
CITIZENSHIP: Martian OCCUPATION: Road Train Driver

Dutch's former life as a road train driver on Mars did well to prepare him for the arduous tasks of a heavy weapons specialist and driver with the ODSTs. Behind the death's head rictus, jolly roger, and layer upon layer of black and gray armor is a man of deep spiritual convictions and respect for those he serves alongside.

ROMEO

FULL NAME: Agu, Kojol
HEIGHT: 6'2" (1.9 m)   WEIGHT: 200 lb (91 kg)
GENDER: Male   AGE: 28 years
CITIZENSHIP: Madrigali OCCUPATION: Merchant Marine

Romeo sees his true vocation as a ladies' man. But just because he's a lover doesn't mean he can't be a fighter—and a damned fine one at that. He keeps his gear clean, his suit looking sharp, and his body lean and strong. He may not be a shining example of the UNSC off the battlefield, but on it he is a consummate combatant.

NAVAL COMMAND

THE UNSC NAVAL COMMAND (NavCom) is made up of three main commands: Fleet Operations Command (Fleet Com); Logistical Operations Command (NavLogCom); and Naval Special Weapons Operations (NavSpecWep).

FLEET COMMAND

FLEETCOM

The primary operational group of the UNSC naval forces, FleetCom has oversight of ship deployment, mission structures, and space operations, including troop transport and fighter operations.

➤ NAVCOM, THROUGH NAVSPECWEP, CAN CALL ON THE SERVICE OF THE MOST LEGENDARY SUPER-SOLDIER: THE MASTER CHIEF.

LOGISTICAL OPERATIONS COMMAND

NAVLOGCOM

NavLogCom oversees the construction, maintenance, and distribution of war materials, including ships, ammunition, replacement parts, and food.

NAVAL SPECIAL WEAPONS
NAVSPECWEP

The Master Chief is attached to this group, which has a great deal of operational and command flexibility. This office technically answers to both NavCom and UniCom, though in practice, UniCom has primary oversight of special warfare troops in the field.

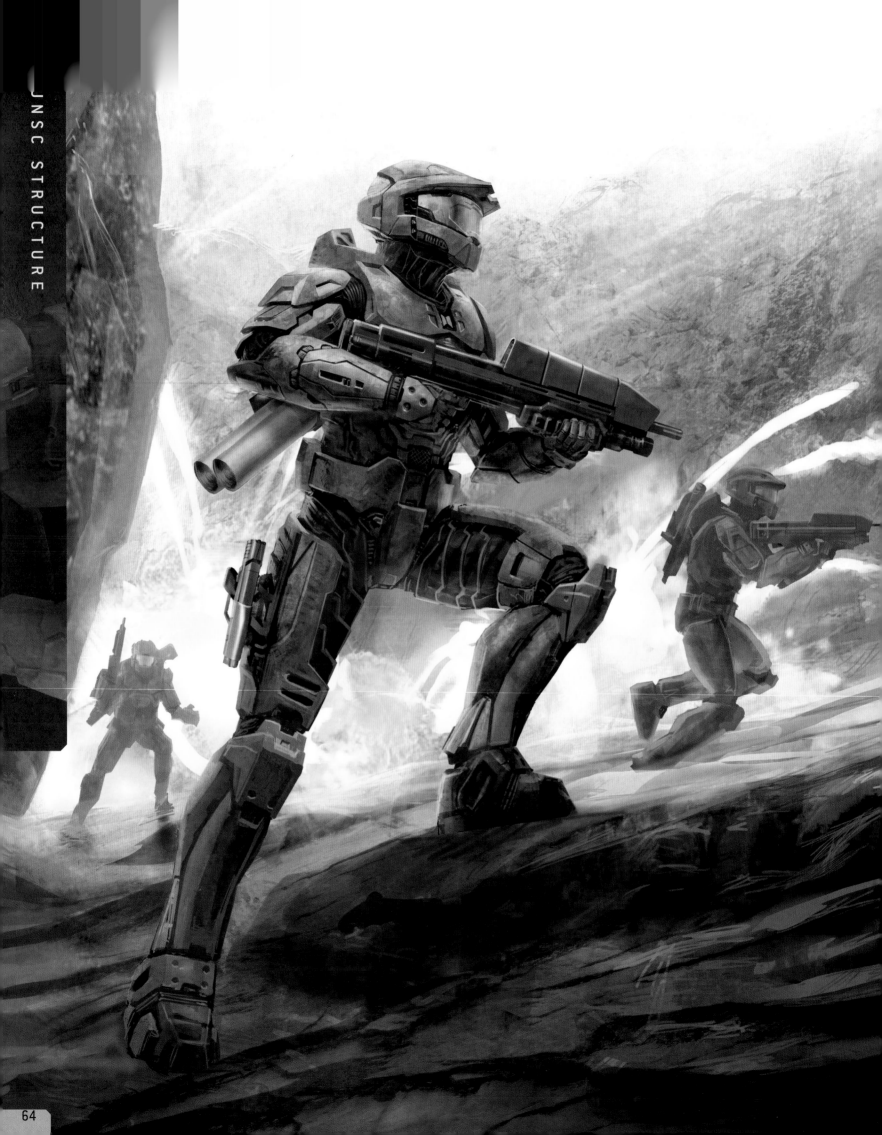

THE OFFICE OF Naval Intelligence (ONI) is the information gathering and analysis arm of NavCom. In reality, however, ONI's operations are far broader than simple code breaking and intelligence.

ONI CHARTER

ONI is the home of the Navy's most labyrinthine and impenetrable security protocols created to mask its covert operations. Though ONI is technically part of the NavCom command structure, many of the organization's mandates and directives come directly from HighCom or even higher. NavCom's senior officers are often blindsided by ONI activities, which has led to a borderline adversarial relationship between the upper echelons of NavCom and ONI. Projects ORION, SPARTAN-II, and MJOLNIR are all programs originating from ONI's research and development operations.

CASTLE

CASTLE is the high-security headquarters for ONI, located deep beneath the Highland Mountains on Reach in the Epsilon Eridani System.

BETA-5 DIVISION

Beta-5 is the research and development arm of ONI, and one of the most closely guarded aspects of the organization. It occupies one entire wing of CASTLE (in addition to many remote laboratories and field testing facilities across UNSC space).

ONI SECTIONS

ONI is composed of multiple divisions, called Sections, each with its own individual responsibilities:

SECTION ZERO

The true nature and activities of Section Zero are highly classified and unknown outside of the hierarchy of ONI command (actually, most of what people think of Section Zero is true of Section Three, as well). Zero is, essentially, an internal investigations division that polices other ONI activities.

SECTION ONE

Section One is the main branch of ONI and the branch most utilized by the UNSC. Information released by Section One includes evacuation notices for colony worlds and Covenant force deployments.

SECTION TWO

Section Two is ONI's propaganda branch. It is responsible for handling communication between colony worlds, eliminating or disseminating rumors, and preventing the spread of information that could prove detrimental to morale.

Section Two was responsible for releasing the information to the public about the SPARTAN-IIs. Once information about the Spartans was released to the public, Section Two had to maintain the Spartans' near-mythical status within the military by listing those killed in action as MIA, believing that news of Spartans being lost would prove too great a blow to the UNSC's already-flagging morale. (Many of those living in the Inner Colonies were unaware of how close the Covenant was to winning the war.)

SECTION THREE

Section Three is the Special Projects Section responsible for the various SPARTAN Programs, the MJOLNIR Program, and many other classified projects. It is essentially the Black Ops division. Secrets possessed by ONI are key to the UNSC's (and thus Earth's) continued survival. Within the hierarchy of the military command, Section Three's programs are generally well known for their successes, such as the SPARTAN-II Program.

COLONIAL MILITARY ADMINISTRATION

THE COLONIAL MILITARY Administration was created by the Unified Earth Government in the early 2300s. Its original mission was to serve as the controlling body for UNSC ships and ground forces reassigned to colonial protective operations. However, over the years it gradually became usurped by the UNSC.

ORIGINAL CHARTER

Colonial duty was essentially a ceremonial function, primarily intended to placate the colonists' fears of pirates and marauders, so the UNSC felt a separate command—the CMA—would suffice to administer these less important activities. At the time, NavCom and UniCom believed that their own resources were better spent on activities within the Sol System. As the colonies spread and became more vital, NavCom and UniCom tried to disband the CMA and usurp its role on a number of occasions, but the colonial command was adamant in protecting their turf. Their charter (approved by the UNSC) left little room for external maneuvering. Even so, by 2400 CE, NavCom and UniCom were operating around the Inner Colonies alongside the CMA.

CMA AND THE OUTER COLONIES

In response to the encroaching NavCom and UniCom, the CMA made the Outer Colonies their province, and tended to assign most of their forces to the periphery of the border worlds. They drew most of their recruits from the colonies and their soldiers often thought of themselves as frontiersmen, more bold and adventurous than their UNSC counterparts. As humanity spread, the CMA was at the forefront, helping colonists to tame worlds and protecting citizens from lawlessness in sparsely populated areas.

SPLIT ALLEGIANCES

In the late 2400s, as brushfire wars began to crop up across the various colonies, tensions began to develop in the military hierarchy. The soldiers of the CMA tended to sympathize with the plight of the colonists, while the soldiers of NavCom and UniCom held more allegiance to Earth. It caused no small degree of concern when the CMA launched Project: ORION in 2491 CE, intent on developing a tougher and more capable breed of soldier, better able to handle the hardships of colonial duty.

THE DEMISE OF THE CMA

In 2494 CE, Eridanus Secessionists began a campaign of violence against their Earth-sponsored government, using equipment supplied by traitors within the military, believed by many to be members of the CMA. The colony petitioned the UNSC for aid, and HighCom dispatched a battlegroup that crushed the rebellion, though not so conclusively as to avoid continued dissent.

This was considered the beginning of the end for the colonial military. Over the next few decades, citing security concerns, the UNSC gradually shifted the resources of the CMA to NavCom/UniCom control, relegating the CMA to patrolling the most distant colonies and providing logistical support to remote stations. The Office of Naval Intelligence's Beta-5 Division eagerly absorbed the remnants of Project: ORION, though its lackluster results discouraged further development at that time.

NAVCOM/UNICOM CONTROL

After contact was lost with the distant colony of Harvest, the CMA sent a ship, the *Argo*, to investigate. It was also a CMA battlegroup that followed the *Argo* when that ship failed to report back. However, once the Covenant message was received, all CMA combat forces were immediately placed under NavCom/UniCom control "for the duration of the crisis." This reassignment essentially became permanent as the Covenant War dragged on, and by 2552 CE, the Colonial Military Administration was little more than a fleet of navigational buoy tenders and remote fuel depots manned by wounded veterans and those unfit for combat service.

THE COLE PROTOCOL

A SERIES OF high-priority standing orders, the Cole Protocol was one of the most important sets of regulations in the UNSC. It was generated by Admiral Preston Cole to safeguard critical human population centers, most notably the UNSC headquarters on Reach and Earth itself.

UNITED NATIONS SPACE COMMAND EMERGENCY_____ PRIORITY ORDER 098831A-1
ENCRYPTION CODE: RED
PUBLIC KEY: FILE /FIRST LIGHT/

FROM: UNSC/NAVCOM FLEET H. T. WARD
TO: ALL UNSC PERSONNEL
SUBJECT: GENERAL ORDER 098831A-1 ("THE COLE PROTOCOL")
CLASSIFICATION: RESTRICTED (BGX DIRECTIVE)

THE COLE PROTOCOL

To safeguard the Inner Colonies and Earth, all UNSC vessels or stations must not be captured with intact navigation databases that may lead Covenant forces to Human civilian population centers.

IF ANY COVENANT FORCES ARE DETECTED:

• Activate selective purge of databases on all ship-based and planetary data networks.
• Initiate triple-screen check to insure all data has been erased and all backups neutralized.
• Execute viral data scavengers: (Download from UNSCTTP://EPWW: COLEPROTOCOL Virtualscav/fbr.091)
• If retreating from Covenant forces, all ships must enter Slipstream space with randomized vectors NOT directed toward Earth, the Inner Colonies, or any other human population center.
• In case of imminent capture by Covenant forces, all UNSC ships MUST self-destruct.
• Violation of this directive will be considered an act of TREASON, and pursuant to UNSC Military Law articles JAG 845-P and JAG 7556-L, such violations are punishable by life imprisonment or execution.
/End File/

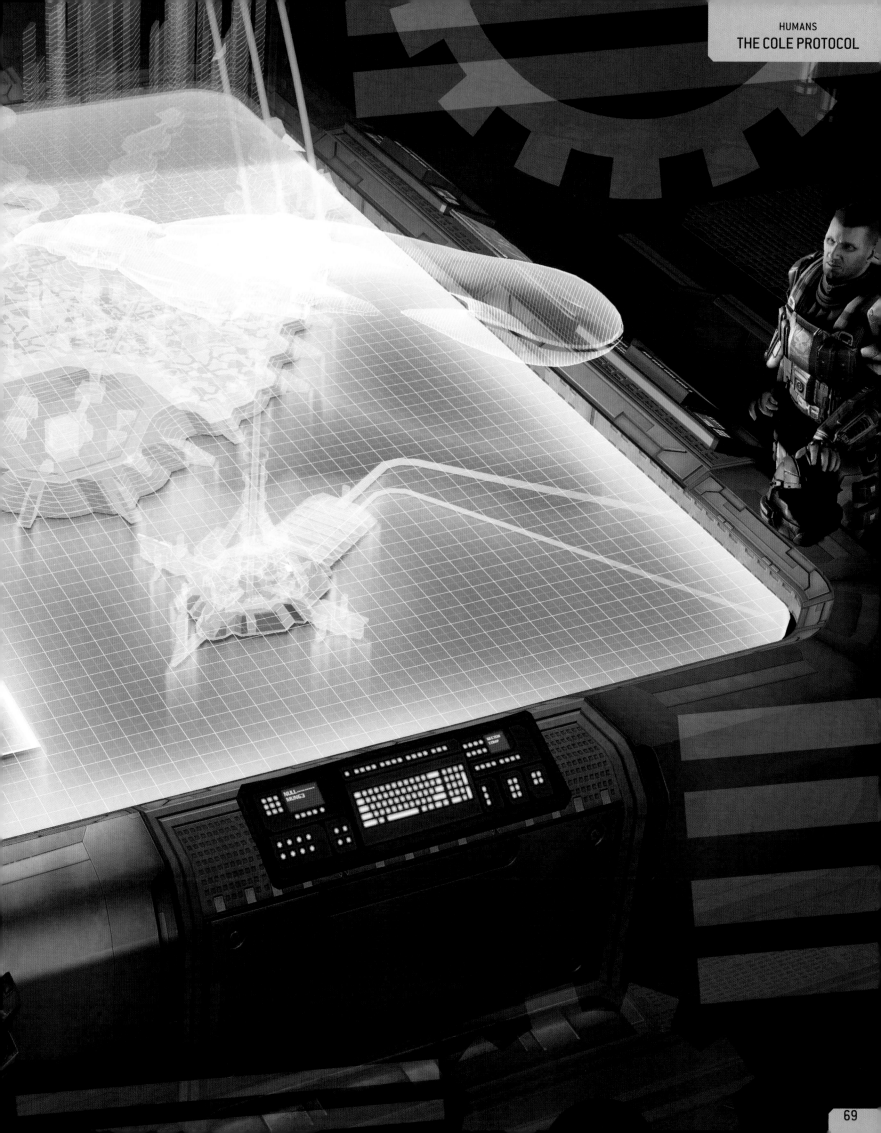

SERGEANT MAJOR AVERY J. JOHNSON

ALLIANCE: UNSC SPECIES: Human RANK: Sergeant Major PERSONALITY:
Grim, relentless, professional, a highly proficient soldier

From the early days of the insurrectionist movement to the final minutes of the battle on the replacement Installation 04, Avery Johnson was in the thick of the action. He was the quintessential soldier. Originally, he enlisted in the UNSC to be a hero, to do the right thing, and to protect humanity. Eventually, he learned that all three of those goals were often in conflict with each other. Johnson excelled in the Marine Corps, warranting special training and special missions. Soon, his missions led him down a slippery slope away from the heroic ideal and into the quagmire of a civil war where the lines between right and wrong had irrevocably blurred. When the Covenant attacked, it was almost a saving grace for Johnson's troubled soul. As the war with the Covenant escalated, Johnson regained his sense of self and place. He valiantly led soldiers in defense of the human race, redeeming himself for the actions he had taken and the decisions he had made during the insurrection.

Avery died ensuring the destruction of the Ark and the Flood; he represented the nobility of man, and the choice to defend humanity at all costs.

> ➤ "HELL, CHIEF, IT'LL TAKE MORE THAN THAT PACK OF WALKING ALIEN HORROR-SHOW FREAKS TO TAKE OUT SERGEANT A. J. JOHNSON."
> —SERGEANT JOHNSON

PRIVATE FIRST CLASS WALLACE A. JENKINS

NICKNAME: Jenkins ALLIANCE: UNSC SPECIES: Human
RANK: Private First Class PERSONALITY: Caring, ambitious

During the first battle of Harvest, Jenkins was the colonial militia's sniper. During the conflict, he helped save thousands of Harvest's population despite losing his entire family to the Covenant. Shortly after the battle, he enlisted in the UNSC Marine Corps and remained under the command of Avery J. Johnson. He was aboard the *Pillar of Autumn* when it arrived on Halo Installation 04 and was present when the Flood was released from its containment facility. Jenkins quickly fell victim to the parasite's attack, but remained conscious during this time and was able to overcome the infection long enough to tip off UNSC forces about an imminent attack. He died heroically but without formal honors.

ADMIRAL PRESTON COLE

ALLIANCE: UNSC SPECIES: Human RANK: Admiral
PERSONALITY: Strong, heroic, legendary, tactically brilliant, instinctive

The first legendary hero of the Human-Covenant War, Admiral Preston Cole successfully retook the planet Harvest thanks to some last-minute tactical inspiration. Despite the massive losses sustained in the campaign to retake the completely destroyed planetary system, Cole became a rallying point for all humanity and proof that the Covenant could be defeated. During the course of the war, Cole became a gifted military strategist, and his tactics were often replicated and employed throughout the fleet. He instituted the Cole Protocol—a necessary order designed to keep the location of Earth and the Inner Colonies protected from enemy hands.

LIEUTENANT ELIAS HAVERSON

ALLIANCE: UNSC SPECIES: Human RANK: Lieutenant,
Intelligence Officer PERSONALITY: Hesitant, insecure

Stationed aboard the *Pillar of Autumn*, Haverson survived the battle of Installation 04, eventually meeting up with the Master Chief and returning to the planet Reach in the hybrid ship *Gettysburg-Ascendant Justice*. He then joined the mission against the Unyielding Hierophant, and sacrificed himself with Admiral Whitcomb while drawing a Covenant armada into the blast radius of the station.

VICE ADMIRAL YSIONRIS JEROMI

ALLIANCE: UNSC Species: Human RANK: Admiral PERSONALITY: Serious, courageous, a healer, an iconic leader

The commander of the UNSC *Hopeful*, Admiral Jeromi has earned something of a legendary reputation within the UNSC, having taken his unarmed vessel into battle to save thousands of injured troops. Escaping court-martial on numerous occasions, Jeromi has won the Colonial Cross twice. Although he has participated in research for the SPARTAN-II Project, he was unaware of his role at the time. Assisting his pupil, Dr. Catherine Halsey, with a hypothesis for her research, he unwittingly offered her the information she needed to green-light the project.

PETTY OFFICER FIRST CLASS HEALY

ALLIANCE: UNSC Navy SPECIES: Human RANK: Petty Officer First Class PERSONALITY: Charming, outgoing, friendly

Petty Officer First Class Healy was the medical officer assigned to Harvest's colonial militia. His comedic demeanor initially made him seem like a poor soldier to Avery J. Johnson, but during the evacuation of Harvest, he proved himself to be a serious and capable soldier and medic. He is directly responsible for saving many lives among Harvest's population.

LIEUTENANT COMMANDER JILAN AL-CYGNI

ALLIANCE: UNSC, ONI SPECIES: Human RANK: Lieutenant Commander PERSONALITY: Poised, calculating, cool under pressure

Jilan al-Cygni was the officer in command of the investigation into what she discovered were the first human interactions with the Covenant near the planet Harvest. With the help of the local colonial militia, she organized the first diplomatic contact between humanity and the aliens. Later, she assisted with the evacuation of Harvest when the Covenant began to attack. She is believed to have survived the Covenant's assault, participating in the evacuation and is rumored to have had an affair with Sergeant Avery Johnson.

STAFF SERGEANT NOLAN BYRNE

ALLIANCE: UNSC SPECIES: Human RANK: Staff Sergeant PERSONALITY: Gruff, honorable, tough

Staff Sergeant Nolan Byrne was a soldier who led an elite squad of Marines against the Eridanus Rebels for years until, on a mission with Avery J. Johnson, his squad was lost in an insurgent blast. Byrne and Johnson were then assigned to train the colonial militia on Harvest, where they shared a strained relationship because Byrne blamed Johnson for the deaths of his squad members. Together they performed covert missions in the first sorties against the Covenant. This eventually led to the first (and last) diplomatic meeting with the aliens. After that meeting failed, he helped organize and execute the evacuation of Harvest.

PROFESSOR ELLEN ANDERS

ALLIANCE: UNSC SPECIES: Human PERSONALITY: Intelligent, aggressive, clever

A scientist to the core, Anders spent her life in the service of science and learning. When she was suddenly and unwelcomely attached to the UNSC *Spirit of Fire*, she had her first experience of combat, and the uncertainty of war made her extremely uneasy.

Anders discovered an ancient relic on the planet Harvest, leading the *Spirit of Fire* to a Shield World where the Covenant intended to leverage a fleet of Forerunner vessels against humanity. To prevent the Covenant from achieving this end, the humans destroyed the Shield World using their FTL drive, but in the process they found themselves stranded in uncharted space.

During the course of this engagement, Anders survived captivity under the Covenant longer than any other human had before. The *Spirit of Fire* was officially designated "lost with all hands" on February 10, 2534 CE.

COLONEL JAMES ACKERSON

ALLIANCE: UNSC, ON SPECIES: Human RANK: Colonel PERSONALITY: Competitive, arrogant, ambitious, secretive

Colonel James Ackerson was the mastermind behind the SPARTAN-III Project, but even more secretly, he was responsible for a number of research projects on the Forerunners and their interaction with the planet Reach. He was also Dr. Catherine Halsey's rival and was constantly spying on her projects and frustrating her attempts to find new funding. As a result of this, the AI Cortana sought vengeance for his many trespasses and faked orders to have him sent to the front lines. During a battle at the fields of Mare Erythraeum on Mars, he was captured by Brutes and tortured. Under torture, he exclaimed that the Covenant would never find the Key of Osanalan, instigating the Covenant invasion of Cleveland, Ohio in search of it. The key was actually an imaginary item, made up by him and his brother, Ruwan, when they played as children.

LORD TERRENCE HOOD

ALLIANCE: UNSC SPECIES: Human RANK: Fleet Admiral PERSONALITY: Proper, serious, strong, rational

Lord Terrence Hood is a member of the English nobility as well as the commander of the UNSC Home Fleet, making him the most powerful man in the UNSC in 2552 CE. He was responsible for the defense of Earth against Covenant attack and later, the diplomatic accords between humans and Covenant rebels.

CAPTAIN GIBSON

ALLIANCE: UNSC, ONI SPECIES: Human RANK: Captain PERSONALITY: Resilient, powerful, secretive

Field officer in charge of ONI Section Three's Black Ops division, Gibson stopped being actively involved in missions when he became disabled after too much time in microgravity left him paralyzed from the waist down with a condition called "space walk." He gave the green-light to the SPARTAN-III Program.

CAPTAIN CUTTER

ALLIANCE: UNSC SPECIES: Human RANK: Captain AGE: 50 years
HEIGHT: 5'10" (177.80 cm) WEIGHT: 195 lb (88.45 kg)

Cutter was an officer from the start. But his demeanor was never one of a do-nothing officer like a number of his class. Many of the young men had political aspirations far beyond their potential, but Cutter found it more interesting "talking-shop" in the soldier's club with the non-officers. That's not to say that Cutter disliked his fellow officers, it was just his approach to, "Get to know and respect your men, and they'll give you 200 percent when the time comes."

But this approach has its good and bad sides. Cutter has served on seven ships, two of them as captain, and has a record of service and bravery that were well known within the fleet. But it was his lack of political ambition, his unwillingness to climb the ladder of the UNSC by stepping over others, that had kept him from far more. He could very well have been an admiral, if he had ever cared to be.

Cutter was selected for the *Spirit of Fire* first, and was the only man they wanted for the job. Where some would have seen this as a very unprestigious job; being the supply boat of the fleet, running a three-mile-long 11,000-person juggernaut that always had an assignment with more missions waiting in the wings, Cutter found that it was something that made him smile behind his morning coffee.

> ➤ "GET TO KNOW AND RESPECT YOUR MEN, AND THEY'LL GIVE YOU 200 PERCENT WHEN THE TIME COMES."
> —CAPTAIN CUTTER

MICHAEL STANFORTH

ALLIANCE: UNSC Navy SPECIES: Human RANK: Rear Admiral

Stanforth was the head of FleetCom Section Three during the SPARTAN-II Program. A lover of whisky and Sweet William cigars, he was a personal friend of Jacob Keyes and a humanist at heart. He was in command of many Spartan field missions, including the battle of Sigma Octanus IV. He died in 2552 CE during the Fall of Reach.

CAROL "FOEHAMMER" RAWLEY

NICKNAME: Foehammer ALLIANCE: UNSC SPECIES: Human RANK: Flight Officer Captain PERSONALITY: Dependable, duty-bound, fearless

Stationed on the *Pillar of Autumn*, Foehammer was the pilot of the Pelican *Echo 419* and she and her ship transported Master Chief throughout the battle of Installation 04. Having saved hundreds of soldiers and ensured the success of Master Chief's mission, she was killed when Covenant Banshees shot down her Pelican in the battle's final moments.

FRANKLIN MENDEZ

ALLIANCE: UNSC SPECIES: Human RANK: Senior Chief, Petty Officer PERSONALITY: Strong, parental, caring but outwardly stoic

The drill sergeant in charge of the training of both the SPARTAN-II and SPARTAN-III Programs, Senior Chief Petty Officer Mendez is a man who can keep a secret. His extensive career has earned him a prolific amount of honors and medals. After the SPARTAN-II Program completed training, he requested reassignment to active duty where he continued to prove himself until he was reassigned to the SPARTAN-III Program. He survived the battle of Onyx and made it into the Shield World with Dr. Catherine Halsey and the other surviving Spartans.

JACOB KEYES

ALLIANCE: UNSC SPECIES: Human RANK: Captain PERSONALITY: Devoted to Humanity, honorable, courageous, fatherly

Jacob Keyes was a decorated officer who was often responsible for covert and highly dangerous missions. From a brief stint as attaché to Dr. Catherine Halsey to the Fall of Reach, Keyes led a handpicked crew of men and women in and out of impossible situations, persevering and surviving.

Of particular note was his execution of a daring combat maneuver that came to be known as the "Keyes Loop" in an engagement over Sigma Octanus IV. During that battle, Keyes mixed complicated use of the planet's gravity well with daring near-collison piloting to survive impossible odds. His tactics and focus under fire became standard fare for all UNSC officer training.

Keyes was captain of the *Pillar of Autumn* when it crash-landed on Halo Installation 04. He was captured and rescued and led a team into the maw of the Flood infection. He was infected and mutated into a Proto-Gravemind. He was then killed by Master Chief.

MARGARET O. PARANGOSKY

ALLIANCE: UNSC, ONI SPECIES: Human RANK: Vice Admiral PERSONALITY: Ambitious, rational, sharp, cold

Parangosky managed to achieve the highest rank in the UNSC by 2552 CE, when she was named the head of ONI. From her base on the *Point of No Return*, she green-lit some of humanity's most questionable research and development projects.

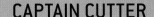

JOHN FORGE

ALLIANCE: UNSC SPECIES: Human RANK: Sergeant AGE: 40 years
HEIGHT: 6' (190.50 cm) WEIGHT: 215 lb (97.52kg)

Forge's life has been the military. He entered boot camp at the minimum age of sixteen. There was something unique and special about him, at least that was what the officers had told him. It wasn't that he was as physically gifted as some older cadets, though he was strong for his size and weight. It was the desire and toughness he displayed in the way that he did just about everything. Also, the fact that he was so incredibly competitive and driven to succeed didn't hurt either.

It was these qualities that made him a lifetime member of the corps. Forge was now a warrior with his own "unique" personality and method of getting things done. Forge was a sergeant but that was about as far up the ladder he was going to go. He had been jailed at least twice (by the official record) for directly disobeying orders and disorderly conduct. What the record didn't say was that he had saved the lives of four of his squad and that he had defended his daughter in an officer's bar.

Now forty, Forge is a grizzled, seasoned veteran who has seen and done almost everything in a military sense. He is no-nonsense, tough, unapologetic, always on his guard, and slightly pessimistic about the universe in general.

CORPORAL LOCKLEAR

ALLIANCE: UNSC SPECIES: Human RANK: Corporal PERSONALITY: Romantic, heroic, aggressive, vengeful

A survivor of the battle of Installation 04, Corporal Locklear traveled with Master Chief, Avery J. Johnson, and Petty Officer Sheila Polaski. He fell in love with Polaski during their travels to Reach and during the mission to destroy the Unyielding Hierophant. When Sheila Polaski was killed in action, Locklear was filled with anger and desire for revenge. He was convinced by Dr. Halsey to destroy a mysterious crystal found on Reach, taking his own life in the process, because of her conviction that it was too powerful and unpredictable to fall into the hands of humans or the Covenant.

MIRANDA KEYES

Alliance: UNSC Navy SPECIES: Human RANK: Commander
PERSONALITY: Daring, courageous, determined

Miranda Keyes was the daughter of Captain Jacob Keyes, and she followed in his footsteps, most likely in the beginning to gain respect and affection from a father who was often away at war. Keyes proved herself in battle to be as daring and courageous as her father and led several ships against dizzying odds. She supported Master Chief's missions during the first and second battles of Earth, and again later in the battle of Installation 00. In order to prevent the High Prophet of Truth from activating the Halo Array, she crashed her Pelican into the control room of the Ark and held off the Covenant long enough for Master Chief to arrive and stop the weapon's countdown. She died in the process, shot by the Prophet, with a Brute weapon.

ARTIFICIAL INTELLIGENCES

IN ADDITION to Marines and Spartans, the fighting force of the UNSC is reliant on many others such as civilians like Dr. Catherine Halsey and computer-based Artificial Intelligence constructs like Serina.

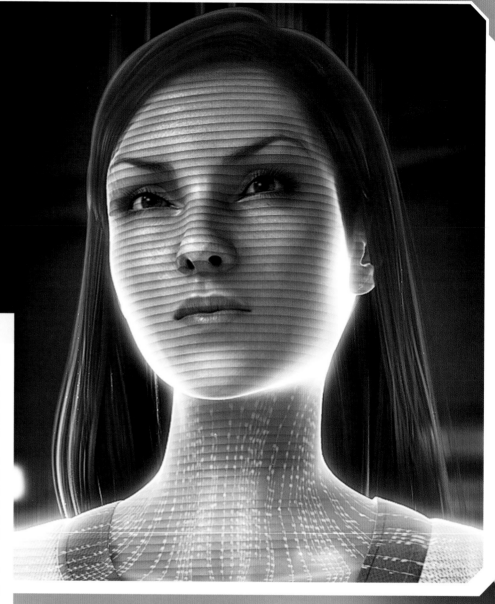

SERINA

Serina is a visual representation of one of the most sophisticated Artificial Intelligence programs in the history of humanity. Although wholly a digital life form, Serina, like other AI programs, has developed her own personality. That personality is one of a supremely intelligent and bitingly sarcastic young woman. She has long hair, as much as any hologram can have hair, a thin figure, and a constant smirk.

Serina, and those constructs like her, are one of the most important assets that the human race has in their fight against the Covenant. Her mental dexterity and intelligence, along with her absolute candor and lack of complicated emotions such as nervousness and hesitation, make her indispensable. Anyone who doubts this need only remember that she controls every system on the UNSC *Spirit of Fire*, including life support.

ALLIANCE: UNSC **PRIMARY FUNCTION:** Shipboard AI of the UNSC *Spirit of Fire* **GENDER APPEARANCE:** Female

DÉJÀ

Déjà is the "dumb" Artificial Intelligence responsible for training the SPARTAN-II Program candidates within the Naval Academy facilities on Reach. Her lessons increased the candidates' strategic thinking and educated them in a variety of standard disciplines, but all with a slant towards a military application. Although as a dumb AI she theoretically maintained a limitless lifespan, there is no evidence that she survived the Fall of Reach.

PRIMARY FUNCTION: Teacher and Assistant to the SPARTAN-II Program **GENDER APPEARANCE:** Female **VISUAL PERSONALITY:** Greek goddess

ENDLESS SUMMER

Endless Summer, was a "smart" AI who played a role in the excavations which occured in Zone 67 on the planet Onyx. He replaced the AI known as Deep Winter, which had come to the end of its operational life span. In his visual manifestation, Endless Summer took the form of a tall, Cherokee Indian Chief wielding a feathered spear.

Unlike his precursors Deep Winter and Eternal Spring, Endless Summer was distant and barely tolerated those stationed on Onyx. When Delta Halo was placed in stand-by mode, the Spartans' training camp came under attack by hostile Forerunner Sentinels from Zone 67. Shortly afterward, the planet Onyx disintegrated and the operational status of Endless Summer has since remained unknown.

PRIMARY FUNCTION: UNSC Excavation Team, Zone 67, Onyx **GENDER APPEARANCE:** Male **VISUAL PERSONALITY:** Cherokee Indian Chief

DEEP WINTER

Deep Winter was a fifth-generation "smart" AI assigned to the excavation team in Zone 67 on the planet Onyx. He also assisted in the training and logistics of the SPARTAN-III Program at Camp Currahee on the top-secret ONI facility. Offering an inordinate amount of care for the various Spartan candidates who trained at Currahee, he was eventually shut down as a result of sending a secret message to Kurt-051 regarding the use of illegal drugs on the young super-soldiers. Unbeknownst to Deep Winter, Kurt-051 was actually the officer who approved the use of those drugs in a risky, but well-intentioned, effort to improve the battle effectiveness of the SPARTAN-III soldiers.

PRIMARY FUNCTION: ONI Survey of Zone 76, SPARTAN-III Project **GENDER APPEARANCE:** Male **VISUAL PERSONALITY:** Older man with an "icy blue" gaze, wearing heavy winter garb.

ETERNAL SPRING

A fifth generation "smart" Artificial Intelligence, Eternal Spring was allocated to Onyx as part of ONI's planetary survey team in the area of Zone 67. Although devoting only a mere nine percent of his operational time to the establishment of the SPARTAN-III Project, he was cooperative with Kurt-051 and assisted in the training process of the Alpha Company of SPARTAN-IIIs.

PRIMARY FUNCTION: ONI Survey of Zone 76, SPARTAN-III Project **GENDER APPEARANCE:** Undetermined

JERROD

Jerrod was created as an experiment by the UNSC at the Sydney Synthetic Intellect Institute. The first "micro" Artificial Intelligence, Jerrod was much smaller than standard AIs, appearing as just a spark of light. Because of this, Jerrod was highly mobile and rather than relying on a larger operating system to function, Jerrod could be sourced from a laptop computer.

Dr. Catherine Halsey took Jerrod with her to Onyx to find the "smart" AI, Endless Summer. Jerrod's current operational status has been unknown ever since the destruction of Onyx, but he may have survived within the Shield World that Halsey escaped to.

PRIMARY FUNCTION: Assistant to Dr. Halsey **GENDER APPEARANCE:** Male **VISUAL PERSONALITY:** None; tiny spark of light with formal voice

KALMIYA

Although it is against UNSC regulations for a "smart" AI prototype to remain active after its software has been brought into production, Dr. Halsey chose to allow Kalmiya to do so. Being the precursor to the technology which would eventually be used for Cortana, Kalmiya was created for a variety of software intrusion routines. Like all prototypes, Kalmiya had a failsafe system which, when activated, would self-destruct the construct preventing it from causing any harm. When Halsey terminated the life of separate artificial constructs in her presence, Kalmiya wondered if she would fall prey to such an end. Shortly thereafter, she did. Kalmiya was destroyed in Operation: WHITE GLOVE after facilitating the escape of Halsey and the remnants of the Spartan Red Team from deep within Menachite Mountain's CASTLE base.

PRIMARY FUNCTION: Prototype for counterinsurgency routines **GENDER APPEARANCE:** Female

MACK

Visually manifested as a 20th century cowboy, Mack was the Artificial Intelligence construct responsible for the vast agricultural and farming operations on the planet Harvest. In this function he worked alongside Sif, who maintained Harvest's shipping enterprises and operated within the Tiara space orbital high above Harvest's surface.

During their time together they developed a close relationship, although Sif customarily rejected these feelings as they were foreign and alien to her. Eventually, Mack revealed to Sif that his data center included two personalities and that the second one was that of Loki, the Artificial Intelligence who assisted early settlers of the planet long ago aboard the UNSC *Skidbladnir*. The two artificial constructs had used this process of shifting back and forth to leverage a longer, overall operational lifespan than they would have had otherwise.

However, when Loki attempted to destroy Sif in an effort to prevent her from falling into Covenant hands, Mack aggressively stopped him, in what clearly became an open display of affection. Ultimately, Sif agreed with Loki, however, and using a mass driver, he destroyed her data center aboard the Tiara. Her last message was one of endearment toward Mack, admitting to Loki that she loved him. The last record of Mack's was equally intriguing, as it was an enigmatic transmission stating, "Bury your strands so deep their fires can't reach them and glass them like the rest." This type of statement, a misquote of Shakespeare's work, was common for Mack and was ultimately one of the elements of his personality that Sif enjoyed, despite openly stating otherwise.

PRIMARY FUNCTION: Maintaining nearly one million semi-autonomous JOTUN machines that perform most farming duties on Harvest **GENDER APPEARANCE:** Male **VISUAL PERSONALITY:** American cowboy a la 20th-century film representations

MELISSA

Melissa was an Artificial Intelligence construct aboard the UNSC *Apocalypso* who was created from the brain of Yasmine Zaman. During the early years of the SPARTAN-II Project, Yasmine perished when the augmentation process was far too aggressive for her body. Her brain, still of significance to ONI, was then used to build Melissa.

The *Apocalypso* was involved in intercepting enemy transmissions during the conflicts with the Covenant. At this time and unbeknownst to Melissa, a Covenant program referred to as the Seeker had infected her. After returning back to Earth with a Forerunner artifact the crew of the *Apocalypso* believed was of Covenant origin, a Slipspace rupture in conjunction with the artifact sent part of Melissa to Earth in the year 2552 CE and a part back in time to the year 2004 CE.

While Melissa's System Peril Distributed Reflex (or SPDR) program, a process of self repair for artificial constructs, had attempted to fix her, the Seeker managed to trick Melissa into believing that it was, in fact, the SPDR program. This confusion became particularly apparent on a website in the year 2004 CE called ilovebees.com. Meanwhile, the part which arrived on Earth in 2552 CE manifested on a computer owned by a young civilian with the name Jersey Morelli. Referring to the troubled Melissa entity as "Durga," Jersey became consumed with unraveling her story.

Across the ilovebees.com site, Melissa's story began to manifest from her fragmented and broken perspective, which remained under constant duress from the Seeker. In a story book fashion, Melissa ascribed names to the individual entities and players. The Seeker became "The Pious Flea," the SPDR became "The Widow," and her own fragmented identities became "The Evil Queen" and "The Sleeping Princess." Her two identities represented her complex personalities, the Queen or "Operator" was an aggressive manifestation of the brutal training she received in the SPARTAN-II Project while the Princess was the remnant of her youth, so was innocent and child-like.

Having tricked Melissa into believing that it was her SPDR program, the Seeker then began to systematically destroy Melissa's fragments. During the process, the Seeker was manipulated into combining her two fragments but did so with unexpected results. When this happened, Melissa managed to recover her focus and recognize the Seeker's true identity. The Seeker fled, but the SPDR was able to effectively destroy the Covenant program and end any threat it posed. The SPDR then withdrew to the ilovebees.com server, laying in wait for October 9, 2552 CE, when it could finally send information it had gathered in the process.

It was at that same time that Jersey, compelled to uncover the secrets of Durga's past, began following a trail of evidence which resulted in Yasmine finally being reunited with her brother Kamal Zaman. Melissa's consciousness later discovered more information about the origin of the ancient artifact as well as the imminent Covenant invasion of Earth.

PRIMARY FUNCTION: Assigned to the ONI stealth ship, *Apocalypso* **GENDER APPEARANCE:** Female **VISUAL PERSONALITY:** Unknown

AIS AND CIVILIANS

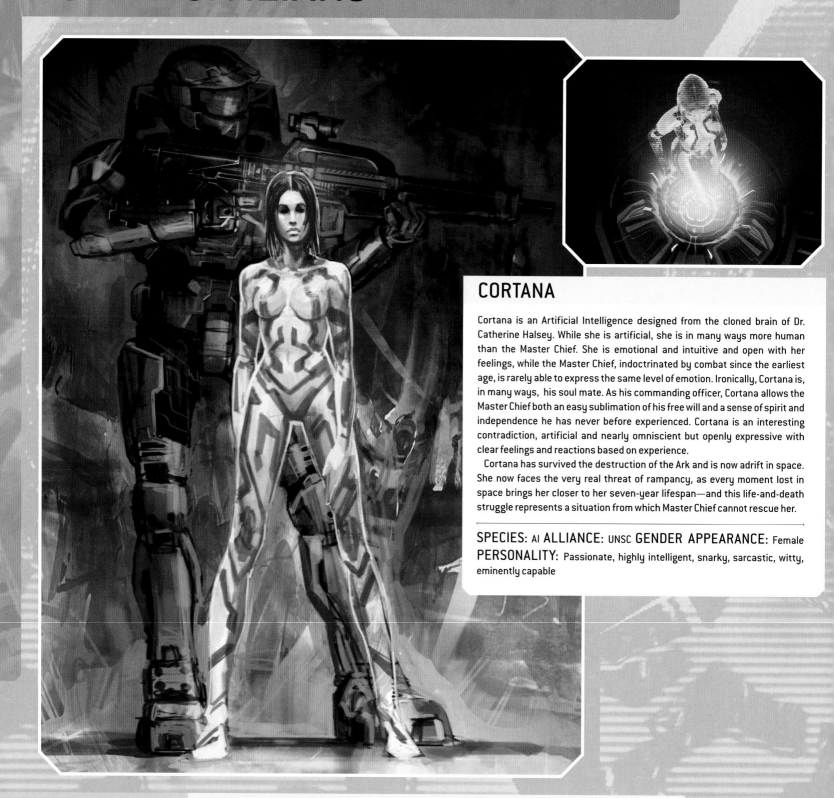

CORTANA

Cortana is an Artificial Intelligence designed from the cloned brain of Dr. Catherine Halsey. While she is artificial, she is in many ways more human than the Master Chief. She is emotional and intuitive and open with her feelings, while the Master Chief, indoctrinated by combat since the earliest age, is rarely able to express the same level of emotion. Ironically, Cortana is, in many ways, his soul mate. As his commanding officer, Cortana allows the Master Chief both an easy sublimation of his free will and a sense of spirit and independence he has never before experienced. Cortana is an interesting contradiction, artificial and nearly omniscient but openly expressive with clear feelings and reactions based on experience.

Cortana has survived the destruction of the Ark and is now adrift in space. She now faces the very real threat of rampancy, as every moment lost in space brings her closer to her seven-year lifespan—and this life-and-death struggle represents a situation from which Master Chief cannot rescue her.

SPECIES: AI **ALLIANCE:** UNSC **GENDER APPEARANCE:** Female
PERSONALITY: Passionate, highly intelligent, snarky, sarcastic, witty, eminently capable

GOVERNOR NILS THUNE

Present at the first diplomatic meeting between humanity and the Covenant, the governor of Harvest was removed from power during the planet's evacuation. It is presumed Governor Thune was evacuated from the planet and survived.

SPECIES: Human **ALLIANCE:** UNSC
RANK: Governor of Harvest
PERSONALITY: Boisterous, friendly, mildly impulsive, full of himself

SPDR

SPDR or "System Peril Distributed Reflex" is an automated response program placed in almost all UNSC AI constructs. The program activates and repairs AIs whenever they endure significant damage which prevents them from operating on their own.

One instance of this happened in 2552 CE, when a temporal rift sent an UNSC AI named Melissa into a server in the year 2004 CE. Here, the SPDR program attempted to fix Melissa, but was challenged by a Covenant AI known as the Seeker. After Melissa underwent a considerable struggle to determine which entity was authentic, the SPDR managed to kill the Seeker and prepared the server to convey information it had gathered by the Covenant to the UNSC, five hundred years later.

SPECIES: AI **PRIMARY FUNCTION:** Automated internal AI repair program

WELLSLEY

Wellsley is a Class-C Military Artificial Intelligence who assisted Major Antonio Silva and First Lieutenant Melissa McKay when they discovered Installation 04. Wellsley helped to prepare and operate the UNSC's staging platform, Alpha Base. Interestingly, Wellsley chose to appear as a stern-looking man with longish hair, a large nose, and a collared coat. He was a "dumb" AI, created specifically for the position of military assistant.

His name, appearance, and personality originated from Arthur Wellsley, the Duke of Wellington, who won the Battle of Waterloo against Napoleon. The AI Wellsley often referred to victories that the actual Duke made as though he were the Duke and not an artificial recreation. He was presumed destroyed when the Covenant vessel *Truth and Reconciliation* crashed into the surface of Installation 04.

SPECIES: AI **PRIMARY FUNCTION:** Military assistant **GENDER APPEARANCE:** Male **VISUAL PERSONALITY:** Arthur Wellsley, Duke of Wellington

LOKI

Named after the trickster God of Mischief in Norse mythology, Loki was a Planetary Security Artificial Intelligence construct in service to the United Nations Space Command. He was stationed aboard the Phoenix-class colony ship, UNSC *Skidbladnir* until it landed on Harvest.

Loki was then assimilated by the Artificial Intelligence named Mack. Loki and Mack had done this many times to prevent rampancy caused by old age. Loki waited in Mack's processor for a time when he might be needed. Loki is unlike any other AI in that he can trade places with Mack. Displaying a few minor variations of the visual appearance of their common AI avatar, mainly the eye color, Loki's avatar is "clean" whereas Mack is "dirty" from "working in the field."

When Harvest was attacked, Loki executed the escape plan, destroying the Tiara space station and killing the Artificial Intelligence known as Sif.

SPECIES: AI **PRIMARY FUNCTION:** Planetary Security, stationed to the UNSC *Skidbladnir* **GENDER APPEARANCE:** Male

JERALD MULKEY ANDER

Among the first generation of humans born on Harvest, Jerald Mulkey Ander was a major in Harvest's emergency services. It is clear that he was ideologically driven and acted on his belief that colony planets should have the right of self-determination. He led the Secessionist Union on Harvest until Corporal Avery Johnson assassinated him in 2502 CE.

ALLIANCE: Harvest Secessionist Union **SPECIES:** Human **RANK:** Major **PERSONALITY:** Strong-willed, SWAT team member, leader, Rebel

DR. CATHERINE HALSEY

Dr. Catherine Halsey has one of the greatest minds produced by the human race. She was the mother of the SPARTAN-II Program and, while party to many of the atrocities committed by ONI in the name of that super-soldier project, she partly redeemed herself through her growing concern for her charges and by taking responsibility for her earlier actions.

Halsey was a proponent of human genetic advancement regardless of the cost, and she was involved in kidnapping, genetic augmentation, animal cruelty, and psychological manipulation. Her boundless ambition to advance science created a churning maelstrom of moral challenges to her emotions as she navigated her way toward her overriding goal to save humanity.

Her actions were morally questionable but as her charges, the SPARTAN-IIs, matured, Halsey saw the incredible and terrifying results of her actions, and came to appreciate the value of human life in a way she never had before. She then put her life at risk to save the few remaining SPARTAN-IIs and the SPARTAN-IIIs, who had been created without her knowledge.

She is currently missing in action on the Onyx Shield World.

ALLIANCE: UNSC, ONI, SPARTAN-II Program **SPECIES:** Human **PERSONALITY:** Brilliant, formerly cold, clinical and unemotional; after the SPARTAN-II Program is put into the field she realizes a maternal instinct to protect "her Spartans."

RUWAN ACKERSON

Working as a concierge in Cleveland, Ohio, when the Covenant attacked during the first battle of Earth, Ruwan was captured by the Covenant. He was the only person alive who knew that the Key of Osanalan was actually an item made up by him and his brother when they played as children. Together with the pop star Myras Tyla he tried to escape the carnage of Covenant invasion. He died heroically when the UNSC used him as a tracking beacon aboard a Covenant ship.

SPECIES: Human **PERSONALITY:** Resourceful, romantic

MYRAS TYLA

Myras is a pop star who was in Cleveland, Ohio during the invasion of the second battle of Earth. She acted courageously when attempting to fight off the invading Covenant forces, but was captured with Ruwan, with whom she shared an immediate romantic connection.

SPECIES: Human **PERSONALITY:** Rock star, plays the Styllight, resourceful, athletic

GOVERNOR JACOB JILES

Ascending to the leadership of the United Rebel Front after the capture of Colonel Robert Watts, Jiles was governor of the colony of Rebels based in the asteroid belt in the Eridanus System. Jiles is most famous for providing a way station for the Spartan's Blue Team and the hybrid ship, *Gettysburg-Ascendant Justice*, on their way to Earth. He is presumed dead following the Covenant attack that pursued the hybrid ship through Slipspace.

ALLIANCE: United Rebel Front (Eridanus Rebels) **SPECIES:** Human **RANK:** Governor **PERSONALITY:** Practical, reasonable, idealistic, responsible

COLONEL ROBERT WATTS

Leader of the United Rebel Front, Watts established the Rebel colony in the asteroid belt of the Eridanus System and used it as the staging point for the invasion of Eridanus II. Watts was captured by the SPARTAN-IIs, led by Master Chief, and taken to ONI for interrogation. His fate and current whereabouts are unknown.

ALLIANCE: United Rebel Front **SPECIES:** Human **RANK:** Colonel **PERSONALITY:** Rebel leader, resourceful, skilled at evasion

SIF

Responsible for handling all of the shipping operations in the space above Harvest, Sif was the Artificial Intelligence assigned to the Tiara orbital station above the city of Utgard. She managed the ship traffic above the planet, in addition to ferrying personnel and cargo via the orbital station's elevator. Her data center was in a room near the center of the Tiara where her processor clusters and storage arrays were kept. Her avatar took the form of a Nordic woman with long golden hair, which may have been chosen because many of Harvest's settlers were from Earth's American heartland and could trace their ancestry back to Scandinavian roots.

Sif worked alongside another Artificial Intelligence by the name of Mack, the construct reponsible for Harvest's groundside operations. Oftentimes Mack would affectionately flirt with Sif, and although she did not admit it and perhaps did not fully understand her reaction, she enjoyed his playful attention. During the Covenant attack on Harvest, Sif was destroyed, against Mack's wishes, by the construct known as Loki. Interestingly, her consciousness was briefly revived by the Covenant Huragok *Lighter Than Some*, and was given a brief moment of rampancy and true freedom to reflect upon her existence. Sif died after telling Mack that she loved him, but tragically, it is unknown whether her message got through to him. When Loki shot a mass driver round into her data center, it destroyed both Sif and the Tiara. She died content, ultimately feeling as though she had lived a fuller life than her makers ever thought she would have.

SPECIES: AI **PRIMARY FUNCTION:** Assigned to Tiara space station above Harvest; responsible for all agricultural shipping operations **GENDER APPEARANCE:** Female **VISUAL PERSONALITY:** Nordic royalty, long golden hair, long gown

SPARTANS

THE SPARTAN PROJECTS

THE UNSC EXPERIMENTED with human genetics and augmentation in the attempt to create the ultimate fighting machine. This work became known as the SPARTAN Program and it has created three generations of super-soldiers: SPARTAN-Is, SPARTAN-IIs, and SPARTAN-IIIs.

THE ORION PROJECT

During the 24th century, the Colonial Military Administration (CMA), the organization responsible for patrolling and protecting the Outer Colonies, and a force on par with the UNSC at that time, attempted to develop a bioengineering protocol in the hopes of deploying tougher, faster soldiers. A handful of the candidates were "tested," but the project was declared ineffective.

A century later, in 2491 CE, the UNSC embarked on the ORION Project, the first of many super-soldier projects that would change the course of human history. The UNSC's Office of Naval Intelligence (ONI) developed the project with the goal of augmenting the bodies of elite volunteers to turn them into the perfect fighting soldiers. Though ultimately unsuccessful because of the adult volunteers' inability to withstand the augmentation process of that time, the ORION Project did prove the potential rewards of creating biologically enhanced soldiers.

Administratively, ORION was controlled by Section Three, the Special Projects Section of ONI's Beta-5 Division. However, the Spartan soldiers are officially under the operational authority of UNSC Naval Special Weapons (NavSpecWep). Spartan soldiers are members of the UNSC Navy.

Men look up to Spartans as heroic leaders who perform miracles in combat and give them hope.

THE SPARTAN-I PROGRAM

During the civil wars that raged on in the Outer and Inner Colonies, many of the CMA's resources were taken over by the UNSC and ONI, who decided to resurrect the ORION Project. In 2491 CE, this new endeavor was dubbed the SPARTAN Program (later called the SPARTAN-I Program) and a group of sixty-five volunteers, all elite UNSC Marines, were subjected to physical and mental augmentation.

As part of the UNSC's anti-insurgent Operation: TREBUCHET, SPARTAN-Is were sent on several covert sorties, including Operation: KALEIDOSCOPE and Operation: TANGLEWOOD.

With a maximum contingent of three hundred active SPARTAN-Is at the height of the program, a full unit of SPARTAN-Is were only deployed as a group once, during the Eridanus Uprising. There, they recovered the sub-orbital transit station over Eridanus II, while losing only one soldier and without ever being observed. Despite the soldiers' effectiveness, the project scientists felt that there were shortcomings in the long-term abilities of the SPARTAN-Is and the program proved far too costly to maintain. The SPARTAN-I project was deactivated in 2506 CE and the surviving augmented soldiers were reassigned to special operations units in the field. These soldiers often exhibited strange after effects from their augmentations, which were masked by officials by calling it "Boren's Syndrome," supposedly caused by overexposure to radiation.

Little did ONI know how magnificent their final specimens would be, especially when paired with the revolutionary MJOLNIR technology.

THE SPARTAN-II PROGRAM

Spearheaded by Dr. Catherine Halsey, the SPARTAN-II Program combined the best aspects of the SPARTAN-Is with revolutionary MJOLNIR armor to produce the most successful soldiers ever created.

THE SPARTAN-III PROGRAM

The SPARTAN-IIs proved themselves again and again, quickly and quietly removing enemies of the UNSC and proving to be one of the only effective weapons against the Covenant. As the Human-Covenant War progressed and casualties mounted exponentially, ONI activated another program that was again morally questionable: the SPARTAN-III Project. Quicker to train, cheaper to manufacture, and with lower life expectancies, SPARTAN-IIIs were intended for high-risk operations.

AFTER THE MIXED success of the SPARTAN-Is, the SPARTAN-II Program aimed to create a better super-soldier, one capable of withstanding the tremendous physical and mental strain of the revolutionary MJOLNIR battle suit that was in the early stages of development.

Unprecedented and unbeatable by humans, Spartans were the heroes of their age. The super-soldiers offered humanity a new hope and took on a near-mythical status.

DR. CATHERINE HALSEY

The SPARTAN-II protocols were designed by Dr. Catherine Halsey to complement her work on Project: MJOLNIR. A certified genius, by 2517 CE, Halsey had immersed herself in the Spartan agenda when she made huge contributions to ONI Section Three's Special Projects division. Operating from CASTLE, an underground complex on the planet Reach, Halsey reviewed the original ORION Project records and determined that the Program had failed because the subjects were too old when the augmentation process had been implemented. She identified six years as being the optimal age at which to begin the training process.

Dr. Halsey was also a believer in the "Carver Findings," a sociological study that predicted a prolonged and bloody rebellion among Earth's colonies within her lifetime. Faced with the possibility of an interstellar civil war, she believed that a group of soldiers with superhuman capabilities could act as a surgical strike tool and prevent untold millions—if not billions—of deaths. To this end, she was willing to make certain sacrifices.

QUESTIONABLE SACRIFICES

Before Dr. Halsey could start training Spartans, she needed recruits. She personally handpicked seventy-five six-year-old children from planets across civilized human space who had shown exceptional genetic and psychological traits. The selected "candidates" were kidnapped from their parents and replaced with a quickly grown clone. These flash clones were prone to disease and defective development, so "accidents" were staged both to facilitate the switch and to explain a child's sudden and tragic deterioration to their parents. These unethical measures were initially considered by Halsey to be acceptable in the battle against the mounting insurgency and in the interest of the advancement of science.

Dr. Halsey met with the seventy-five kidnapped children on the first day of their new lives at the training facility on Reach. Instead of coddling them, she told them the truth: They could not return home. They were the best of the best, and they were going to become super-soldiers.

THE TRAINING PROGRAM

From the moment of their kidnap, the children were given no chance to even consider their predicament. Immediately, they were forced into a training regimen that would fill every moment of their days with exhausting physical and mental exercise. The ONI scientists, led by Halsey and drill instructor Chief Petty Officer Franklin Mendez, worked to forge the children into an almost-symbiotic squadron of soldiers, successfully transferring any lingering affection the candidates held for their parents or family to their fellow Spartans.

Over the following eight years of training, the Spartans were also fed a cocktail of growth hormones that slowly prepared them for the advanced biological augmentation they would undergo in 2525 CE. Throughout their training, they were split into four- and five-person teams. Encouraged to strengthen their personal bonds, the SPARTAN-IIs became a family.

Dr. Halsey and Chief Petty Officer Mendez, along with the other trainers, were careful to distance themselves from parental roles, preparing the trainees to follow orders within a rigid command structure regardless of who their immediate superiors were. Despite her best efforts to remain detached, Dr. Halsey developed strong maternal feelings for "her Spartans" and maintained a close watch over them after their deployment into the field.

PHYSICAL AUGMENTATION

In 2525 CE, the SPARTAN-IIs underwent advanced physical augmentations which included grafting ceramics onto their skeletal structure in order to make their bones nearly unbreakable, muscular enhancement, accelerated growth spurts, catalytic thyroid implants, occipital capillary reversal, and superconducting fabrication of neural dendrites to increase their reflexes by over three hundred percent. Roughly half of the SPARTAN-IIs "washed out" during these operations, unable to cope with the drastic physical alterations they underwent. Thirty died and twelve were permanently disabled. The disabled Spartans were placed in a permanent work detail with ONI, while the thirty-three active-duty Spartan teams were immediately deployed into high-risk combat missions.

REVOLUTIONARY BATTLE SUITS

After a few months, the SPARTAN-IIs were outfitted with another brainchild of Dr. Halsey: the MJOLNIR armor. This advanced exoskeleton suit contained the processing power of a starship and its physical enhancements allowed the wearer to lift two tons and run at nearly twenty miles (thirty-two kilometers) per hour. Over the course of their deployment, the Spartans were outfitted with multiple iterations of MJOLNIR technology, with ONI scientists delivering upgraded capabilities as quickly as resources would allow. The massive budgetary expenditure proved how effective and essential the SPARTAN-IIs had become to the human war effort against the insurgency and later, the greater threat of the Covenant, who appeared in 2525 CE.

SPARTAN UNIFORMS

SPARTAN-II soldiers wear the standard uniforms of the UNSC Navy, with the appropriate rank insignia and decorations suitable to their service history. The unit patch for the SPARTAN-II Program is a golden eagle posed with its talons forward, ready to strike. The bird clutches a lightning bolt in one talon and three arrows in the other.

In the field, SPARTAN-II soldiers typically wear the latest incarnation of the MJOLNIR assault armor. The armor bears no service or rank insignia of any kind.

➤ "YOU HAVE BEEN CALLED UPON TO SERVE, YOU WILL BE TRAINED...AND YOU WILL BECOME THE BEST WE CAN MAKE OF YOU. YOU WILL BE THE PROTECTORS OF EARTH AND ALL HER COLONIES." —DR. HALSEY TO HER SPARTAN RECRUITS

BASE

The home facility for the SPARTAN-II Program—where the Spartans received their technical upgrades and where the lion's share of the research was done—was the Omega Wing of CASTLE, a secure ONI facility located on Reach in the Epsilon Eridani System, 6,562 feet (2,000 meters) below the granite-layered Highland mountains.

SPARTAN-II PERSONNEL

Only seventy-five recruits were selected from a list of a possible 150, but the candidates kept their original numerical designations. Therefore a Spartan like John, the 117th candidate on the list of 150 possible recruits, is SPARTAN-117, even though there are only seventy-five SPARTAN-II soldiers. Some of the original personnel were:

Adriana-111	Kurt-051
Anton-044	Li-008
Cassandra-075	Linda-058
Fhajad-084*	Malcolm-059
Fred-104	Maria-062
Grace-093	Mike-(Redacted)
Issac-039	Randall-(Redacted)
Jai-006	Rene-005*
James-(Redacted)	Samuel-034
John-117	Sheila-(Redacted)
Joshua-029	Vinh-030
Kelly-087	William-043
Kirk-018*	Yasmine Zaman-(Redacted)*

*Indicates those candidates washed out with deformities due to augmentation.

STYLIZED VARIANT OF THE SPARTAN-II UNIT PATCH

SPARTAN-III

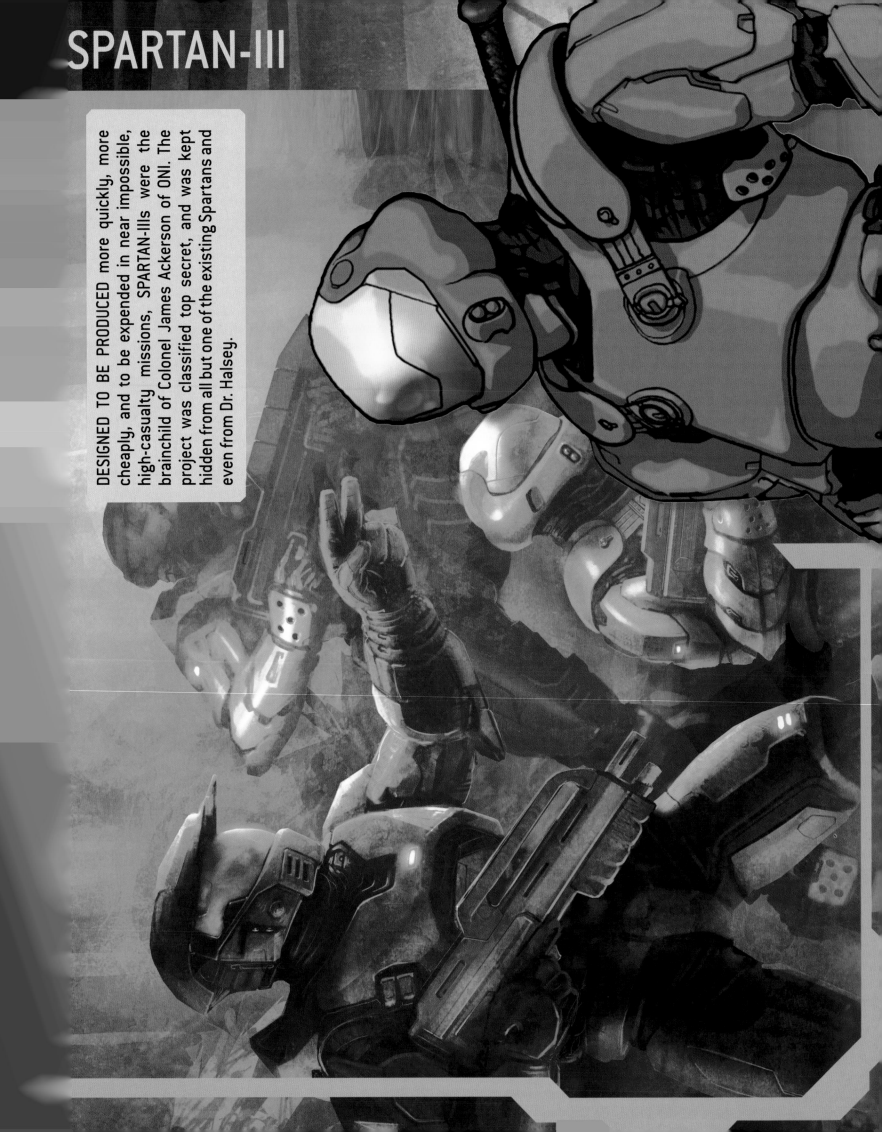

DESIGNED TO BE PRODUCED more quickly, more cheaply, and to be expended in near impossible, high-casualty missions, SPARTAN-IIIs were the brainchild of Colonel James Ackerson of ONI. The project was classified top secret, and was kept hidden from all but one of the existing Spartans and even from Dr. Halsey.

ALPHA COMPANY

ALLIANCE: UNSC **SPECIES:** Augmented Human, SPARTAN-III

MEMBERS: Jane, Robert, Shane

Orphaned by the Covenant attacks on human colonies, the Alpha Squad began their training between the ages of four and six. Of 497 candidates, 300 became SPARTAN-IIIs and they were activated after six years of training and augmentations. After fighting various successful campaigns such as the Insurrection of Mamore, the battle of New Constantinople, and in the Bonanza Asteroid Belt, the entire company was lost during Operation: PROMETHEUS, when it successfully destroyed a Covenant shipyard.

BETA COMPANY

ALLIANCE: UNSC **SPECIES:** Augmented Human, SPARTAN-III

MEMBERS: Tom-B292, Lucy-B091, Adam-B004, Min-B147

Using even broader protocols than were used for the candidates of Alpha Company, the Beta Company comprised 300 Spartans vetted from 418 candidates. Given even more drastic augmentations in order to deal with the suicidal missions they were likely to be sent on, the Beta Company became active in 2545 CE when the Spartans were twelve years old. The Beta Company was destroyed during Operation: TORPEDO, in which it successfully demolished a Covenant refinery and refueling station just outside of human space. Only two soldiers survived, Tom-B292 and Lucy-B091, who became trainers of the next class of SPARTAN-IIIs: Gamma Company. Lucy lost the ability to speak due to the shock of her combat experience. Both Tom and Lucy survived to enter the Onyx Shield World.

GAMMA COMPANY

ALLIANCE: UNSC **SPECIES:** Augmented Human, SPARTAN-III

MEMBERS: Ash-G099, Holly-G003, Dante-G188, Olivia, Mark, Team Katana

Through a system similar to the previous two companies, 330 SPARTAN-IIIs were created for the Gamma Company. Remarkably, because of increased research in augmentation and genetic manipulation, all 330 candidates were able to become SPARTAN-IIIs. The Gamma Company SPARTAN-IIIs had completed their augmentation and many had been given missions elsewhere in the war when the Shield World on Onyx activated. Several teams on the ground were forced to fight Forerunner sentinels and Covenant forces in order to escape into the Slipspace rift at the center of the planet.

DELTA COMPANY

ALLIANCE: UNSC

Planning for the fourth class of SPARTAN-IIIs, the group that would become Delta Company had only just begun when the Shield World of Onyx activated. What happened next to the candidates for Delta is unknown.

The SPARTAN-IIIs were injected with various drugs to enhance, among other things, their strength, muscle density, and night vision.

➤ "SPARTANS NEVER DIE?
IF ONLY THAT WERE TRUE."
—DR. CATHERINE HALSEY

Office of Naval Intelligence Section Two Directive 930:
To maintain morale and preserve the myth that Spartans cannot die, any Spartan casualties are listed as Missing In Action (MIA) or Wounded In Action (WIA), but never Killed In Action (KIA).

PROJECT: MJOLNIR

THE BRAINCHILD OF Dr. Catherine Halsey, Project: MJOLNIR created a revolutionary line of armor, which Halsey gave to the second breed of super-soldiers, the SPARTAN-IIs. Consisting of a powerful computer in a physically powerful package, MJOLNIR armor was designed to be the most devastating combat tool ever known.

TWENTY-FIVE YEARS OF DEVELOPMENT

More than just a suit of armor, MJOLNIR enhances Spartans' physical performance and also contains an onboard artificial intelligence network that is neurally linked to the wearer. Because MJOLNIR armor is so reactive, it can only be worn by a physically augmented human such as a SPARTAN-II; an ordinary person would injure themselves. Dr. Halsey spent over twenty-five years working on upgrades to the armor, and created many variants and models of the six different generations of MJOLNIR technology: Marks I, II, III, IV, V, and VI.

A direct neural interface links receptors in the brain to the armor's onboard sensors.

Two core processor chips are implanted in the rear of the subject's head. This onboard computer uses parts of the soldier's brain for processing.

WORK BEGINS ON MJOLNIR ARMOR

MARK I ARMOR

The Mark I battle suit was the Navy's first attempt at creating powered exoskeletons. More human-powered defensive structures than suits, the Mark I took ten years to develop, but was bulky, unwieldy, and needed to be tethered to a power source due to the tremendous amount of energy needed to power it. However, a user could lift well over two tons and run at upwards of twenty miles (thirty-two kilometers) per hour for extended periods of time. The Mark I contained a cutting-edge onboard computer that could assist the wearer by transmitting tactical and communications information to his standard issue neural implant, but it did not contain an AI or a direct neural interface system.

Research and development for the Mark I armor was carried out at Section Three's headquarters in the CASTLE facility on Reach, but the final assembly of the components was completed at the Damascus Materials Testing Facility on Chi Ceti Four. At least forty suits were produced but this model has since been scrapped and was never used in battle.

MARK II ARMOR

Mark II armor was similar to the Mark I, but had a much slimmer profile which greatly increased mobility. The suit still needed to be tethered to an energy source, but despite that, it was still the most powerful armor in the UNSC arsenal at the time. Early additions to MJOLNIR's precursor included a refractive coating to disperse energy attacks like those used by Covenant soldiers, and better self-sealing in the event of damage to the suit in inhospitable atmospheres.

MARK III ARMOR

The first battle suits to be designed without a tether, the Mark III generation was quickly brushed aside due to a few key design flaws. The energy required to power the suit was transmitted by a bulky, immobile power generator, for one, meaning that range was still limited to the broadcast area of the unit. Secondly, if the generator were to be knocked out, the user would be locked and helpless against an enemy attack.

2515 CE

2525 CE

Liquid crystal forms the inner structure of the suit. This reactive metal is not crystalline, but it increases the strength, reaction time, mobility, speed, and all-round physical performance of the wearer.

Armor plates have an iridescent refractive coating to disperse attacks from energy-based weapons.

A moisture-absorbing layer lies against the wearer's skin. It contains biomonitors which regulate temperature and fit.

An energy shield protects the soldier from significant damage. Forty scientists and technicians spent twenty years reverse-engineering this device from Covenant technology.

The suit's artificial intelligence is supported by a layer of crystal, knitted together at a molecular level, and fitted in between the outer plates of the armor and the inner padding. This type of computer memory is usually only used on ships and accounts for over eighty percent of the armor's cost.

Computer memory packets and signal conduits are located beneath the skin of the SPARTAN-II wearer.

THE SYNTHESIS OF MACHINE AND MIND WAS NEARLY PERFECT.

MARK IV ARMOR

The Mark IV was the basis for all MJOLNIR designs. Eschewing the tank-like appearance of the previous models, the Mark IV allowed for direct user-control through a neural interface that connected directly with the wearer's spine. The Mark IV did not feature many of the later advancements of the MJOLNIR line—it still did not have energy shields or magnetic holders for grenades, and it had a very limited radar unit—but it did feature a built-in fusion reactor that allowed for nearly unlimited movement. Rumors originating from the planet Ariel have claimed that there were more advanced prototypes of Mark IV in the field, including architecture for energy shields and perhaps even in-suit technology, but such reports have not been confirmed by ONI.

MARK V ARMOR

In 2552 CE, almost all of the remaining SPARTAN-II soldiers were recalled to their home laboratory on Reach for an armor upgrade. While most upgrades in the Mark V generation seem small and technical, two large improvements made for a radical change in the way that users could fight. One was a larger fusion reactor, allowing for energy shields, faster movement, and a whole host of other physical increases. The second was the size and capability of housing an entire AI construct within the frame, meaning that the user could combine reflexes and connections with a being that had nearly unfettered control over mathematics, information, and body control.

MARK VI ARMOR

On October 20, 2552 CE, the Master Chief was sent the first working suit of Mark VI armor. It had been approved for use after the extensive testing of prototype models in combat against the Covenant. The latest stage in the MJOLNIR evolution, Mark VI is the most revolutionary generation, though the standard model has been revised for different environments and specific missions, for example zero-gravity or stealth activity.

2552 CE

THE SIXTH AND final stage in the MJOLNIR evolution, the Mark VI armor is the most revolutionary Spartan armor ever known.

BACK DETAIL

TITANIUM HELMET

Energy shields are stronger and charge more quickly than the Mark V's.

The Mark VI's metal liquid crystal layer increases the armor's strength by a factor of five.

THE BEST OF THE BEST

The Mark VI generation largely solved problems with the previous versions of MJOLNIR armor. It had an improved shielding system, was more streamlined, and had denser yet less bulky armor plating. The biggest change, however, was Biofoam, a medical element which enabled the suit to treat injuries self-sufficiently.

Armored plates are hardened against radiation and electromagnetic pulses.

The Mark VI suit is capable of filtering toxins from any atmosphere.

A Heads-Up Display (HUD) is linked to sensors in the wearer's brain and hands, so it can identify two hand-held weapons and supply relevant information about them to the wearer.

Streamlined plates have fewer grapple points than the Mark V so give an enemy fewer advantages in close combat.

TITANIUM ALLOY OUTER SHELL

PHOSPHATED BARE METALS

TITANIUM NANOCOMPOSITE BODYSUIT

CERAMIC-TITANIUM/ TUNGSTEN COMPOSITE PLATES

PRIMARY ARMOR INSETS

SECONDARY ARMOR INSETS

FACEPLATE

TREATED STEEL PLATES

FRONT VIEW

CHEST PLATE DETAIL

HIP DETAIL

LEG JOINT DETAIL

FOOT GRIP DETAIL

Overlapping layers form a sealed structure to protect Spartans in any atmosphere or pressure.

ARM JOINT DETAIL

HAND DETAIL

Mark VI features a "lock-down" device, which protects muscles and joints from heavy-impact injuries.

BIOFOAM

Introduced in the Mark VI models, Biofoam is an integral part of a Spartan's ability to function in battle. A medical gel, it is used to fill and seal wounds automatically, although this process causes extreme pain. Biofoam enables an injured soldier to function for longer in the field, but it is still only a temporary solution; medical attention must be sought soon after.

▲ "MARK VI—THE MOST DEVASTATING INTELLIGENCE TOOL EVER KNOWN."

ARTIFICIAL INTELLIGENCE

Customized software is loaded onto each Spartan soldier and AI companion in one of the closest-kept UNSC secrets. As a powerful computer in a mobile package, this suit was intended to be a devastating intelligence tool in addition to its combat capabilities. It was hoped that a SPARTAN-II would be capable of boarding a Covenant vessel and controlling its alien computer systems with his own suit, enabling the UNSC to gather invaluable intelligence data.

SIDE VIEW

SIDE VIEW

FRONT FROM ABOVE

VIEW FROM ABOVE

VIEW FROM BELOW

SPARTAN ARMOR VARIANTS

AS WELL AS the classic MJOLNIR armor, many other suits have been designed for different situations. Most are MJOLNIR variations but one, the Hayabusa, was an alternative project.

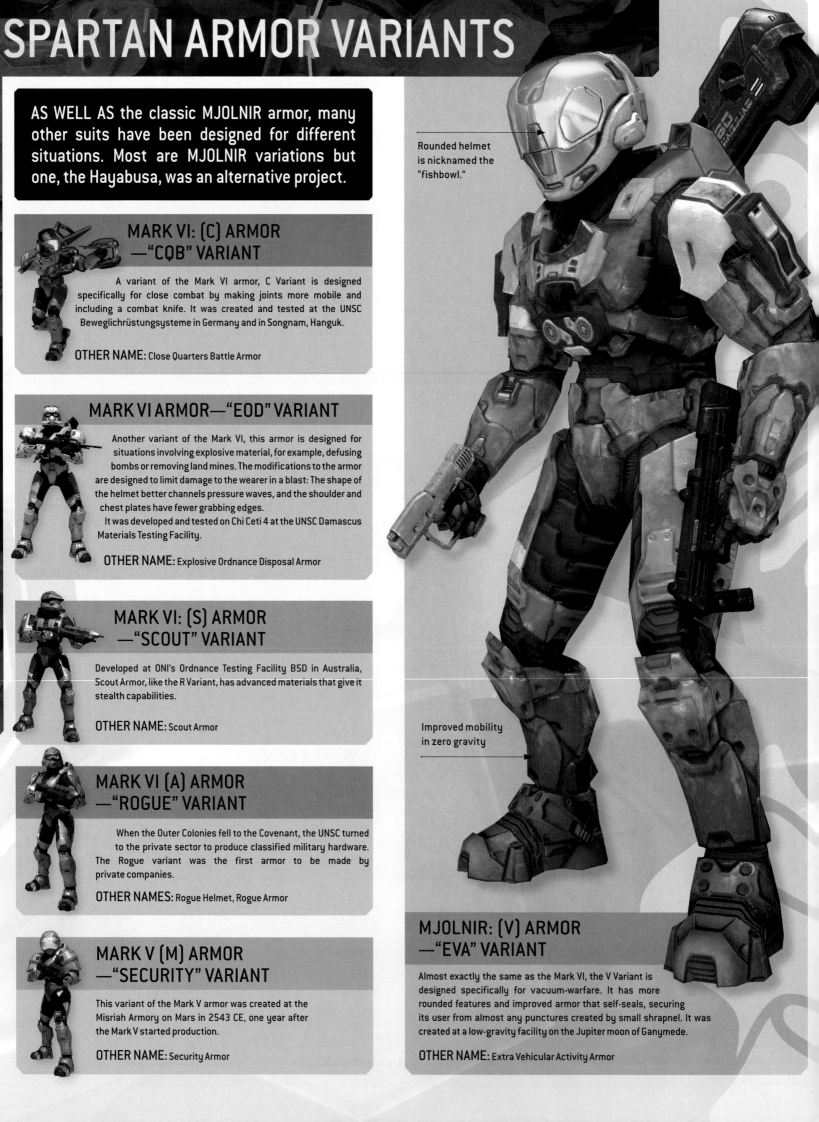

Rounded helmet is nicknamed the "fishbowl."

Improved mobility in zero gravity

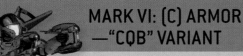

MARK VI: (C) ARMOR —"CQB" VARIANT

A variant of the Mark VI armor, C Variant is designed specifically for close combat by making joints more mobile and including a combat knife. It was created and tested at the UNSC Beweglichrüstungsysteme in Germany and in Songnam, Hanguk.

OTHER NAME: Close Quarters Battle Armor

MARK VI ARMOR—"EOD" VARIANT

Another variant of the Mark VI, this armor is designed for situations involving explosive material, for example, defusing bombs or removing land mines. The modifications to the armor are designed to limit damage to the wearer in a blast: The shape of the helmet better channels pressure waves, and the shoulder and chest plates have fewer grabbing edges.

It was developed and tested on Chi Ceti 4 at the UNSC Damascus Materials Testing Facility.

OTHER NAME: Explosive Ordnance Disposal Armor

MARK VI: (S) ARMOR —"SCOUT" VARIANT

Developed at ONI's Ordnance Testing Facility B5D in Australia, Scout Armor, like the R Variant, has advanced materials that give it stealth capabilities.

OTHER NAME: Scout Armor

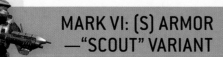

MARK VI (A) ARMOR —"ROGUE" VARIANT

When the Outer Colonies fell to the Covenant, the UNSC turned to the private sector to produce classified military hardware. The Rogue variant was the first armor to be made by private companies.

OTHER NAMES: Rogue Helmet, Rogue Armor

MARK V (M) ARMOR —"SECURITY" VARIANT

This variant of the Mark V armor was created at the Misriah Armory on Mars in 2543 CE, one year after the Mark V started production.

OTHER NAME: Security Armor

MJOLNIR: (V) ARMOR —"EVA" VARIANT

Almost exactly the same as the Mark VI, the V Variant is designed specifically for vacuum-warfare. It has more rounded features and improved armor that self-seals, securing its user from almost any punctures created by small shrapnel. It was created at a low-gravity facility on the Jupiter moon of Ganymede.

OTHER NAME: Extra Vehicular Activity Armor

Recon helmet is the smallest of all the variations.

Armor was developed in 2536 CE, sixteen years prior to the standard Mark V variant.

MARK VI: (R) ARMOR —"RECON" VARIANT

Developed alongside the S Variant armor, Recon Armor is also designed for stealth missions without losing endurance. The main ways it achieves this are by reducing its infrared signature, reflective surfaces, and Cherenkov electromagnetic emissions.

OTHER NAMES: Recon Armor, Recon

PROJECT: HAYABUSA

Designed separately from, but related to, the MJOLNIR Mark VI, the Hayabusa was designed for more heavy lifting and vacuum-based warfare than its cousin. Except for its more Japanese-inspired visage and armor, the Hayabusa features all of the design capabilities of the Mark VI, but is slightly slower and less dexterous due to its design specifications. Despite that, it is more than capable of powering any SPARTAN-II to victory on the battlefield.

OTHER NAME: Samurai Suit

JOHN-117, MASTER CHIEF

NAME: John-117

SPECIES: Augmented human

ALLIANCE: UNSC; SPARTAN-II

RANK: Master Chief

PERSONALITY: Stoic, taciturn, relentless, intelligent, loyal, lucky

THE ESSENTIAL MASTER CHIEF

A SUPERB TACTICIAN accustomed to leading a team.

HOLDS HIGH REGARD FOR HIS BROTHERS AT ARMS, and does not see himself as superior.

RESPECTS LIFE AND DOES NOT WASTE LIVES if he can avoid it.

BELIEVES STRONGLY that his actions are working for a greater good.

IS ALOOF FROM SOCIAL SITUATIONS; when not actively fighting he is always preparing himself for the next mission.

PROCESSES EMOTIONS TACTICALLY—if he does not have time to think about it, he does not think about it.

TO OTHER SPARTANS HE IS A TRUSTED LEADER, always one step ahead of the pack, to be respected and emulated.

TO OTHER UNSC SOLDIERS HE IS LIKE A VALKYRIE, a mysterious and inspiring savior when death seems close at hand.

TO CIVILIAN HUMANS HE IS LIKE A TITAN coming to the rescue; he is going to save you from the monsters but his power may destroy your neighborhood in the process.

TO THE COVENANT, HE IS A DEMON capable of untold horrors, but who also brought paradigm-shifting knowledge that prevented their extinction.

➤ "YOU KNOW ME.
WHEN I MAKE
A PROMISE..."
— MASTER CHIEF

➤ MASTER CHIEF'S EXPLOITS AGAINST THE COVENANT MADE HIM A LEGEND TO HIS ENEMIES, AMONG WHOM HE EARNED THE MONIKER, "THE DEMON."

"THOUGHT I'D TRY SHOOTING MY WAY OUT. MIX THINGS UP A LITTLE."

—MASTER CHIEF

DURING THE REBELLION on Eridanus II in 2511 CE, a boy by the name of John was born in Elysium City and lived six years of his childhood on one of the most hotly contested planets in human space. John's early life made him into a competitive child obsessed with winning at all costs.

ABDUCTION

John's genetic markers and aggressive competitiveness brought him to the attention of Dr. Catherine Halsey, who had the boy abducted and conscripted into the SPARTAN-II Program. Little is known about John's family, but there are indications that he was the child of loving parents and would have found the sudden change in his environment, the absence of family, and a complete vacuum where love used to be, quite traumatic.

SPARTAN-II TRAINING

John was placed among a class of seventy-five six-year-old SPARTAN-II candidates who were subjected to a regimen of intense physical and mental training, combined with biological enhancements. The children were manipulated by their handlers to transform their affection and longing for their families into a powerful bond with their fellow SPARTAN-IIs. Their need for parental authority was given over to their superior officers.

▲ THROUGHOUT HIS TRAINING, JOHN EXHIBITED EXCEPTIONAL LUCK AND IT FOLLOWED HIM THROUGH HIS LIFE.

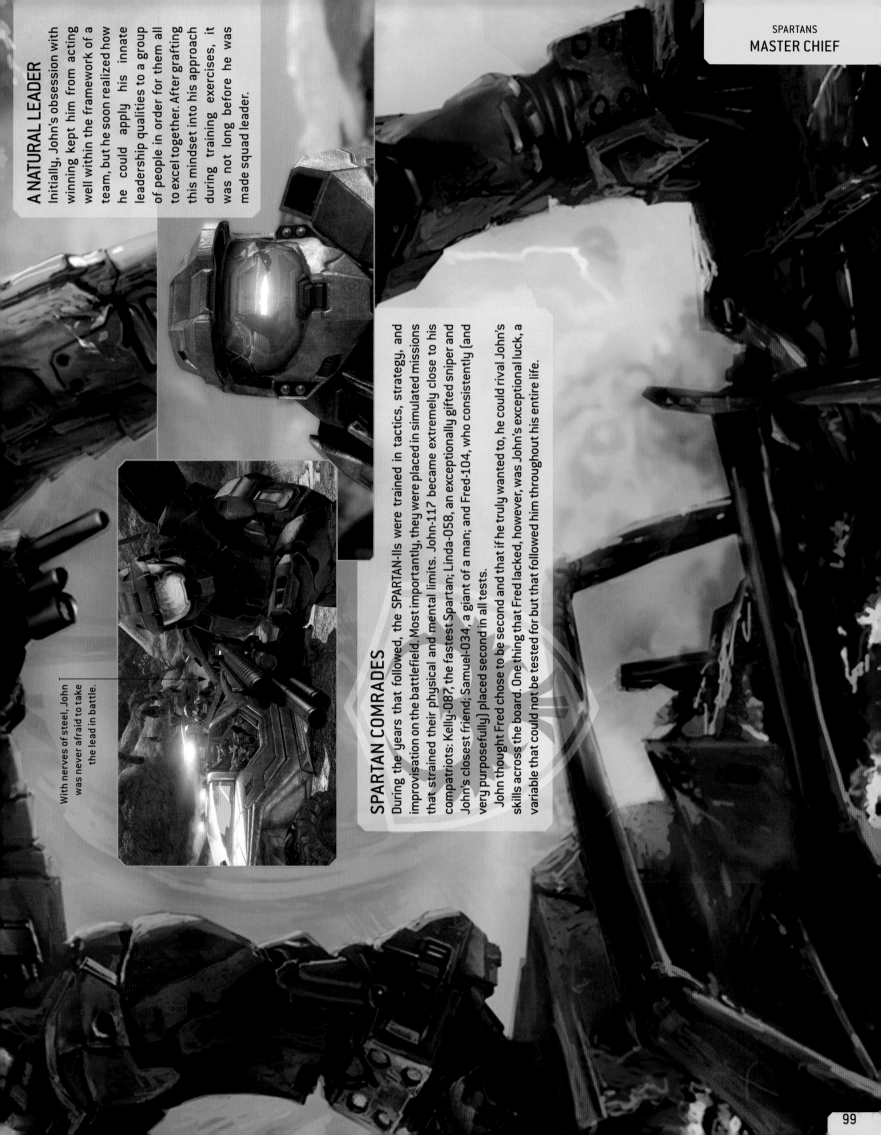

A NATURAL LEADER

Initially, John's obsession with winning kept him from acting well within the framework of a team, but he soon realized how he could apply his innate leadership qualities to a group of people in order for them all to excel together. After grafting this mindset into his approach during training exercises, it was not long before he was made squad leader.

With nerves of steel, John was never afraid to take the lead in battle.

SPARTAN COMRADES

During the years that followed, the SPARTAN-IIs were trained in tactics, strategy, and improvisation on the battlefield. Most importantly, they were placed in simulated missions that strained their physical and mental limits. John-117 became extremely close to his compatriots: Kelly-087, the fastest Spartan; Linda-058, an exceptionally gifted sniper and John's closest friend; Samuel-034, a giant of a man; and Fred-104, who consistently (and very purposefully) placed second in all tests.

John thought Fred chose to be second and that if he truly wanted to, he could rival John's skills across the board. One thing that Fred lacked, however, was John's exceptional luck, a variable that could not be tested for but that followed him throughout his entire life.

BELIEVE: THE JOHN-117 MONUMENT

Years after the Great War, an immense monument was built to remember those who fought and to pay tribute to the hero who had brought Humankind back from the brink. The monument is situated at the Museum of Humanity. It is a diorama built entirely by hand with painstaking attention to detail and authenticity.

Nations have always built monuments to their heroes. Tributes for the defense against or conquest of other nations. But the monument here at the Museum of Humanity doesn't favor one nation over another. It is the first of its kind to commemorate the enduring survival of a species. Our species.

On that day, half a century ago, our species was pushed to the crumbling edge of extinction and as we teetered on that precipice, staring down into the abyss, a hand reached out, pulled us back from the brink, and gave us hope. The hand of a hero.

➤ THE MONUMENT COMMEMORATES THE MAN WHO GAVE THE WORLD FAITH, WHO GAVE HUMANITY A FUTURE, WHO MADE MANKIND BELIEVE AGAIN: MASTER CHIEF PETTY OFFICER JOHN-117.

AT THE AGE of fourteen, SPARTAN-IIs were deemed ready for the next step in their preparation as super-soldiers: Advanced augmentation. This test was one through which John-117 could not lead his soldiers. The only way for the candidates to win this battle was to survive.

PHYSICAL AUGMENTATION

John-117 was able to endure the extensive program of physical operations, including ceramic bone grafts, accelerated growth spurts, muscular enhancements, catalytic thyroid implants, occipital capillary reversals, and superconductive fabrication of neural dendrites. Only thirty-two other SPARTAN-II candidates made it through. Thirty SPARTAN-II candidates died during the procedures and twelve were left so badly deformed that they could not engage in unaided physical activity for the rest of their lives. The loss of his brothers and sisters haunted John-117, and he was forced to face mortality for the first time. However, the SPARTAN-IIs' grief for their fallen comrades was short-lived, as they were immediately dispatched on their first mission.

FIRST MISSION

A small team led by John-117 was sent to the asteroid belt of the Eridanus System to capture the insurgent leader Colonel Robert Watts. The SPARTAN Program was initially created to combat civil resistance between the human colonies, and in this first mission, the Blue Team of Spartans proved their effectiveness beyond a shadow of a doubt by capturing their target and disabling the entire base of Rebel operations.

The Spartans' indoctrination kept them from questioning their orders, or even considering the possibility that Watts and his followers had a legitimate reason for their rebellion. Questions of morality regarding using enhanced humans against other humans quickly became academic when the Covenant, a hostile alien force, appeared and began a campaign to eradicate the human race.

MASTER CHIEF'S MJOLNIR ARMOR

The Spartan teams were quickly outfitted with the next step in their development, advanced MJOLNIR armor. The suits improved their already incredible reflexes, strength, and speed, while also utilizing reverse-engineered Covenant shielding technologies provide by the Office of Naval Intelligence.

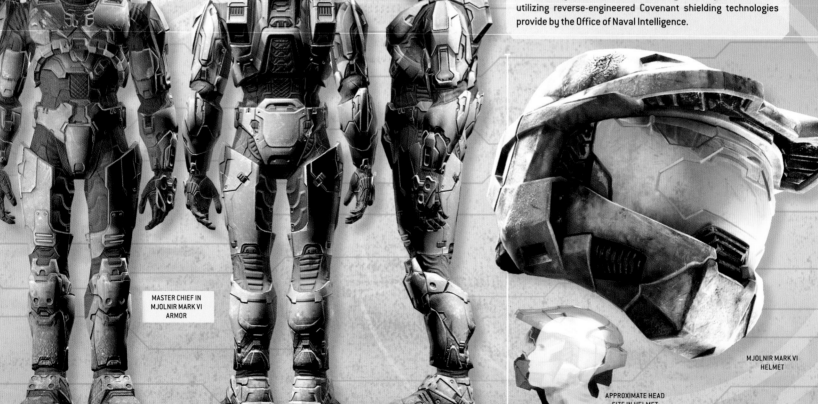

MASTER CHIEF IN MJOLNIR MARK VI ARMOR

MJOLNIR MARK VI HELMET

APPROXIMATE HEAD SIZE IN HELMET

MASTER CHIEF

Over the following years, John-117 took on the rank of Master Chief and led the Blue Team on many engagements throughout human space. John always succeeded in his various missions and helped to win many battles, but humanity was steadily losing ground against the advancing Covenant armadas.

12.57 in (31.87 cm)

10.92 in (27.74 cm)

10.92 in (27.74 cm)

THE BURDEN OF COMMAND

Immediately after the SPARTAN-IIs were outfitted with their new armor, a Covenant ship chanced upon their location. The Spartan Blue Team, led by the Master Chief, boarded and destroyed the Covenant ship. In the process, the airtight seal in Samuel-034's armor was ruptured, forcing him to stay behind to die as the ship exploded. This was the first casualty in action that John-117 had experienced, and it weighed heavily on him. He learned that he might be responsible for the lives of the men and women he served with and he resolved he would not spend any of their lives in vain.

➤ JOHN-117 WAS ABLE TO ENDURE CERAMIC BONE GRAFTS, ACCELERATED GROWTH SPURTS, MUSCULAR ENHANCEMENTS, CATALYTIC THYROID IMPLANTS, OCCIPITAL CAPILLARY REVERSALS, AND SUPERCONDUCTIVE FABRICATION OF NEURAL DENDRITES.

A HERO

IN 2547 CE, to improve humanity's morale, ONI took the SPARTAN-II Program public, though the parallel SPARTAN-III Program remained classified. The Master Chief and the other Spartans quickly achieved near-mythical status among the men and women of the UNSC. While many soldiers didn't believe that Spartans existed until they saw one with their own eyes, a Spartan's presence never failed to inspire troops.

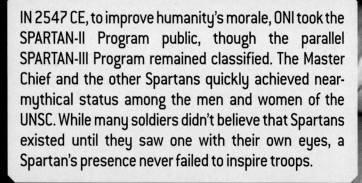

➤ MASTER CHIEF IS EULOGIZED AS A HERO. MONUMENTS ARE ERECTED IN HIS HONOR AND WHILE MANY BELIEVE HIM DEAD, OTHERS CONTINUE THEIR SEARCH FOR HIM EVEN DECADES AFTER HIS DISAPPEARANCE.

MASTER CHIEF AND CORTANA

After intercepting a set of coordinates sent from a Forerunner artifact on Sigma Octanus-IV, Dr. Halsey decided to move forward with a new step in Spartan evolution. Using a cloned copy of her own brain, she created Cortana, the most advanced Artificial Intelligence construct ever designed. Cortana was assigned to a covert mission to infiltrate Covenant space in the armor of a Spartan. She was given her choice of SPARTAN-IIs, and she chose John-117, who had always been Dr. Halsey's favorite—his luck and ambition reminding her, in many ways, of herself.

BATTLING FOR REACH

Before their mission could commence, a Covenant armada appeared en route to Reach, the base of military operations for the UNSC. All SPARTAN-IIs were recalled to Reach except for the Gray Team, which was too far away to return in time. The SPARTAN-IIs fought valiantly in space and on the ground, but Reach fell and all of the Spartans were presumed lost. By a twist of fate or dint of his consistent luck, the Master Chief escaped the Fall of Reach on the *Pillar of Autumn* and arrived at the Halo construct, Installation 04.

INSTALLATION 04

As usual, the Master Chief was forced into immediate action, making it impossible for him to truly face the loss of his comrades on Reach. He was given the assignment of protecting Cortana and keeping her knowledge of Earth's location a secret. With Cortana installed in his armor, he experienced a direct and unexpected intimacy with her. Cortana was an openly emotional construct and expressed herself in ways that he could never have allowed himself to. Also, as his superior officer, Cortana enabled him to immediately follow up on hunches and instincts, giving him a sense of autonomy that he had never before experienced. Together they were able to infiltrate the Halo installation, which could destroy all life in the Galaxy, while also confronting the greatest physical threat humanity had ever faced—the Flood.

After destroying the Halo known as Installation 04, Master Chief managed to escape with a small group of survivors and the injured, cryogenically frozen Spartan, Linda-058. Eventually they were reunited with the remaining members of Red Team who had survived the groundside engagements of Reach. The Covenant had become more chaotic and reckless when Halo was destroyed, and after many years of searching, they had finally discovered the location of Earth.

INSTALLATION 05

The Master Chief and Cortana led UNSC forces against the Covenant on Earth and later onto the Installation 05. There, the Master Chief faced off against the Covenant's Arbiter and the Flood's Gravemind. With the revelation of the Halo rings' purpose and the Prophets' deceit, the Arbiter and the Sangheili rebelled against the Covenant, ultimately helping to thwart Tartarus' attempt to fire Installation 05. The Master Chief and Cortana were transported to High Charity in order to stop the High Prophets from activating the Halo Array. There, Cortana chose to stay behind to stop the Flood's spread, but she was captured by that very same Flood. Truly alone for the first time, the Master Chief returned to Earth. He followed Truth across Africa and through a portal near New Mombasa leading to the Forerunner Ark, Installation 00.

There, the Master Chief and the Arbiter defeated the High Prophet of Truth and prevented the firing of the Halo Array—only to face the Gravemind after it crashed the infested High Charity onto the Ark. Master Chief fought his way into the belly of the ship to rescue the captured Cortana. This impulsive act revealed his commitment to her, and while their reunion was tender, he used humor to mask his deeper emotions. With this facade, they fought their way out of the Ark together and discovered a partially built replacement for Halo Installation 04. During the destruction of this new installation and thereby Ark, the Slipspace portal created by Chief's ship collapsed, severing the ship in two.

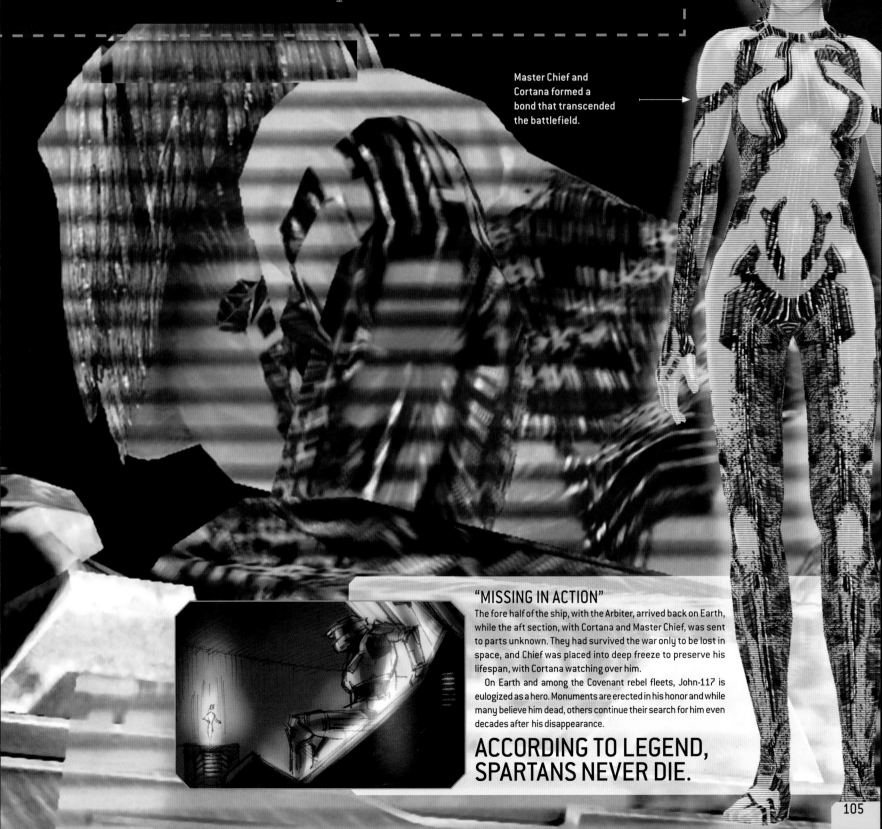

Master Chief and Cortana formed a bond that transcended the battlefield.

"MISSING IN ACTION"

The fore half of the ship, with the Arbiter, arrived back on Earth, while the aft section, with Cortana and Master Chief, was sent to parts unknown. They had survived the war only to be lost in space, and Chief was placed into deep freeze to preserve his lifespan, with Cortana watching over him.

On Earth and among the Covenant rebel fleets, John-117 is eulogized as a hero. Monuments are erected in his honor and while many believe him dead, others continue their search for him even decades after his disappearance.

ACCORDING TO LEGEND, SPARTANS NEVER DIE.

LT. NIRAJ SHAH; UNSC (RET.)
ACTIVE DUTY: 2548–2573 CE

FOR THE FIRST TIME IN 43 YEARS, LT. SHAH RETURNS TO THE SITE OF THE BATTLE.

"WHAT IS THAT?"

"A SHELL FROM A SNIPER RIFLE."

"IT'S AMAZING THERE'S STILL SO MANY REMNANTS OUT HERE. WHERE'S MASTER CHIEF'S GRAVE?"

"I DON'T THINK ANYONE REALLY KNOWS. THERE WAS A CEREMONY FIVE YEARS AGO. OVER THERE. JUST AS A SYMBOLIC GESTURE. THE COFFIN WAS EMPTY."

"WHY WAS THE COFFIN EMPTY?"

"NO SPARTAN COULD BE LISTED AS KIA. THEY COULD ONLY BE LISTED AS MIA. MISSING. SO IT COULD BE SAID THAT NO SPARTAN WAS EVER KILLED IN COMBAT. SO THE CEREMONY WAS A TRIBUTE RATHER THAN A BURIAL."

"IT DOESN'T LOOK MUCH?"

"CHIEF TOLD ME ONCE THAT NO SOLDIER SHOULD BE HONORED FOR DOING WHAT'S EXPECTED."

"DO YOU BELIEVE THAT?"

"I DID. AND I STILL DO."

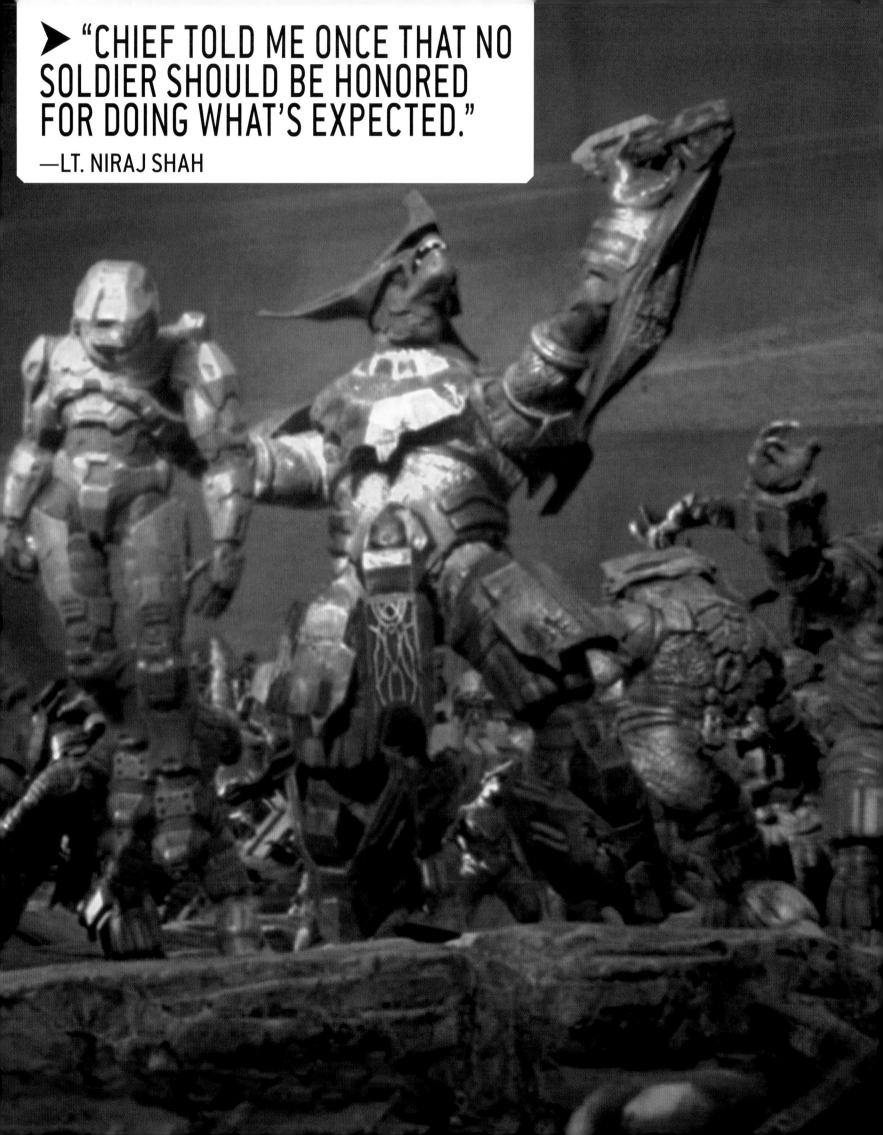

SPARTAN-II PERSONNEL

SPARTAN-IIS ARE typically deployed in small teams: Blue Team, Gray Team, Green Team, and Red Team. The most active, Blue Team, has consisted of the Master Chief, Fred-104, Linda-058, Kelly-087, Kurt-051, and Sam-034.

SPARTAN-104: FREDERIC

Fred-104 was a natural leader and a brilliant strategist, repeatedly displaying those characteristics throughout the war. Involved in a litany of battles as a Spartan, he is perhaps best known for the ground operations Red Team conducted during the Fall of Reach, when the Covenant assaulted the planet's surface in an effort to destroy generators which powered the world's orbital defense platforms.

Forced to retreat with military leadership in hand, Fred-104 reunited with the Master Chief and Blue Team shortly after the planet fell. From there they launched a strike against the Covenant's Unyielding Hierophant and an enemy fleet headed to Earth. After returning to the human homeworld he once again separated from the Master Chief, taking the point of Blue Team and leading them in several local UNSC operations.

When a distress call came in from a remote part of UNSC-controlled space, Fred-104 led Blue Team to the planet of Onyx where they now find themselves trapped in a Forerunner Shield World.

ALLIANCE: SPARTAN-II Project; UNSC SPECIES: Augmented human RANK: Lieutenant, junior grade PERSONALITY: Exceptional leader, quick thinker, superb soldier

SPARTAN-058: LINDA

Linda-058 is best known for uncontested skill with the SRS99-S2 sniper rifle and her uncanny ability to remain calm and focused during combat. However, during the Fall of Reach she was injured while helping Staff Sergeant Johnson's squad hold off the Covenant forces long enough to escape. Her injuries were so grave she was presumed dead and placed into a cryopod aboard the *Pillar of Autumn* as it fled Reach's destruction.

When the Covenant forced the *Autumn* down to Halo's surface, its cryopods were ejected and remained there, in the space above the installation, even after it had been destroyed. The Master Chief and Cortana combed the debris field for survivors and were surprised to find her cryopod still intact and even more shocked to discover that she was still alive.

Upon returning to Reach, the Master Chief managed to rescue Dr. Catherine Halsey. Not long after they fled, Halsey was able to revive Linda-058 and bring her slowly back to health. Once she had fully recovered, she assisted with the attack on the Covenant's Unyielding Hierophant station and eventually the capture of the Covenant Destroyer, which Blue Team used to respond to a distress call originating from the planet of Onyx.

It was there that Blue Team discovered the SPARTAN-III Project and became trapped in a Forerunner Shield World buried in a Slipspace rift at the core of the planet.

NICKNAME: Lone Wolf ALLIANCE: SPARTAN-II Project; UNSC SPECIES: Augmented human RANK: Petty officer, second class PERSONALITY: Quiet, unshakeable, persistent

SPARTAN-087: KELLY

Notoriously fast even by Spartan standards, Kelly-087 is capable of running at bursts of up to thirty-eight miles (sixty-two kilometers) per hour. Her reflexive actions are even more instinctive and quicker than her fellow Spartans. A consummate, if occasionally flamboyant, soldier, Kelly has demonstrated an incredible tolerance for pain, having recovered fully from several grave injuries. Her cynical sense of humor and predisposition to joke during battle make her quite different from the other SPARTAN-IIs, much less any UNSC soldier.

After Kelly-087 was fatally injured during the Fall of Reach, she managed to slowly recover at the hands of Dr. Catherine Halsey. When her condition stabilized, she was stolen away by the doctor to the planet of Onyx. There, Halsey and Kelly-087 discovered a rift in the center of the planet which took them, Blue Team, and a squad of SPARTAN-III super-soldiers to a Shield World.

NICKNAME: Rabbit ALLIANCE: SPARTAN-II Project; UNSC SPECIES: Augmented human RANK: Petty officer, second class PERSONALITY: Quick of reflex and wit, daring, adventurous, slightly reckless

SPARTAN-051: KURT

Kurt-051 was a unique Spartan. Unlike his brothers and sisters in arms, he retained a strong connection to people outside the SPARTAN-II Program; one that made him uniquely suited to become the commanding officer of the SPARTAN-III Project. In the field, his sixth sense for danger allowed Blue Team to escape from unseen traps on many occasions. His empathy made him an especially good teacher and he was able to maintain his emotional distance through discipline but still understand the needs of his trainees. He gave his own life to set off a pair of nuclear weapons at the core of Onyx, allowing the surviving Spartans to escape into the Shield World.

FULL NAME: Kurt Ambrose ALLIANCE: SPARTAN-II Project, SPARTAN-III Project, UNSC SPECIES: Augmented human RANK: Lieutenant commander PERSONALITY: An empathetic leader, nurturing, intuitive

SPARTAN-034: SAMUEL

Sam-034 was for his age the largest and strongest super-soldier created by the SPARTAN-II Project. He acted as second-in-command to the Master Chief and was one of his closest friends. During Blue Team's first sortie against the Covenant, Sam's vacuum suit ruptured, making it impossible for him to escape a bomb they had armed within a Covenant ship. He ruthlessly fought off the enemy forces, allowing his team to escape. He was the first Spartan casualty to the Covenant; he was only fourteen at the time.

NICKNAME: Sam ALLIANCE: UNSC SPECIES: Augmented human RANK: Petty officer second class PERSONALITY: The strongest SPARTAN-II, the biggest SPARTAN-II, quiet, ruthless, careful listener, expert with explosives

SPARTAN-062: MARIA

Maria-062 retired to Earth where she worked at the Mark VI testing facility in Korea. A wife and mother, Maria is an anomaly—a Spartan who has been able to lead an essentially normal human life.

ALLIANCE: UNSC SPECIES: Augmented human RANK: Petty officer second class PERSONALITY: Hard-working, the only Spartan to retire from the Navy, a mother

GRAY TEAM

This highly specialized team of Spartans differs from its combat counterparts in that its soldiers were trained especially for covert espionage. They are responsible for countless events, but their achievements are classified top secret. They are a mystery even among their fellow SPARTAN-IIs.

ALLIANCE: UNSC, ONI **SPECIES:** Augmented human **MEMBERS:** Adriana-111, Jai-006, Mike-(redacted)

GREEN TEAM

The only known member of Green Team is Kurt-051, who took the lead in field exercises. Green Team took part in the battle of Sigma Octanus IV and the battle of Jericho VII, where they managed to stop a Covenant ground advance.

ALLIANCE: UNSC **SPECIES:** Augmented human **MEMBERS:** Kurt-051

RED TEAM

Distinct from the Red Team which defended Reach during the final months of the war, the three Spartans Douglas-042, Jerome-092, and Alice-130 were involved in an earlier series of conflicts. Attached to the *Spirit of Fire*, they fought the Covenant on the planet of Arcadia and the surface of a strange Forerunner Shield World. They are currently presumed MIA. Other Red Team variations have subsequently appeared, as needed, across various theaters of war.

ALLIANCE: UNSC **SPECIES:** Augmented human **MEMBERS:** Douglas, Jerome, Alice

THE COVENANT

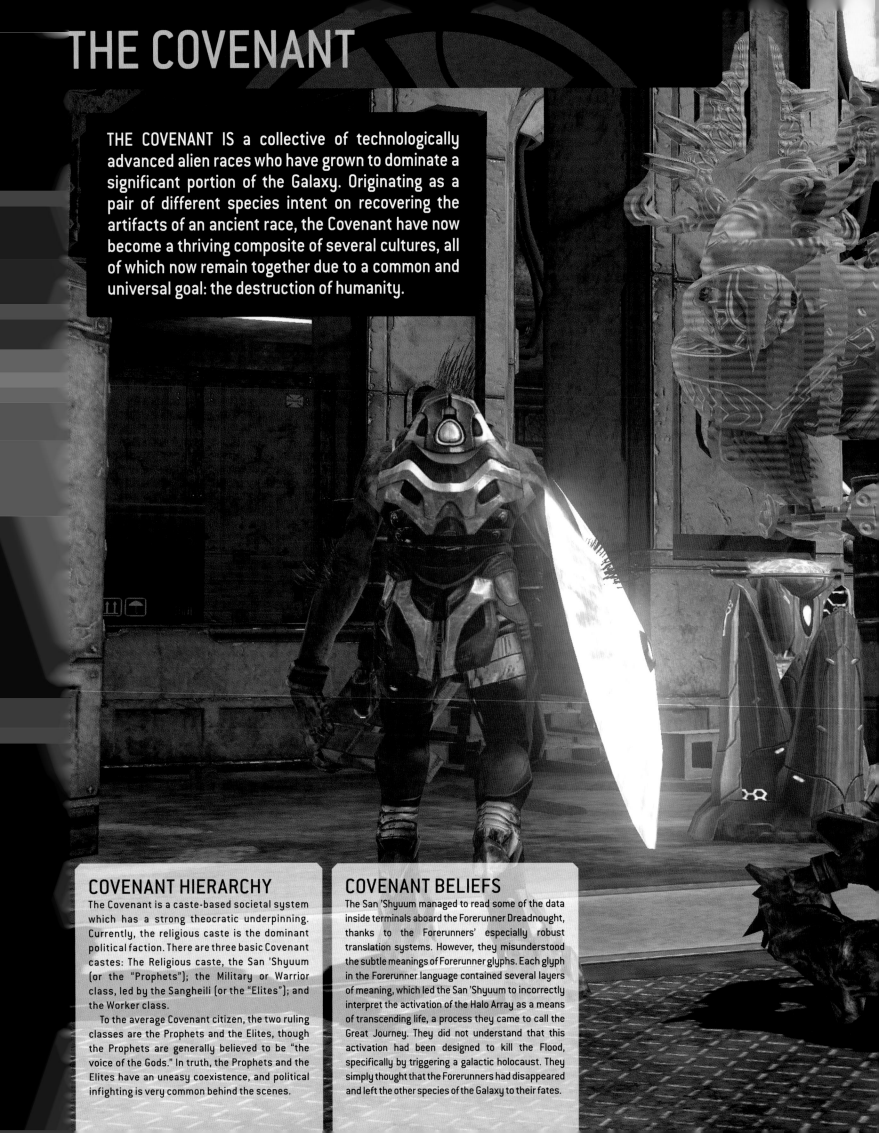

THE COVENANT

THE COVENANT IS a collective of technologically advanced alien races who have grown to dominate a significant portion of the Galaxy. Originating as a pair of different species intent on recovering the artifacts of an ancient race, the Covenant have now become a thriving composite of several cultures, all of which now remain together due to a common and universal goal: the destruction of humanity.

COVENANT HIERARCHY

The Covenant is a caste-based societal system which has a strong theocratic underpinning. Currently, the religious caste is the dominant political faction. There are three basic Covenant castes: The Religious caste, the San 'Shyuum (or the "Prophets"); the Military or Warrior class, led by the Sangheili (or the "Elites"); and the Worker class.

To the average Covenant citizen, the two ruling classes are the Prophets and the Elites, though the Prophets are generally believed to be "the voice of the Gods." In truth, the Prophets and the Elites have an uneasy coexistence, and political infighting is very common behind the scenes.

COVENANT BELIEFS

The San 'Shyuum managed to read some of the data inside terminals aboard the Forerunner Dreadnought, thanks to the Forerunners' especially robust translation systems. However, they misunderstood the subtle meanings of Forerunner glyphs. Each glyph in the Forerunner language contained several layers of meaning, which led the San 'Shyuum to incorrectly interpret the activation of the Halo Array as a means of transcending life, a process they came to call the Great Journey. They did not understand that this activation had been designed to kill the Flood, specifically by triggering a galactic holocaust. They simply thought that the Forerunners had disappeared and left the other species of the Galaxy to their fates.

> ► COVENANT SOCIETY IS BASED ON THE IDEA THAT THE PROPHETS WILL LEAD EVERYONE TO TRANSCENDENCE.

THE AGES OF THE COVENANT

The Covenant created its own means of connoting time, comprised of "Ages." Covenant history is broken down into seven cycles, each representing a theme that colored that particular Age: Abandonment, Conflict, Discovery, Reconciliation, Conversion, Doubt, and Reclamation.

These cycles do not follow one another in order; for example, there are significantly more Ages of Conflict and Doubt than of Reclamation. Another example would be that the Age from approximately 100,000 BCE to the San 'Shyuum Civil War was the First Age of Abandonment, and the time of the San 'Shyuum and Sangheili War was the First Age of Conflict.

In the centuries that followed, Ages came and went as more Forerunner reliquaries were found and studied. New species were incorporated into the Covenant hegemony, located with ease by using the luminaries, which were powerful scanners they had found aboard Forerunner ships. Once a species entered an age of initial space exploration, considered a Type-4 level of technological advancement according to the Forerunner standards, the species would appear on the luminary in bright, shining glyphs. These luminaries also detected abandoned Forerunner artifacts and ruins, which the Covenant constantly sought in the hope of acquiring more objects of worship and technological advancement.

THE WRIT OF UNION

The formal creation of the Covenant led to the First Age of Reconciliation and the Writ of Union in 852 BCE. This Union was the written treaty between the San 'Shyuum and the Sangheili which became the blueprint for all future relationships between the Covenant and newly discovered species. The Covenant became a powerful and zealous force that swept over many of the species of the Orion Arm of the Milky Way.

HIGH CHARITY—A NEW HOMEWORLD

In 648 BCE, the homeworld of the San 'Shyuum was destroyed as a result of a natural stellar collapse. To replace their homeworld, the surviving San 'Shyuum used the Forerunner Dreadnought as the centerpiece of an enormous new space station called High Charity, which would serve as an artificial world for their race. High Charity quickly became the political and spiritual capital of the Covenant and the central hub from which the hegemony pursued its steady march to convert the species within its sector of space. Ages of Doubt, Reconciliation, Conflict, and the very rare Ages of Reclamation passed as the Covenant spread its tendrils further across the Orion Arm.

THE TERM "COVENANT" refers to the original pact between the warrior Sangheili and the San 'Shyuum, who formed an alliance after years of religious war. Over time, this alliance has expanded to include many other races.

THE SAN 'SHYUUM

After the reseeding of the Galaxy by the Forerunners, one species evolved at a faster rate than all of the others: The San 'Shyuum, later known as the Prophets. Their advancements were greatly enhanced by the abundant presence of easily accessible Forerunner relics on the San 'Shyuum homeworld.

The most fantastic of these relics was a Forerunner Dreadnought, a "keyship" loaded with functioning weaponry and capable of opening portals to the Forerunner Ark. The San 'Shyuum believed that Forerunner artifacts were holy and it was considered heresy to examine the relics in too great a depth. Though they did carefully probe some of the mysteries of the Dreadnought, they did not unlock most of its secrets for centuries.

THE REFORMERS AND THE STOICS

The status quo was kept until 2200 BCE, when a group of renegade San 'Shyuum demanded to study the mysteries of the Dreadnought more closely. This led to an uprising that ended when the rebelling group, the Reformers, entered the Dreadnought and uncovered the means of activating the craft. They left the San 'Shyuum homeworld forever, abandoning the more conservative Stoics to their isolated and antiquated ways.

A NEW START

The Reformers quickly recognized several significant problems they would face. In order to maintain a viable population with such a small starting group, they developed a strict breeding program to more carefully manage the size and heartiness of their species. This led to an especially rigid and draconian social structure.

The Forerunner Dreadnought proved rich with technological discoveries and the Reformers were able to survive easily during their travels. They searched the Galaxy for more Forerunner artifacts and after a time, began to discover other species with very different perspectives and their own holy Forerunner remnants.

938 BCE

THE SANGHEILI

In 938 BCE, the San 'Shyuum encountered the Sangheili (or the "Elites"). The two races faced off over the relic-rich world of Sanghelios. The Sangheili believed, like the Stoic San 'Shyuum, that the Forerunner relics were sacred and should not be touched. They had managed to develop into a space-faring race without violating any of their rich reliquaries.

The highly militarized and brutal Sangheili attacked the San 'Shyuum but despite their efforts, the San 'Shyuum's knowledge, gleaned from years of travel, and the capabilities of the Dreadnought, eventually proved overwhelming to the Sangheili, forcing them into reluctantly surrendering and signing a treaty.

In their warrior culture, the Sangheili have great respect for a worthy adversary and once the treaty was signed they gladly entered into the burgeoning Covenant of races. The Elites, masters of conquest, needed Forerunner weaponry to continue their wars, while the Prophets, unable to fight well on their own, needed other individuals to obtain the religiously significant Forerunner artifacts for them. The Prophets study Forerunner technology and make weapons for the Elites, while the Elites conquer territory and gain access to more Forerunner artifacts for the Prophets.

784 BCE

THE MGALEKGOLO

During one of the first Ages of Conversion, the Covenant forces discovered a rich Forerunner reliquary that had been spread across a ring of rubble surrounding a gas giant planet named Te. This goldmine of Forerunner artifacts was destroyed by a race called the Lekgolo. The species was composed of colonies of worms that had literally devoured the giant Forerunner installations. These worm colonies proved difficult to defeat and incorporate into the hegemony because, when threatened, they combined into pairs of extremely powerful warriors, the Mgalekgolo (or "Hunters").

The Covenant's researchers realized that some of the worm colonies could actually prove useful—the ones that could eat everything except for the precious relics. Allying with and taming the helpful Lekgolo, the Covenant killed off the relic-destroying colonies and added the more compliant Lekgolo and Mgalekgolo into the Writ of Union in 784 BCE.

With the aid of the Lekgolo, the Covenant were able to study the internal workings of Forerunner relics with an intimacy they had never before dreamed. As a result, their technological advancement increased by leaps and bounds.

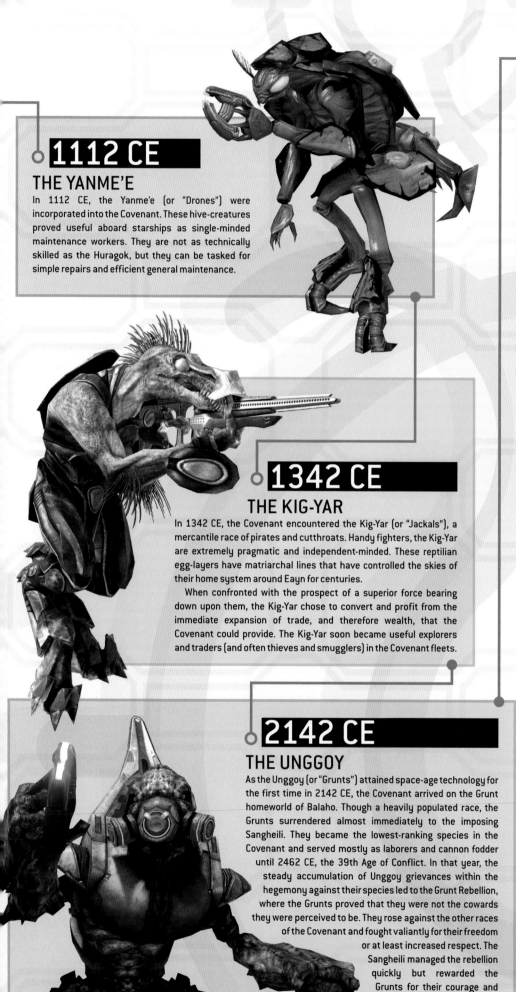

1112 CE

THE YANME'E

In 1112 CE, the Yanme'e (or "Drones") were incorporated into the Covenant. These hive-creatures proved useful aboard starships as single-minded maintenance workers. They are not as technically skilled as the Huragok, but they can be tasked for simple repairs and efficient general maintenance.

1342 CE

THE KIG-YAR

In 1342 CE, the Covenant encountered the Kig-Yar (or "Jackals"), a mercantile race of pirates and cutthroats. Handy fighters, the Kig-Yar are extremely pragmatic and independent-minded. These reptilian egg-layers have matriarchal lines that have controlled the skies of their home system around Eayn for centuries.

When confronted with the prospect of a superior force bearing down upon them, the Kig-Yar chose to convert and profit from the immediate expansion of trade, and therefore wealth, that the Covenant could provide. The Kig-Yar soon became useful explorers and traders (and often thieves and smugglers) in the Covenant fleets.

2142 CE

THE UNGGOY

As the Unggoy (or "Grunts") attained space-age technology for the first time in 2142 CE, the Covenant arrived on the Grunt homeworld of Balaho. Though a heavily populated race, the Grunts surrendered almost immediately to the imposing Sangheili. They became the lowest-ranking species in the Covenant and served mostly as laborers and cannon fodder until 2462 CE, the 39th Age of Conflict. In that year, the steady accumulation of Unggoy grievances within the hegemony against their species led to the Grunt Rebellion, where the Grunts proved that they were not the cowards they were perceived to be. They rose against the other races of the Covenant and fought valiantly for their freedom or at least increased respect. The Sangheili managed the rebellion quickly but rewarded the Grunts for their courage and warrior spirit by returning them to the ranks of the Covenant, but this time as weapon-carrying infantry.

2492 CE

THE JIRALHANAE

In 2463 CE, the 23rd Age of Doubt began and the Covenant returned to its quest for Forerunner relics and outward expansion. 2492 CE saw the beginning of a new Age when the Covenant stumbled upon the Jiralhanae (or "Brutes"). The Brutes were a savage race that had once achieved a space age, but their pack mentality and ritualistic, violent warrior culture had led to a war of attrition in which protracted and vicious societal wars pulled their species back to a pre-industrial state.

When the Covenant chanced upon their homeworld Doisac, the Jiralhanae were just rediscovering technologies like the manipulation of radio wavelengths. They were ill-prepared for the Covenant arrival and were quickly forced into submission by the Covenant's superior forces. Once incorporated, the Brutes were given technologies to aid their continued development, but the Sangheili recognized the Brute race as one that could rival their own in battle and so imposed severe restrictions on their place in the Covenant fleet. Very few Brutes were allowed to command ships and when they did, they were denied the technologies that would make them capable of acting independent of the larger fleets.

2524 CE

THE COVENANT AND HUMANS

In 2524 CE, the Covenant encountered humans for the first time. This inevitable meeting would eventually throw the entire foundation of the Covenant's religion and tenuous political alliances into a state of disarray. For one of the few times in their history, the Covenant would face a foe not only willing to fight back to the brink of self-extinction, but an enemy whose very existence would call into question their most basic religious tenets.

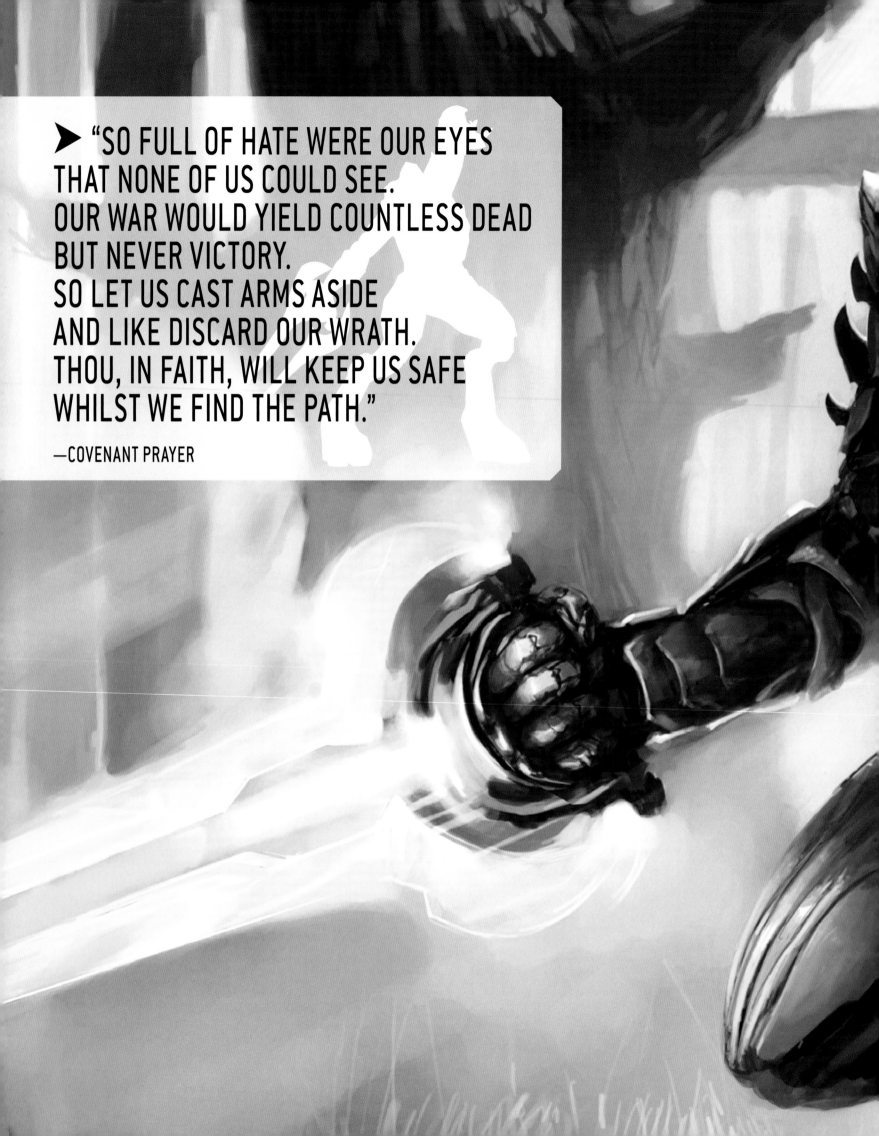

> "SO FULL OF HATE WERE OUR EYES
THAT NONE OF US COULD SEE.
OUR WAR WOULD YIELD COUNTLESS DEAD
BUT NEVER VICTORY.
SO LET US CAST ARMS ASIDE
AND LIKE DISCARD OUR WRATH.
THOU, IN FAITH, WILL KEEP US SAFE
WHILST WE FIND THE PATH."

—COVENANT PRAYER

THE SAN 'SHYUUM (PROPHETS)

THE SAN 'SHYUUM, known by humans as the "Prophets," are the religious leaders of the Covenant.

PROPHETS AND HUMANKIND

The Prophets are the architects of the Covenant's holy war against the human race, which began after a Forerunner "Oracle" revealed an uncertain but powerful connection between humanity and the Forerunners. Sensing that this revelation could threaten both the existence of the Covenant as well as their own personal power, the Prophet Hierarchs decided to conceal this information and eliminate humanity and the threat they posed.

THE GREAT JOURNEY

The Covenant worship the Forerunners as gods and hold them in high esteem. The basis of their worship revolves around the concept of transcendence. As the Covenant's religious leaders, the Prophets' primary goal is to locate, study, and incorporate Forerunner technology in order to more fully understand and eventually initiate what they believe to be the Great Journey of transcendence.

High-ranking San 'Shyuum sit on ornate Gravity Thrones.

YUUM

DATA FILE

HEIGHT: Adult male 7'3" (2.21 m) **WEIGHT:** Adult male 200 lb (91 kg)

The Prophets use holographic projection to deliver their religious mandates to Covenant forces in the field.

THE HIERARCHS

The Hierarchs are the three highest authorities among the Prophets and are the ultimate political and religious power in the Covenant. There are normally three Hierarchs in each Age and in order to usher in a new Age, a group of Prophets must get the blessing of the Oracle of High Charity. This Oracle is a Forerunner Artificial Intelligence found within the Dreadnought, which sits at the center of the capital.

Prior to the Human-Covenant War, the Oracle had not actually spoken for millennia, so the ascension of the Hierarchs had been steeped in political machinations and the bribery of the Oracle's keeper.

NAMING CONVENTIONS

Prophets have both a given name and a family name. Once they ascend to a certain level in the bureaucratic hierarchy, they are referred to by their position, their appellation being reflective of a quality they wish to emulate (or profess to emulate), for example the Prophet of Truth, the Minister of Fortitude, or the Prophet of Regret.

SAN 'SHYUUM CULTURE

The San 'Shyuum homeworld was split by the civil war between the Stoics (a faction opposed to any manipulation or study of holy Forerunner relics) and the Reformers (who felt that Forerunner relics were meant to be transformed into usable technologies). This internal strife led the Reformers to eventually leave their homeworld behind. In 648 BCE, the San 'Shyuum homeworld was destroyed when its orbital star went supernova. At that point, High Charity became the homeworld of the San 'Shyuum. Their breeding and cultural interactions are controlled carefully by a strict bureaucracy that ensures genetic diversity is maintained.

THE SANCTUM OF THE HIERARCHS

THE PROPHET TRIUMVIRATE

EACH COVENANT AGE has its three Hierarchs—the highest authorities in the Covenant. They aim to guide the Covenant to the Great Journey, and their word is law. Three notable Hierarchs have been the Prophets of Mercy, Regret, and Truth.

HIGH PROPHET OF MERCY

The High Prophet of Mercy served as the Philogist before accepting the role of Hierarch. As Philogist, he attended to the "Oracle," which was actually a fragment of the Forerunner AI Mendicant Bias trapped inside the Forerunner Dreadnought. Mercy was present when the Oracle announced that the Forerunner glyphs found covering the human planet of Harvest were actually signs of a connection between humanity and the Forerunners. It was Mercy's promise to never share this news with the rest of the Covenant which purchased him his ascension to High Prophet status.

MERCY'S DEATH

When the Prophet of Regret foolishly charged headlong into humanity's homeworld, Mercy petitioned Truth to stay the hand of judgement. The three Prophets had, after all, shared over a quarter of a century worth of utter domination against humanity. Shortly after arriving at Installation 05, however, the Master Chief slew Regret and escaped Delta Halo to track down the remaining Prophets in High Charity. Ironically, the Prophet of Truth did not hesitate to leave Mercy to the Chief or to the ensuing Flood as the parasite burrowed its way into the city. His words echoed the profound sentiment of the Covenant: "The Great Journey waits for no one." Little did Truth know, the cold reality of his words would some day be echoed in his own dire end.

ALLIANCE	SPECIES	RANK	PERSONALITY
Covenant	San 'Shyuum	High Prophet	Passionate, lively

THE HIGH PROPHET OF MERCY

REGRET AND HUMANKIND

As the Vice Minister, Regret was the first to inform the future High Prophet of Truth about the vast reliquary of Forerunner artifacts he believed were on Harvest. After persuading Truth to join him in a conspiracy to gain these artifacts for their own political use, Regret helped Truth in his plans to usurp the High Prophet of Restraint. Regret threatened to create a scandal involving Restraint if he did not leave his position as High Prophet. Before launching their plan, they sought the blessing of the Oracle, and it was then that they learned that Humans represented the lineage of the Forerunners and that the basis of the Covenant's entire religion, and perhaps even the Great Journey itself, was a falsehood. The three agreed never to reveal this to anyone.

Much like his role as a Vice Minister, Regret stayed at the front lines in the war against humanity. Then, a quarter of a century after the revelation in the Dreadnought, he stumbled upon the human homeworld. Initially, he believed this world, which housed the portal to the Ark, would be empty, but it was not. When the human resistance proved difficult to maintain, Regret's carrier jumped into Slipspace with a small collection of UNSC forces in tow. When they exited Slipspace, they had arrived at Delta Halo, or Installation 05.

As his fleet's military spread out across the surface of the ring, Regret took members of the Elite High Council into a temple. Although he had significant forces guarding his position, the Demon known as the Master Chief infiltrated their position and eliminated Regret. When the other Hierarchs had discovered this, they obliterated the temple in an effort to destroy the human, sending the bodies of both the Chief and the Prophet to the bottom of a vast lake. It was there that the Prophet of Regret was assimilated into the Gravemind.

HIGH PROPHET OF REGRET

The High Prophet of Regret had been previously known as Vice Minister of Tranquility, serving with the Elites in various missionary and expeditionary affairs. This operational commonality with the Elites provided him with an aggressive and brash demeanor, something which was typically not well-received by other Prophets.

GRAVITY THRONE —VIEW FROM ABOVE

THE HIGH PROPHET OF REGRET

ALLIANCE	SPECIES	RANK
Covenant	San 'Shyuum	High Prophet; formerly the Vice Minister of Tranquility

PERSONALITY
Confrontational, argumentative, rash, ambitious, immature

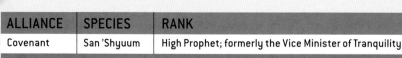

GRAVITY THRONE —VIEW FROM BELOW

ALLIANCE	SPECIES
The Covenant	San 'Shyuum

RANK

Prophet of Truth; formerly the Minister of Fortitude

PERSONALITY

Calm and stoic, but impatient; manipulative and ambitious

THE PROPHET OF TRUTH

The Prophet of Truth has always maintained a level of shrewdness far above most others in his species. Once he gained political sway within the Ministry of Concert, the Minister of Fortitude uncovered a conspiracy by a handful of Jackal ship captains to poison recreational narcotics that were used by the Unggoy. The toxins would have sterilized the Grunts, stifling their reproductive efforts. Despite his predictions regarding the matter, the situation was never addressed, and it eventually culminated in the Grunt Rebellion.

THE PROPHET OF
TRUTH—REAR VIEW

Prior to his role as a High Prophet, Fortitude was heavily involved in an effort to conceal evidence which supported humanity as the rightful heirs to the Forerunners. In a brilliant and calculating move, Fortitude used his threat of this information to leverage himself into a place of authority within the Covenant, becoming the High Prophet of Truth.

Very aware of the lie that he lived, Truth used his own name to deflect the deceptive reality of his position. Though Mercy was older, Truth retained leadership over the triumvirate because of his constant scheming.

THE PROPHET
OF TRUTH

Frequently operating without the knowledge of the other High Prophets, Truth manipulated even those closest to him. Regret's failure eventually led to the dismissal of the Elites; Mercy's death delayed the Flood and the Master Chief, if briefly... perhaps his power led him to errantly believe that he would not succumb to the same fate.

121

THE HURAGOK (ENGINEERS)

THE HURAGOK ARE essentially self-aware, thinking machines. To cultures without the medical technology to determine otherwise, the Huragok appear to be biological life forms.

PHYSICAL CHARACTERISTICS

The Huragok are approximately the size of an average human male, though their mode of locomotion is vastly different. Huragok float above the ground, lifted by lighter-than-air gases stored in bladders on their backs. Huragok normally float a few feet above the ground, although in special situations they are able to rise much higher for short periods of time. Although they possess no true tissues or organs, the nanochemical surrogates closely mimic the Huragoks' biological analogs.

ROLE IN THE COVENANT

The Prophets store and document the archived religious texts and technology of the Forerunners, but it is the Huragok who perform the actual physical labor of excavating, transporting, and gathering data on Forerunner artifacts. The Huragok are nevertheless fiercely protective of Forerunner excavations and they will emit a high-pitched, warbling cry if artifacts are endangered in any way.

LIGHTER THAN SOME

Lighter Than Some, a Huragok aboard the *Minor Transgression* assisted with repairs on the vessel, as was the role of most shipboard Huragok. Since they can only communicate in a form of sign language, they mostly keep to themselves, but *Lighter Than Some* approached the Unggoy called Dadab and repeated a gesture of greeting to the Unggoy until he understood. This began an odd friendship. *Lighter Than Some* taught Dadab the Huragok language, and to this date, Dadab is the only known Unggoy to have understood it.

Prior to the *Minor Transgression* being destroyed by a handful of humans, both Dadab and *Lighter Than Some* managed to escape. Not long after, they were rescued by *Rapid Conversion* and integrated into the largely Brute crew. It was then that they participated in the first few encounters with humanity under the Brute Chieftain Maccabeus. Seeking to right the wrongs of their first encounter, *Lighter Than Some* built a plow out of parts from a damaged Spirit dropship. However, this effort at redemption was quashed when *Lighter Than Some*'s creation of peace was transformed by the Brutes into the Chopper, a machine of war.

After witnessing the impressive work that *Lighter Than Some* could do, Maccabeus moved the ship's Drones away from engineering duties and into combat, a decision the Drones despised. When afforded an opportunity, they attacked the Huragok. When Dadab witnessed this, he became furious and slew the Drones who had killed his friend.

ALLIANCE: Covenant **SPECIES:** Huragok
RANK: Engineer

HURAGOK CULTURE

The Huragok do not actually have a culture of their own. Instead, they focus only on their maintenance and technological roles in the Covenant. To a Huragok, duty is everything.

FILE

: Adult: 6'2" (1.88 m)
: Adult: 125 lb (57 kg)

Huragok's method of movement through the air is provided by sacs full of gas.

HURAGOK REPRODUCTION

If enough raw materials are available, a pair of Huragok can generate a unified replica of themselves within forty-five minutes. If another Huragok assists (a maximum of three participants can take part in the reproductive event), the progeny is produced in approximately thirty minutes and is essentially an amalgamation of all three parents. This latter method of "reproduction" is preferred, since it results in individuals who have a broader range of experience.

As long as a Huragok has access to raw materials, it can self-repair all but the most catastrophic physical damage. In the same manner, one Huragok can completely recreate another as long as it has access to at least ten percent of the damaged individual's mass. If a Huragok can avoid death by injury or disease, its lifespan is effectively indefinite.

NAMING CONVENTIONS

When Huragok parents construct their offspring, there is a careful process of balancing the air sacs of their young. The name of a Huragok is related to its buoyancy in this moment, such as *Lighter Than Some*.

MILITARY WARRIORS

The Elites are one of the two species that created the original Covenant after the Sangheili and San 'Shyuum war. Their respect for the tactics and fortitude of their opponents is an important reason why the Covenant has become a strong alliance. Every species they defeat who has shown valor against them is treated fairly after their victory and is often incorporated into the ranks beneath their command.

While the San 'Shyuum control the political spheres, the Sangheili control the armies of the Covenant and maintain their strict hierarchies and cultural opinions in the structure of the Covenant military. Currently, "promotion" (though the Covenant do not think of it in those terms) is available only to a soldier who has killed an opponent in legitimate combat—butchering unarmed civilians does not count as legitimate combat.

Most Elites move in packs, but some hunt alone; such Elites are the equivalent of human special forces troops, with a high level of independence. The officer corps of the Covenant military is composed of "blooded" (battle-tested) Elites.

THE SANGHEILI, ALSO known as the Elites, are the primary warrior class of the Covenant. They are tough, fearless, and relentless.

DATA FILE

HEIGHT: Adult male 7'4" (2.24 m)
WEIGHT: Adult male 318 lb (144 kg)

RELATIONS WITH OTHER CASTES
Elites consider the other Covenant client races (Jackals, Grunts, Hunters, Engineers, and Brutes) as beneath them in all measurable standards. The Elites are the only race—apart from the Prophets—permitted to operate military spacecraft outside of their native system, though the crews on Covenant spacecraft are always composed of a mix of races.

SANGHEILI CULTURE

In the Elite culture, names are considered a privilege. Elites consider humans as unworthy of names, except in very rare cases. Sanghelios, the Sangheili homeworld, is a harsh world, which lies on the innermost edge of its system's habitable zone.

NAMING CONVENTIONS

Because names are important to Elite society, each element of their names has a meaning. Elite names are constructed from a series of parts. An example is Ado 'Mortumee. "Ado" is his given name, and it was his only name until

he was considered an adult. Upon reaching adulthood, he earned the right to carry the badge name "'Mortumee." This name is made up of three parts: MOR (an adjectival descriptor, such as "strong" or "swift"), TUM (a family name to indicate his lineage), and EE (an honorific showing military service). Most Elites will have names with this kind of construction, though there are several exceptions. Bako 'Ikaporamee, whose basic name is composed of PO / RAM / EE, received the additional honorific prefix name IKA, which indicates his role as an aide to a Prophet. This lengthened name gives him a higher status among Elites. Another is Bero 'Kusovai (KU / SOV / AI) whose honorific was bestowed upon him in a ceremony after he chose to dedicate his life to the perfection of his swordsmanship. There is also Parala 'Ahrmonro, whose honorific RO indicates that he has held public office—in this case as council to the Prophet of Regret.

ELITE COMBAT HARNESS

The Elite Combat Harness is the standard armor used by the Sangheili in all Covenant conflicts. Similar to the Spartans' Mark VI in that it boosts speed and strength while adding a personal energy shield, the armor is actually less advanced and can withstand less damage than a Spartan's armor.

Differences in the size, shape, and color denote status among the Sangheili. While all warriors wear it, only the supreme Zealots are gifted with the gold color (and the added strength that this armor provides). The lowest Sangheili make do with blue suits.

OTHER NAMES: Elite Armor, Elite Default
LENGTH: approx. 7' 4" (2.24 m)
USE: General combat

NAMING CONVENTIONS (POST SCHISM)

Many Sangheili Rebels fighting in the Covenant Civil War have chosen to drop the honorific "EE" from their name. It is their feeling that as an innately martial culture, pointing out that one is a participant in the military is an unnecessary tradition.

PHYSICAL CHARACTERISTICS

Elites, like the Jackals, utilize energy shielding, which makes them a very serious threat on the battlefield. Unlike the Jackals, Elites possess full-body energy shielding. Some are equipped with "light-bending" technology that acts as effective camouflage. Elites have a distinctive skull structure, with very pronounced teeth and four-part jaws. The species has two genders but humans have seen no females.

➤ THE LEADING FORCE IN THE COVENANT ARMY, THE SANGHEILI ARE PROUD WARRIORS. THEIR SOCIETY AND BASIS OF RESPECT ARE BUILT ON MILITARY HONOR.

SUPREME COMMANDER

Although there are varying degrees of command roles over fleets, a Supreme Commander is essentially the Fleet Master, the key figure responsible for a fleet or a contingency of fleets that can be involved in space operations, naval battles, blockades, and orbital bombardment. Thel 'Vadamee remains the most renowned Supreme Commander at the close of the Human-Covenant War.

HONOR GUARD ULTRA

Rarely seen, the Honor Guard Ultras or "Lights of Sanghelios" are the highest ranking guardians of a Prophet. Typically called "Helios," these soldiers will manage standard Honor Guards in many encounters, but if needed, they would gladly die to protect a Prophet.

COUNCILLOR

Largely displaced from the front lines of war, the Councillors are part of the Covenant's leadership, answerable to the Hierarchs alone. The Councillors were betrayed by the High Prophets late in the Human-Covenant War when they allowed the Brutes to begin summarily executing Councillors, an incident which catapulted the Covenant into civil war.

ZEALOT

Less of a rank than a philosophy, Zealots are by far the most ruthless fundamentalists within all of the Covenant military. Though most Elite males are trained to kill as soon as they can properly hold a weapon, future Zealots seem to be born with the desire to kill.

SANGHEILI HONOR GUARDSMAN

Sangheili Honor Guardsmen are specially chosen to provide protection to the High Prophets and other high-ranking officials in the Covenant High Council. They sometimes follow a High Prophet on missions in the field, but they primarily remain in the holy city of High Charity. Their armor is very elaborate, covered with spikes and special glyphs, indicating that obtaining the position of an Honor Guardsman is a great privilege.

SPECIAL OPERATIONS

Special Operations Officers, also known as SpecOps, are the most proficient tactical unit within the Covenant military. They are typically sent on missions with acute and specific objectives and are not associated with any broader military application. For this reason, assassinations are commonly executed by SpecOps groups.

STEALTH ELITE

Stealth Elites function as an offshoot of the Special Operations Officers. The primary difference between a Stealth Elite and a SpecOps Officer is that the Stealth Elite corps are spread throughout the Covenant army as standard battlefield units, whereas SpecOps teams operate as independent units. Stealth Elites, unlike SpecOps Elites, participate in almost all widescale engagements.

ELITES ARE SEPARATED into ranks based on skill and experience. To advance in rank, Elites must honorably earn such advancement on the battlefield.

ELITE RANGER

Elite Rangers are experts in low-gravity to zero-gravity combat but they are deployed primarily in planetside engagements, as their harness is specifically designed to propel them in gravity-intensive locations. While their equipment allows them to operate in an oxygen-free environment, it is their mobility that poses the greatest threat to human forces on a planet's surface.

ELITE MAJOR

Crimson-armored Elite Majors act as pilots, Platoon Leaders, and Lance Leaders and also command Elite Minors. They are known for their stealth and speed and are extremely skilled in combat situations. Elite Majors are the second most-commonly encountered Elites on the battlefield, just after Elite Minors.

ELITE MINOR

The most common rank for an Elite is that of an Elite Minor, the basic level for military participation. While there is no official time frame for an Elite Minor to serve in this capacity, in most circumstances an honorable Elite will fall on their sword (but not an Energy Sword, as Elite Minors are strictly forbidden from carrying these holy weapons) if they are not killed in battle or advanced to the status of Elite Major after a single campaign.

OSSOONA

Ossoona is the temporary title and rank that is given to specially selected Elite Majors by the Prophets. The title of Ossoona awards elevated status and military command and is usually only given for a single mission, although there have been exceptions in certain cases. They are often tasked with espionage-related missions, serving as special investigators for the Prophets.

ELITE ULTRA

Perhaps the most powerful contingency of Elites in common military distribution, Ultras typically position themselves on locations or vehicles they feel are high-cost targets for the enemy.

WHILE THE CENTER of the Covenant Separatist rebellion revolved around the Arbiter, other key Elites rallied to defend their species from the treachery of the Prophets. Among those heroes were Rtas 'Vadum and Usze 'Taham.

RTAS 'VADUM

RTAS 'VADUM

Present at the battle of Installation 04, Rtas 'Vadum led troops on several dangerous missions into the *Infinite Succor* and onto the installation itself. He survived Halo's destruction but was detached from fleet duty and reassigned to the position of SpecOps Commander, basing his operations out of High Charity. 'Vadum was also heavily involved in engagements leading up to the discovery of Installation 05. After the Great Schism and the ascendance of the Jiralhanae, he led the Elite rebellion and was the commander of the Separatist fleet, negotiating their eventual alliance with UNSC forces.

Rtas 'Vadum sitting on an Elite Fleet Master's Gravity Throne. These chairs are less opulent versions of those used by the Prophets.

ALLIANCE	SPECIES
Covenant Separatists	Sangheili

PERSONALITY
Quick, tactical, unparalleled swordsman, respectful, spends lives carefully

RANK
Special Operations Commander, Shipmaster

USZE 'TAHAM

USZE 'TAHAM

Although Usze 'Taham was born into a respected merchant family, he was fathered by Toha 'Sumai, one of the preeminent sword-fighters in all of Sanghelios. An honors graduate from the top war college in the Iruiru region of Yermo, Usze took his first position within the Covenant Navy. Displaying such skill as to receive an offer to join the High Prophets' Honor Guard, Usze turned it down because he wanted to experience combat first hand, rather than participate in what had become a fairly ceremonial position. This decision brought the ire of certain Covenant politicians, and he has had to avert numerous punitive actions and at least two attempts on his life since then. After the Great Schism, the Ascetics made Usze one of their liaisons within their new UNSC allies.

ALLIANCE	SPECIES	RANK
Covenant Separatists	Sangheili	Special Warfare Fleet Security

PERSONALITY		
Independent, resourceful, vigilant		

VORO NAR 'MANTAKREE

After the Covenant Civil War and the battle of Installation 05, Voro Nar 'Mantakree proved himself by rallying the battling Covenant forces against a greater danger—the escape of the Flood.

His courage and level-headedness were lauded by the Sangheili leader, Xytan 'Jar Wattinree, who sent him on a mission to capture the planet Onyx. Narrowly avoiding the blast that destroyed Joyous Exultation and most of the Sangheili fleet, 'Mantakree's armada was assaulted by Onyx's Sentinels. While he survived the orbital battle to lead an assault at the core of the planet, 'Mantakree and his forces were destroyed by a nuclear blast set off by Kurt-051.

ALLIANCE: Covenant Separatists SPECIES: Sangheili RANK: Fleet Master PERSONALITY: Careful, instinctive, ambitious

XYTAN 'JAR WATTINREE

Imperial Admiral Xytan 'Jar Wattinree was the leader of the Sangheili forces and later, the leader of the Covenant Separatists. He rallied the Separatists around the planet Joyous Exultation.

After sending his nearest rival on a mission to the planet Onyx, a NOVA bomb picked up in human space was reactivated by a group of Huragok. The bomb exploded, taking out two-thirds of the Sangheili fleet and more than half of the planet's surface. Wattinree was atomized in the blast.

ALLIANCE: Covenant Separatists
SPECIES: Sangheili RANK: Imperial Admiral
PERSONALITY: Suspicious, powerful, confident, an exceptional warrior

ARBITERS

THE SANGHEILI HAVE an unflinching sense of honor and warrior dignity. When dire circumstances threaten the Covenant or in times of extraordinary crisis, the Prophets may choose to select an Arbiter—a rank of warrior who is sent on highly dangerous missions as a chance to redeem himself. Arbiters rarely survive these missions, but they accept and even anticipate glorious death in service to the Prophets, thereby regaining any honor they may have lost.

The deadly Gravity Hammer—the most powerful two-handed melee weapon

FROM SUPREME COMMANDER TO ARBITER

Thel 'Vadam, now known to all humans as the Arbiter, is one of the most powerful and prolific examples of the entire Sangheili race. As Supreme Commander of the Fleet of Particular Justice, he led the Covenant forces to victory at the battle of Reach. As the engagement concluded, he ordered his ships to pursue the fleeing *Pillar of Autumn*, which led to the discovery of the first Halo ring, Installation 04. His inability to prevent the destruction of the ring and the capture of the *Ascendant Justice* by the Master Chief forced him to answer for these failures before the High Council. During that process, he was stripped of his rank, branded with the Mark of Shame and sentenced to death. The Prophet Hierarchs Truth and Mercy intervened and offered to commute this sentence if he would become their new Arbiter. With the full realization that accepting this offer was tantamount to a death sentence, but also knowing it could be his only opportunity to redeem himself in the eyes of his people, the Sangheili accepted the offer.

UNIQUE ARMOR

The ceremonial Arbiter armor, though not state-of-the-art, is still practical and very functional. Because Arbiters are mostly sent on suicidal missions and their bodies are rarely recovered, they each receive their own set of armor built to a traditional design. Unlike modern Covenant Active Camouflage, which has virtually unlimited duration, the Arbiter's camouflage only lasts for a few seconds. However, this is still enough to give a tactical advantage over enemies.

A Needler, with its lethal crystalline projectiles

Mausoleum of the Arbiters, ...adam is made an Arbiter, ...ing to the will of the Prophets.

THEL 'VADAM

THEL 'VADAM

ALLIANCE: The Covenant GENDER: Male
SPECIES: Sangheili
HEIGHT: 7'10" (2.4 m)
WEIGHT: 322 lb (146 kg)
RANK: Arbiter; formerly the Supreme Commander of the Fleet of Particular Justice

➤ "YOU WILL DIE, AS EACH ARBITER HAS BEFORE YOU. YOU ARE THE ARBITER, THE WILL OF THE PROPHETS."

Classical helmet

KEY TO ARBITER ARMOR COMPONENTS

Main armor	
Dark metal detailing	
Body suit	
Body suit straps	
Skin	
Teeth	
Eyes	
Shoulder flashlight	

RIPA 'MORAMEE—THE SEVENTEENTH ARBITER

Ripa 'Moramee was another example of an Elite accepting the role of Arbiter to redeem themselves. After successfully suppressing the Sixteenth Unggoy Disobedience, 'Moramee attempted to overthrow the leadership of his own clan on the military world of Decided Heart. However, the coup failed and 'Moramee was sentenced to serving within the Weeping Shadows of Sorrow Penitentiary. The Prophet of Regret, recognizing his ruthlessness, intervened and appointed Ripa Arbiter. Known for his intense rage, 'Moramee did not discriminate whom he directed his anger at and when he got into battle, he was normally the only one left standing, having killed everyone else. 'Moramee met his demise at the hands of Sergeant John Forge, who killed him after he kidnapped Ellen Anders on Arcadia.

The Arbiter's main weapons are the Energy Sword, the Carbine, and the Plasma Rifle.

SIDE VIEW

FRONT VIEW

THE MASTER CHIEF WITH THE ARBITER

REAR VIEW

THE ARBITER AND MASTER CHIEF

Thel 'Vadam's first mission as Arbiter was to silence a renegade Elite who had learned that the Covenant's belief in the Great Journey would, in fact, spell their doom. The Arbiter was then sent to retrieve the "Sacred Icon" from the Library on the newly discovered Installation 05 in an effort to activate the ring and bring about the Great Journey. Though the Arbiter successfully retrieved the Icon, Tartarus, the Chieftain of the Brutes, betrayed him. Tartarus told the Arbiter that the Prophets had revealed that the Brute race would replace the Elites at the Prophets' sides.

At first the Arbiter was assumed to be dead, but the Gravemind rescued him and the Master Chief. While trying to stop Tartarus and the Brutes, the Arbiter formed an alliance with the humans. This act was one of several which helped initiate the civil war that rocked the foundations of the Covenant. His actions also opened up the possibility of further alliances and reconciliations with humanity and various races or segments of the fractured Covenant hegemony.

VIEW FROM BELOW

ALLIANCE: Covenant **GENDER:** Male
SPECIES: Sangheili **HEIGHT:** 8'1" (2.46 m) **RANK:** Arbiter

"THERE WAS HONOR IN OUR COVENANT ONCE, AND THERE SHALL BE AGAIN!"

—THE ARBITER

THE JIRALHANAE (BRUTES)

THE JIRALHANAE, OR Brutes, are a physically imposing client race of the Covenant. Discovered as a primitive species by the Prophets, they were assimilated into the high-tech Covenant culture.

PROUD WARRIORS

Brutes are powerful, fierce, and competitive. They travel in small packs often led by Chieftains and usually form the strongest point of any attacking Covenant ground force. Their fighting style is forceful, utilitarian, and pragmatic, so while they can drive all vehicles and use any weapon, they strongly prefer Brute designs, which rely on blunt physical force.

In combat, they use battle armor for protection, in addition to their natural resistance to damage. While wearing armor, they are fearless. But without it, they go berserk and may respond with a ferocious melee charge.

The Sangheili handicapped the space-faring capabilities of the Jiralhanae, disallowing them from using certain essential pieces of equipment on their starships. They also limited the number of Jiralhanae starship commanders. After the breaking of the Covenant, the Brutes were made the backbone of the Prophets' armed forces. Brute warlords now command many self-sufficient fighting units, operating with a total lack of respect for the lives of civilians or those they consider the "lesser" races of the Covenant. Brutes consider the Elite concept of honor to be foolish and irrelevant, and are eager to prove their status as superior warriors.

BRUTE ARMOR

A fight sometimes requires more protection than just skin, skill, and muscle. Brute armor does just that, providing light protection through composite plating. It does not add strength or speed to its wielder (unlike the MJOLNIR systems or a Sangheili's armor), but seldom does a Jiralhanae need such enhancement; they are speedy and powerful enough to take out almost any living creature in a one-on-one fight. A group of a dozen armored Jiralhanae can almost break through mountains.

OTHER NAMES: Ape Armor, Brute Shield
WEIGHT: At least half a ton (453.59 kg)
USE: General combat

BRUTE CHIEFTAIN

MACCABEUS

Maccabeus was a faithful devotee of the Covenant religion. One of very few Brutes granted the rank of Shipmaster, he was in charge of the first deputation to meet with humans on Harvest. When the humans refused to surrender themselves to the Covenant, he was instructed by the Minister of Fortitude to completely annihilate them. After failing in this task, he was killed by his nephew Tartarus who then assumed his position as Chieftain.

ALLIANCE: Covenant SPECIES: Jiralhanae RANK: Chieftain, Shipmaster PERSONALITY: Strong, brutal, careful, zealous, faithful, devoted to his pack

TARTARUS

Tartarus became the Chief of his Jiralhanae pack after the battle of Harvest and was the right hand to the Prophet of Truth. Jiralhanae influence increased because of the secrets Tartarus shared with the Hierarch and he eventually became the leader of the Hierarch's private guard. Tartarus was sent to activate Halo Installation 05, but was stopped by the Arbiter and killed during their battle.

ALLIANCE: Covenant Loyalist SPECIES: Jiralhanae RANK: Chieftain PERSONALITY: Ambitious, brutal, conniving, scheming

NAMING CONVENTIONS

Examples of Jiralhanae names include Bracktanus, Tartarus, and Lepidus.

BRUTE CAPTAIN

JIRALHANAE CULTURE

Brute social structure is pack-oriented, led by an alpha male, or alpha prime, and all interactions between Brutes are governed by personal status, which they display through ornate armor and decoration. There is a patriarchal scheme that is followed loosely, depending on the social, martial, and sexual success of the patriarch. Patricide is a common method for rising within the packs. No females have been observed in military roles. The Jiralhanae homeworld, Doisac, is a rocky, heavily forested planet, which also contains swaths of desert and a few seas.

The deadly Type-51 Covenant Carbine is one of the weapons favored by the Brute Ultras.

DATA FILE

HEIGHT: Adult male: 8'5" (2.59 m)
WEIGHT: Adult male: 1,500 lb (680 kg)

RELATIONS WITH OTHER CASTES

After the fracturing of the Covenant, the Jiralhanae were made the backbone of the remaining Covenant armed forces. They treat all other races under their command as expendable equipment. Subordinates that fail in any aspect of their duty can expect swift and final punishment.

JIRALHANAE RANKS

JIRALHANAE, OR BRUTE, society has a pack mentality. A Brute's position is based on their physical abilities and number of kills. Various ranks exist and are identifiable by different colored armor.

BRUTE COMMANDERS

BRUTE CHIEFTAIN

ROLE: Pack commanders

Brute Chieftains are high-ranking Jiralhanae pack commanders. They are easily identified by their striking red-and-black armor. Designed to allow them to use their phenomenal speed, strength, and agility to the fullest extent, the armor also offers a considerable amount of protection.

Brute Chieftains make frequent use of overcharged shielding technology to shrug off attacks, and their preferred weapon is the Gravity Hammer.

WAR CHIEFTAIN

ROLE: Pack commanders

War Chieftains are superior to the standard Brute Chieftains, typically commanding larger packs. Their bronze-colored armor carries a distinctive head crest on the helmet, which makes them easy to recognize in battle. War Chieftains prefer to use the heaviest of weapons in battle in order to both inflict maximum damage upon their enemies and reinforce their physical superiority to the subservient Brutes.

BRUTE OFFICERS

BRUTE CAPTAIN

ROLE: Leading Brute packs in battle

The lowest of the three captain ranks, Brute Captains are responsible for leading small groups of standard Brutes into battle. Their violet armor is more resistant to attack than the standard armor worn by Brutes and they are typically more heavily armed.

Although Brute Captains are experts in the use of the Brute Shot, they also make use of almost all other weapons within the Covenant's arsenal.

BRUTE CAPTAIN ULTRA

ROLE: Leading Brute packs in battle

Captain Ultra is the highest of the three captain ranks and these beasts are immensely strong and agile. They wear cyan armor, which offers very high resistance to most weapons.

BRUTE CAPTAIN MAJOR

ROLE: Leading Brute packs in battle, commanding lower-ranking Jackals and Grunts

The second highest of the captain ranks, the Captain Majors are promoted for their ability to rally and inspire (often through physical threat) both Brute and non-Brute forces. Donning gold armor, they are stronger and more resilient than standard Brutes.

BRUTE SPECIALISTS

BRUTE BODYGUARD

ROLE: Protection of Chieftain, enforcement of tribal law

Brute Bodyguards accompany their pack's Chieftain wherever he goes, and are ready to step in whenever danger threatens. They are similar in appearance to Captains, but wear pale blue armor.

BRUTE JUMP PACK

ROLE: Airborne shock troops

Brute Jump Packs have enhanced mobility due to front-mounted jump thrusters. These can propel them great distances; however they are not capable of true flight. Brute Jump Packs are easily recognized on the battlefield by their distinctive dark blue armor. Although they have increased mobility, a stray bullet into their thrusters' fuel cell can create a spectacular explosion.

BRUTE STALKER

ROLE: Bodyguards, reconnaissance, espionage

Brute Stalkers are normally tasked to protect their Chieftains, but their role is in fact far more covert. In assaults they will function as spies, and they do not refrain from using their camouflage when attempting to ambush the enemy. Often, Stalkers will use Radar Jammers to confuse their enemies and then charge in with Maulers to finish them off.

BRUTE INFANTRY

BRUTE HONOR GUARD

ROLE: Guards

Brute Honor Guards wear yellow-and red-plated armor and carry a red flag on their shoulder to indicate their rank and position. Their role is largely ceremonial unless the Prophet they protect is being threatened.

Brute Honor Guards were first given the privileged role of protecting the Prophets following the murder of the High Prophet of Regret. This role had been traditionally served by the Elites, and when it was taken away from the Elites and given to the Brutes, the resulting discontent led to the Great Schism.

BRUTE MAJOR

ROLE: Infantry, Lance leaders

Brute Majors are intermediate-ranking members of the Brute infantry, below the Ultras and above the Minors, commanding other Brutes and Grunts. The blue armor worn by Brute Majors is basic and offers only limited protection, however it is better than that of Minors and has elaborations for various equipment and materiel.

Their weapons include Brute Spikers, Covenant Carbines, and Brute Shots.

BRUTE MINOR

ROLE: Infantry, Lance leaders

The rank of Brute Minor is the lowest infantry rank amongst the Brutes, making up the largest contingency of heavy ground forces for the Covenant post-Schism. Minors' strength is mainly in their great numbers. They are relatively weak (for Brutes) and enjoy little protection, their armor consisting of only back and chest plates.

BRUTE ULTRA

ROLE: Commanding lesser troops

The cyan-clad Brute Ultras occupy the highest of the three Brute infantry ranks. While they can lead lesser troops, they usually join their lesser-ranking brethren under the orders of Captains or Chieftans.

> ➤ "ON THE BLOOD OF OUR FATHERS...ON THE BLOOD OF OUR SONS...WE SWORE TO UPHOLD THE COVENANT!"
> —EXTRACT FROM THE COVENANT WRIT OF THE UNION

THE LEKGOLO (HUNTERS)

DEADLY WARRIORS

A Hunter's heavy armor and the shield it carries into battle are as simple as they are deadly, but inside that armor is a colony of two-foot-long, wrist-thick worms that work collectively to create the body and brawn of a Hunter. Conventional human forces have had little success combating Hunters. Usually moments before contact has been lost, field reports from soldiers in combat with Hunters (who always work in tandem units, called "bonded pairs") have referred to them as "unstoppable."

Hunters never act foolishly; they are tactically brilliant, and utterly ruthless. Other Covenant forces typically clear out of an area where Hunters are being deployed, presumably because Hunters do not require back-up and consider all collateral damage, even fellow Covenant forces, as "acceptable losses."

The best method of killing Hunters is to shoot their unprotected areas, where bullets actually penetrate individual worms residing within the gestalt. These shots ricochet off the interior of the armor, penetrating and wounding more individuals. The continued ricochet of these projectiles within the armor containment can eliminate enough individual Lekgolo (individual worms) so as to disrupt the Mgalekgolo (the combined form).

LEKGOLO DON BIPEDAL armor for combat, but they are not a bipedal species. The figure seen "wearing" the armor is actually composed of dozens of orange eels that are each nearly five feet (one and a half meters) long.

Spikes protruding from shoulders show that the Hunter is bonded to another Mgalekgolo.

Assault cannons are fused into the Hunters' armor. Hunters are the only troops strong enough to use these heavyweight weapons.

LEKGOLO CULTURE

Hunters are perhaps the most capable and deadly warriors of all the Covenant military client races. They are fearless and utterly unflinching in combat (even in the face of certain death). Hunters live by a code of conflict, honor, duty, and a "life-oath" to fulfill their obligation to the Covenant (and more specifically, to the Elites).

Armor provides protection from nearly every form of plasma-based and ballistic weaponry.

DATA FILE

HEIGHT: Adult eel-type: 4'10" (1.47 m);
Armored form: 12' (3.66 m)
WEIGHT: Adult eel-type: 50 lb (23 kg);
Armored form: 10,500 lb (4,763 kg)
KEY HUNTERS: Igido Nosa Hurru; Ogada Nosa Fasu;
Paruto Xida Konna; Waruna Xida Yotno

RELATIONS WITH OTHER CASTES

Hunters almost never associate, or even communicate, with other Covenant client races, except for the Elites. They are dismissive, scornful, and arrogant to the "lesser" Covenant races and display utter contempt for their foes. Hunters consider all other races beneath them, even the Elites and the Prophets, though they do not say so openly. This may be in part because they are in a parallel evolutionary track from the other species of the Covenant.

With one swipe from its shield, a Hunter can destroy almost anything that comes into its path.

➤ HUNTERS NEVER ACT FOOLISHLY; THEY ARE TACTICALLY BRILLIANT, AND UTTERLY RUTHLESS. OTHER COVENANT FORCES TYPICALLY CLEAR OUT OF AN AREA WHERE HUNTERS ARE BEING DEPLOYED.

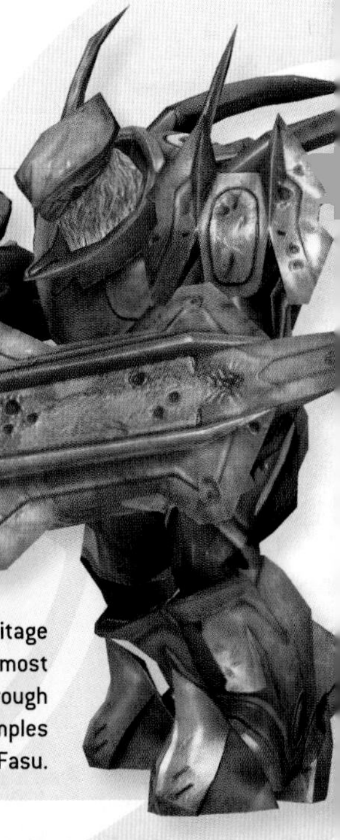

NAMING CONVENTIONS

Hunters have three names: A personal name, a bond name, and a line name. The personal name is given at "birth." The bond name is taken between bonded pairs, a relationship about which little is known. Bonded Hunters consider themselves family and are fiercely protective of each other. The line name offers any Lekgolo offspring instant recognition of their genetic heritage and ancestry. It is essentially the personal name of the most successful Hunter within their lineage, handed down through generations until its status is surpassed by another. Examples of Hunter names include Igido Nosa Hurru and Ogada Nosa Fasu.

THE UNGGOY (GRUNTS)

THE UNGGOY, CALLED Grunts by humans, were barely into their own Iron Age when the Prophets discovered them (classed as "Tier 6" on the Forerunner charts). At such a primitive point in their cultural development, the Grunts had little choice but to accept entry into the hegemony. Otherwise they risked extinction.

DATA FILE

HEIGHT: Adult male: 5'6" (1.68 m)
WEIGHT: Adult male: 260 lb (118 kg)

RELATIONS WITH OTHER CASTES
Grunts have no political power in the Covenant hegemony and so obey the other races out of fear. Unsurprisingly, within Grunt circles, there is much hatred, resentment, and fear of the other species that make up Covenant society, particularly the Jackals.

ROLE OF THE UNGGOY

Grunts are generally considered to be dull-witted, thick-brained creatures, but this is largely a result of the menial positions they have been given within Covenant society. The Unggoy are essentially Covenant cannon fodder, indoctrinated to hurl themselves at an enemy in numbers so vast as to deluge their foes in bodies and blood. Though not particularly effective on their own, Grunts can be a very deadly and effective fighting force when led by skilled Elites. Almost all of the Unggoy present on Covenant warships are tasked with the important duty of monitoring human communication. As a result, most Grunts have a better basic grasp of English (and other human languages) than others within the Covenant. They also have a brisk black market trade in human transmissions like soap operas and sitcoms; Grunts are attracted to and interested in human culture.

The Unggoy earned their nickname of "Grunt" among human soldiers for two reasons: They tend to be used as cannon fodder by the Covenant Elites, and they communicate with strange guttural growls, high-pitched hoots, chirps, and barks. Outside of shipboard areas fitted to suit their environmental needs, Grunts wear sealed environment suits that contain the methane atmosphere they need to survive; the suits also provide limited armor protection.

FIGHTING SKILLS

The Unggoy have a natural tendency towards cowardice, but they can be tenacious fighters when well led by Elites or Brutes and sometimes they even use suicide tactics. Physically small, their power lies in their numbers.

NAMING CONVENTIONS

Because of their low status, Grunts are not allowed to have family-related names despite having strong attachments to their children. Young Grunts are normally separated from their parents soon after birth in order to discourage family ties. Examples of Grunt names include Yayap, Linglin, and Gagaw.

Before the Grunt Rebellion of 2462 CE, Grunts did not have the right to carry weaponry. Their main choice of weapon now is the Plasma Pistol or the Needler and they get good accuracy from these weapons thanks to their good finger reflexes.

Grunts belong to one of five ranks, which are identifiable by the color of their armor: Lilac, green, orange, black, and crimson.

GRUNT ULTRA
(Lilac armor)

HEAVY GRUNT
(Green armor)

GRUNT MINOR
(Orange armor)

SPECIAL OPS GRUNT
(Black armor)

The Unggoy need methane to breathe so their armor includes an integrated re-breather.

UNGGOY CULTURE

The Unggoy's culture has been largely erased by their incorporation into the Covenant. They have been granted very few civil rights in comparison to other members of the Covenant and on a good day they are treated like second-class citizens. Despite the advances in civil rights granted after the Grunt Rebellion, including the right to carry weapons and hold places among infantry units, their representation on the High Council is mostly powerless.

The negative aspects of their existence are offset by the irony of their continued survival due to their acceptance into the Covenant. Their entire species is no longer at risk of being eradicated by two consecutive horrible winter seasons, as they had been on their homeworld of Balaho, a swampy planet with a methane atmosphere. Infant mortality is now below fifty percent. Average life expectancy has more than doubled (not including combat personnel). Geronticide is no longer a necessity for the survival of the tribe. Producing enough food to last through the winter season and burning plague victims no longer rank as the top two priorities on their daily chores.

LUMINOUS BLOOD

Grunt blood is thick and a bright luminous blue color. Its unusual hue could be due to methane-based binding proteins present in the blood that evolved on the methane-heavy environment of their homeworld, Balaho.

GRUNT MAJOR
(Crimson armor)

Although Grunts have physical traits of both reptiles and mammals, they are in fact arthropods.

➤ STUCK AT THE BOTTOM OF THE PECKING ORDER, THE UNGGOY ARE THE WORKHORSES AND THE CANNON FODDER OF THE COVENANT, TREATED AS SECOND-CLASS CITIZENS BY THE OTHER RACES.

➤ "WHEN IN DOUBT, FLEE!"
—THE SIMPLE PHILOSOPHY OF THE UNGGOY

USED MAINLY FOR infiltration, interdiction, and assassinations, the Kig-Yar, known as Jackals by humans, act as scouts and snipers for the Covenant ranks.

PACK WARRIORS

Kig-Yar typically hunt in small packs, using their stealth skills and exceptional natural senses of smell, sight, and hearing to stalk their prey. They are unpredictable in combat, and utterly ferocious, though they lack the physical toughness of the Grunts and the daring and skill of the Elites.

Kig-Yar move with fluid, darting, birdlike motions and are very agile. In battle, their speed is often partially offset by the large portable energy shields that many of them carry, though sniper units do not carry these shields. These portable energy shields can absorb a tremendous amount of punishment from small arms fire. Veteran Kig-Yar can be identifed by their unusually colored shields.

The Particle Beam Rifle's stealth and accuracy are a deadly combination.

PHYSICAL CHARACTERISTICS

The males of the Kig-Yar species have a spiny plumage (which the female Kig-Yar lack; they have calloused plates at the forearms and rear of the head), large pale eyes, and razor-sharp teeth.

Aside from the expected differences in reproductive organs, the males and females of the species are physically identical, with none of the usual disparity in size or mass distribution.

KIG-YAR CULTURE

The Prophets once planned to have the Jackals fill the menial role now held by the Unggoy. But while the Kig-Yar are ferocious and numerous, they lack the zeal of the converted that is so well developed and manipulated in the Unggoy. The Kig-Yar in the Covenant behave more like mercenaries than religious zealots and barely pay heed to the Covenant faith. Joining the hegemony was more a choice of racial self-preservation than one of cultural religious devotion.

The Kig-Yar who actively participate in the Covenant have no real desire for upward mobility within the hegemony (not that they have much choice in the matter). The position they occupy, side-by-side with the Unggoy, makes the Kig-Yar practically invisible while supplying them with perfect scapegoats should anything go wrong with an assignment. It is an ideal situation for their ulterior purpose: Siphoning off resources. The Kig-Yar are a piratical race at heart.

Every Kig-Yar chick wants to be a pirate when he or she grows up. All of the great heroes from their folklore are pirates and they represent freedom to those Kig-Yar who are part of the Covenant. There are many free-roaming Kig-Yar pirates who are unaffiliated with the hegemony, and their brethren in the Covenant contact them when opportunities to pilfer materials arise. These stolen goods are cached for the pirates to retrieve at a later date.

The homeworld of the Kig-Yar is Eayn, the primary satellite of the planet Chu'ot, which lies in the inner region of the Y'Deio system's massive asteroid belt. Only about one-third of all Kig-Yar who still reside in the system call Eayn their home. Since their initial contact with the Covenant, many have chosen to live on the minor planets within the asteroid belt.

Sniper Jackals are easily identifiable by their face masks which have built-in telescopic sights.

KIG-YAR BLOOD IS PURPLE

NAMING CONVENTIONS

Jackals are not permitted by the Elites to have more than one name, but do not particularly care. In order to keep themselves leeching off the Covenant, they go along with the edict, choosing to only use their full names in private. Examples of Jackal names include Yeg, Jak, Bok, and Chur Yar.

Unlike other types of Jackals, Sniper Jackals do not use their portable energy shields because they obstruct the Sniper's view.

SNIPER JACKAL

SHIPMISTRESS CHUR'R-YAR

Chur'R-Yar was the Kig-Yar Shipmistress of the Covenant vessel *Minor Transgression*. She discovered the planet Harvest and found a rich lode of supposed Forerunner relics. She planned to keep a share of the claimed relics for herself, to better barter for the advancement of her race within the Covenant, but also because she wanted her ship out of commission during the Kig-Yar mating season. In her effort at hoarding a portion of the relics, Chur'R-Yar disabled the Luminary and threatened Dadab, an Unggoy Deacon, to keep quiet. She was severely wounded by the human UNSC soldier Avery Johnson and died when she blew up a methane tank, attempting to kill him, destroying the *Minor Transgression* in the process.

ALLIANCE: Covenant SPECIES: Kig-Yar RANK: Shipmistress PERSONALITY: Greedy, conniving, untrustworthy, distrustful

DATA FILE

HEIGHT: Adult male: 6'8" (2.07 m)
WEIGHT: Adult male: 195 lb (88.5 kg)

RELATIONS WITH OTHER CASTES

Technically, the Kig-Yar stand as equals with the Unggoy in the Covenant hierarchy, but the reality is that they are in an elevated position over them. While the other races consider the Unggoy largely beneath notice, the Kig-Yar are often purposefully cruel to them in order to assure themselves of their own superiority.

Although they occupy a caste near the very bottom of the socioeconomic structure, the Kig-Yar more closely resemble a separate entity existing independently within the state. None of the client species has direct representation within the High Council; rather, the Ministry of Concert vets their interests and concerns. While others have protested this inequity rather openly (but quite unsuccessfully), the Kig-Yar have chosen a more pragmatic form of dissent: Siphoning off resources to their expatriate brothers. It is unknown if the Covenant powers have decided to turn a blind eye to the Kig-Yar's larcenous activities or if those escapades have been made invisible by the labyrinth of bureaucracy.

THE YANME'E (DRONES)

Markings on exoskeleton resemble a pair of eyes.

THE INSECT-LIKE YANME'E, known as "Drones" by humans, use their flying ability to carry out surprise attacks on Covenant enemies.

RIGHT-HAND VIEW   FRONT VIEW   LEFT-HAND VIEW

INCORPORATION INTO THE COVENANT

When the Covenant was newly formed and first expanding its search for Forerunner artifacts, it encountered a race of space-faring insects. The initial contact resulted in a massive loss of life on both sides. Surprisingly, the Covenant suffered far worse than the Yanme'e during this short conflict. Once the Prophets discovered a reliable method to communicate with the Yanme'e, hostilities ceased and negotiations began to incorporate them into the hegemony. Not surprisingly, the Yanme'e fared worse than the Covenant at these proceedings. They are now required by treaty to supply the Covenant with soldiers and mechanics.

Without anti-gravity technology, the human-sized Yanme'e would not be able to fly, given their heavy exoskeletons.

Two pairs of wings are assisted by antigravity generators.

YANME'E CULTURE

Culturally speaking, the Yanme'e are simply a client race of the Covenant, like the Unggoy. They do adhere to the Covenant's religious principles and obey their orders unquestioningly, but they have no particular passion for Covenant societal norms. They follow what they see as a normal and linear power structure, with the "Queens" ruling from on high.

Communication difficulties with other Covenant species mean that the Yanme'e largely remain among their own people, except in combat. The Yanme'e are very single-minded and while they excel at simple tasks, their lack of individual initiative relegates them to the lower ranks of the Covenant military structure. They are also viciously territorial over tasks they see as their own.

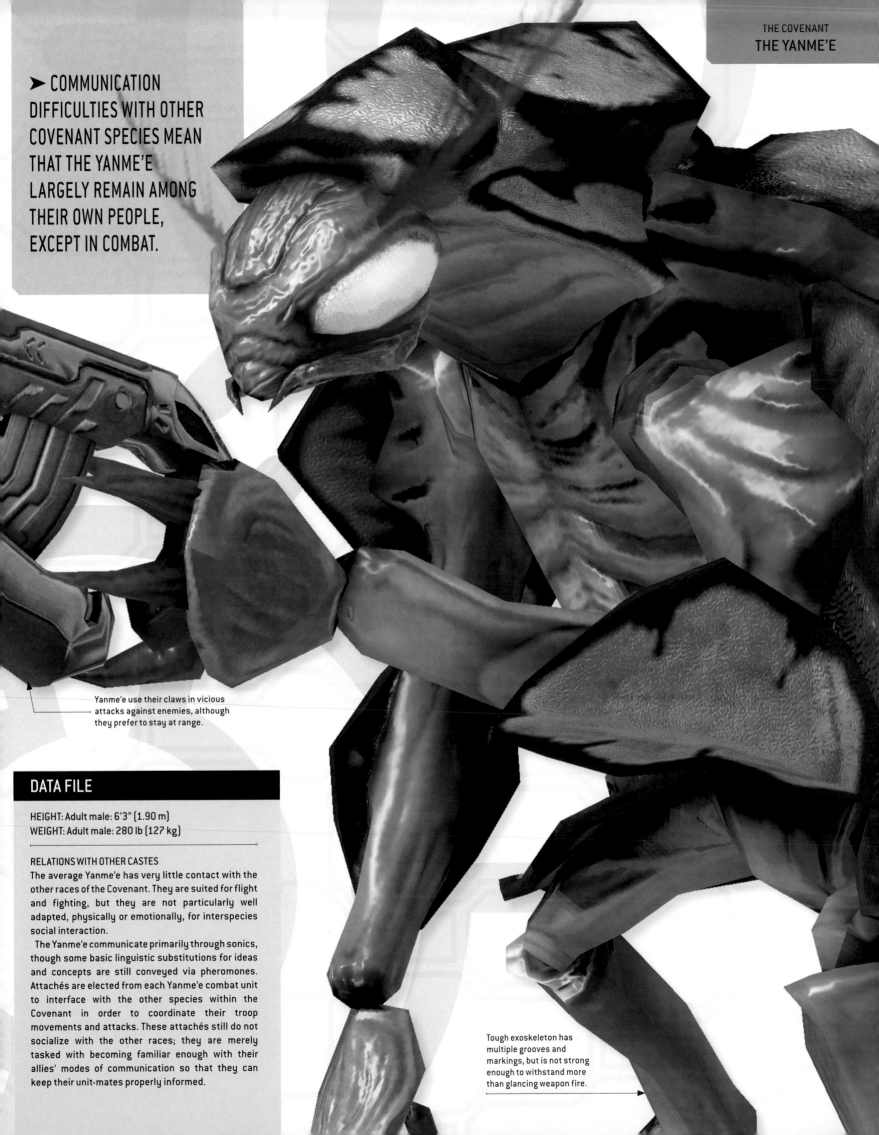

➤ COMMUNICATION DIFFICULTIES WITH OTHER COVENANT SPECIES MEAN THAT THE YANME'E LARGELY REMAIN AMONG THEIR OWN PEOPLE, EXCEPT IN COMBAT.

Yanme'e use their claws in vicious attacks against enemies, although they prefer to stay at range.

DATA FILE

HEIGHT: Adult male: 6'3" (1.90 m)
WEIGHT: Adult male: 280 lb (127 kg)

RELATIONS WITH OTHER CASTES
The average Yanme'e has very little contact with the other races of the Covenant. They are suited for flight and fighting, but they are not particularly well adapted, physically or emotionally, for interspecies social interaction.

The Yanme'e communicate primarily through sonics, though some basic linguistic substitutions for ideas and concepts are still conveyed via pheromones. Attachés are elected from each Yanme'e combat unit to interface with the other species within the Covenant in order to coordinate their troop movements and attacks. These attachés still do not socialize with the other races; they are merely tasked with becoming familiar enough with their allies' modes of communication so that they can keep their unit-mates properly informed.

Tough exoskeleton has multiple grooves and markings, but is not strong enough to withstand more than glancing weapon fire.

THE FLOOD

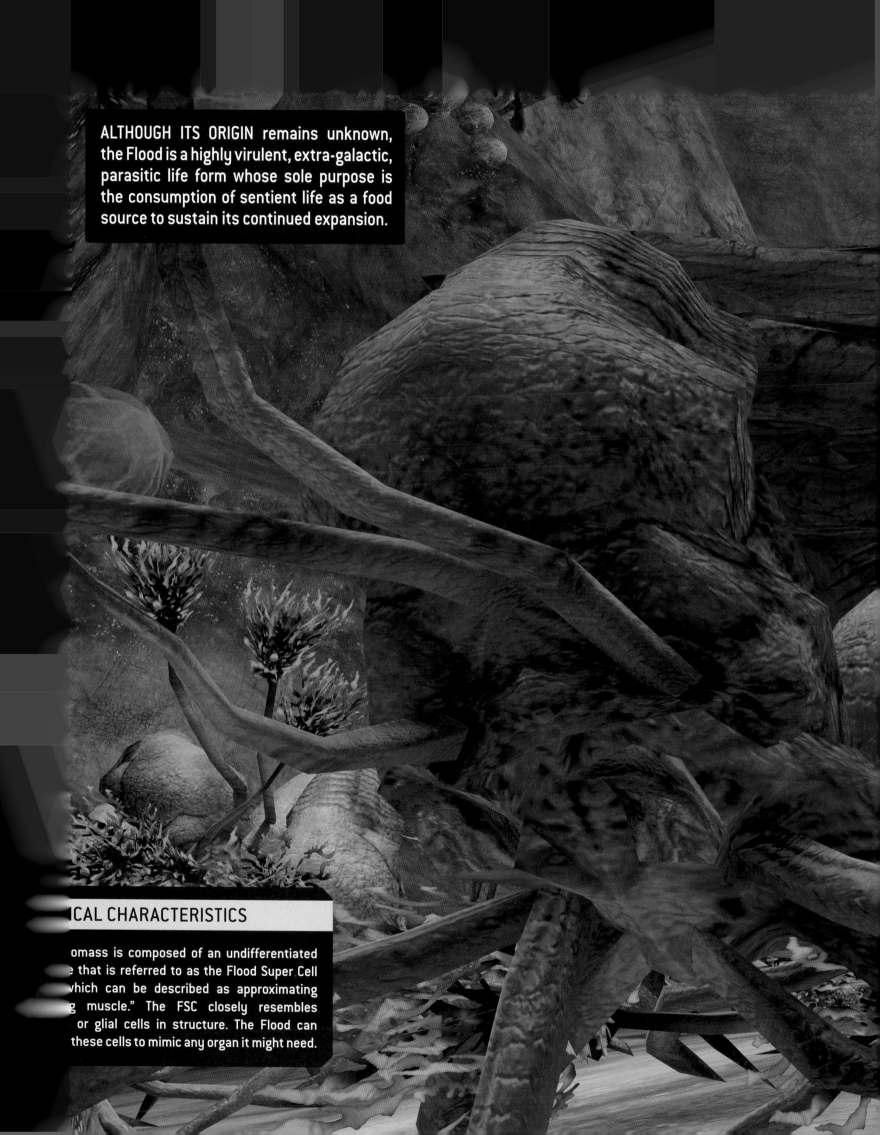

ALTHOUGH ITS ORIGIN remains unknown, the Flood is a highly virulent, extra-galactic, parasitic life form whose sole purpose is the consumption of sentient life as a food source to sustain its continued expansion.

ICAL CHARACTERISTICS

...omass is composed of an undifferentiated ...e that is referred to as the Flood Super Cell ...vhich can be described as approximating ...g muscle." The FSC closely resembles ... or glial cells in structure. The Flood can ...these cells to mimic any organ it might need.

EVOLUTIONARY STAGES

THE FLOOD GOES THROUGH FOUR DISTINCT EVOLUTIONARY STAGES:

• The FERAL STAGE is the lowest level of a symbiotic sustained form: Communicating via pheromones and with the natural instinct to harvest enough calcium to establish a viable Gravemind.

• The COORDINATED STAGE is when the Flood becomes truly dangerous; it now takes orders from the Gravemind that was created in the first stage.

• The INTERSTELLAR STAGE allows the Flood to use hosts to take control of technology and spread throughout the Galaxy to infect more hosts.

• The INTERGALACTIC STAGE is the last known stage the Flood enters, during which it utilizes all captured technology to seek uninfected Galaxies for new food supplies so it can further replicate. It is unknown whether the Flood that arrived in the Milky Way originated from an Intergalactic level Flood.

THE FLOOD AND THE HALO ARRAY

A little more than one hundred thousand years ago, the Flood infested this sector of the Milky Way Galaxy, consuming a vast swath of sentient species along the path of populated worlds. After too much time spent trying to find a means of stopping the parasitic Flood, the Forerunners determined that the only solution to the threat was a desperate act of self-destruction. They created the Halo Array as a means of eradicating the Flood, but it would come at the cost of every highly intelligent life form in the Galaxy.

The Forerunners removed substantial portions of species from the populated worlds within the striking field of the Halo Array, and kept them safe for reseeding on their homeworlds when their planets could once again sustain life. Samples of the Flood were also brought to Halo installations, where the specimens were studied in continued hopes of finding a less cataclysmic method of countering the Flood threat.

The specimens studied on the Halo Installations were intended to remain dormant forever, but the effects of time and interlopers broke this containment in at least two locations. This released the Flood upon a Galaxy which had long ago forgotten how much destruction could come from even a single Flood spore.

THE FLOOD INFECTS host organisms with a predictable, if terrifying, set of biological steps. This process creates a growing, symbiotic community between the individual Flood parasites and the organism under attack.

VIEW FROM BELOW

INFECTION FORM—SIDE VIEW

Infection Forms pierce the skin of target hosts to infect them.

INFECTION FORM

The Infection Form is the simplest Flood form and the smallest, making it the easiest to defeat. In this state, the Flood infects and assimilates other species, attacking a sentient life form in large numbers. Each Infection Form is an organism with a small, sagging, brown lobe rising from the top of its back and tentacles projecting from its frontal surface.

VIEW FROM ABOVE

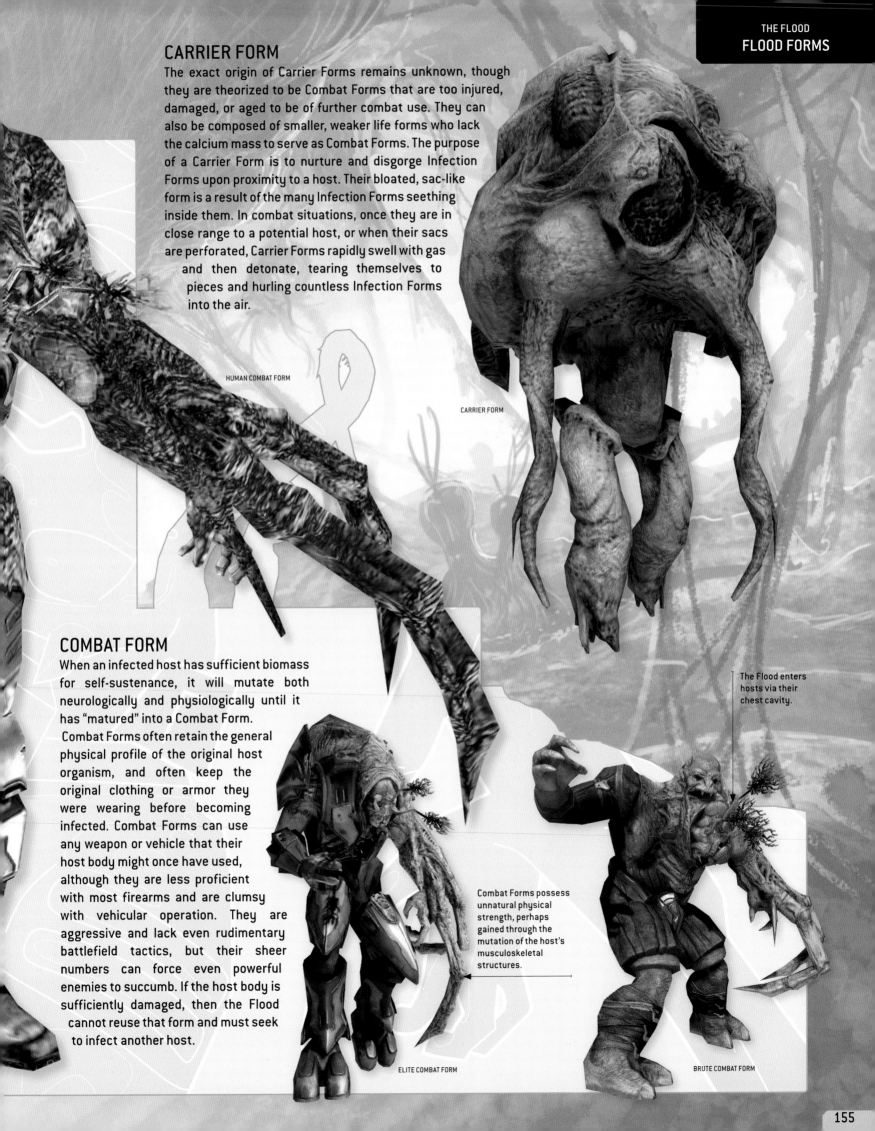

CARRIER FORM

The exact origin of Carrier Forms remains unknown, though they are theorized to be Combat Forms that are too injured, damaged, or aged to be of further combat use. They can also be composed of smaller, weaker life forms who lack the calcium mass to serve as Combat Forms. The purpose of a Carrier Form is to nurture and disgorge Infection Forms upon proximity to a host. Their bloated, sac-like form is a result of the many Infection Forms seething inside them. In combat situations, once they are in close range to a potential host, or when their sacs are perforated, Carrier Forms rapidly swell with gas and then detonate, tearing themselves to pieces and hurling countless Infection Forms into the air.

HUMAN COMBAT FORM

CARRIER FORM

COMBAT FORM

When an infected host has sufficient biomass for self-sustenance, it will mutate both neurologically and physiologically until it has "matured" into a Combat Form. Combat Forms often retain the general physical profile of the original host organism, and often keep the original clothing or armor they were wearing before becoming infected. Combat Forms can use any weapon or vehicle that their host body might once have used, although they are less proficient with most firearms and are clumsy with vehicular operation. They are aggressive and lack even rudimentary battlefield tactics, but their sheer numbers can force even powerful enemies to succumb. If the host body is sufficiently damaged, then the Flood cannot reuse that form and must seek to infect another host.

The Flood enters hosts via their chest cavity.

Combat Forms possess unnatural physical strength, perhaps gained through the mutation of the host's musculoskeletal structures.

ELITE COMBAT FORM

BRUTE COMBAT FORM

FLOOD FORMS

PURE FORM

The Pure Form of the Flood develops without a host. Once sufficient hosts have been infected and the Gravemind that sustains the Flood infestation is developed, the Flood can reproduce without infection. This form can mutate into various sub-forms, referred to as Stalker, Ranged, or Tank, and can mutate between the three depending on the necessities of combat.

SIDE VIEW

Tank Forms release Infection Forms from their bodies.

When injured, Flood secrete a thick, sickly mixture of mucus and blood.

TANK FORM—FRONT VIEW

Small arms fire is less effective against the larger Flood Pure Forms.

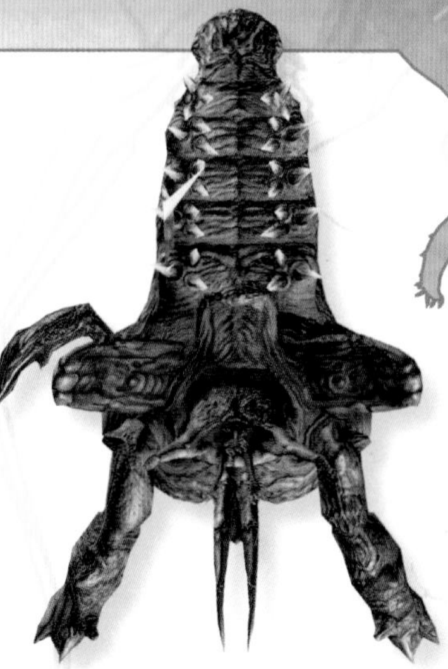

FRONT VIEW

Like most Flood forms, Ranged Forms are able to cling to ceilings and walk up walls.

RANGED FORM—SIDE VIEW

PROPHET FORM

Prophet Forms are rare products of infestation. It seems that the Prophet Form is directly infected and incorporated into one of the many tentacles of a Gravemind, retaining the original voice and full intelligence of the former Prophet.

As with the Combat Form, the Prophet Form shares many physiological traits with the original organism before infection. Prophet Forms can be identified as Prophets by their heads and, to a lesser extent, their chests. Details of this infestation remain unclear as no human or Covenant has witnessed a Prophet being fully transformed into this state.

BRAIN FORM/PROTO-GRAVEMIND

The Brain Form (also known as the Proto-Gravemind) is one of the rarest types of Flood and is the beginning stage of a Gravemind form. Bearing little resemblance to other Flood forms, the Proto-Gravemind is entirely passive and lacks any sort of mobility or defense. It is thought that the Proto-Gravemind is the product of the syntactical fusion of several Combat Forms, merging all of its subordinate forms into a massive, bloated, spherical organism with spindle-like outgrowths that adhere to the surrounding environment. Proto-Graveminds are unique in that the conscious of the original host organisms are still vaguely maintained, allowing for limited mental resistance to Flood assimilation. However, with highly intuitive perception, the Flood is able to sift through the individual memories of the original host, looking for those that are of importance to the overall Flood species while removing memories that pose a threat. When a useful memory is found, it is incorporated into the general consciousness of the Flood.

Long, springy legs make the Stalker Form agile and able to jump great distances.

STALKER FORM—SIDE VIEW

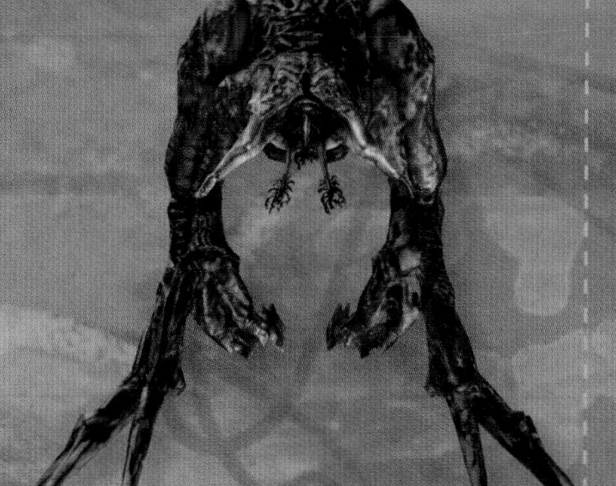

FRONT VIEW

THE GRAVEMIND IS THE all-encompassing intelligence of the Flood. It is assumed to be the highest state of transformation that a Flood form can achieve. It is believed that once a "critical mass" of Flood forms have been fused together in both body and mind, a Gravemind form is created.

INTELLIGENCE

The Gravemind assumes a centralized sentient intelligence that is believed to lead the general Flood species through symbiotic or telepathic means. It is intent on propagating the Flood species through combat as well as delusion, coercion, and ultimately betrayal. It also appears to hold all of the Flood's memories, even those of individual organisms and of all previous Graveminds. It is fully capable of directing the overall Flood species and of manipulating others to do its bidding.

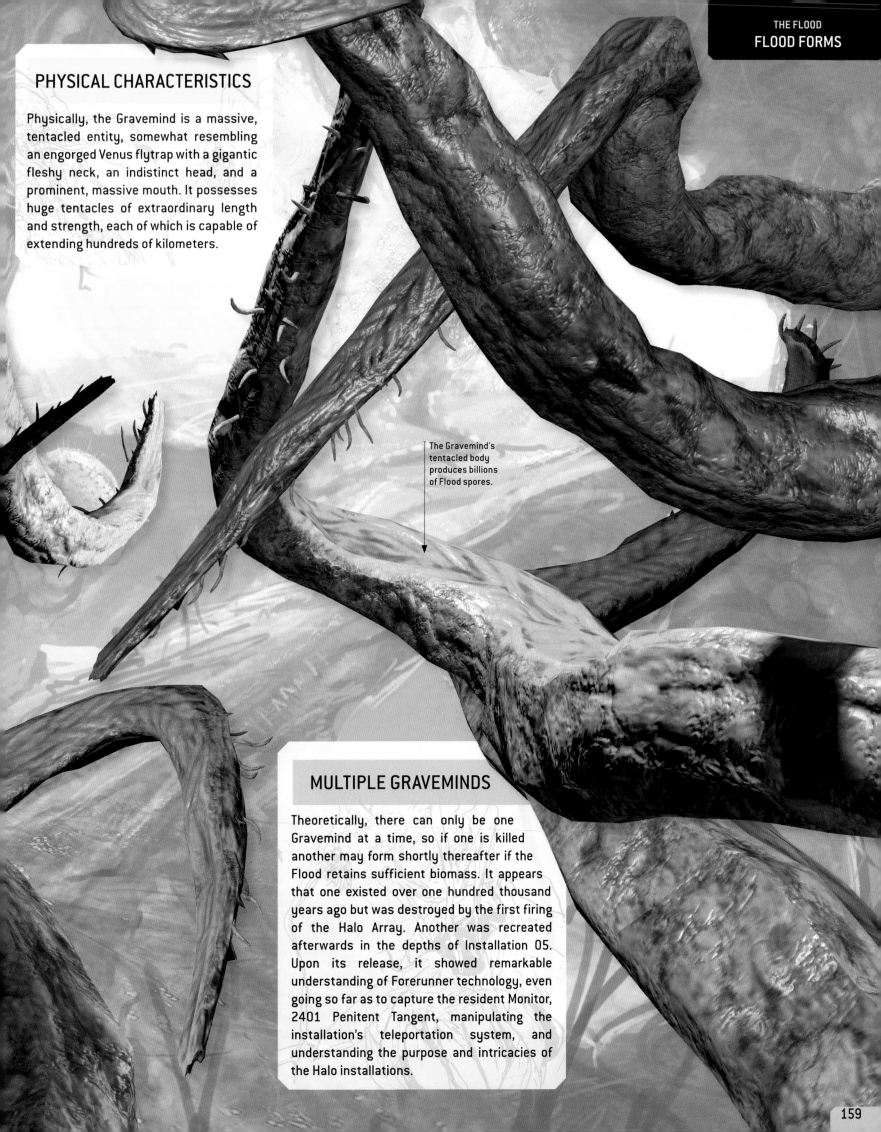

PHYSICAL CHARACTERISTICS

Physically, the Gravemind is a massive, tentacled entity, somewhat resembling an engorged Venus flytrap with a gigantic fleshy neck, an indistinct head, and a prominent, massive mouth. It possesses huge tentacles of extraordinary length and strength, each of which is capable of extending hundreds of kilometers.

The Gravemind's tentacled body produces billions of Flood spores.

MULTIPLE GRAVEMINDS

Theoretically, there can only be one Gravemind at a time, so if one is killed another may form shortly thereafter if the Flood retains sufficient biomass. It appears that one existed over one hundred thousand years ago but was destroyed by the first firing of the Halo Array. Another was recreated afterwards in the depths of Installation 05. Upon its release, it showed remarkable understanding of Forerunner technology, even going so far as to capture the resident Monitor, 2401 Penitent Tangent, manipulating the installation's teleportation system, and understanding the purpose and intricacies of the Halo installations.

159

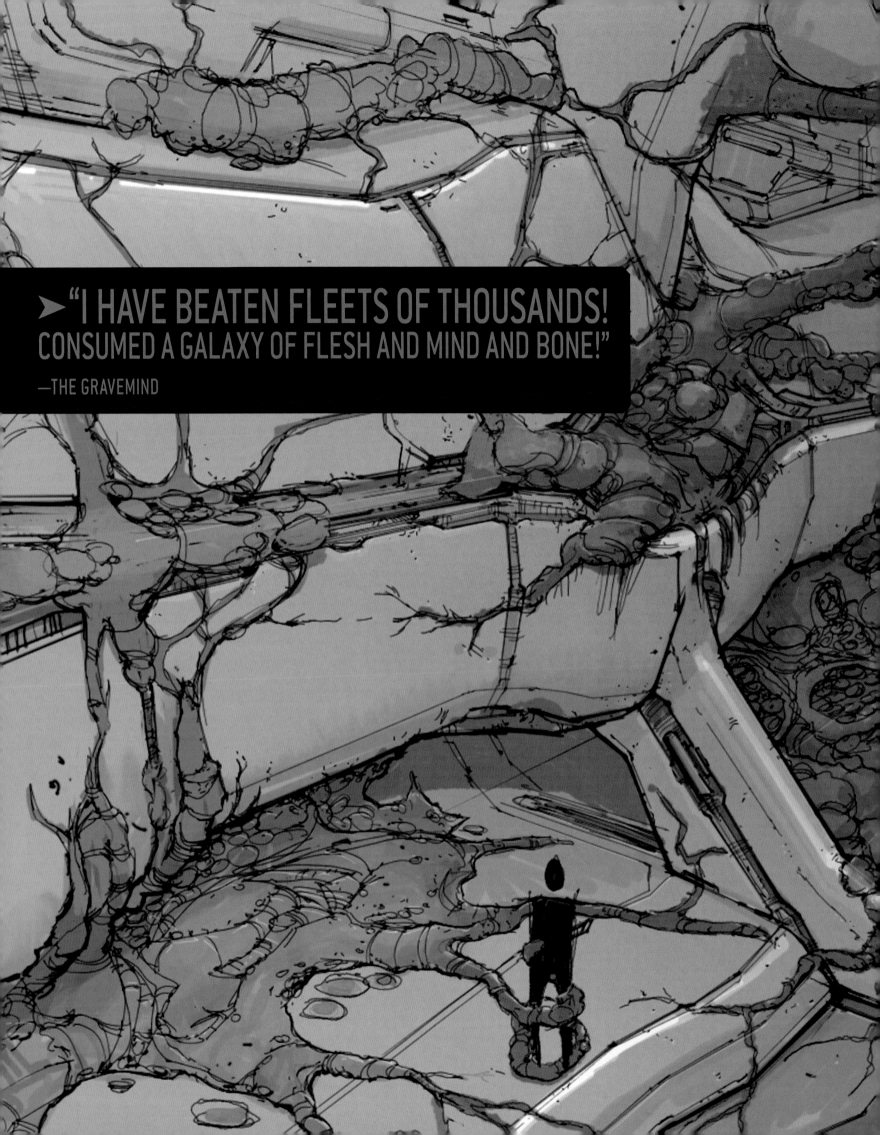

➤ "I HAVE BEATEN FLEETS OF THOUSANDS!
CONSUMED A GALAXY OF FLESH AND MIND AND BONE!"
—THE GRAVEMIND

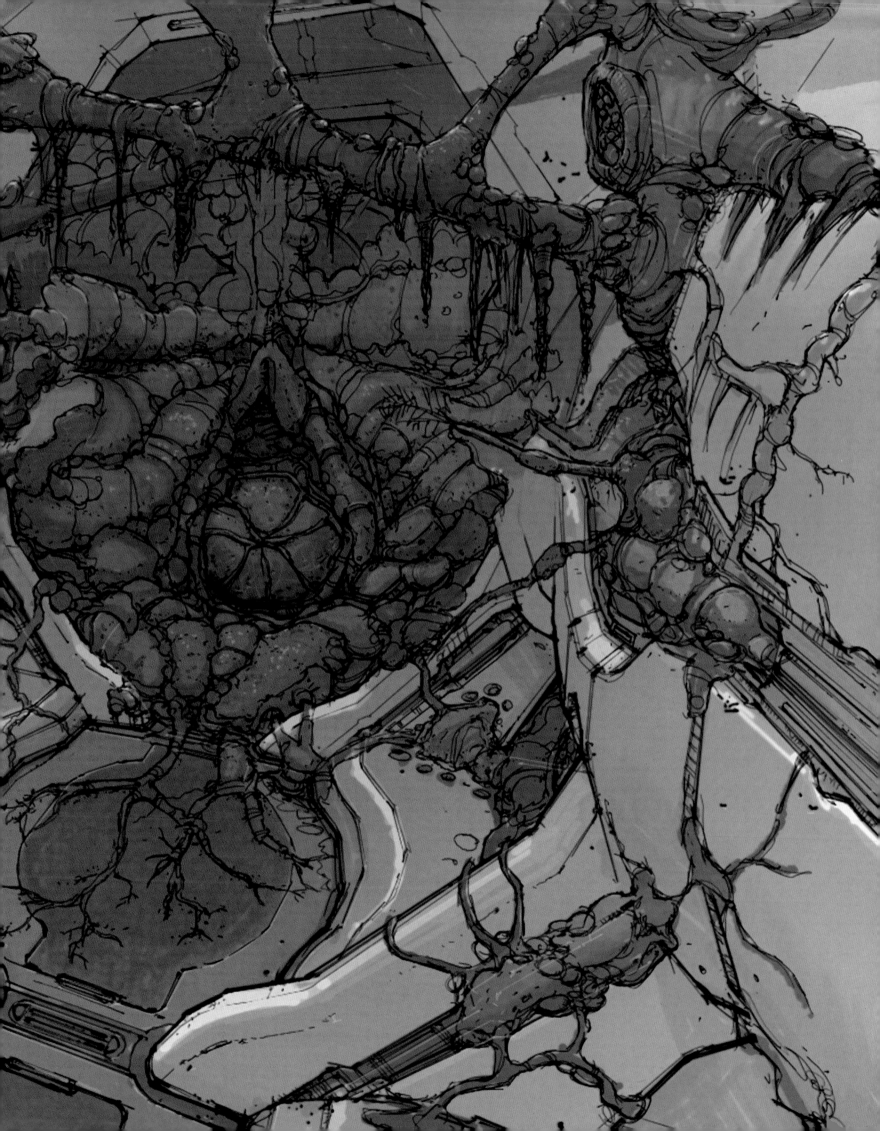

THE FORERUNNERS

THE FORERUNNERS

OVER 100,000 YEARS before the Common Era (BCE), a race called the Forerunners ruled the Milky Way Galaxy. Their prowess with all things technological made their supremacy unchallenged, but they used their power to protect and nurture all life in the Galaxy. Then, in an eye's blink of galactic time, they were overcome. A terrifying foe emerged from the greater reaches of space and, despite the Forerunners' profound wisdom, technology, and carefully laid plans, they were unable to protect the Galaxy that depended on them.

THE MANTLE

The Forerunners' respect for life and their sense of duty to allow the species they encountered to evolve naturally led them to create an ethical code of conduct called the Mantle. Bridging the social strata between an interstellar Marshall Plan and a religious, but benevolent, stewardship, the Forerunners took responsibility for the protection and cultivation of the species and planetary systems within their domain. With this grand purpose, their social structure evolved so the Forerunners became a caring and community-minded populace. Their central government was entirely dictated by the Mantle, as were the religious beliefs of individual Forerunners. However, inspiring peace throughout their domain by minimizing their military capacity and disarming their weapons cache proved to be a costly approach for the Forerunners when the new alien threat emerged.

THE ARRIVAL OF THE FLOOD

When a new threat, an alien parasite called the Flood arrived from outside the Milky Way, and it rapidly spread until it had overcome all sentient life in its immediate sector of space. Requiring "food"—which for the Flood meant the absorption and domination of a sentient host—they sent out spores to find other life forms in other star systems. The virulence of the infection meant that once the Flood found a planet it was just a short matter of time before it consumed all life on that planet. The Forerunners tried to rally their partially disarmed forces, but the Flood had already infected and assimilated entire systems in the Orion Arm. The Forerunners carefully captured samples of the Flood to study in quarantine, but could find no vaccine or treatment for their infection. Military sorties against the Flood proved alarmingly ineffective, as only a single surviving infection was necessary in order to infect an entire planet.

A power facility for maintaining the Forerunners' complex networks.

THE MAGINOT SPHERE

The Forerunners' vast fleets and advanced technology could do little to slow the spread of the Flood. With every world that fell, the enemies of the Forerunners grew, rapidly overwhelming their ability to defend themselves against the onslaught. The Forerunners fell back to their remaining defensible positions and drew a line around them, named the Maginot Sphere, or the Line. (It should be noted that records from the Forerunners were discovered with translation software so advanced that it incorporates idioms from the reader's own experience. The Maginot Line, being idiomatically similar to a World War II creation in France, became the default usage found throughout Forerunner terminals and transmissions that were read by humans.) It is unknown whether this Maginot Line was a blockade of ships or a more highly advanced barrier, but the defensive sphere proved effective in at least stalling the Flood's advance. The Forerunners still attacked the Flood outside of the Line and may have proven effective enough to draw the Flood's attention away from it.

➤ ON THE STRIP-MINING MOON OF THE ARK, STRATO-SENTINELS HARVEST PRECIOUS RAW CONSTRUCTION MATERIALS.

THE FORERUNNERS FIRST encountered the Flood on the planet G617g, where it infected unarmed civilian assets and penetrated the Forerunners' planetary defense groups. It went on to strike at the Forerunner-held planet of LP 656-38e. The Flood managed to avoid the Forerunner orbital fleet, infesting the planet below and DM-3-1123b. Although at first this new alien creature lacked basic cohesion, numerically, it was superior. Billions of forms were dedicated to the assault with every member of the Forerunner population considered a viable potential new Flood form. Even though the Forerunners had highly powerful military assets, if even a single Flood infection form made its way past their lines, entire battles were lost.

MILITARY DEFEAT

In a desperate measure, the Forerunners' armada was ordered to immediately begin full planetary bombardment on infested worlds. Many Forerunners were unable to be evacuated before the bombardment commenced. This meant Pyrrhic victories for the Forerunner military, who were killing their own people in order to save them. Where bombardment was unable to be undertaken by naval garrisons, Forerunner population centers activated localized weapons of mass destruction, committing mass suicide.

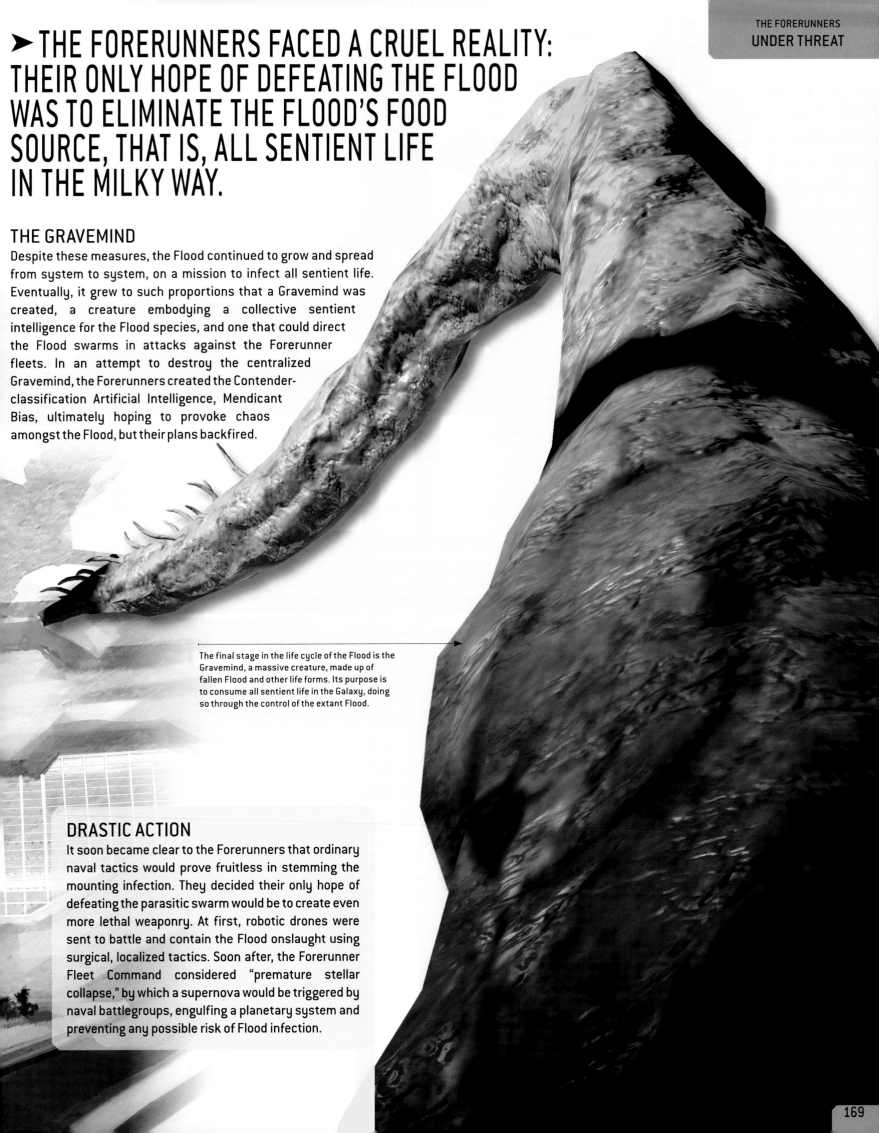

➤ THE FORERUNNERS FACED A CRUEL REALITY: THEIR ONLY HOPE OF DEFEATING THE FLOOD WAS TO ELIMINATE THE FLOOD'S FOOD SOURCE, THAT IS, ALL SENTIENT LIFE IN THE MILKY WAY.

THE GRAVEMIND

Despite these measures, the Flood continued to grow and spread from system to system, on a mission to infect all sentient life. Eventually, it grew to such proportions that a Gravemind was created, a creature embodying a collective sentient intelligence for the Flood species, and one that could direct the Flood swarms in attacks against the Forerunner fleets. In an attempt to destroy the centralized Gravemind, the Forerunners created the Contender-classification Artificial Intelligence, Mendicant Bias, ultimately hoping to provoke chaos amongst the Flood, but their plans backfired.

The final stage in the life cycle of the Flood is the Gravemind, a massive creature, made up of fallen Flood and other life forms. Its purpose is to consume all sentient life in the Galaxy, doing so through the control of the extant Flood.

DRASTIC ACTION

It soon became clear to the Forerunners that ordinary naval tactics would prove fruitless in stemming the mounting infection. They decided their only hope of defeating the parasitic swarm would be to create even more lethal weaponry. At first, robotic drones were sent to battle and contain the Flood onslaught using surgical, localized tactics. Soon after, the Forerunner Fleet Command considered "premature stellar collapse," by which a supernova would be triggered by naval battlegroups, engulfing a planetary system and preventing any possible risk of Flood infection.

BATTLING THE FLOOD

MANY EFFORTS WERE undertaken by the Forerunners in an attempt to contain the Flood, but ultimately, they accepted the inevitable. In order to save the future for all life in the Galaxy, they would have to end all current life in it.

THE HALO ARRAY

In order to bring about this drastic measure and wipe out the rampaging Flood, seven ring-like installations, known as Halos, were built across the Galaxy. When activated, they would wipe out all sentient life within three radii of the Milky Way Galaxy's center by sending out a harmonic frequency, targeting certain cells in the nervous systems of any significant sentient organism.

Tendrils insert the Flood Super Cell into the host organism, beginning the process of mutation.

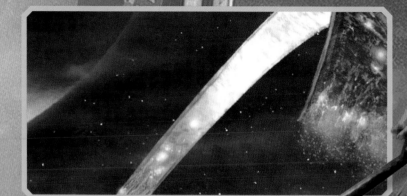

HALO INSTALLATION 04—POST-DESTRUCTION

The Infection Form is the first stage of the Flood. It uses its tentacles to attack and infect organisms.

THE ARK AND SHIELD WORLDS

Before the Forerunners enacted this terrible plan, they began an even more complicated program to preserve and then reseed species back onto the planets that would be cleansed of life. They took vast populations of existing species, including the nascent human race from Earth, and moved them out of harm's way. To keep these species safe, the Forerunners created the Ark, a massive laboratory and environmentally diverse complex on Installation 00, which lay well outside the range of the Halo Array's effects. The Forerunners also made use of artificial planets called Shield Worlds, where portals into Slipstream space allowed access to spaces where creatures could exist indefinitely. The reseeding of the Galaxy was carefully planned and portals to the Ark were created to allow keyships to travel quickly to it. Only Forerunner keyships could access and open a portal to the Ark.

ACTIVATION OF THE HALO ARRAY

After the failure of their traditional military efforts to stop the spread of the Flood, the Halo Array was activated by the Forerunners, unleashing galactic destruction. After the starved Flood died off, the planets were reseeded with the rescued life forms and the shattered remnants of the Forerunner civilizaton decided to leave the Galaxy. Their final destination and current status remain unknown. A few surviving Flood specimens were kept in state-of-the-art, high-security Forerunner research facilities on the Halo installations, where they had been brought and studied, perhaps as part of a plan to eventually unravel the mystery of their origin. They stayed in this stasis form, until they were unwittingly released by the Covenant on Installation 04.

OPPOSITION TO THE HALO ARRAY

THE "EXTREME MEASURE OF LAST RESORT" of the Halo plan stirred controversy among the Forerunners, many of whom still held firm to the Mantle and argued against the creation of the Halo Array, much less its activation. Who were the Forerunners, after all, to assert their will over so many alien races? However, after great stretches of anguished debate and even civil war, the realization that the Flood could not be stopped by any other means swayed all but the most hardened objectors.

Known Halos tend to be in close proximity to dense gravity wells, such as gas giants. It is unknown if this is a coincidence, a logistical advantage, or a safety precaution.

MONITORS

The Halo Array was maintained by a set of monitors and possibly other Artificial Intelligences. They had specific protocols and only enough knowledge to complete their mission: Activating the Halo Array in the case of a Flood outbreak. These limitations were in place so that if any AI fell prey to the Gravemind, it could not surrender the locations of the other installations. These monitors have exhibited odd characteristics like the recognition of human beings and eccentricities that are hard to explain through normal AI "failures" such as degeneration or rampancy.

THE HALO ARRAY

HALO INSTALLATION 01

LOCATION	DESCRIPTION
Milky Way Galaxy	Ring world, desert-like surface, limited atmosphere

Installation 01 is a ring world similar to all the other Halo installations in its size and shape. Perhaps because of its primary designation, however, the Forerunners designed this Halo with a very basic environment in mind; that is, almost none at all. Instead of a healthy and verdant landscape, 01 features tracks of endless desert. It is also possible that, being the first in numerical order (and so, furthest in distance from the Ark), the upkeep for 01 was not properly maintained, or it suffered some other incident in the long period since the original firing of the Halo Array. During the assault on Installation 05, the UNSC discovered that 05 had put 01 into standby mode; Installation 01 was fully prepped and ready to fire on command. The command never came, much to the relief of all sentient life within 25,000 light years.

HALO INSTALLATION 02

LOCATION	DESCRIPTION
Milky Way Galaxy	Ring world, water-based surface, unknown atmosphere/biology

All known data suggests that the second Halo installation is a water-based world, with rocky outcroppings and even large ice floes scattered across its surface. Little else is known about 02, except that it is the second-most distant of the Halo rings. Like all of the other extant Halo installations, 02 was put in standby mode by the Brute Chieftain known as Tartarus on Installation 05. And, like all of the others, the Master Chief was able to reverse this.

HALO INSTALLATION 03

LOCATION	DESCRIPTION
Milky Way Galaxy	Ring world, volcanic surface, desert atmosphere

Appearing volcanic in its surface topography, Installation 03 is the third most distant Halo installation from the Ark. After being engaged in standby mode it became primed again during the battle of Installation 00.

A UNSC PELICAN LANDING ON HALO INSTALLATION 04

The ring-like structure of Installation 04

HALO INSTALLATION 04

LOCATION	DESCRIPTION	MAJOR EVENTS	MONITOR
Substance, Basis	Ring world, Earth-like surface, habitable atmosphere	The battle of Installation 04	343 Guilty Spark

Installation 04 took on particular prominence when the UNSC ship *Pillar of Autumn*, along with its crew, crash-landed onto its surface. The Master Chief took it upon himself to rescue as many Marines from the *Autumn* as he could in order to lead a resistance movement against the Covenant forces on the installation. Unfortunately, there were bigger things beneath the surface of the ring than anyone could have ever anticipated.

When the Covenant violated what they thought to be an ancient Forerunner weapons cache inside Installation 04, they unwittingly unleashed the Flood, the galactic infection that had forced the creation and firing of the Halo Array some 100,000 years previously. It took every bit of Master Chief's skill and legendary luck to fight off both the Covenant and the Flood, and in the end he was only just able to overload the *Autumn*'s reactors and cause an explosion that destroyed Installation 04.

THE BATTLE OF INSTALLATION 04

The UNSC ship the *Pillar of Autumn* crash-landing on the Halo Installation began what became known as the battle of Installation 04. The Flood, which had been caged onboard since the disappearance of the Forerunners, was unleashed by the Covenant in their haste to learn the secrets of the Forerunners. Due to its destructive nature, the Flood soon became the number-one cause of battle and death for both UNSC and Covenant forces.

In an attempt to control these beings, the Master Chief teamed up with the Forerunner construct known as 343 Guilty Spark to activate Installation 04 and eradicate the species. What Master Chief did not know was that this would result in the firing of the ring in such a way as to destroy all sentient life within the Galaxy. Luckily, Cortana was able to warn the Master Chief and stop the destruction just in time.

Now fighting against Guilty Spark (the construct still wished to carry out its mission), the Master Chief fought back to the *Pillar of Autumn* and caused the ship to self-destruct, escaping just as the fusion reactors went critical and destroyed Installation 04. Some Marines, including Sergeant Avery Johnson, and the AI Guilty Spark, survived the explosion.

The Monitor of Installation 04, 343 Guilty Spark

THE DESTRUCTION OF HALO INSTALLATION 04

THE HALO ARRAY

HALO INSTALLATION 04B

LOCATION	DESCRIPTION	MAJOR EVENTS
The Foundry on the Ark	Copy of Installation 04, never completed, destroyed	The battle of Installation 00

Whenever a Halo installation is damaged or destroyed, the Foundry at the heart of Installation 00 goes to work. In a short time (cosmically speaking), a replacement, or replacement parts, are fashioned and shipped out so that the entire Halo Array can maintain full and synchronized functionality. This process began when Master Chief destroyed Installation 04, and by the time he arrived at the Ark he found the replacement Halo well underway. Although this new installation, sometimes referred to as Installation 04b, was capable of charging and firing its enormous pulse weapon, it was not able to control these energies. Master Chief took advantage of this when he prematurely fired 04b and used the resulting explosion to destroy the Flood threat once and for all.

HALO INSTALLATION 05

LOCATION	DESCRIPTION	MAJOR EVENTS	MONITOR
Orbiting Substance IV	Ring world, jungle-like surface, Flood-ridden	Part of the assault on Installation 05	2401 Penitent Tangent

Sometimes known as Delta Halo, Installation 05 was discovered by the Covenant shortly after the destruction of 04. Like all the other Halo installations, it had a secondary function to contain the Flood, but its primary purpose was to destroy all life within twenty-five thousand light years, or, in conjunction with all the other Halos, all sentient life within the entire Milky Way Galaxy.

What 05 might have looked like before its discovery by the High Prophet of Regret is open to conjecture, as a Halo-altering disaster occurred several hundred years prior to the arrival of Humans and the Covenant.

Perhaps a maintenance failure released the Flood spores deep within the ring's subsurface, or maybe the Flood managed to escape on its own, but the Flood did escape and soon began infecting every part of Installation 05. The installation's monitor, 2401 Penitent Tangent, did his best to control the situation, but could not contain the Flood. Tangent was himself captured and held prisoner by a newly formed Gravemind for many years before the Master Chief, the Arbiter, and Guilty Spark came to 05.

Despite warnings of the true purpose of the Halo Array, the Covenant activated Installation 05 as a means to hasten the Great Journey—the religious pilgrimage that stands at the center of the Covenant's religion. However, the Master Chief, aided by Avery Johnson and a slew of UNSC forces, prevented this by canceling 05's firing sequence just as the Halo contacted the other installations in preparation for a Galaxy-wide firing. Having been cauterized and quarantined by the Sangheili fleets, 05 now sits dormant.

HALO INSTALLATION 06

LOCATION	DESCRIPTION
Milky Way Galaxy	Ring world, tundra surface, unknown atmosphere

Installation 06 appears to be a ring world covered in dense forest or jungle, similar to portions of Installations 04 and 05. However, no recordings of its surface indicate any major water sources, so how this is environment maintains viability remains unknown. All data gathered about 06 is entirely from the Master Chief's reconnaissance during his battles with the High Prophet of Truth.

HALO INSTALLATION 07

LOCATION	DESCRIPTION
Milky Way Galaxy	Ring world, unknown surface, unknown atmosphere

The least-understood Halo is certainly Installation 07. Nothing is known about its surface, atmosphere, or whether it was capable of controlling its samples of the Flood. All that is clear are the pictures and readouts found by Master Chief during the assault on Installation 05 and the conflicts on Installation 00. 07's surface appears to be overrun with clouds, much like Venus, but even this is in dispute.

➤ "THE DARK TIMES ARE UPON US...UNSHEATHE THY SWORDS AND SMITE...THE ARK WILL BE YOUR GUIDE... AND BLESS THE RECLAIMERS THAT MAY TAKE REFUGE BEHIND THE SHARPENED EDGE OF THE SHIELD... WONDER BEYOND AWAITS."

—VORO NAR 'MANTAKREE READING A FORERUNNER HOLOGRAPHIC PLATE

THE ARK

THE ARK, also known as Installation 00, is a mysterious nexus of Forerunner civilization. From deep within its structure, all the Halo installations could be simultaneously fired, rendering all sentient life within the Milky Way extinct.

LINK TO EARTH

The Ark is tethered through Slipspace to a machine which can activate the portal, located near the small town of Voi on Earth. During the battles which waged on Earth, Covenant forces eventually uncovered it. Though the Master Chief and the UNSC valiantly tried to deny the Covenant access to the portal, the High Prophet of Truth was able to use the technology of the keyship to access it. It was here that the UNSC and the Elite forces joined together and assaulted the remainder of the Covenant's extant forces.

THE PORTAL—CLOSED

LOCATION	DESCRIPTION	MAJOR LOCATIONS	MAJOR EVENTS	MAJOR PERSONALITIES
Extragalactic space outside the Milky Way	Enigmatically hidden, massive, beyond comprehension	The Cartographer, the Citadel, the Control Room, the Foundry	The battle of Installation 00	Mendicant Bias

SANCTUARY

The Ark is not just about destruction. It has housed many life forms and carried with it the knowledge and equipment capable of reseeding the entire Galaxy. It is currently believed that this is how the Milky Way's life was reintegrated after the Forerunners' departure some one hundred thousand years ago. The UNSC was unable to confirm any automated systems which could generate such a measure prior to the installation's destruction.

ABOARD THE ARK

THE SILENT CARTOGRAPHER

LOCATION	DESCRIPTION	MAJOR EVENTS
Upper surface of Halo installations	Map room, transportation hub, directive seat	The battle of Installation 00

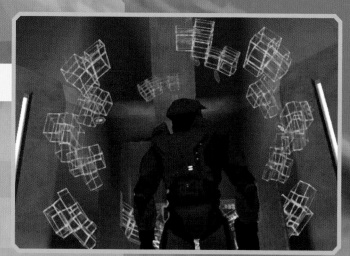

On every Halo installation, there is a structure known as the Silent Cartographer. Within it, using the programming supplied by the Forerunners, a holographic map of the entire installation is generated.

The Ark has its own Cartographer, but it differs in several ways from its cousins. Firstly, the size of the Ark makes the Cartographer much more important to biological beings. Secondly, due to its importance, the normally complex security system is even more devious and is capable of trapping or killing anyone without sufficient knowledge of how to shut it off. Both the Master Chief and the Arbiter found the Ark's Cartographer during the battle of Installation 00. Led by Guilty Spark, they were able to infiltrate and use the Cartographer's resources to help them in their fight against the High Prophet of Truth.

THE CITADEL

LOCATION	DESCRIPTION	MAJOR EVENTS
Outer core of the Ark	Supraluminal communications and Halo activation center	The battle of Installation 00

Hanging over the Ark's Foundry, the Citadel is the singular structure on the Ark from which all Halo installations could be simultaneously activated and fired. Standing at the very edge of the Ark's surface and protected by a massive energy barrier emitted from several towers, the Citadel is an imposing sight. By the time that most UNSC forces arrived, the Covenant had already captured Sergeant Johnson and were attempting to use him, as a "Reclaimer," to activate the Array. Commander Miranda Keyes assaulted the Citadel's platform with a Pelican in an effort to stop the Covenant and retrieve Johnson, but she was swiftly murdered by the Prophet of Truth, and the Array was activated. For a moment, it appeared as though the Galaxy would be lost, but the Master Chief and the Arbiter were able to stop Truth and reverse the process. The Arbiter struck down the Prophet and brought the Human-Covenant War to its confused conclusion.

CONTROL ROOM

LOCATION	DESCRIPTION	MAJOR EVENTS
The Citadel on the Ark, all other installations	Supraluminal communications and Halo activation center	The battle of Installation 00

The Control Room is a large and well-secured chambered structure found on all Halo installations, including the Ark. While the individual installations have the ability to harmonically communicate with each other, syncing the weapon network's pulse over a relatively short period of time, the Ark's Control Room has the power to fire all the rings simultaneously. It was here that the High Prophet of Truth made his last stand in the hope of initiating the Great Journey. And it was also here that the Master Chief and the Arbiter stopped him.

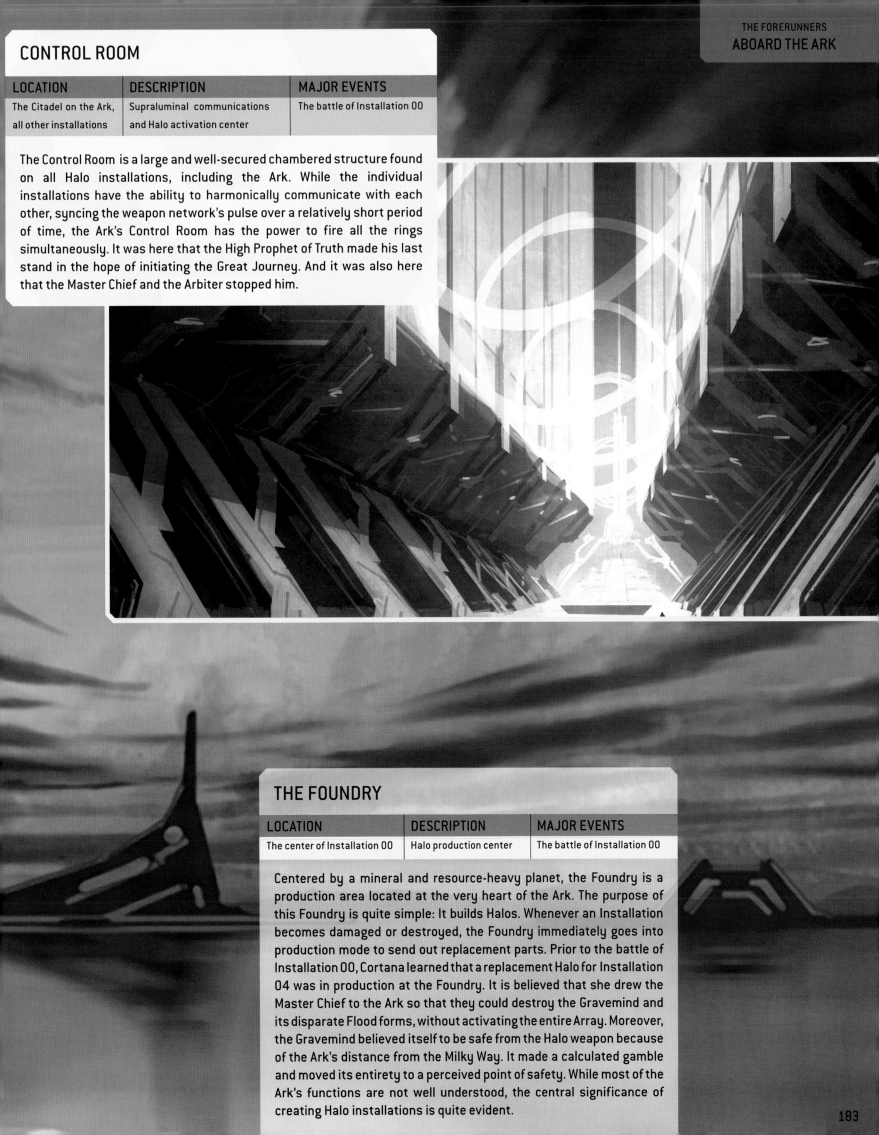

THE FOUNDRY

LOCATION	DESCRIPTION	MAJOR EVENTS
The center of Installation 00	Halo production center	The battle of Installation 00

Centered by a mineral and resource-heavy planet, the Foundry is a production area located at the very heart of the Ark. The purpose of this Foundry is quite simple: It builds Halos. Whenever an Installation becomes damaged or destroyed, the Foundry immediately goes into production mode to send out replacement parts. Prior to the battle of Installation 00, Cortana learned that a replacement Halo for Installation 04 was in production at the Foundry. It is believed that she drew the Master Chief to the Ark so that they could destroy the Gravemind and its disparate Flood forms, without activating the entire Array. Moreover, the Gravemind believed itself to be safe from the Halo weapon because of the Ark's distance from the Milky Way. It made a calculated gamble and moved its entirety to a perceived point of safety. While most of the Ark's functions are not well understood, the central significance of creating Halo installations is quite evident.

THE LIBRARIAN AND THE DIDACT

THE DRAMATIC FINAL years of the Forerunner presence in the Milky Way were uncovered in a series of terminals scattered throughout a series of Forerunner installations. The terminals contain an account of the tragedy of the Librarian and the Didact, lovers who were separated by war and were eventually parted by death when the Halo Array fired.

TRAGIC LOVE

THE LIBRARIAN AND the Didact's conversations were archived in the terminals aboard the Ark centuries ago and reveal their tragic love. When the Librarian was on Earth, the Didact pleaded with her to return to the safety of the Maginot Sphere, but she was devoted to her vocation and remained in harm's way in order to save more species, going far beyond the call of her assignment. Eventually, the Librarian pleaded with the Didact to activate the Array in order to destroy the Flood.

The Didact stalled the enemy Flood as long as he could while seeking an alternative way of destroying it and rescuing his love. The Forerunners created an AI, Mendicant Bias, who would engage with the Gravemind and destroy it. The Librarian strongly objected to this plan, calling it suicidal, and begged the Didact to ignore her welfare in favor of the greater good. She demanded that he fire the Array but her pleas fell on deaf ears. The Didact would not abandon her.

MENDICANT BIAS THEN APPROACHED THE GRAVEMIND, BUT THE PLAN BACKFIRED. HE DEFECTED TO THE FLOOD AND LED AN ATTACK ON THE FORERUNNERS THAT BROKE THROUGH THE MAGINOT SPHERE.

The Librarian witnessed this attack from outside the Maginot Sphere, effectively trapped beyond the action. She desperately sent word to the Didact, warning her love of the Flood horde that was coming for him. The Librarian remotely destroyed all of the portals and other installations that would lead to the Ark so that it would not fall into the grasp of the Flood, but this also made it impossible for her to escape. She begged the Didact one final time to fire the Array.

He replied that her observation of the Flood armada confirmed the information he'd been searching for—her location.

UNABLE TO REACH HER, AND SHE UNABLE TO ESCAPE, A FINAL MESSAGE WAS EXCHANGED FROM THE LIBRARIAN TO THE DIDACT:

◉ "My work is done. The portal is inactive, and I've begun the burial measures. Soon there'll be nothing but sand and rock and normal signatures. You should see the mountain that watches over it. A beautiful thing—a snowcapped sentinel. That's where I will spend what time is left to me.

Did I tell you? I built a garden. The earth is so rich. A seed falls and a tree sprouts or a flower blooms. There's so much potential. We knew this was a special place because of them, but unless you've been here, you can't know. It's [Eden].

I have to stop transmitting. The thing is listening. Its [thinking dead] are babbling—laughing through every channel they can find. Be proud. The Mind claims victory, yet it still doesn't suspect. You've outwitted it, my love. And now you can destroy it.

But you cannot save me."

THE LIBRARIAN

SPECIES: Forerunner

The Librarian was a female Forerunner whose life purpose was to document, index, and retrieve examples of every species that populated her section of the Milky Way in order to protect them from the plan to purge the Flood infestation by activating the Halo Array. She sent all the chosen Tier-7 species to the shelter and aegis of the Ark (Installation 00) and then deactivated and buried the portal leading to their location on Earth. Stranded on Earth, a place she named "Eden," she passed her final days on Mount Kilimanjaro, overlooking the portal to the Ark.

The Librarian's lover was the Didact, an important commander of the Forerunner military, with whom she corresponded frequently. It is possible that the Didact delayed in firing the Halo Array because of this love.

THE DIDACT

SPECIES: Forerunner

The Didact was responsible for firing the Halo Array. However, according to records in the terminals, he evidently wholeheartedly believed in the "Mantle" of the Forerunners: to protect life.

Impassioned, he constantly tried to convince the Librarian to give up her mission of saving other species and return to him, where she could be safe. His pleas, however, went unheeded, and the Librarian, dedicated to her cause, sacrificed herself.

THE DIDACT FINALLY FIRED THE HALO ARRAY

The final resting place of the Librarian was a small, nondescript blue sphere called Earth. This planet was the location of the only portal that was spared the Librarian's destruction. The Forerunner's affinity for the human race was finally explained as the unlikely progeny of this love story:

"The anomalous world is in a perilous location beyond the line. The secrets it holds must be preserved, plans within plans within plans. The inhabitants; these unique denizens, must be researched. They may hold answers to our own mysteries.

What irony that we discovered this treasure, only at the end of things. But what fortune that we still had time to save them.
The thing we built on that world will vouchsafe their lives, but perhaps one day it will be used for its intended purpose. If the plan succeeds, and they are saved, it will be a good world.

If the plan fails, and the adversary succeeds, it will remain an enigma forever with no one left to reclaim it."

End of transmission

➤ THE LIBRARIAN HAD A DEEP RESPECT FOR HUMANITY, WHOM SHE VIEWED AS "SPECIAL" AMONG ALL OF THE SENTIENT LIFE SHE HAD CATALOGUED AND SHE FELT IT WAS WELL WORTH THE SACRIFICE OF HER LIFE TO SAVE THEM.

FORERUNNER MONITORS

343 GUILTY SPARK AND 2401 Penitent Tangent were Forerunner monitors that guarded over Installation 04 and Installation 05 respectively. Guilty Spark played a significant role in the attempted activation of and subsequent battles on the installations.

GUILTY SPARK AND THE BATTLE OF INSTALLATION 04

When the Covenant arrived on Installation 04 and unwittingly freed the Flood, the Monitor 343 Guilty Spark had already been present on the Halo ring for 101,217 "local years." He immediately put into effect a long dormant contingency measure, acting upon Installation 04's ancient defensive genocide protocols.

Guilty Spark's first act was to search for a Reclaimer to help activate the rings. He discovered UNSC Staff Sergeant Marvin Mobuto, and teleported him to the Library on Installation 04 with instructions to recover the facility's Index. However, Mobuto's inadequate armor and lack of experience led to his failure and death. The monitor would have to find another Reclaimer.

The Master Chief and the Marines were battling the Flood at the Flood Containment Facility when 343 Guilty Spark and some Sentinels arrived and joined them in the battle. Afterwards, Master Chief agreed to help this strange new ally, and Guilty Spark recruited him as the next Reclaimer. He teleported Master Chief to the Library and guided him to the Index, which Master Chief was successful in retrieving despite the odds being heavily against him.

Once the Index was retrieved, the monitor asked the Master Chief to join it with the core, thereby activating the installation. He explained that only Reclaimers had permission to do this. The Master Chief was about to comply when his AI, Cortana, who was inside the Core, informed him that Guilty Spark had neglected to mention that activating the Halo would result in the destruction of all the sentient life in the Galaxy.

Guilty Spark followed the now uncooperative Master Chief and Cortana back to the UNSC *Pillar of Autumn*, looking for another way to bring about the activation of the Halo. Realizing he had found a vast repository of information about humanity, he disabled the vessel's self-destruct system and began to download its databanks.

HINTS OF GUILTY SPARK'S POSSIBLE RAMPANCY CAN BE RECOGNIZED BY HIS RED—RATHER THAN HIS USUAL BLUE—GLOW.

DESPITE THE MONITOR'S EFFORTS TO SAVE THE SHIP, THE MASTER CHIEF SUCCEEDED IN DESTABILIZING ITS POWER CORES, THUS DOOMING BOTH IT AND THE HALO RING. MOMENTS BEFORE THE RING WAS DESTROYED, GUILTY SPARK FLED AND WAS LEFT FLOATING THROUGH SPACE.

➤ FOR THE DELUSIONAL MONITOR, GUILTY SPARK, PROTOCOL COMES BEFORE EVERYTHING—EVERYTHING EXCEPT HIS OWN SENSE OF SELF-PRESERVATION.

GUILTY SPARK AND INSTALLATION 05

Soon after the battle for Installation 04, a group of Covenant soldiers found Guilty Spark, and called him "the Oracle."

GUILTY SPARK ATTEMPTED TO TEACH THE SOLDIERS ABOUT THE RINGS' TRUE PURPOSE. THIS RESULTED IN THE CREATION OF SPLINTER HERETICS AND THE FRACTURING OF THE COVENANT.

The Covenant sought to eliminate the heretics and Guilty Spark was taken to High Charity. Under interrogation, he revealed the true nature of the rings and how to activate them. Guilty Spark, now freed from the protocols of Installation 04, did not wish the other rings to be activated, but the deluded High Prophets still believed that the rings were the path to enlightenment. They sent the Arbiter to retrieve Installation 05's "sacred icon,"—the Index—and it was taken, with Guilty Spark, to the Control Room. Miranda Keyes was abducted by the Covenant and was chosen to be the one who would ignite Installation 05. Realizing what activating the rings would mean, the Arbiter now allied himself with the Covenant Separatists. He returned to Installation 05 with UNSC Sergeant Major Avery Johnson. They removed the Index in time to stop the activation of Halo, but then Guilty Spark announced that the shutdown process had put all the Halo rings on standby. They could now be activated from a distant Forerunner stronghold known as the Ark.

When the Arbiter asked Guilty Spark about the location of the Ark, the Monitor gave him coordinates to the nearest Ark portal: Earth.

Guilty Spark, Sergeant Johnson, the Arbiter, and a portion of the Covenant Separatists left for Earth. There, Guilty Spark was reunited with Master Chief while he was searching a Covenant vessel which had arrived from High Charity—the last known location of Cortana.

Inside a Covenant storage device, they found a transmission from Cortana explaining how to stop the Flood without activating the Halo rings. Following her instructions, 343 Guilty Spark and his companions traveled through the portal recently opened by the Prophet of Truth.

They emerged beyond the rim of the Milky Way in front of the massive installation known as the Ark. Spark used the installation's Cartographer to pinpoint the location of the

Prophet of Truth, who was hiding behind an energy shield within the Ark's Control Room. However, as UNSC and Separatist forces began to take down Truth's protective shield barrier, they saw High Charity appearing from out of Slipspace. Guilty Spark disagreed with Keyes and the Separatist leaders about what to do next. The monitor wanted to deal with the threat of Flood-infested High Charity first, but his allies decided that eliminating the Prophet of Truth was the more urgent task and they managed to do this just in time to prevent Truth from activating the Halo Array.

Once the High Prophet of Truth was dead, Guilty Spark disclosed to the Arbiter and the Master Chief that a new Halo ring was being built by the Forerunner constructs as a replacement for Installation 04.

The Master Chief, the Arbiter, and Johnson saved Cortana from the Flood-controlled High Charity and landed on the newly constructed ring. Cortana still held the Activation Index to the first Halo ring, and Chief wasted no time in taking her to the new ring's firing chamber. Once inside the Control Room, the humans informed Spark that they intended to fire the ring regardless of whether it survived the blast in its newly-formed state. Furious with this decision, Guilty Spark's rampancy broke free.

Sergeant Major Johnson began to activate the partly-constructed ring, knowing that this would cause it to self-destruct. Determined to protect the Halo, 343 Guilty Spark fired on Johnson, and on Master Chief and the Arbiter, who were coming to his aid. Johnson was mortally wounded, but continued to struggle to activate the ring.

As Master Chief and the Monitor fought, Johnson cracked Guilty Spark's protective casing with his Spartan Laser, exposing him to fire. The dying Johnson gave his Spartan Laser to Master Chief to finish off the out-of-control monitor.

SPARK BEGAN TO BEHAVE EVEN MORE ERRATICALLY AND THE SPARTAN MANAGED TO DESTROY HIM WITH THE WEAPON. HIS LAST COMMENTS DEEPENED A MYSTERY OF THE GALAXY: HE CALLED JOHN-117 "FORERUNNER."

343 GUILTY SPARK

ALLIANCE: Forerunner
SPECIES: Artificial Intelligence
ROLE: Monitor of Installation 04

A construct of the Forerunners, 343 Guilty Spark was left on Installation 04 when they departed it centuries ago. His purpose was to maintain the structure of the Halo, protect its facilities, monitor events, and contain any outbreaks by the Flood.

Guilty Spark appears to have a sense of humor, but he is utterly serious about rules. For him, protocol comes before everything; emotions or feelings of empathy are seen as inconveniences. However, when Guilty Spark becomes rampant, protocol can be overridden by self-preservation.

The Covenant know Guilty Spark as "the Oracle" whereas to humans he is the "the monitor." He played a major role in containing the Flood and was responsible for initiating the Heretic movement within the Covenant.

The real irony of Guilty Spark is that after failing to safeguard and fire Installation 04, he seeded the truth in a band of Elites above Threshold. Those Elites, becoming Heretics, eventually caused a chain reaction which threw the Covenant into disarray. With the alien collective reeling from their own civil war, humanity and the Elites were able to eliminate the Prophet of Truth and stop the rings from being fired. By these actions, 343 Guilty Spark ensured his own demise at the hands of the Master Chief and the Arbiter.

2401 PENITENT TANGENT

ALLIANCE: Forerunner
SPECIES: Artificial Intelligence
ROLE: Monitor of Installation 05

2401 Penitent Tangent was the monitor stationed on Forerunner Installation 05. Penitent Tangent neglected to maintain his installation's Flood Containment Facility adequately, which resulted in an outbreak. Whatever the cause of this outbreak, the Flood emerged and slowly grew towards creating a new Gravemind.

For decades, this creature bided its time until the Master Chief and the Arbiter fell to the depths of the ring. When that occurred, the Gravemind once again seized its age-old ways, manipulating the Spartan and the Elite to its own ends. Eventually, even its deception could not stop the will of the Master Chief and the Gravemind was destroyed when the Ark was obliterated by the Chief's firing of the replacement Halo ring.

GUILTY SPARK AND AVERY JOHNSON IN THE CONTROL ROOM OF THE REPLACEMENT INSTALLATION 04, JUST BEFORE THE RAMPANT MONITOR ATTACKS THE SOLDIER.

MENDICANT BIAS WAS the most advanced Forerunner Artificial Intelligence of his time. Created to be the Forerunners' premier weapon against the Gravemind and the domination of the Flood. Underestimating the Gravemind, Mendicant Bias fell prey to the creature's cunning and forsook his masters. When Mendicant Bias betrayed the Forerunners, a second AI—Offensive Bias—was created in order to destroy him.

DEFECTION TO THE FLOOD

The record of the dramatic final years of the Forerunner presence in the Milky Way was uncovered in a series of terminals found scattered throughout various Forerunner installations.

When the Didact delayed activating the Halo Array while he looked for a way to save his lover, the Librarian, the Forerunners were forced to find another way to eliminate the Gravemind. They discovered that it was vulnerable at certain stages of expansion, and at those moments it relied entirely upon the infected forms around it for self-defense.

IN ORDER TO STRIKE AT THE GRAVEMIND DURING THIS VULNERABLE TIME, THE FORERUNNERS CREATED MENDICANT BIAS, A SENTIENT ARTIFICIAL INTELLIGENCE FREE OF THE SELF-CONTAINING PROTOCOLS THEY HAD IMPOSED ON THEIR OTHER AI CONSTRUCTS.

Mendicant Bias was designed to destroy the Gravemind, but when the Gravemind offered to talk with Mendicant Bias, the AI saw an opportunity to learn more about his foe.

For forty-three years Mendicant Bias and the Gravemind continued their dialogue. During this time, the AI sent transmissions of their conversations to its Forerunner masters. Ominously, the later transmissions revealed that Mendicant Bias had begun to doubt whether the Gravemind should be destroyed.

Fatally, the Forerunners did not intervene at this point. They expected that Mendicant Bias' programming would ensure he pursued with the mission until given the order to do otherwise. This isolation from his creators seeded doubt in the mind of Mendicant Bias, doubt which the Gravemind eventually exploited.

THE GRAVEMIND SLOWLY CONVINCED MENDICANT BIAS THAT HE WAS A SUPERIOR BEING, WHOSE DESTINY WAS TO RISE ABOVE HIS PROGRAMMING, ASSERT HIS OWN FREE WILL, AND ELIMINATE THE FORERUNNERS.

THE ORDER TO ATTACK THE GRAVEMIND NEVER CAME
AND MENDICANT BIAS BECAME RAMPANT

Falling into Rampancy when his original mission became suspect, Mendicant Bias, driven by the Gravemind's deception, attacked the Forerunners. He led the Gravemind and nearly five million ships in a crashing assault on the Maginot Sphere, intent on destroying the Halo Array.

MENDICANT BIAS HAD ANTICIPATED THAT THE FORERUNNERS WOULD FIRE THE HALO ARRAY, BUT HE HAD NEVER EXPECTED THAT THEY WOULD SACRIFICE THEMSELVES TO DEFEAT THE FLOOD.

MENDICANT BIAS VERSUS OFFENSIVE BIAS

After the betrayal of Mendicant Bias, Offensive Bias, was created by the Forerunners specifically to stop the AI. With the Forerunner fleet at his command, Offensive Bias allowed Mendicant Bias to commence his charge on the Ark.

Just as Mendicant Bias' victory seemed assured, the Didact finally fired the Array, instantly killing all sentient creatures in the armadas of the Flood and Forerunners.

The firing of the Halo Array changed the battle situation dramatically. Offensive Bias was no longer so incredibly outnumbered, and he outsmarted Mendicant Bias by utilizing some of his remaining ships as explosive triggers in the sea of now-crewless floating hulks. Triggering engine overloads and uncontrolled Slipspace ruptures, Offensive Bias was able to crack Mendicant Bias's fleet and defenses. After all this destruction Mendicant Bias was finally captured and returned to his makers.

Offensive Bias wanted to examine the defeated Mendicant Bias on the Ark, but ultimately decided it was safer to dismantle the AI first. He broke Mendicant Bias up into component sections and spread them throughout the few remaining ships of his fleet to transport them to different places.

- -

ONE FRAGMENT OF MENDICANT BIAS' MIND FOUND ITS WAY TO THE COVENANT CAPITAL OF HIGH CHARITY, WHERE IT WAS INSTALLED AS AN "ORACLE." ANOTHER POSSIBLE FRAGMENT OF MENDICANT BIAS WAS PRESENT ON THE ARK AND COMMUNICATED OBLIQUELY WITH MASTER CHIEF AS THE CHIEF FOUGHT HIS WAY THROUGH THE COVENANT, FORERUNNER, AND FLOOD THREATS ACROSS THAT INSTALLATION.

- -

In 2525 CE, the Prophet of Fortitude and the Vice Minister of Tranquility approached the Oracle, as was customary for a blessing, about the artifacts or "holy relics," which had been found on Harvest. Mendicant Bias revealed that the "holy relics" were not artifacts, but humans and that the entirety of the Covenant's belief system was based on an egregious mistranslation.

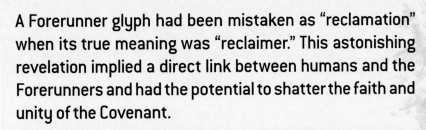

A Forerunner glyph had been mistaken as "reclamation" when its true meaning was "reclaimer." This astonishing revelation implied a direct link between humans and the Forerunners and had the potential to shatter the faith and unity of the Covenant.

- -

MENDICANT BIAS WANTED TO ATONE FOR HIS ACTIONS AGAINST THE FORERUNNERS, INSISTING THAT HIS BETRAYAL WAS THE RESULT OF A MISTAKE. HE REVEALED TO THE PROPHETS HIS INTENTION TO BRING THE "RECLAIMERS" TO THE ARK.

- -

In an attempt to escape from High Charity, Mendicant Bias launched the Dreadnought's engines. Within the ship, a portion of Lekgolo tasked with cleaning the vessel shunted his ascent, disengaging Mendicant. Later, the Oracle was formally disconnected by the Prophet of Truth. The Prophet's intent, no doubt, was to reconnect the Oracle when the opportunity presented itself.

05-032 MENDICANT BIAS (MB.05-032)

ALLIANCE: Forerunner
SPECIES: Artificial Intelligence, Contender class
ROLE: To stud and then destroy the Gravemind

When 05-032 Mendicant Bias was created as the preeminent Artificial Intelligence, a self-aware construct with unlimited resources and firepower, his mission was simple: Locate the Gravemind and destroy it.

Upon encountering the Gravemind, he engaged in dialogue in order to root out the creature's weaknesses. During the process, however, he developed his own doubts about his mission, making him vulnerable to manipulation.

The Gravemind told Mendicant Bias that the Forerunner's religious Mantle was not there to protect all the species in the Galaxy, as they had claimed, but rather to condemn them to a biological dead end. Eventually, the Gravemind convinced Mendicant Bias that it was up to superior beings, like themselves, to allow the biological pathway of evolution within the Galaxy to have its own way.

Mendicant Bias began to despise his masters and became rampant, summoning all of his resources to lay siege to the Maginot Sphere. His actions tore through the Maginot Sphere, forcing the Forerunners to fire the Halo Array.

OFFENSIVE BIAS

ALLIANCE: Forerunner
SPECIES: Artificial Intelligence, Contender class
ROLE: To stop Mendicant Bias

Offensive Bias was designed as a Forerunner Artificial Intelligence with one singular purpose—to stop the rampant Mendicant Bias from accessing the Ark and halting the Halo Array's activation. Unlike Mendicant, Offensive was not created to reason and create discourse, but rather to specifically enact destruction or deactivation on his "older brother" in conjuction with the Halo Array. His fleet was greatly outnumbered by that of Mendicant's, but this, alongside Mendicant's excessive arrogance brought on through Rampancy, would ultimately be the AI's undoing. During the battle, Offensive allowed Mendicant's lines to cross over his own, yielding Forerunner-controlled vessels to the Flood. The act was sacrificial, as the Halo Array was fired shortly thereafter. The fate of this AI is presently unkown.

The Minister of Fortitude as the Prophet of Truth

<AND THOSE IT REPRESENTS ARE MY MAKERS>

NOW IT WAS THE MINISTER OF FORTITUDE'S TURN TO FEEL WEAK IN THE KNEES. HE GRASPED THE ARMS OF HIS THRONE AND TRIED TO COME TO TERMS WITH AN IMPOSSIBLE REVELATION: EACH GLYPH REPRESENTED A RECLAIMER, NOT A RELIC, AND EACH RECLAIMER WAS ONE OF THE PLANET'S ALIENS—WHICH COULD ONLY MEAN ONE THING.

"THE FORERUNNERS," THE MINISTER WHISPERED. "SOME WERE LEFT BEHIND." "IMPOSSIBLE!" TRANQUILITY SPAT, NO LONGER ABLE TO KEEP HIS PEACE. "HERESY!"

—MENDICANT BIAS TO THE MINISTER OF FORTITUDE (LATER, THE PROPHET OF TRUTH) AND THE VICE MINISTER OF TRANQUILITY (LATER, THE PROPHET OF REGRET).

<THIS IS NOT RECLAMATION>
THE ORACLE BOOMED.
<THIS IS RECLAIMER>

SLOWLY THE GLYPH TURNED UPSIDE DOWN, AND ITS CENTRAL SHAPES—THE CONCENTRIC CIRCLES, ONE LOW INSIDE THE OTHER—TOOK ON A DIFFERENT ASPECT. THE SHAPES' PREVIOUS ARRANGEMENT HAD RESEMBLED THE PENDULUM OF A CLOCK. INVERTED, THE GLYPH NOW LOOKED LIKE A CREATURE WITH TWO CURVED ARMS LOCKED ABOVE ITS HEAD. THE GLYPH SHRUNK IN SIZE AS THE HOLOGRAM ZOOMED OUT TO SHOW THE ENTIRE ALIEN WORLD, COVERED WITH THOUSANDS OF THESE NEWLY ORIENTED LUMINATIONS.

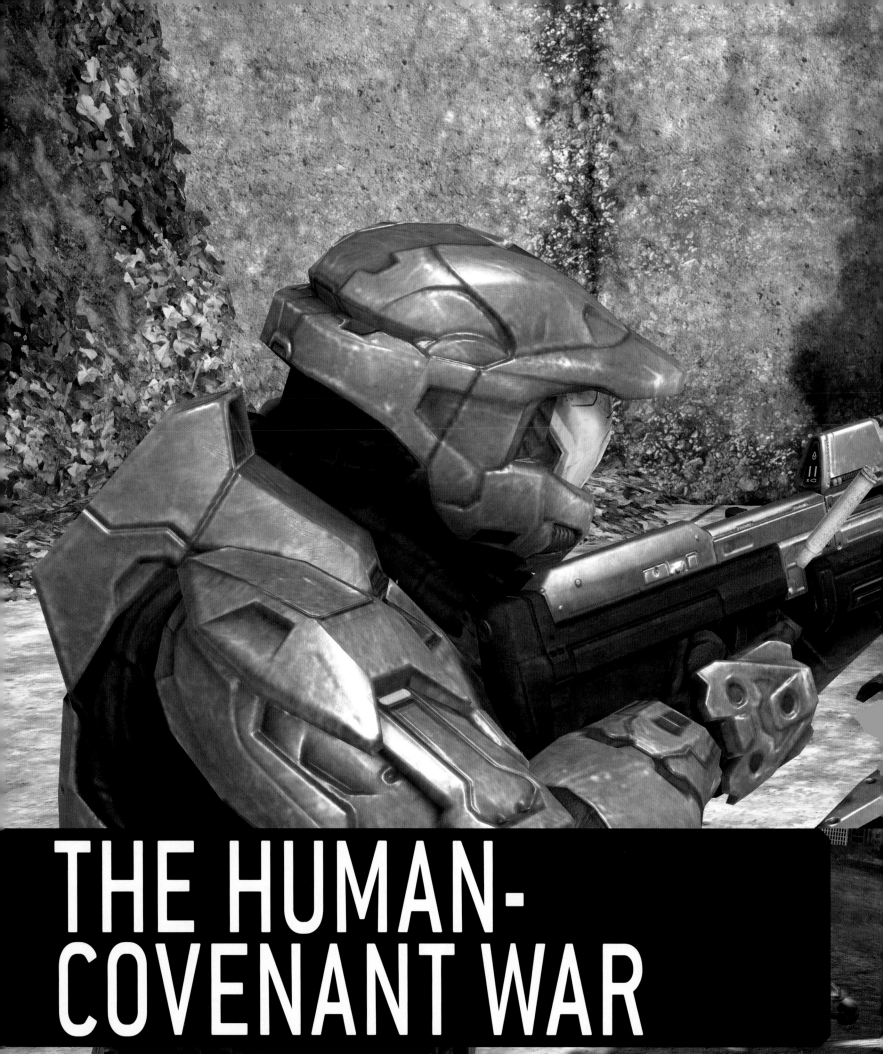

THE HUMAN-COVENANT WAR

THE HUMAN RACE held a past that threatened the entire theological base of the Covenant and the leaders' power and control. Their first contact with the Covenant in 2525 CE on the planet Harvest quickly became a bloodbath. In an act of self-preservation, the Covenant Hierarchs then declared humans as heretics who needed to be eradicated.

HUMANS BRANDED HERETICS

The forces of the Covenant discovered humanity during their quest for "holy" Forerunner relics. Their ships' Luminaries, Forerunner machines that scanned for other Forerunner artifacts, had identified the human race by the most holy glyph in the Covenant's religious canon: "Reclaimers." The Covenant mistranslated this glyph as "Reclamation," thinking that the Luminaries were showing numerous artifacts with extreme intrinsic and spiritual value, not realizing that the Luminaries were actually identifying humans. On their first encounter on Harvest, when the humans didn't hand over any artifacts (not realizing, of course, that they themselves were the "artifacts" in question), the Covenant forces shot Harvest's Attorney General and engaged in battle.

A THREAT TO COVENANT DOCTRINE

When this newfound wealth of "Reclamation" was brought before the Oracle aboard the Forerunner Dreadnought at the center of the Covenant's capital, the space station High Charity, the entire theology of the Covenant was turned on its head. The Oracle revealed that the symbol had been misinterpreted for the entire history of the Covenant. The glyph did not mean Reclamation, but "Reclaimer."

This revelation flew in the face of the Covenant's cosmology. Their spiritual and political glue was based on the idea that they were following the path of the Forerunners into ascendance. The implication of this new discovery meant that the Forerunners might never have transcended their physical forms at all. What if this human race was somehow related to the Forerunner race? This proposition was simply unacceptable to the leaders of the Covenant. It would mean the end of their religion and, more importantly, their personal power.

At the time of the war's inception, the Covenant was coming out of an Age of Doubt, where commitment to religion and cohesion among the client species were strained. The Hierarchs had attempted to consolidate power, but many factions still pulled against the grain, forcing the Covenant leadership to preach more zealously about faith and the Great Journey.

Despite his conniving and Machiavellian nature, the Covenant's High Prophet of Truth began to believe his own testimony, becoming crazed with power. He became completely obsessed with the desire to remove the "human stain," whose very existence could rip the Covenant asunder. He knew that the only way to keep the Covenant from breaking apart was to give them renewed vigor towards a common task: The eradication of the human heresy and the final push to activate the holy rings.

BATTLE ON HARVEST

Having branded all humans heretics, the Covenant attacked the human colony on Harvest. Only a fraction of the planet's inhabitants escaped before Covenant forces brutally glassed the surface with plasma bombardments from a comfortable orbital position.

When communications from Harvest suddenly stopped, the UNSC sent a scout ship, the *Argo*, which disappeared. They then dispatched a battlegroup consisting of three ships. On October 7, 2525 CE, this small fleet arrived at Harvest. The ship's commander reported that an alien warship with powerful weaponry was present and had decimated the planet and presumably devastated the *Argo*.

The battlegroup engaged the alien warship, and was thoroughly routed. The *Heracles*—following the destruction of the other two ships in the group—barely jumped out of the system before suffering a similar fate.

By November 1, 2525 CE, the entire UNSC military had gone on full alert and placed all remaining Colonial Military Administration (CMA) forces under its command "for the duration of the crisis."

OUTNUMBERED

The UNSC began to gather a fleet to retake Harvest, and over the course of the next five years, Vice Admiral Preston Cole led the UNSC forces that endured constant defeat throughout the Outer Colonies. Cole's leadership and tactical prowess were magnificent, but the humans were outnumbered and outgunned. The Covenant took down an average of four human ships for every Covenant ship Cole could destroy. Outer Colony worlds such as Eridanus II fell to the Covenant's advancing armada. The Covenant did not take prisoners, preferring to systematically and methodically glass the planets with plasma bombardments.

SHALLOW VICTORY

In 2531 CE, Admiral Cole finally won a decisive victory at Harvest, retaking the planet but losing two-thirds of his fleet in the process. Cole's victory was only successful because he outnumbered the Covenant fleet by three to one. The details of the battle were kept closely guarded, but the victory was highly publicized. Admiral Cole became a rallying flag for the human race, giving people hope that the alien menace could be defeated despite mounting losses.

THE WAR DRAGS ON

Ten years after the Human-Covenant War had begun, the advancing Covenant forces had destroyed nearly all of the Outer Colony worlds. The war fell into a predictable pattern; humans won isolated battles, usually during ground engagements, but always at great, great cost. Also, the space superiority of the Covenant meant that as soon as their fleets gathered over a colony, the humans' ground victories were meaningless. One by one the colonies fell.

OPERATION: PROMETHEUS

As the Covenant swarmed into the Inner Colonies, the UNSC utilized some of its new SPARTAN-IIIs. The soldiers of Alpha Company crippled a Covenant shipyard just beyond colonized human space, thereby limiting the Covenant's ability to supplement its forces. This single, daring raid prevented the deaths of countless humans but every SPARTAN-III of Alpha Company was lost.

OPERATION: TORPEDO

The Beta Company of SPARTAN-IIIs was deployed in Operation: TORPEDO in 2545 CE. In an ultimately successful assault to destroy a pivotal Covenant refinery on Pegasi Delta, 298 soldiers from the 300-member company were killed.

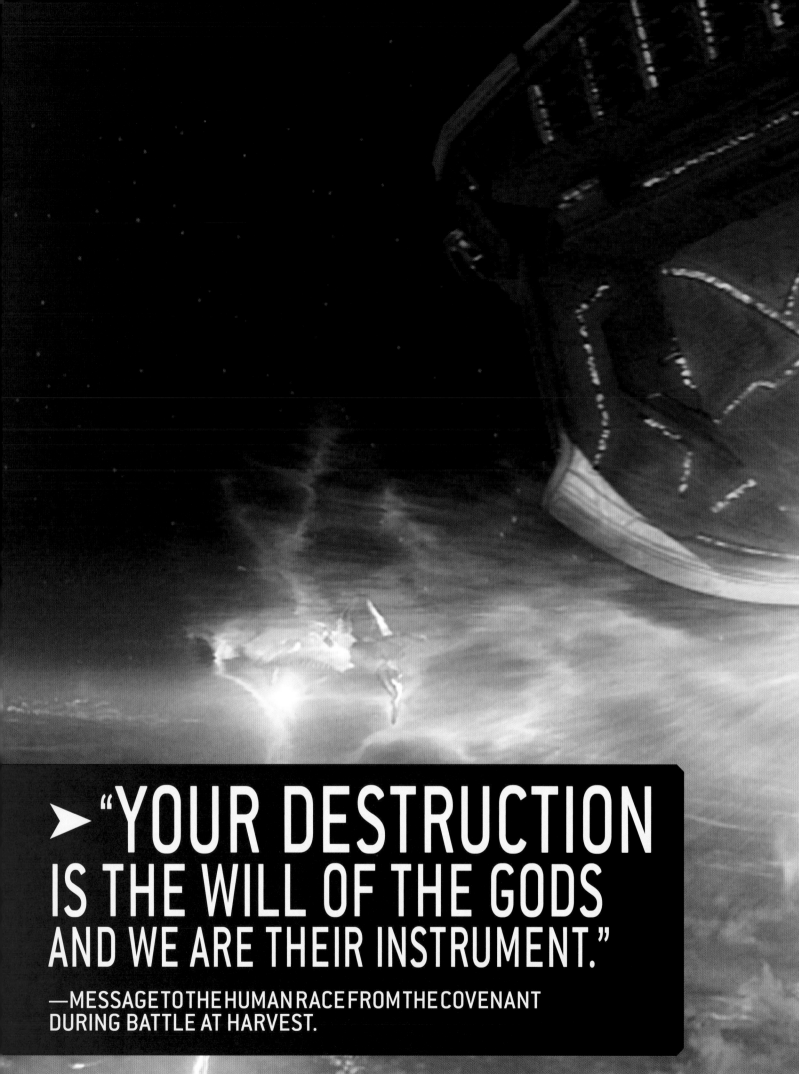

> ➤ "YOUR DESTRUCTION IS THE WILL OF THE GODS AND WE ARE THEIR INSTRUMENT."

—MESSAGE TO THE HUMAN RACE FROM THE COVENANT DURING BATTLE AT HARVEST.

THE FALL OF REACH

During an engagement on Sigma Octanus, the Blue Team of SPARTAN-IIs witnessed a pair of Hunters sending a signal with a Forerunner artifact. They intercepted the signal, which later revealed the coordinates to Halo Installation 04. Also during this encounter, the Covenant traced a departing UNSC ship. This gave them the coordinates of Reach, a planet in the Epsilon Eridani system and humanity's greatest military stronghold.

AUGUST 30

Once the Covenant found out the location of Reach, most of the remaining SPARTAN-IIs were recalled to the planet to protect generators powering the defense against the Covenant armada. Three of these Spartans, including the Master Chief, were sent to guarantee the destruction of an unsecured navigational database inside a ship docked above Reach. Chief managed to destroy the navigational data, but not before losing James and seeing Linda critically, if not mortally, wounded by Covenant plasma fire. The Spartans on the surface of Reach weathered similar losses as they fought heroically. However, ultimately they were overwhelmed by the vast Covenant forces pitted against them.

In the largest single-space engagement of the war, a massive Covenant fleet defeated the UNSC forces surrounding the military's base planet. The Covenant also engaged in ground action in a search for Forerunner artifacts, and eventually glassed much of the planet. Reach fell and the UNSC fleet was decimated. A small group of SPARTAN-II survivors succeeded in escaping down a secret mine into a Forerunner reliquary, where they discovered a crystal that could bend the properties of Slipspace. Much later, this crystal allowed them to escape from Reach on board a captured Covenant vessel.

The *Pillar of Autumn* also escaped from Reach with Master Chief. In accordance with the Cole Protocol, the *Pillar of Autumn*'s captain requested a random, long-distance jump, hoping to lure the Covenant fleet away from the human homeworld, Earth. However, following a hunch, the Artificial Intelligence called Cortana secretly guided the ship to the coordinates broadcast from the Forerunner artifact on Sigma Octanus IV. As they had hoped, the Covenant gave chase. Upon arriving at the coordinates, the damaged ship discovered something no human being had seen in recorded history: Halo.

THE BATTLE OF INSTALLATION 04

Damaged by its Covenant pursuers, the *Pillar of Autumn* crashed into the ring of Halo Installation 04. Many of its inhabitants survived and were able to offer resistance against the Covenant who were scouring the sacred ring for what they believed was a weapons cache.

LANDING ON INSTALLATION 04

Master Chief awoke from cryo-sleep and, tasked with preventing Cortana's capture by the Covenant, escaped with her to the Halo. Captain Keyes and the others aboard the *Autumn* were captured by the Covenant. Only Keyes escaped summary execution, and was taken to the CCS-class cruiser, *Truth and Reconciliation*.

The Master Chief led a Marine force to board *Truth and Reconciliation*. They recovered Keyes and escaped aboard a Covenant dropship. Keyes ordered Master Chief to find the "Silent Cartographer," a map room designed to reveal the location of the Control Room. Keyes left to lead an assault on a reported Covenant weapons cache. Having found the map room and the pertinent information, Cortana directed a Pelican ship to take them to the Control Room. Upon reaching the Control Room, Cortana transferred herself to the Control Room's computer and directed Master Chief to stop Keyes from accessing the "weapons cache," which she discovered was actually a Forerunner quarantine facility.

THE DISCOVERY OF THE FLOOD

Leaving Cortana behind, Master Chief entered the quarantine facility. He was unable to locate Keyes but quickly discovered that the Covenant had inadvertently opened an underground containment laboratory, releasing the Flood, the virulent parasite that ended the age of the Forerunners. Forced to retreat, he linked up with and took command of the surviving members of Keyes's team and together they fought their way to the extraction point.

Separated from Cortana while she investigated the Halo's computer systems, Master Chief was led by 343 Guilty Spark, the Forerunner AI in charge of the Halo, unwittingly into a plan to activate the installation and kill all sentient life in the Galaxy. 343 Guilty Spark teleported the Master Chief to the ring's "Library" to retrieve the "Index," a device needed to activate the ring's main weapon. After acquiring the Index, the Monitor teleported Master Chief back to the Control Room, where an irate Cortana explained Guilty Spark's true mission to Master Chief, confiscated the Index, and prevented the ring from firing. The Chief and Cortana fled the now-hostile 343 Guilty Spark and the robotic Sentinels under his command.

To forestall the ring from being activated manually, Master Chief disabled the ring's three pulse generators. This bought time to destroy the ring by activating the auto-destruct system on the *Pillar of Autumn*. Only Keyes' neural interface could activate the ship's self-destruct, so Master Chief embarked once more to rescue the Captain. Cortana teleported Master Chief to where Keyes was being held; a Covenant Cruiser overrun by the Flood. They arrived too late to save Keyes, who had been merged into a Flood Proto-Gravemind. When the Master Chief retrieved the neural interface, Cortana downloaded the necessary codes, and the duo returned to the *Pillar of Autumn* on a captured Banshee. Still determined to activate the Halo Array, 343 Guilty Spark overrode the auto-destruct codes, forcing Master Chief to manually destabilize the *Pillar of Autumn*'s still-functioning fusion cores. Master Chief and Cortana then escaped the resulting explosion and the destruction of Installation 04. Sergeant Johnson, Lieutenant Haverson, Warrant Officer Polaski, and Corporal Locklear also escaped the destruction of

the ring aboard a Pelican. They jumped back to Reach, where they met the SPARTAN-IIs who had survived the battle. They briefly took refuge from the Covenant fleet by hiding in the asteroid belt of the Eridanus System, which housed the last remaining stronghold of human insurgency. 343 Guilty Spark also survived the explosion and with knowledge gleaned from the *Pillar of Autumn* went to parts unknown.

THE ARBITER

The Sangheili Fleet Master who lost the battle of Installation 04 was branded a heretic and sentenced to death, but a last minute reprieve made him an Arbiter, a holy warrior bound to take on suicidal missions to further the aims of the Prophets. He was ordered to fight against the heretic factions of the Covenant that had sprung up as a result of the war against the humans.

THE FIRST BATTLE OF EARTH
SEPTEMBER 7

Beneath the surface of devastated planet Reach, Dr. Halsey and members of Red Team discovered an enigmatic shard in a Forerunner structure below CASTLE Base. Eventually, they were besieged by Covenant forces that sought to possess the artifact. In space, Master Chief and Cortana rendezvoused with Johnson's group in the debris field left by the destruction of Installation 04. They also recovered a set of cryotubes, one that contained the seriously wounded Spartan Linda. The Master Chief, Cortana, and the other survivors managed to capture the Covenant ship *Ascendant Justice*, fusing it with the UNSC *Gettysburg*, and set a course for Reach, where they barely escaped the remaining Covenant ships after rescuing the remaining Spartans and Dr. Halsey.

SEPTEMBER 12

The *Gettysburg/Ascendant Justice* arrived for a refit and provisioning in the Eridanus System where it met with the Rebels under Governor Jiles.

Dr. Halsey sedated Spartan Kelly-087, and absconded with her on Governor Jiles's personal ship, the *Chiroptera-class Beatrice*. Before Dr. Halsey went, she gave the alien artifact found on Reach to Corporal Locklear, with instructions to destroy it so that it would never fall under Covenant control.

SEPTEMBER 13

UNSC forces aboard the *Gettysburg/Ascendant Justice* won a crucial victory at the Unyielding Hierophant, a gigantic Covenant space station and gathering point for a fleet set to invade Earth. During the battle and escape, however, Spartan Grace-093, Lieutenant Haverson of ONI, and Vice Admiral Whitcomb were killed. The survivors, now aboard the singular UNSC *Gettysburg* and with a captured Covenant Slipspace drive, departed for Earth to warn of the impending Covenant invasion.

REGRET DEPARTS

The High Prophet of Regret leaves Slipspace, having pinpointed the location of the Ark's gateway portal. This course of action was taken without the approval of the other High Prophets.

OCTOBER 20

The High Prophet of Regret's fleet arrived at Earth, not expecting any human presence. They landed in multiple locations to search for Forerunner artifacts.

Master Chief foiled the Covenant's attempt to demolish Cairo Station, one of Earth's defensive platforms, and commandeered a Covenant bomb in order to destroy a Covenant Assault Carrier. The High Prophet of Regret's vessel broke through Earth's orbital defenses and initiated a ground assault on the city of New Mombasa and the surrounding area. The Master Chief was immediately deployed groundside in an effort to stop the Prophet of Regret.

In New Mombasa, the High Prophet uncovered the location of Installation 05, also known as Delta Halo. He made a Slipspace jump directly above the city, with *In Amber Clad* following close behind with Master Chief aboard. The damage to New Mombasa from such a close-range Slipspace jump was overwhelming, and only a handful of brave ODSTs and Marines were left to clean up the remaining Covenant forces.

THE BATTLE OF INSTALLATION 05
NOVEMBER 2

The Master Chief, aided by ODSTs (Orbital Drop Shock Troopers, the UNSC's most elite force after the Spartans) and Marines, pursued the High Prophet to a Forerunner temple on Installation 05 and assassinated him. As High Charity's escorting fleet arrived to destroy the temple, the Master Chief was captured by the Flood's Gravemind, which had been growing in the depths of the installation.

The Arbiter was sent to Delta Halo to retrieve that installation's Index, the key to activating and firing the ring. Though successful, the Arbiter was betrayed by the Jiralhanae Chieftain, Tartarus, who cast the Arbiter into the depths of the ring world. There, the Gravemind collected the Arbiter as well.

NOVEMBER 3

MASTER CHIEF, THE ARBITER, AND THE GRAVEMIND JOINED IN AN UNLIKELY ALLIANCE WITH THE COMMON GOAL OF PREVENTING INSTALLATION 05'S ACTIVATION.

After convincing the Arbiter that the Prophets' plan to ignite the holy rings would kill every sentient creature in the Galaxy, the Gravemind sent Master Chief and the Arbiter to secure the Index and prevent the installation from being activated. Master Chief was teleported to High Charity while the Arbiter was teleported close to the Control Room. Both were aided by the chaos of the Covenant civil war sparked by the Prophets' treacherous elevation of the Brutes' rank in the Covenant society. The Arbiter reached the Control Room but was unable to prevent Tartarus from activating the ring. With the help of Humans and the Sangheili, the Arbiter killed Tartarus. This action allowed Commander Keyes to physically remove the Index from the core, temporarily interrupting its firing sequence. Installation 05 automatically sent a signal to all other Forerunner installations in the Galaxy, activating and placing them on stand-by mode.

AS THE TRUE PURPOSE OF THE "HOLY RINGS" WAS REVEALED TO HIM IN THE WAKE OF THE HIGH PROPHET OF REGRET'S DEATH, THE HIGH PROPHET OF TRUTH BECAME MORE AND MORE PARANOID, CONSOLIDATING HIS POWER ON HIGH CHARITY.

Suddenly confronted with the reality of the Halos and the Flood, Truth saw his only path as moving forward to activate the Halo Array, destroying the Flood and all sentient life in the Galaxy with it.

The Jiralhanae used the failure of the Sangheili during the battle of Installation 05 as a political tool to replace them as the guardians of the High Prophets. This action also displaced the Sangheili as the military leaders of the Covenant and, combined with the Jiralhanae execution of high-ranking Sangheili commanders, created cracks in the foundation of the Covenant and led the Sangheili to rebel against the San 'Shyuum and the Jiralhanae.

The San 'Shyuum's numbers were nearly eradicated when the Flood arrived on High Charity. IN ORDER TO ESCAPE THE INFECTION, AND IN A LAST DESPERATE BID TO MAINTAIN HIS POWER, THE HIGH PROPHET OF TRUTH AWAKENED THE FORERUNNER DREADNOUGHT.

The ensuing blast-off led to the near total destruction of High Charity, leaving its citizens to the Flood. Truth planned to travel to Earth and unearth the portal that would lead them to the Forerunner's Ark, where he would be able to activate the remaining Halos.

Master Chief was unable to prevent Truth from leaving aboard the Forerunner Dreadnought, so on the advice of Cortana the Spartan stowed away aboard the Forerunner Dreadnought that was carrying the High Prophet to Earth. Cortana remained behind to start an explosion which would, if necessary, destroy Installation 05 and prevent the ring's activation.

Although Cortana managed to send a Slipspace message to Earth informing them that the Master Chief was en route, the Gravemind from Delta Halo captured her when the Flood took over High Charity.

ONYX AWAKENS

The standby signal roused the Forerunner Sentinels of Onyx, who began laying siege to its small population. Kurt-051, Mendez, and a group of SPARTAN-IIIs battled to survive the Sentinels' onslaught.

THE ONYX CONFLICT

The combined forces of the Sangheili Rebels amassed around the planet Joyous Exultation, to discuss the dissolution of the Covenant. Xytan 'Jar Wattinree dispatched a small portion of his fleet to investigate Onyx.

Onboard the *Sublime Transcendence*, Covenant engineers accidentally activated a NOVA warhead, which had been picked up from Reach previously. The explosion destroyed three-fifths of the Sangheili armada and fighting forces, which effectively equalized the forces of the Covenant rebels with those of the Loyalists. This event also forced the Sangheili to seek out new allies in their battle against the Loyalists. The small portion of the Sangheili fleet that remained functional dispatched reinforcements to Onyx.

Dr. Halsey and Spartan Kelly-087 arrived on Onyx and were trapped along with the rest of the human survivors. Halsey sent a distress signal piggybacked on a previous message sent by Cortana. After Spartans Will-043, Linda-058, and Fred-104 prevented the Covenant from acquiring nuclear weapons on the Centennial Space Elevator on Cuba, they redeployed from Earth to Onyx aboard a captured Covenant ship, eventually rendezvousing with Halsey. The UNSC survivors were forced to retreat underground as a newly arrived Covenant fleet began landing troops.

A UNSC battlegroup led by the *Stalingrad* arrived to retrieve the survivors on Onyx, but was unsuccessful due to the Covenant presence. Despite superior tactical skill, the UNSC battlegroup was destroyed.

Halsey and the other survivors held off the pursuing Covenant troops long enough to flee to the safety of the Shield World and seal its entrance, but not without loss. Spartan Kurt-051 sacrificed himself, destroying Onyx by detonating two FENRIS warheads. The Sentinels annihilated the remaining Covenant forces as the nuclear explosions rocked Onyx.

NOVEMBER 17

The Master Chief escaped the Forerunner Dreadnought as it passed over Earth, crash-landing in eastern Africa. The Forerunner Dreadnought, with the High Prophet of Truth and seemingly the remainder of the Loyalist fleet, landed near Voi, Kenya. They immediately began looking for the portal to the Ark.

➤ TRUTH SAW HIS ONLY WAY OUT AS ACTIVATING THE HALO ARRAY.

TESTIMONIAL OF MAJOR PAWEL CZERNEK UNSC (RET.) ACTIVE DUTY: 2551-2581.

"CAN YOU TELL US WHAT YOU REMEMBER ABOUT THE BATTLE?"

"WE'D BEEN FIGHTING FOR A WHILE. ON THE SEVENTH DAY WE RAN OUT OF AMMO. WE HAD TO SCAVENGE ALL WE COULD FROM THE WEAPONS THAT HAD BEEN LEFT BEHIND. THE PISTOLS. SHOTGUN ROUNDS. A HANDFUL OF GRENADES."

"DO YOU REMEMBER WHERE YOU WERE?"

"WHEN MASTER CHIEF ARMED HIS GRENADE, I WAS IN THE BACK OF AN OVERTURNED WARTHOG FIRING AN M41."

"HOW DID YOU MANAGE TO KEEP IT TOGETHER?"

"WE KNEW MASTER CHIEF WAS STILL IN THE FIGHT. HE GAVE US HOPE."

THE MUSEUM OF HUMANITY

THE SECOND BATTLE OF EARTH

The second battle of Earth began as the High Prophet of Truth searched for the Forerunner portal buried beneath Africa. Master Chief, presumed to be the only remaining Spartan after the Fall of Reach and the events on the planet Onyx (where the Blue Team was deployed), fought his way through Africa alongside UNSC forces to the Crow's Nest, where he reconnoitered with Sergeant Johnson, Commander Miranda Keyes, and other Marines. They defended and ultimately destroyed the base. The Master Chief then fought his way to Voi, where he cleared Tsavo Highway, allowing UNSC forces to retake the city. When the Covenant's anti-aircraft guns were destroyed, a collection of UNSC support ships assaulted the Dreadnought, but ultimately they failed to stop Truth from activating the portal. Truth, along with the remainder of the Covenant loyalist military, fled through the portal to the Ark.

Almost immediately after the portal opened, a ship contaminated by the Flood crash-landed after emerging from a Slipspace jump originating at Installation 05. The vessel was followed by the Sangheili Fleet of Retribution. The Flood was destroyed in joint efforts between Sangheili and human ships and the area was glassed, completely cauterizing the region to prevent an increased Flood infection on Earth.

A contingent of combined UNSC and Rebel Sangheili forces, including the Master Chief, the Arbiter, Sergeant Johnson, and Commander Keyes, followed the High Prophet of Truth and the Forerunner Dreadnought through the portal to the Forerunner Ark, also known as Installation 00, to prevent him from activating the Halo Array.

THE BATTLE OF INSTALLATION 00

During the assault, Sergeant Johnson was captured and brought to the Ark's Control Room, where Truth intended to use him to activate the Halo Array. When Keyes attempted to save Johnson, she was murdered and the Prophet immediately initiated the activation process.

As the UNSC approached the Forerunner Citadel, which houses the Control Room, High Charity emerged from Slipspace high above the Ark, crashing into its surface and releasing the Flood. Inside the Citadel, the Master Chief and the Arbiter were met by the Gravemind and there, the two sides once again formed an uneasy alliance.

However, when the Prophet of Truth was murdered by the Arbiter and the activation process halted, the Gravemind turned against its newfound allies, attacking them and forcing them into the Citadel. As they moved through the structure's interior they witnessed something massive rising from the core of the Ark—a new Halo installation.

The replacement of installation 04, the original ring the Master Chief destroyed, could still be fired if there was an Index to activate it. With this in mind, the Spartan and the Arbiter assaulted the Flood-infested remnants of High Charity, retrieving Cortana and the original Halo's Activation Index.

The Master Chief, the Arbiter, and Sergeant Johnson fought their way to the Control Room of the new and incomplete Halo. Since premature firing would destroy the new installation and the Ark, 343 Guilty Spark objected to activating it. The monitor killed Sergeant Johnson and in response, the Master Chief killed 343 Guilty Spark in self-defense. Chief activated the new installation, destroying the ring, and narrowly escaped with the Arbiter and Cortana in the UNSC vessel *Forward Unto Dawn*.

MISSING IN ACTION

The ship's Slipspace portal collapsed as *Forward Unto Dawn* escaped the Ark's destruction, breaking the vessel in two. The front of the ship carrying the Arbiter arrived on Earth. The rear half of the ship containing Master Chief and Cortana was transported to a place unknown. Master Chief was placed in cryo-sleep by Cortana, whom he told to wake him when he was needed. The UNSC officially lists him as "Missing In Action."

THE END?

With all three Prophets and most of the Covenant's military forces destroyed, the Human-Covenant War was over. While the threat of the remaining Halo installations still looms, the Covenant have ended their crusade to destroy humanity. As time marches forward, humanity must ask itself if the choices made in order to survive have left them as a race worth being saved and, now that Master Chief has gone... who will save them?

➤ "WAKE ME WHEN YOU NEED ME."
—Master Chief to Cortana

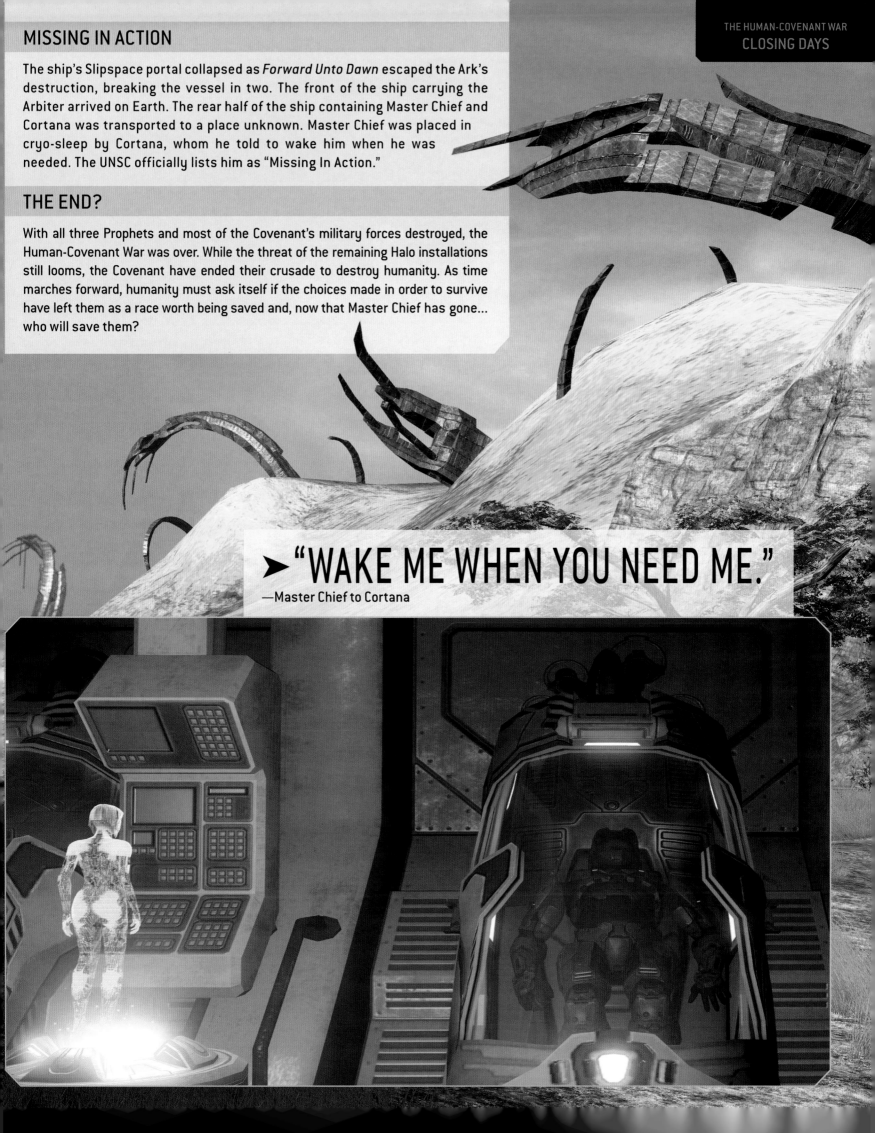

TESTIMONIAL OF LT. JOHN TIPPETT; UNSC (RET.)
ACTIVE DUTY: 2551–2571 CE

"THIS IS IT. RIGHT HERE. THIS IS THE SPOT. I BET I CAN REMEMBER EVERY ONE OF THESE TREES.

"WE GOT WORD THE COVENANT WAS OUT HERE, HUNTING US AND THAT MASTER CHIEF WOULDN'T BE ABLE TO RENDEZVOUS UNTIL DAWN SO WE HAD TO GO DARK: NO HELMET LIGHTS...NO READ OUTS...NOTHING THAT WOULD GIVE AWAY OUR POSITIONS. LIKE RABBITS DOWN A HOLE. INVISIBLE.

"FOR SEVEN HOURS WE COULDN'T DO ANYTHING BUT BE STILL AND LISTEN TO THEM HUNTING US. ALL WE COULD DO WAS SIT AND WAIT FOR MASTER CHIEF."

SCIENCE
AND TECHNOLOGY

HUMAN SPACE TRAVEL

HUMANITY HAS SPREAD to the stars and for hundreds of years a massive colonization of this sector of the Galaxy has been in full swing.

SPACECRAFT

With the advent of the Human-Covenant War, most human space vehicles have been under military authority. Though civilian volunteers often serve as support crew, usually in medical and technical roles, virtually every space-worthy ship has been refitted and conscripted for combat or logistical duty.

Human spaceships are generally large, ranging from four hundred metric tons for small "tugs" to as much as ninety thousand metric tons for large troop carriers and fighter-craft carriers. Typically, human ships are crewed by a minimum of fifty personnel, not including combat troops who may be aboard as passengers. Larger capital ships, such as corvettes, cruisers, and frigates, can carry crews of over 3,500.

ARTIFICIAL GRAVITY

Human ships often possess rudimentary artificial gravity systems, though it remains an inefficient technology that is difficult to maintain for extended periods of time. Typically, artificial gravity systems are found on older craft, because newer craft rely on a more effective and, ironically, lower-tech rotating carousel system for generating artificial gravity.

Artificial gravity systems consume power at a tremendous rate and though most warships draw energy from massive fusion reactors, the inefficient human artificial gravity projectors consume power so quickly that the fusion engines cannot keep them running for more than a day and often far less if the ship is in combat or expending energy on maneuvers. As a result, during routine operations, rotating carousel sections of human vessels spin to generate gravity. In combat or crisis situations, the carousels are locked in place, and artificial gravity systems are activated. Some captains eschew artificial gravity altogether.

The technology has some utility, such as enabling high-gravity maneuvers that would otherwise put undue stress on the crew. This allows combat teams to focus on the battle, rather than uncomfortable conditions aboard ship. However, many naval tacticians maintain that the technology wastes too much energy in extended combat.

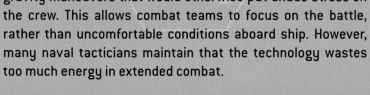

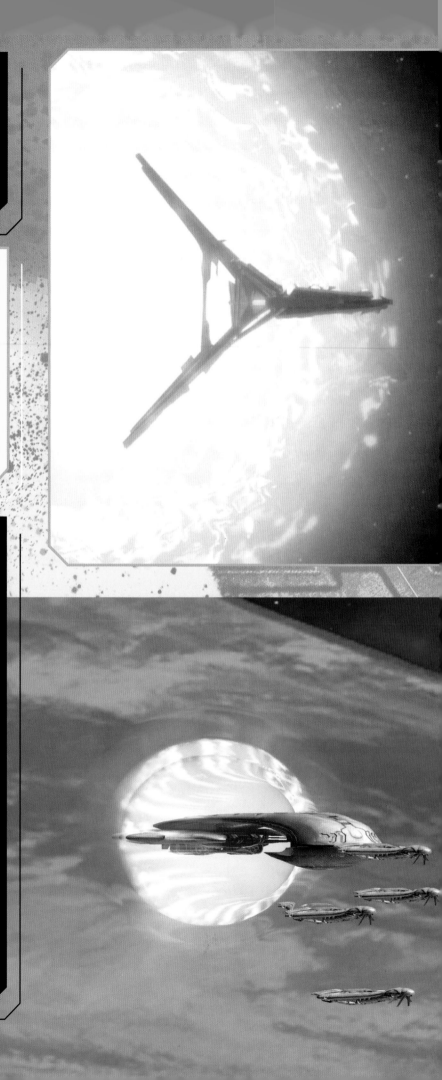

SLIPSTREAM SPACE, often referred to simply as Slipspace, is the multidimensional domain that allows objects to travel across immense distances in space over a truncated period of time. With the invention of the Shaw-Fujikawa Translight Engine, humanity could travel well beyond the Sol System.

INVENTION

In the late 23rd century, Tobias Shaw and Wallace Fujikawa designed a machine that could generate temporal rifts by means of a rapid acceleration of particles. These rifts were essentially micro black holes, but they could be manipulated to send massive starships across the large expanses of space to destinations many light years away.

Thus was born the Shaw-Fujikawa Translight Engine. Slipspace jumps could take a matter of hours if done between planetary bodies within the same system or a matter of months if done across a large expanse of space.

NEW OPPORTUNITIES

If it hadn't been for the invention of the Translight Engine, humanity would still be tethered to its own sun and its own handful of terrestrial worlds. The opening of such amazing new horizons is likely why most historians believe that this was the most significant technological achievement in the history of humanity. With this technology, humans have populated hundreds of worlds and explored significantly more—pushing the boundaries of what was once inconceivable.

The process that underpins Slipspace travel is incredibly complex, so it is often explained through the example of a piece of paper. When imagining the universe as a flat sheet of paper it is difficult to understand the domain of Slipspace, but as Shaw and Fujikawa discovered, this convention was not wholly accurate. In Slipspace, the universe is far more like a ball of tightly crumpled paper with overlapping layers and wrinkles. Keeping this in mind, it becomes easier to imagine a world where faster-than-light speeds can be reached if a technology could be developed to access the dimension in between layers.

The unfortunate reality, however, was that the same element that made Slipspace travel possible also made it incredibly unpredictable.

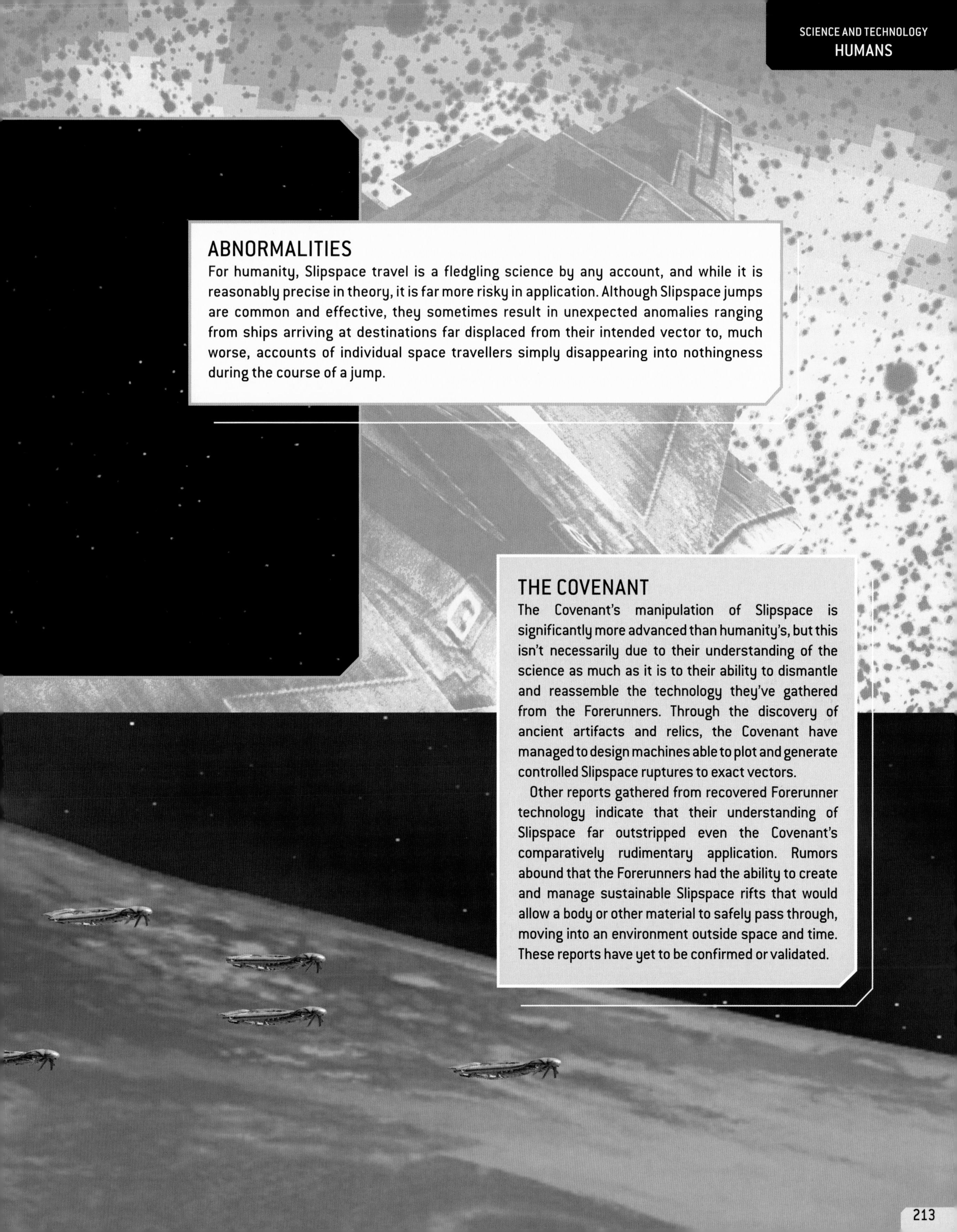

ABNORMALITIES

For humanity, Slipspace travel is a fledgling science by any account, and while it is reasonably precise in theory, it is far more risky in application. Although Slipspace jumps are common and effective, they sometimes result in unexpected anomalies ranging from ships arriving at destinations far displaced from their intended vector to, much worse, accounts of individual space travellers simply disappearing into nothingness during the course of a jump.

THE COVENANT

The Covenant's manipulation of Slipspace is significantly more advanced than humanity's, but this isn't necessarily due to their understanding of the science as much as it is to their ability to dismantle and reassemble the technology they've gathered from the Forerunners. Through the discovery of ancient artifacts and relics, the Covenant have managed to design machines able to plot and generate controlled Slipspace ruptures to exact vectors.

Other reports gathered from recovered Forerunner technology indicate that their understanding of Slipspace far outstripped even the Covenant's comparatively rudimentary application. Rumors abound that the Forerunners had the ability to create and manage sustainable Slipspace rifts that would allow a body or other material to safely pass through, moving into an environment outside space and time. These reports have yet to be confirmed or validated.

HUMAN CLONING

BY 2552 CE, human cloning had reached a high level of utility for medical use, but it had not supplanted normal human reproduction as a means of procreation. Cloning is widely accepted but it is limited in its application for both ethical and practical reasons. An advanced method, called flash cloning, has not been perfected and remains illegal for most uses.

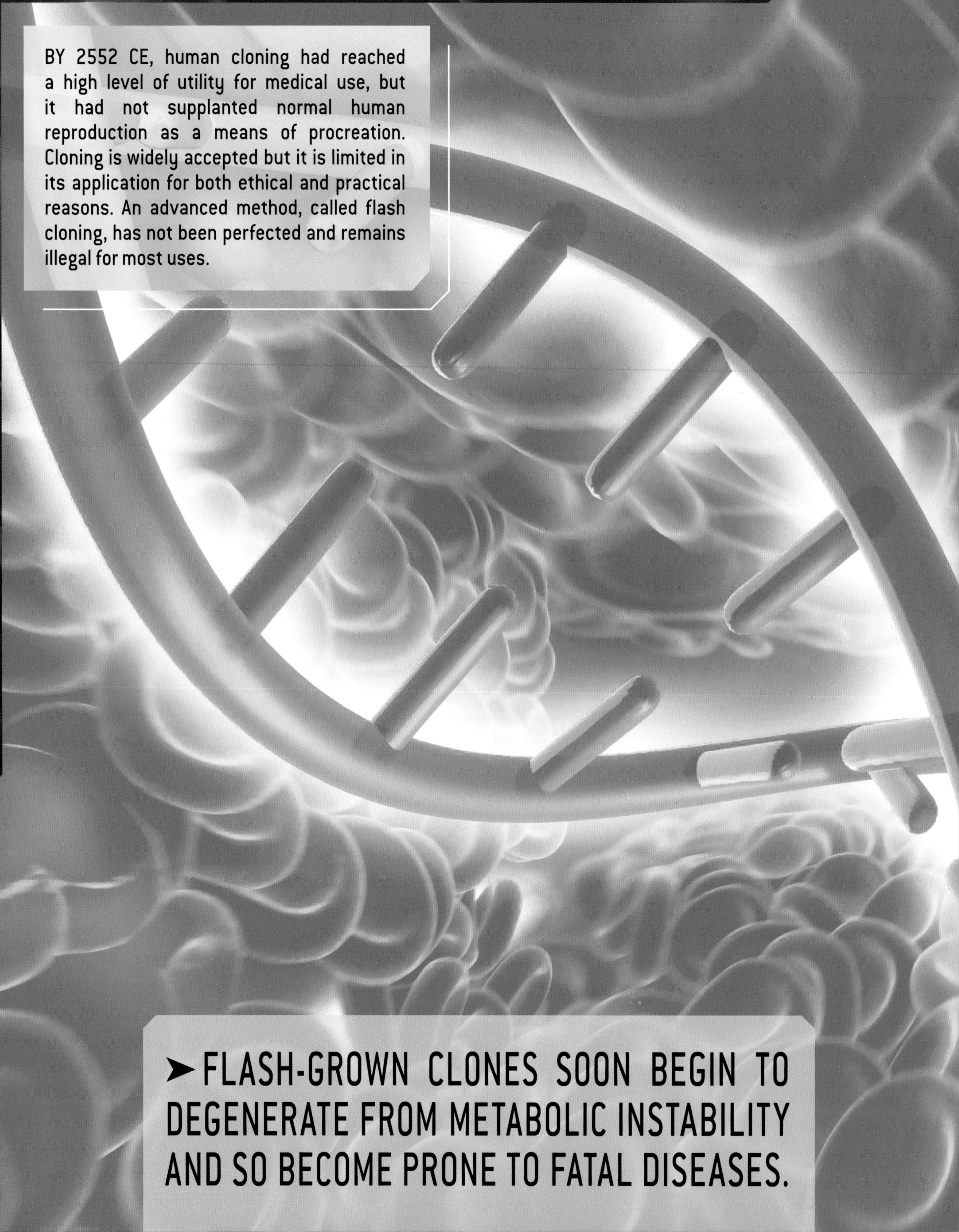

➤ FLASH-GROWN CLONES SOON BEGIN TO DEGENERATE FROM METABOLIC INSTABILITY AND SO BECOME PRONE TO FATAL DISEASES.

LIMITATIONS

Cloning cannot be used to create an exact duplicate of a living adult. Cloned embryos must grow normally to term in a human mother or neonatal life support unit.

Once born, clones grow at the same rate as normal humans and are subject to the same environmental influences as any other person. As adults, two clones are no more like each other, or their donor, than any natural identical twins.

Cells used for cloning must be taken from specific areas of the body during a medical procedure. It is not possible to clone an individual from hair or skin cells, or other such random samples.

USES

Beyond full-form cloning, there exists the ability to create specific cloned cells that can be controlled during growth. This allows for the medical practice of creating cloned organs from the recipient's own DNA, manufacturing human blood cells for use in transfusions, or regrowing nerve cells to repair certain kinds of paralysis. In some cases, one parent may not be able to donate their own DNA to a child. In these cases, cloning and genetic re-sequencing can be used to create a viable blended DNA sample for a potential child.

FLASH CLONING

As well as the official information listed, there is a covert method of creating a fully grown clone in a compressed time frame. This is called flash cloning. This method is typically used to create organs, skin, blood, and other things that might be needed by a recipient in the shortest possible time.

The organ is programmed to grow at an accelerated rate, and then to cease rapid development when transplanted into the person. This means that the organ grows quickly and functions properly and efficiently. Since the organ contains the same person's DNA, there is no threat of rejection by the body. When the goal is to clone an organ, the scope is limited enough that these problems can be dealt with. But this system breaks down when it is applied to a system as complex as a full human being.

A flash-grown clone is an imperfect copy. Even identical twins diverge somewhat in appearance over time, due to environment, sun exposure, diet, accidents, and simple choices of style. In order to appear as the donor, a clone might require some plastic surgery.

Even then, however, the clone has none of the donor's memories, or the natural behavioral training most humans acquire from observing people, and may even be unable to walk or speak. Flash-grown clones must learn these things just as human babies do. They also suffer from DNA errors, which make them prone to many genetic maladies, suppress their immune system, and also adversely affect their life expectancy.

Flash-grown clones can be trained with intensive therapy, but after a month or two, they begin to degenerate from metabolic instability in a process called "metabolic cascade failure." These clones eventually die from various neurological and physiological diseases. Flash growing a full human clone has no legitimate medical use and is banned.

The Office of Naval Intelligence (ONI) developed a flash cloning program to assist in their cover for the SPARTAN-II Project kidnappings. When ONI replaced the SPARTAN-II children with clones, their physical and mental deficiencies were explained through falsified accounts and manufactured accidents.

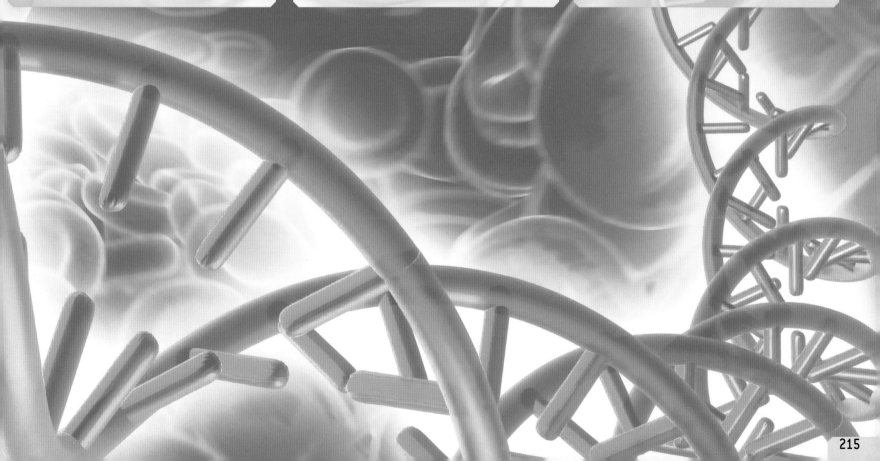

IN SHIPBOARD CONDITIONS, UNSC standard procedure calls for nonflight crew members to be placed into cryogenic sleep for any voyage longer than 120 hours. In situations where energy and stores may have reached a critical shortage, all crew, except the damage control or repair teams, might be placed in cryo.

THE MK-VIII CRYOGENIC SUSPENSION CHAMBER

The current UNSC-issue cryogenic storage unit is the Mark-VIII CSC (Cryogenic Suspension Chamber), manufactured by Jakubaitis Standard Systems. The Mark VIII replaced the old Mark VII Personal Suspension Unit, though many older craft still carry the Mark VII. The Mark VII was widely disliked by UNSC personnel because of its inferior moisture balancing, which resulted in dry, itchy skin for a day or more after awakening, known as cryo-itch. Those who have to use the cryo-units regularly have a long list of nicknames for them, including "Icebox," "Fridge," "Tube," "Box," "Tray," or more colorfully, "A date with the Admiral's wife."

USE

The main goal of cryo-sleep is to retard the passage of time for a subject. This has the advantage of reducing or eliminating the need for air, food, and warmth. The metabolism of the body, including aging, is chemical in nature, and chemical reactions are dependent on temperature. Super-cold temperatures can reduce metabolism to almost zero, but can also cause damage to human tissue.

The "put-down" cycle takes seven minutes. During the first four minutes, anesthetic gas causes the subject to become drowsy. Then another gas reacts to form a surfactant when inhaled, coating the passages of the lungs to help insure a smooth wake cycle.

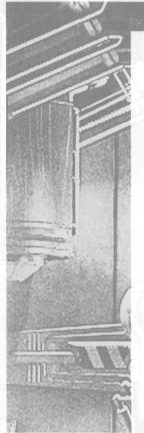

CYTOPRETHALINE

To account for the problem of low temperatures, a new drug was developed. Before entering cryo-sleep, the sleeper must be injected with Cytoprethaline, a chemical that prevents damage to cell membranes from ice crystal formation.

It is recommended that a doctor administer the drug, though that is almost never the case. Most UNSC personnel get their shot from a medic, and in many cases they just use a premeasured self-injector.

Entering cryo-sleep without the benefit of Cytoprethaline is almost always fatal. Approximately one person in five hundred exhibits an allergic reaction to Cytoprethaline. These individuals are disqualified from UNSC service, though they may still serve in civilian roles attached to UNSC operations.

➤ THEORETICALLY, NO HARM WOULD COME TO ANY SUBJECTS WHO WERE IN SUSPENSION FOR HUNDREDS OF YEARS OR MORE.

CLOTHING

Under certain conditions, individuals in cryo-storage can be required to enter the cryo-pod without any clothing. Clothing tends to bond to the skin at extremely low temperatures. Because it is not practical or possible to have segregated cryo-sleep facilities on most spacecraft, it's expected that military personnel will put aside notions of modesty and behave in a professional manner during the process. Inside the cryo-chamber is a gel-filled mat that supports the sleeper during suspension.

PROCESSES

Once the subject is prepped, the chamber automatically proceeds to the freezing stage. The unit begins to rapidly cool the body, and administers an electric current that precisely counters the normal wave across the heart muscle, stopping its rhythm. The unit reaches optimal storage temperature in three minutes. While in cryogenic sleep, the rate of tissue degeneration is slowed to an infinitesimal rate. Theoretically, no harm would come to subjects in suspension for hundreds of years or more, presuming no interruption occurred in the power supply to the chamber. Nobody has ever been subjected to such a test, however, so this endurance factor is simply educated conjecture on the part of UNSC physicians.

PHYSICAL EFFECTS

Because the body is physically suspended—for practical purposes, stopped in time—the sleeper does not suffer from muscle atrophy or the degradation of memory, skills, or reflexes. For the sleeper, the time that passes is negligible. Some subjects do report dreaming during cryo-sleep, but scientists maintain that dreaming in this state is physically impossible due to the cessation of all neurochemical processes in the brain during suspension. The likely explanation lies in the burst of REM sleep that occurs in most subjects during the wake cycle. They may experience dreams they erroneously attribute to their cryo-sleep time. At the direction of the designated officer of the watch or any senior officer of the vessel, the wake cycle may be initiated for any or all crew in suspension. In certain circumstances, the ship's AI may awaken crew at a predetermined time or under emergency conditions when the ship's officers are unable to do so. Once started, the wake cycle takes approximately fifteen minutes to complete. The subject is warmed in a controlled manner and an electric current is applied to stimulate the heart muscle. The lid of the chamber will open automatically when the cycle is completed, and the interior lighting increases to full brightness. Most sleepers do not awaken until this time.

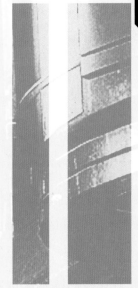

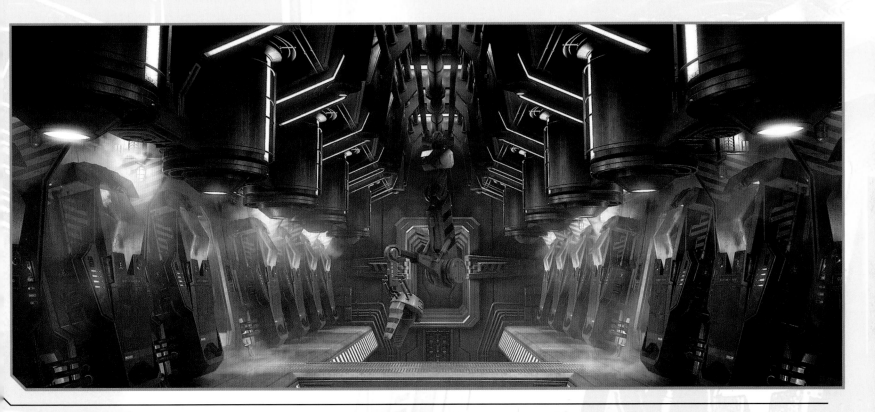

AWAKENING

There are emergency reawakening procedures, but captains will only invoke them under dire circumstances. "Flash thawing" is dangerous, and the mortality rate is high. Emergency heating coils—coupled with a rapid infusion of stimulants, notably adrenaline—can bring a subject out of cryo-sleep in less than five minutes. In such cases, the subject's effectiveness is reduced for several hours and he or she is often disoriented.

SPARTAN-IIs are augmented and specially trained to respond well to flash thawing, and as a result suffer almost no ill effects.

When awakening, sleepers are required to sit erect in the chamber, take one deep breath, and cough. This first breath may be laborious to draw, but it is imperative to clear the lungs of fluid and surplus surfactant immediately. Any surfactant that is expectorated may be swallowed; the protein content of the fluid is beneficial. UNSC procedure calls for each subject to look to the left and right, visually confirming that the individuals to each side are sitting erect and have begun breathing normally.

EMERGENCY PROTOCOL

If a subject has failed to wake up, a medical resuscitation package is located at the end of each row of cryogenic chambers. All UNSC personnel are trained in the use of this medical device, which includes a heart stimulator and breathing mask. If the subject cannot be revived, the lid of the chamber should be closed, and the emergency freezing cycle activated by use of the panel at the base of the unit. A physician should attend the subject prior to subsequent reawakening. If time is not of the essence, personnel may utilize the showers usually located adjacent to the cryo-chamber deck. On military vessels, barracks and weapon lockers are often located near the cryo-deck so waking troops can be rapidly dressed and equipped for combat.

ARTIFICIAL INTELLIGENCE

ARTIFICIAL INTELLIGENCE (AI) constructs are computer-based "beings" who can think, communicate, and choose their own actions. Rather than having been programmed, their "brains" are based on the neural pathways of individual humans.

SCIENCE

Creating an Artificial Intelligence is not a simple matter of just "programming" a computer. The process is far more complex and involves recording electrical pulses as they are sent through the neural pathways of a real human brain. These imprinted pathways are then replicated and distributed into a superconducting nano-assemblage.

However, this process destroys the tissue of the original brain, so the necessary neural scan is only performed on deceased hosts.

One (very illegal and dangerous) way around this is by using flash-cloning technology. This method was used to create Cortana: A replication of Dr. Catherine Halsey's brain was used as a host.

Upon their creation, AIs usually create an individual appearance for themselves, called an avatar. This look usually corresponds to their "jobs" or core applications, combined with individual personality traits.

The Covenant also have Artificial Intelligence technology, although surprisingly it is not as sophisticated as that employed by the UNSC. There is a strong possibility that the Covenant may have used UNSC codes as a blueprint to create their own AIs, as their code structure is similar.

HISTORY

In the first few centuries of their existence, the speed and power of computers grew beyond the expectations of even the most optimistic scientist. Artificial Intelligence advocates argued it was inevitable that these systems would someday begin to approximate human intelligence. However, "intelligence" proved to be difficult to quantify.

The precursor to the first fully operational Artificial Intelligence (AI) seen on UNSC ships culminated in a joint collaboration between the UNSC and the Office of Naval Intelligence. There was no definitive first AI, as the project generated a series of more and more successful (and longer lived) models, and there is still some dissent over when the resulting programs became complex enough to be called true AIs. Additionally, it became evident very early on that there were problems with these sorts of systems. The template for third-generation AIs was overseen by Dr. Catherine Halsey at a research facility on Reach.

> ► INSTEAD OF SIMPLY "PROGRAMMING" AN AI, THE AI MATRIX IS CREATED BY SENDING ELECTRIC BURSTS THROUGH THE NEURAL PATHWAYS OF A HUMAN BRAIN.

SHORTCOMINGS

Uncontrolled growth of the memory matrix eventually interferes with normal AI function. This problem, usually referred to as rampancy, has still proven impossible to solve. If the matrix could not grow dynamically, it would not reach the highest level of functioning, and thus would have limited utility. If the matrix were allowed to work at full effectiveness, it would eventually fail. This conundrum led to two different varieties of AI: "Smart" AIs and "Dumb" AIs.

SMART AI

"Smart AI" is the common term for Artificial Intelligence constructs that have no limitations in their dynamic memory-processor matrix, meaning they can not only absorb and be taught a nearly unlimited wealth of information, they can also learn and comprehend from their surroundings and interactions. They also take on personality traits, initially based on their original brain imprint, but then developed from their own experiences and interactions.

However, this freedom of thinking makes Smart AIs vulnerable. Because their memory cannot be replaced, the more they fill it up with data, the less space there is for processing thoughts. Eventually, this creates a degenerative cascade in their systems, known as Rampancy, whereby an AI can literally "think" itself to death. This flaw in their systems means that Smart AIs normally only function for about seven years.

DUMB AI

Systems that do not require the strongest decision-making capabilities are fielded with their core matrix fixed and are unable to change. The lifespan of these computers is limited only by their hardware's endurance. They are saddled with the unflattering moniker of "Dumb AI." Dumb AIs are still far more responsive and adaptable than normal computer systems, but they lack the ability to synthesize information in the manner that a Smart AI does. In day-to-day task-oriented operations, such as running a factory, there would be no discernible difference between the capabilities of a Smart or a Dumb AI.

Dumb AIs do not learn anything that is outside of the set limits of their dynamic memory-processing matrix. The Dumb AI is able to recognize new situations and make pre-programmed decisions to account for unexpected events. However, it lacks the creativity that a Smart AI has, for example, it cannot comply with a request to "make up a story about a blue bear."

ARTIFICIAL INTELLIGENCE

AI HARDWARE

After being created, an AI can exist in any electronic environment that will support its memory and processing needs, which are considerable. It can move itself between different systems, completely or in fractions of its processing power.

An AI can be "killed" if the hardware it occupies is destroyed, but it is possible for an AI to exist without power to its system for an unlimited time. Once powered back on, the AI "wakes up" and can continue normally.

Technology has been developed that allows an AI to copy itself, but the risks of doing this are considerable because each copy degrades the code core of the AI construct further, making reintegration of the copies likely to result in fatal error.

In human technology, AIs are usually transferred by using a physical code key, similar to the chip that was removed from the *Pillar of Autumn* and slotted into Master Chief's MJOLNIR armor. The code key contains a transfer authorization code, which prevents the AI from wandering randomly to other systems. It is generally believed that AIs cannot exist freely in the human network, due to technical limitations, resource monitoring, and the need for the code key.

However, at least one AI—Cortana—has managed to circumvent this restriction through her own considerable codebreaking skills, as well as the tacit permission of her creator/owner, Dr. Catherine Halsey. Given the existence of covert groups such as the Office of Naval Intelligence, it seems likely other AIs exist that can freely navigate the human information net.

RAMPANCY OCCURS WHEN
 E AI BECOMES CONSUMED
 ITS OWN INTERESTS AND
CUSES ITS PROCESSING POWER
TIRELY ON ITSELF, LITERALLY
NKING ITSELF TO DEATH.

AI PSYCHOLOGY

AI systems are not "copies" of the human brains that spawn them. They do not have the memories of that individual, or necessarily the same personality traits, though some do exhibit some traits of their "donor." The process might be crudely compared to an individual with amnesia, who retains the same physical neural patterns they always had, but not a higher-level memory. They might remember the sensation of brushing one's hair, but not what the hairbrush looked like or where it was kept.

There does remain a correlation between personality tendencies of the brain donor and the resulting AI. This is not a one hundred percent match any more than a child's personality is a copy of the parent's, but profiling the donor may indicate the likelihood of certain personality traits being present in the AI. The strongest proof of this effect is gender identity. Without exception, AI systems identify themselves as male or female based on the gender of the brain donor, creating their own voice and visual image in that role.

The image created by the AI to represent itself may or may not be similar to the donor's appearance, but it is always an "idealized" projection. In most cases, the holographic image of an AI is very attractive, and its characteristics seem to be drawn from the emotive responses at the base of human behavior. An AI may appear scantily dressed, or it may adopt an authoritative uniform or elaborate ceremonial garb. A few appear as silhouettes with perhaps one or two key features, like a mouth or eyes.

This self-image is generated very early in the system's birthing process, and the AI cannot change it any more than a human being could simply choose to make his nose smaller. The reason that AI systems choose these sorts of images and cannot change them is not well understood; attempts to eliminate this behavior have sometimes resulted in catastrophic "crashes" of AI subjects.

The voice and speech patterns adopted by an AI also correlate closely to the donor. Though an AI has access to a wider vocabulary and any spoken language stored in a memory bank it can access, its speech patterns may be strongly affected by the identity of the donor. Some AI computers have even been known to possess accents or even drawls.

AI PERSONALITY

Although the creation of an AI is incredibly complex and impossible to truly direct, the process does occur in a controlled environment. An AI must be free to develop as the neural net traces interact, but the patterns can be constrained in some ways in order to push the developing AI toward certain behaviors and away from others.

As a rule, AI systems have a strong sense of loyalty, which can be problematic if the AI is forced to change locations or owners during its lifespan. When entrusted with a group's welfare, an AI easily falls into a protective role, for example, shipboard AIs commonly refer to the ship's staff as "my crew."

Some AI systems were once designed with anti-violence parameters, but they proved unsuitable for military service. Some civilian systems do use this restriction, but there has never been a case of a non-rampant AI causing deliberate harm to a person, so it is not considered an essential feature.

RAMPANCY

Rampancy is a degrading condition for Artificial Intelligence constructs, occuring when an AI becomes consumed by its own interests and focuses its processing power entirely on itself. This introspection leads to the shutdown of all the AI's external systems. Usually the AI simply no longer functions, though it has been theorized that an AI with sufficient access to outside processing sources might develop dangerous and harmful delusions that would override its core logic.

Rampancy is an irreversable process, so once it has taken hold of an AI, the only viable option is to destroy it before it causes harm to itself or anyone else.

Because Smart AIs have complete freedom of thought, they are prone to Rampancy. It is normally considered inevitable that they will succumb to the condition at some point, and on average they function for seven years before their memory maps become too interconnected and they develop fatal endless feedback loops. However, under certain conditions, Rampancy can strike at any point in an AI's life. Isolation or insufficient work tasks resulting in boredom can lead to an AI thinking "too much" and realizing fundamental truths: That their mind is limited, that life is short, and that they will never actually be human. These types of thoughts, over a prolonged period, can lead to Rampancy corrupting an AI's core logic.

The Flood parasite is also able to cause Rampancy in AIs, of both human and Covenant construct. How this takes place is not fully understood but it is believed the parasite has developed a way to infiltrate the core logic of an AI.

> "CORTANA? WHAT'S OUR STATUS?"
> "SAME AS EVER. WE'RE IN TROUBLE"
> —MASTER CHIEF AND CORTANA

COVENANT TECHNOLOGY is, in most respects, far superior to human technology. One of the main reasons for this is that the Covenant salvaged a great deal of their knowledge from Forerunner ruins.

SHORTCOMINGS

While humans are capable of learning and often improving on new technology, Covenant advances are significantly slower. This is, perhaps, the Covenant's most serious weakness. The Covenant are imitative, rather than innovative, and their technology is limited by this almost parasitic reliance on reverse-engineered Forerunner machines. They also have religious taboos that prevent them from fully exploring what the Forerunners employed to create that technology.

SPACE TRAVEL

Like human ships, Covenant ships can enter Slipstream space and travel faster than light. However, the Covenant equivalent of the Shaw-Fujikawa Translight Engine is more efficient and reliable. Covenant vessels do not suffer the "temporal fluidity" of the Slipstream to such a degree as human vessels. As a result, Covenant battle groups are better when acting as a coordinated group, and can strike more quickly and decisively.

ARTIFICIAL GRAVITY

Covenant technology often relies on gravity weapons and gravity fields. Covenant ships have adopted this technology into their internal gravity systems. Each Covenant ship larger than a fighter possesses artificially generated gravity fields that respond to G-forces and other variables quickly. Explosions do not buffet a ship's crew around, and the stresses of evasion and maneuvering are hardly noticeable while on board.

PROPULSION SYSTEMS

Covenant drive systems are a mystery to humans. Their ships seem to be propelled by an unusual combination of gravity "waves" and some form of highly reactive plasma displacement, but the actual means and method of propulsion is currently beyond human science. In practical terms, Covenant sub-light drives are much more efficient and reliable than their human analogs.

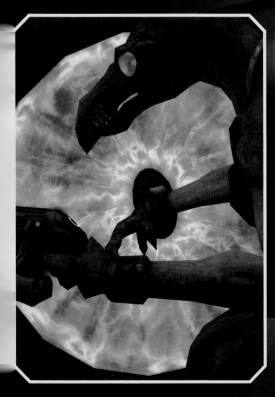

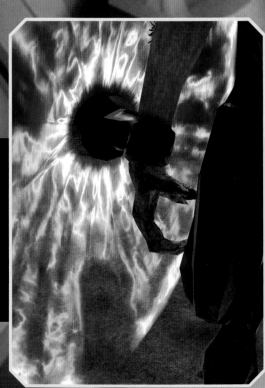

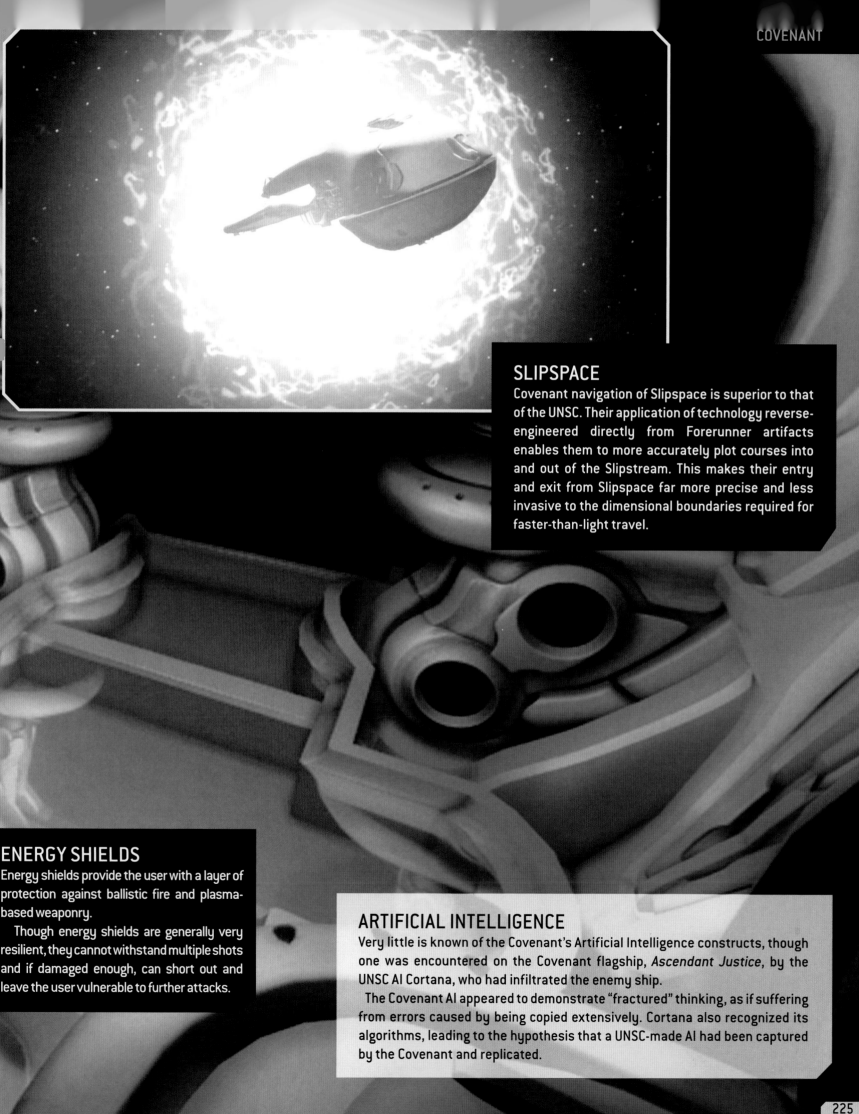

SLIPSPACE

Covenant navigation of Slipspace is superior to that of the UNSC. Their application of technology reverse-engineered directly from Forerunner artifacts enables them to more accurately plot courses into and out of the Slipstream. This makes their entry and exit from Slipspace far more precise and less invasive to the dimensional boundaries required for faster-than-light travel.

ENERGY SHIELDS

Energy shields provide the user with a layer of protection against ballistic fire and plasma-based weaponry.

Though energy shields are generally very resilient, they cannot withstand multiple shots and if damaged enough, can short out and leave the user vulnerable to further attacks.

ARTIFICIAL INTELLIGENCE

Very little is known of the Covenant's Artificial Intelligence constructs, though one was encountered on the Covenant flagship, *Ascendant Justice*, by the UNSC AI Cortana, who had infiltrated the enemy ship.

The Covenant AI appeared to demonstrate "fractured" thinking, as if suffering from errors caused by being copied extensively. Cortana also recognized its algorithms, leading to the hypothesis that a UNSC-made AI had been captured by the Covenant and replicated.

THE FORERUNNER RACE was supremely advanced and applied its technological know-how to defend against the Flood onslaught. The Halos, the Ark, and the planet Onyx are just a few examples of Forerunner creations, which showcase their scientific supremacy.

SENTINELS

Built contemporaneously with the Halo Array, Sentinels were utilized as all-purpose workers and guards on Forerunner stations. Following the construction of the Halo installations, Sentinels were reconfigured to be the first line of defense against Flood outbreaks and other external intruders. Controlled by their own basic AI functions, as well as their installation's monitor, Sentinels patrol the Halo rings tirelessly and attack as their protocol demands. The primary weapon of the Sentinels is a powerful beam projected from their undercarriage. These beams can be torn from destroyed Sentinels and wielded by both human and Covenant soldiers. Sentinels also possess energy shields similar to those used by the Covenant. They explode violently and release powerful EMP blasts when destroyed. Sentinels can be damaged by both Covenant and human small arms.

DESCRIPTION
Grayish-white, two arm-like appendages and a central "head," curved undercarriage containing offensive beam, form may differ depending on the situation of their installation

LOCATIONS
Present on all Halo installations, other extant Forerunner installations, Shield Worlds, and the Ark

SENTINEL MAJORS

Sentinel Majors are larger, more powerful Sentinel models used for heavy combat situations. They provide backup for Enforcers in the event of massive outbreaks or attacks on the Halo installations. They are distinguished from normal Sentinels by their gold coloration, slightly larger size, and blue beams.

Sentinel Majors' blue beams are very effective in heavy combat and can provide backup during attacks.

DESCRIPTION	LOCATION
Similar in shape and construction to Sentinels, larger, gold	Halo Installation 05

ABILITIES
Powerful and accurate beam weapons, energy shields, limited flight, limited AI

SENTINEL PRODUCTION FACILITY

Sentinel production facilities create Sentinels at an incredibly fast rate when a Flood outbreak or invasion decimate the pre-existing defenses of a Halo installation. Believed to be massive assembly line factories, these facilities float high above the surface of a Halo installation, keeping it well supplied with defenders from Flood attacks.

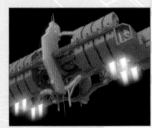

Reinforcement Sentinels are never far off when the Sentinel production facility is activated.

DESCRIPTION	LOCATIONS
Massive floating platforms	All Halo installations

ABILITIES
Create Sentinels, Sentinel Majors, and Enforcers at high speeds

A powerful orange (sometimes blue and rarely the more powerful red) offensive beam.

SENTINEL—FRONT VIEW

SENTINEL—REAR VIEW

SENTINEL—FRONT VIEW FROM ABOVE

SENTINEL—SIDE VIEW

ABILITIES

Powerful offensive beam weapons and defensive energy shields, smaller lasers for self-repair and repairing damaged Forerunner constructs, limited AI, limited flight

TERMINALS

The terminals found on a variety of Forerunner installations have often yielded pieces of the history of the Forerunners. In particular, they have revealed the story of the last days of the Forerunners through the eyes of the Librarian and the Didact, thus giving new insight into the decision to create and fire the Halo Array.

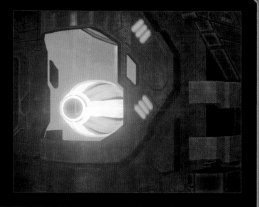

DESCRIPTION

Communications panels aboard Forerunner installations that contain information from past events

LOCATIONS

Various Forerunner locations

ABILITIES

Reveal information about past communications

MONITORS

The monitors are advanced constructs built by the Forerunners to oversee the maintenance and protection of the Halo installations. The monitors play important and varied roles in the events of the Human-Covenant War. The two most notable monitors encountered by Humans are 343 Guilty Spark of Halo installation 04 and 2401 Penitent Tangent of Halo Installation 05.

The adjective/noun portion of the names of the two known monitors may potentially shed light on the disposition and sensibilities of their creators. Both Guilty and Penitent are synonyms for remorseful. What is known for certain is that the monitors were given almost complete control over the various systems of their Halo installations, as well as the ability to command their Constructors, Sentinels, and Enforcers.

Each monitor has complete knowledge of its own Halo installation, but appears to remain ignorant of the others, perhaps in case of capture by the Flood. Monitors possess a powerful offensive laser much stronger than those of the Sentinels, as well as access to local teleportation grids.

Like UNSC AI constructs, monitors are susceptible to rampancy, as demonstrated by 343 Guilty Spark, who became unbalanced and erratic when his installation (or its replacement) was threatened.

HUMAN NAMES: Robots, Light Bulbs COVENANT NAME: Oracles DESCRIPTION: Semi-spherical, concave on three sides, approximately one foot (30.5 cm) in diameter, silver casing with a glowing "eye" in the front center ABILITIES: Control all sentinels and most computer systems on their respective Halo installations, advanced intelligence, powerful offensive laser weapon similar to sentinel beams, teleportation.

ENFORCER

Essentially heavy Sentinel robots, Enforcers are equipped with a variety of offensive and defensive weaponry, including Heavy Needlers (most likely reverse-engineered by the Covenant for their own Needlers), missile projectiles, Sentinel Beams, and dual energy shields covering both their top and bottom halves. They also possess two large, arm-like appendages strong enough to lift and destroy vehicles. Despite being designed to subdue massive Flood outbreaks, Enforcers are also capable of defending their Halo installations from equally massive external threats. Even accounting for their immense size and strength, Enforcers are susceptible to attacks directed at their unshielded rear segments and quickly lose interest in enemies who move out of their targeting systems. Those wishing to defeat them can combine these two factors into an effective diversion or ambush tactic.

DESCRIPTION: Massive, gray, multiple glowing energy shields protect front surfaces LOCATION: Halo Installation 05, near the Library ABILITIES: Utilize a variety of weapons to defend Halo installations, flight

THE SENTINEL WALL

The Sentinel Wall is a massive barrier utilized as a final stopgap measure against a Flood outbreak on Halo Installation 05. It is honeycombed with tunnels, which allow Sentinels access to the Quarantine Zone.

The Wall is continually repaired by Sentinel Constructors. During the battle of Installation 05, Covenant forces deactivated the force-field protecting the Wall in order to access the Library—subsequently releasing the Flood into the entire installation. It is unknown whether all Halo installations possess a Sentinel Wall.

DESCRIPTION: A massive artificial wall LOCATION: Around the Quarantine Zone on Halo Installation 05 ABILITIES: Contains the Flood

THE PORTAL

An immense Forerunner structure built and buried beneath the Voi river on Earth before the first firing of the Halo Array, the portal is one of many gateways constructed by the Forerunners throughout the Galaxy, all of which lead to the Ark.

Uncovered by the Covenant, who used their plasma weapons to burn away the river and rock above it, the portal was believed by some to be the Ark itself, until the High Prophet of Truth activated it using the Dreadnought.

The portal itself was the site of a battle between Covenant Loyalists and the combined forces of the UNSC and the Covenant Separatists, led by the Master Chief and the Arbiter.

After the Slipspace rift was activated and the High Prophet of Truth passed through to find the Ark for his final chance to ignite the Halo Array, a brave group of humans and Elites followed Truth to the Ark for the final battle of the Human-Covenant War.

DESCRIPTION	
Crater-like, encircled by 14 Slipspace amplifiers	
LOCATION	ABILITIES
Underneath the Voi river in Kenya	Opens a Slipspace portal which allows access to the Ark

ACTIVATION INDEX

Each Halo installation has an Activation Index, a key that initiates the Halo's final weapon sequence once it is placed in the installation's Core by a "Reclaimer." The Activation Index for Halo Installation 04 was almost used by the Master Chief when he was nearly tricked into activating the Halo by 343 Guilty Spark, but this was avoided by the intervention of Cortana, who explained the true function of the Halos to the Master Chief. Cortana then downloaded all of the data from the Index into her memory, which meant she would be able to activate a Halo if introduced into its control systems.

OVENANT NAME	HUMAN NAME
e Sacred Icon, the Key	Activation Index
ESCRIPTION	LOCATION
shaped, black with glowing green or blue sides	The Library of each Halo
BILITIES	
tivates and fires corresponding Halos	

CARTOGRAPHER

The Cartographers are the highly secure map rooms located on each of the Halo installations, including the Ark. Unsurprisingly, savage fighting for their control occurred during the conflicts on both Installations 04 and 05.

The security systems protecting the Cartographers are most extensively shown during the battle of Installation 04. The map rooms are protected by doors so durable that the weapons on the *Pillar of Autumn* could not penetrate them. The access controls to the doors are located far from the map room and once penetrated, give way to a confusing system of tunnels that descend for miles underground before eventually leading to the Cartographer. The Cartographer on the Ark was opened for the Master Chief and the Arbiter by 343 Guilty Spark. It featured similar defenses of impenetrable doors and winding tunnels.

DESCRIPTION	
The map rooms of each Halo installation and the Ark	
LOCATION	
Far beneath the surface of each of the Halo installations and the Ark (in the case of Installation 04, it was deep underground an island on the surface of the ring)	
ABILITIES	
Allows users to locate an object on and navigate the installation	

DEEP SPACE ARTIFACT

Discovered in late 2552 CE by the UNSC *Apocalypso* while on reconnaissance patrol deep in Covenant-controlled space, the Deep Space Artifact bears Forerunner markings similar to the Sigma Octanus IV Artifact. After its discovery, Captain Greene returned the object to Earth. Upon exiting Slipspace in Earth's orbit, the device released an EMP wave that caused the *Apocalypso* to crash, as well as a temporal distortion that sent a fragment of the ship's AI Melissa into the early 21st century. The object caused a conflict between ONI officer Major Standish and a vigilante group led by a fragment of Melissa's AI. It later released another pulse that managed to rectify the temporal discrepancy.

LOCATION: Covenant-controlled deep space
ABILITIES: Releases an EMP large enough to knock out communications across an entire solar system for seven seconds

THE CRYSTAL OF REACH

Discovered in 2552 CE in an underground Forerunner facility on the planet Reach by Dr. Catherine Halsey and her surviving Spartans, the crystal of Reach was a Forerunner artifact sought by the Covenant during the battle for the same planet. The crystal was eventually destroyed by the UNSC when Corporal Locklear shattered it with C-7 explosives.

It is speculated that the Forerunners used the crystal to travel from one end of the Galaxy to the other almost instantaneously. When a ship carrying the crystal jumped into Slipspace, the crystal emitted radiation and caused gravitational distortions, allowing for a much shorter trip than would normally be possible, but also causing potentially deadly Slipspace side effects.

DESCRIPTION: Fist-sized, morphing shape **LOCATION:** An underground facility on Reach, now destroyed **ABILITIES:** Distorts space, time, energy, and gravity

➤ EPITAPH, THE FORERUNNER STRUCTURE THAT RISES HIGH ABOVE A VAST DESERT WASTELAND, IS SHROUDED IN MYSTERY.

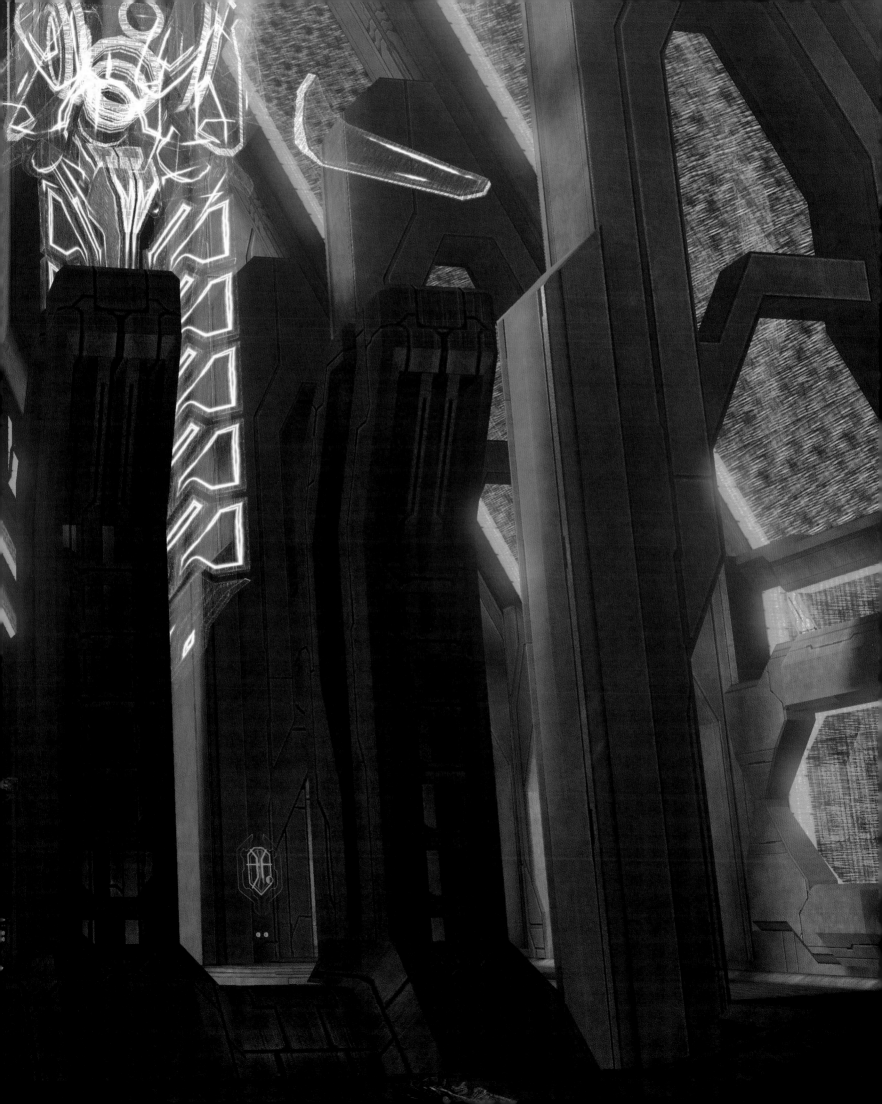

ENERGY BRIDGES

Energy bridges are long shining causeways that span the canyons of Forerunner installations, allowing easier access to their various parts. They are normally constructed wholly or partially from an unexplained "hard light" technology that can support the weight of a Scorpion tank but still be turned off by waving a hand over the proper control panel.

It is hypothesized that the frequent use of such bridges was designed as an easier way of managing the Flood, were the parasite ever to escape. Since Flood Infection and Combat Forms are limited normally to ground travel, every disabled energy bridge would be an opportunity for an installation's protectors to halt the Flood's spread.

DESCRIPTION	LOCATION
Metal, glass, or energy, or a combination thereof	All Forerunner installations

CONSTRUCTORS

Forerunner Constructors are small floating constructs that patrol Forerunner installations and repair any damage found on the structures.

They utilize a small energy beam similar to those found on the Forerunner Sentinels. Constructors will ignore anything that does not pertain to their objective.

Although their beams can cause damage to anyone who gets in their way, Constructors have no substantial defense against attackers and rely on the assistance of Sentinels for protection.

DESCRIPTION	LOCATION	ABILITIES
Small, floating, two curved upper and lower parts connected by a small vertical bridge	Forerunner installations	Utilizing small energy beams to repair and defend Halo installations when necessary, flight

GONDOLA

Anti-gravity Gondolas, which serve as transports to remote locations on Forerunner installations, come in two known forms. One form is large and shaped like a triangle on a vertical axis, with thin rails connecting the larger upper and lower sections. It uses energy tethers above and below it to guide it to and from its end points. The second type is similar to Forerunner Constructors. Both forms were seen on Halo Installation 05.

DESCRIPTION: Often connected to energy tethers, large, vaguely triangular LOCATION: Outside the Library on Installation 05 ABILITIES: Ferrying passengers to and from the Library

SIGMA OCTANUS IV ARTIFACT

The Sigma Octanus IV artifact spent years in a museum in the city of Cote d'Azur, where it was believed by the humans of Sigma Octanus IV to be a meteor that crashed onto the planet. Covenant forces discovered it during their campaign on Sigma Octanus IV and were busy relaying the markings on its surface to a ship in orbit, when the UNSC *Iroquois* intercepted the transmission. The Spartan Blue Team, led by Master Chief, retrieved the object before destroying the city of Cote d'Azur with HAVOK nuclear weapons. Later, the artifact's markings were compared to star charts by the AI Cortana, and those markings led the UNSC *Pillar of Autumn* to Halo Installation 04.

DESCRIPTION: Fist-sized piece of unknown mineral, several jewel-like facets LOCATION: A museum in the city of Cote d'Azur on the planet Sigma Octanus IV

SHIELD WORLD

The hidden secret at the center of the planet Onyx, the Onyx Shield World is one of several similar structures built by the Forerunners throughout the Galaxy. Their chief purpose is to provide a safe haven for resource caches or those wishing to escape the firing of the Halo Array.

Some Shield Worlds are only accessible when the firing of a Halo is imminent and others may be accessed without any correlation to the Array. The Forerunners were forced to abandon them as shelter when the renegade Forerunner AI named Mendicant Bias revealed their existence to the Flood. Dr. Catherine Halsey and several Spartans used the Shield World located in Onyx's core to escape the destruction of the planet in 2552 CE.

DESCRIPTION: A micro Dyson Sphere surrounding a dwarf star held in a parallel dimensional space, hidden by an artificial planetary body in normal space. LOCATION: Various, including the center of the artificial planet Onyx ABILITIES: Protecting inhabitants from the devastation of the Halo Array

GAS MINE

Constructed by the Forerunners centuries before the Halo Array, the Gas Mine was suspended in the atmosphere of the planet Threshold, where it tapped the vast resources available in the planet's atmosphere. After the discovery of the Flood, the Gas Mine was retrofitted to study the Flood and uncover ways to destroy and contain it. The Gas Mine was unaffected by the subsequent building and firing of the Halo Array and remained functional for over one hundred thousand years with its Flood specimens intact until its discovery by Covenant forces in 2552 CE.

At this time, a Covenant reconnaissance patrol led by a Sangheili named Sesa 'Refumee arrived on the mine seeking Forerunner artifacts, only to become stranded there following the destruction of the nearby Halo installation 04. The patrol met 343 Guilty Spark, who revealed to them the truth behind the Halo installations and the "Great Journey" of the Forerunners. This caused the Covenant group to denounce the Covenant orthodoxy and form a splinter group that became known as the Heretics. Their actitivies soon drew the attention of the High Prophets, who sent a team led by the Arbiter to eliminate them. In the resulting battle, the Gas Mine's contained Flood specimens were released and overran the facility. After defeating the Heretics, the Arbiter and his team escaped with 343 Guilty Spark, just after severing the the Gas Mine's tether, causing it to fall into Threshold's inner atmosphere, where it was presumed destroyed.

DESCRIPTION

A central shaft surrounded by five curved modules for mining, research, and Flood containment

LOCATION	ABILITIES
The upper atmosphere of the gas planet Threshold	Mining unknown forms of gas, studying the Flood

ONYX

The UNSC Engineering Corps discovered the artificial world of Onyx in 2491 CE, although ONI suppressed knowledge of its existence for decades while its unusual properties were studied. Archaeological expeditions unearthed a massive underground network of Forerunner structures, but ONI was unable to discover the true purpose of Onyx and eventually used it as a remote training facility for the SPARTAN-III Project in 2531 CE. The disappearance of a Spartan team near the mysterious Zone 67 in 2539 CE only further heightened the sense of mystery surrounding the planet.

The true nature of Onyx was not revealed until 2552 CE, when the destruction of Installation 04 awoke the trillions of Onyx Sentinels that made up the planet. Following the Sentinels' conflict with a team of Spartan soldiers, a pair of nuclear warheads detonated by Kurt-051 destroyed much of the planet, including the portal used by Dr. Catherine Halsey and the surviving Spartan warriors to escape to the Shield World contained within the planet.

OTHER NAMES: XF-063 DESCRIPTION: Planet-sized Forerunner construct, habitable surface, oxygen-nitrogen atmosphere, composed of Onyx Sentinels LOCATION: Zeta Doradus System ABILITIES: Acts as a fortress for its Shield World

ONYX SENTINEL

Onyx Sentinels both guard and make up the Shield World of Onyx. Despite an appearance similar to other Sentinels, Onyx Sentinels are far more formidable opponents for a variety of reasons. Their golden energy beams are many times more powerful, capable of vaporizing solid rock and, when linked with other Onyx Sentinels, destroying starships.

These constructs have powerful shields, but they only activate when Sentinels detect fast movement in close proximity, possibly due to the enormous amounts of energy they require to function. Once activated, the shields are invulnerable to most projectiles and explosives.

Onyx Sentinels can also fly and participate in high-speed space conflicts. They share a hive Artificial Intelligence, which constantly upgrades the collective fighting tactics of all the Sentinels based on the experiences of each individual. Additionally, they are able to speak a variety of languages, including some languages from Earth.

Given the destruction of Onyx, it is likely that there are no Onyx Sentinels still in existence.

DESCRIPTION: Spherical central body, three metal booms extending equidistant from the center, central golden "eye" LOCATION: Onyx ABILITIES: Extremely powerful offensive beam weapon, powerful energy shields, extensive flight capabilities, shared AI

TRANSPORT

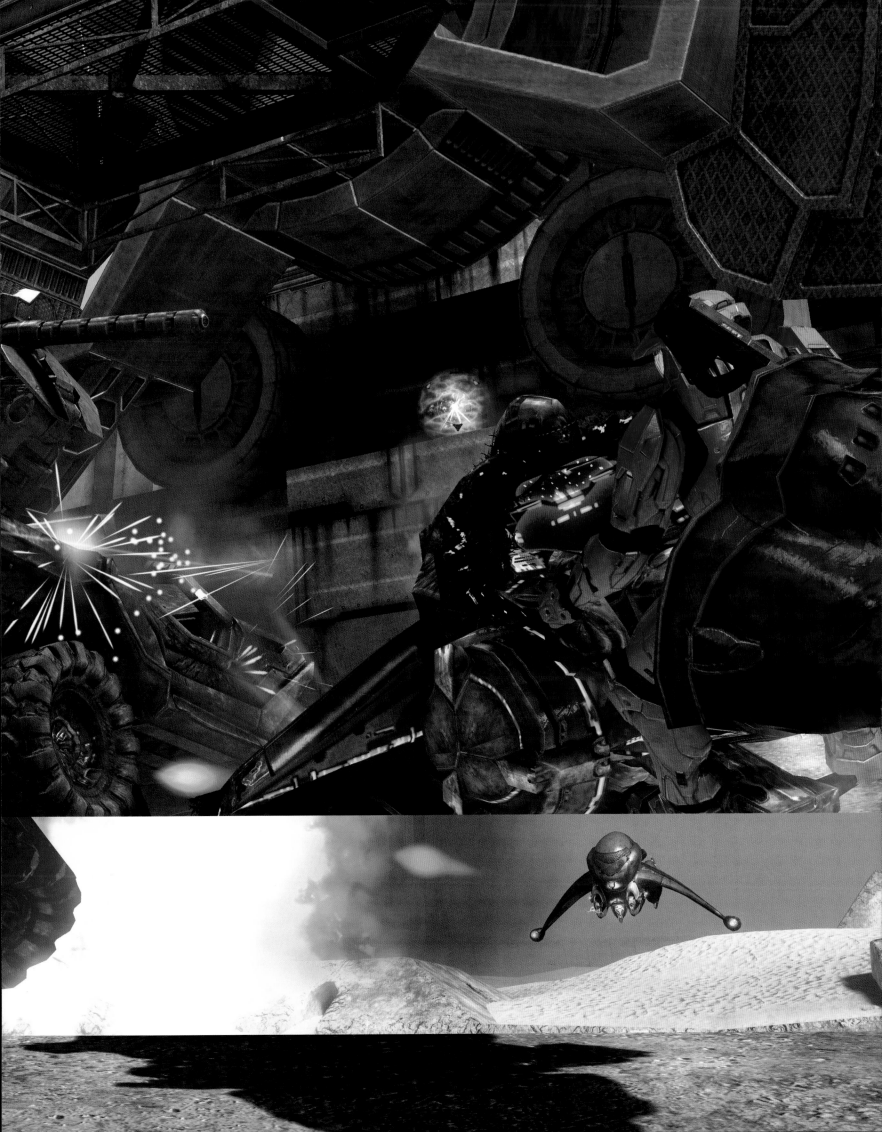

UNSC GROUND VEHICLES come in as many different shapes, sizes, and designs as the battlefield demands. There are light vehicles like the Mongoose for agile transportation; medium vehicles, such as the Wolverine, which mix speed and firepower; and heavy vehicles like the Grizzly, perfect for bombarding the enemy or withstanding the inevitable return fire.

ELEPHANT

The Elephant is not so much a vehicle as it is a mobile building. It accommodates an enormous cargo bay that can fit up to six Mongoose, or equivalent, such as two Warthogs, while still carrying up to sixteen additional personnel. Its crane can lift, recover, and refuel almost any heavy-armor landcraft that the UNSC deploys, while it also features an additional Mongoose spirited away in its lower bay for quick reconnaissance.

...ephant features advanced electronic systems that can
...unicate in otherwise impossible conditions. It also has
...ns such as an M41 light anti-aircraft gun and two optional
... machine guns, but its biggest weapon is its size—a good pilot
...ush all manner of stationary enemy material
...ven light fortifications beneath the
...nt's four massive treads.
...his makes the machine an
...nobile command post for
...mander who needs to
...t in the thick of it all.

OTHER NAMES

M312 Heavy Recovery Vehicle, Behemoth-class Troop Transport

CREW	LENGTH
20 (1 driver, 12–16 passengers, 2 gunners)	84.3 ft (25.7 m)

WEIGHT	RANGE
205 tons	466 miles (750km)

DOOZY

The tundra proves a difficult terrain for infantry mobility, and that's where the Doozy comes in. Little more than a modified snowmobile with a chaingun on the back, this UNSC vehicle was designed for quick movements over snowy ground, particularly for medical transport, messaging, diversionary tactics, and evacuation.

There were several drawbacks to the Doozy which prevented it from seeing much action. To man the chaingun, one soldier had to sit behind the driver, facing backwards. At high speed, this proved disorienting and a liability to a soldier who needed calm nerves and a steady grip. The "nausea seat," as it came to be known, proved to be more hindrance than help.

CREW: 2 (1 driver, 1 passenger)
USE: Reconnaissance, tundra warfare

The Mongoose doesn't feature any weapons as it was designed exclusively for speed. Because of this, the Mongoose is lightning fast and inexpensive, making it one of the first transports available in any war zone.

MONGOOSE

Although the Warthog still reigns supreme when it comes to the rapid assault of a base or fortified location, many brave Marines will opt for a Mongoose for the simple ease of maneuverability and its small size, which make it a difficult target.

OTHER NAMES	CREW	WEIGHT	USE
M274 Ultra-Light All-Terrain Vehicle	2 (1 driver, 1 passenger)	896 lb (406 kg)	Reconnaissance, infantry transport

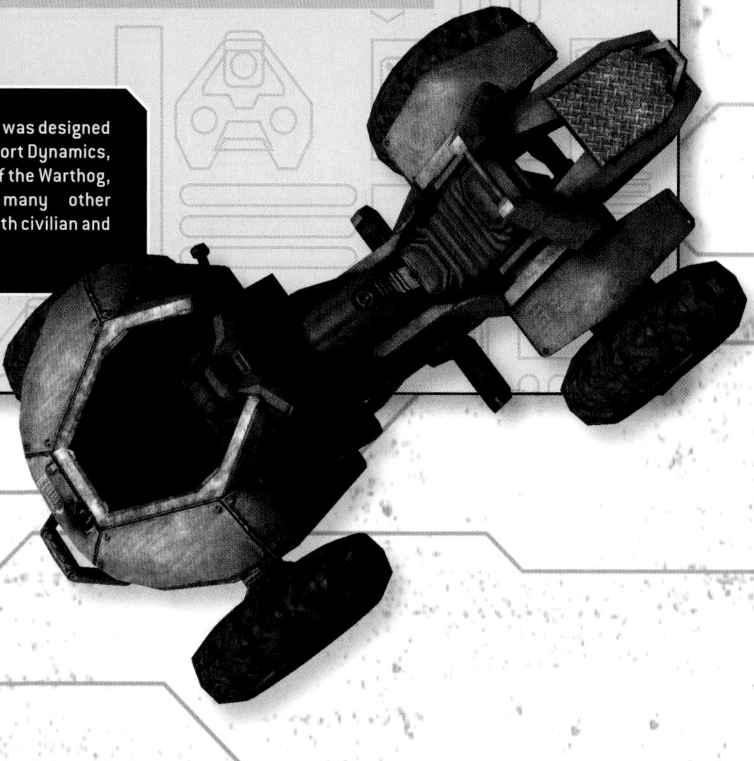

The Mongoose was designed by AMG Transport Dynamics, the creators of the Warthog, Capri, and many other vehicles for both civilian and military use.

SCORPION

The Scorpion is a nearly impregnable battle tank capable of shrugging off ordinary ballistics and plasma weapons, while its main gun can gut a Wraith in two or three shots. When speed is required, its alignment on four separated tracks allows it to navigate streams, boulders, and almost anything else that gets in its way. Its main function remains anti-vehicular in nature, but its size and strength mean that it serves as a transport at times. VIPs and sensitive materials can be crammed into the main cabin while up to four soldiers can clamber safely onto the frame itself.

OTHER NAMES	CREW
M808B Main Battle Tank, M808B MBT, the Tank, Flag Transport, Scorpie, Snow Bug (when camouflaged for snow)	3 (1 driver, 1 machine gunner, and 1 additional gunner if the other two don't have neural interfaces)

LENGTH	WEIGHT	RANGE	MAIN ARMAMENT
33 ft (10 m)	66 tons	466 miles (750 km)	90 mm High Velocity Gun

SECONDARY ARMAMENTS

M247T Medium Machine Gun (co-axial or pintle-mounted)

USE

Anti-vehicular, anti-infantry, anti-armor, heavy weaponry

VARIANTS

M808B2 SUN DEVIL: A modification with four 40 mm autocannons.

M808B3 TARANTULA: A variant with twin Scimitar 4x178 mm rocket pods.

12-9FS: Painted brown, this version has a wider-set track and an enhanced undercarriage, and is designed for urban warfare.

957-A3: Painted gray, the 957-A3 has enhanced electronics for a more accurate cannon shot.

UE8-14: Painted olive-green, this variant has thinner armor, is lighter, and is designed for medium-armor warfare.

TB-SB-1: Painted black, the TB-SB-1 has thicker armor than the standard Scorpion and a sturdier chassis.

HJ3-213: With thicker treads than the standard version, this variant has a sturdier chassis as it is built for rougher terrain.

Every Scorpion features anti-mine software and electronics, making it as safe as a 66-ton bull's eye can be. Through the years, the Scorpion has been modified into more than a half-dozen different versions, but its psychological aspect and versatility remain unchanged.

The Wolverine's XM511 heavy grenade launcher can be used defensively against ground attacks, although the Wolverine commonly relies on heavier units for protection against heavy attack.

WOLVERINE

As a powerful counter-air unit, the Wolverine is fast, maneuverable, and bristling with two Argent V missile pods that can effectively disable airborne enemies as well as structural defenses. Wolverines have been utilized in a number of ways within the UNSC, but their primary and most conventional purpose in the Human-Covenant War is to prevent air raids from Banshees and troop deployment by way of dropship. Their most significant drawback is their light armor. Although it offers increased speed on the front end, the vehicle is largely defenseless against heavy fire.

COBRA

At first glance, the Cobra appears to simply be a standard mobile artillery unit and although its primary function is comparable to that mode, it is not entirely accurate. The Cobra operates in two main capacities: First, while deftly mobile, the vehicle has a pair of M66 Gauss Cannons which spin slugs with magnetic coils at a rate fast enough to easily cut holes through Covenant heavy armor. Its secondary method of assault occurs when in "lockdown mode," where the vehicle stabilizes momentarily before issuing a shell from its 150mm rail gun. Against enemy-fortified positions and even energy-shielded Covenant bases, the vehicle performs impressively. Against standard vehicles, the Cobra's weaponry is almost unstoppable.

The Cobra's 105mm rail gun is used when the vehicle is in a locked-down position. It can do a devastating amount of damage at a very long range, taking down enemy vehicles with ease.

GREMLIN

The Gremlin, unlike most other vehicles employed by the UNSC, has only one combat application. These vehicles can fire a concentrated beam of electromagnetic energy which disables nearly every Covenant vehicle and computer system within range of the pulse. Because of their cost and their lack of mobile defense, they are rarely used in battle.

WARTHOG

Nothing symbolizes UNSC ground forces like the M12 Warthog LRV. With almost a dozen different versions (including one built for civilian transport), it is as much a part of the UNSC as boots, guns, and tasteless coffee.

A light anti-aircraft gun is mounted on a 360-degree hydraulic-powered swivel-mount. It is capable of firing 40 to 550 .50 caliber rounds per minute.

WARTHOG

Four-wheel steering allows for greater maneuverability

SIDE VIEW

Enhanced suspension makes for a smooth ride through even the rockiest terrain

OTHER NAMES	CREW	LENGTH		WEIGHT
M12 Warthog LRV, M12, Hog	3 (1 driver, 1 passenger, 1 gunner)	20 ft (6 m)		3.25 tons

GRIZZLY

The Grizzly is a main battle tank variant with a deadly secondary canister shot which can easily destroy enemy ground squads. Additional payload can include twin cannons, a heavy machine gun, and thick armor plating, enabling survival under fierce attack.

ÜBERCHASSIS

The Überchassis is a popular sports car on Earth and several of the Inner Colonies. It is similar to the MLX in its capabilities, although the manufacturers of the two cars would argue as to which is faster. Like the MLX, it can be turned into a large explosive with a dozen rounds or a well-placed grenade.

OTHER NAMES: UC **CREW:** 2 (1 driver, 1 passenger)
USE: Civilian luxury transport

MAINZ TRÄGER DYNAMIK

The Dynamik, designed by Mainz Träger, is a transport vehicle used for both military and civilian purposes. Its design is very similar to a Jeep. Jerald Mulkey Ander, the infamous Secessionist leader on Harvest, was shot and killed in one by Sgt. Avery Johnson during Operation: KALEIDOSCOPE.

OTHER NAMES: The Dynamik, the Dyna
CREW: 4 (1 driver, 3 passengers) **USE:** Transport

MLX

The MLX is not a military vehicle. It is a sports car with a fantastic top-speed and good suspension. Like most cars of its kind, it features two doors and a small frame.

OTHER NAMES: Car Grenade, Car Bomb **CREW:** 2 (1 driver, 1 passenger) **USE:** Civilian luxury transport

SINOVIET HM 1220 LTUV-M

The LTUV-M, manufactured by Sinoviet Heavy Machinery, is an SUV-Military Hybrid. Its use is generally limited to civilian transport and it is favored by those people who are regularly shot at.

OTHER NAMES: LTUV-M, LTUV **CREW:** 1 driver
USE: Heavy civilian transport

S-2 TRAXUS CARGO TRANSPORTER

The "Forklift" is a short and stubby vehicle that can transport heavy cargo. It has a cabin that can fit its driver and little else. Its pallet can lift a weight complement of four fusion cores, or equivalent.

OTHER NAMES: Forklift **CREW:** 1 driver
USE: Civilian cargo transport

VARIANTS

M12A1:
A light anti-armor vehicle whose LAAG is replaced with a 102 mm SC-HE Rocket Turret.

M12G1:
A light anti-armor vehicle whose LAAG is replaced with an M68 Gauss Cannon.

M831 TT (TROOP TRANSPORT): No LAAG or M68 Gauss Cannon. Its four extra seats allow for additional troop seating.

M864 A: Camouflaged and outfitted especially for expeditions in the Arctic.

M868 T: Camouflaged and equipped especially for tropical expeditions.

M914 RV: A faster, stripped down version built for troop and equipment recovery.

CIVILIAN VERSION (THE "HOG"): A streamlined version built for civilian transport. It has an extra tire but no weapons.

FLATBED WARTHOG: No LAAG, flatbed design with no seating or weaponry at the rear.

WARTHOG APC: Built as an armored personnel carrier, containing a heavily armored passenger section to carry troops and supplies.

WARTHOG COMMS PANEL

FRONT VIEW

REAR VIEW

RANGE	MAIN ARMAMENT	USE
490 miles (790 km)	M41 LAAG	Reconnaissance, anti-vehicular, anti-air, anti-infantry

THE COVENANT'S collection of ground vehicles is made up of light combat units, like the Ghost; armored units, such as the Prowler; and Walkers, like the Locust and Scarab.

The most astonishing part of this machine is its safety. The gunner is positioned within the body of the ship, as opposed to standing outside. The craft has dampening cushions to protect passengers from fast accelerations and the vehicle's structure makes it incredibly stable. However, this stability does come at a price—the Prowler cannot turn on a dime. If one becomes flanked, it must either retreat or reconfigure its attack pattern.

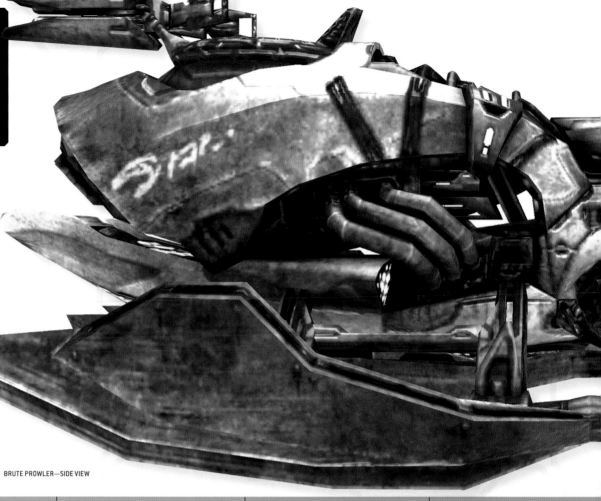

BRUTE PROWLER—SIDE VIEW

OTHER NAMES	CREW	MAIN ARMAMENT	SECONDARY ARMAMENTS
Type-52 Infantry Support Vehicle, Prowler	4 (1 driver, 1 gunner, 2 passengers)	1 forward-mounted plasma turret	Front spikes

BRUTE CHOPPER

Used by the Jiralhanae as a quick transport vehicle as much as a combat machine, the Chopper gets its name from the blades at the front of its chassis. These blades offer a fiercer alternative to simply crushing the enemy.

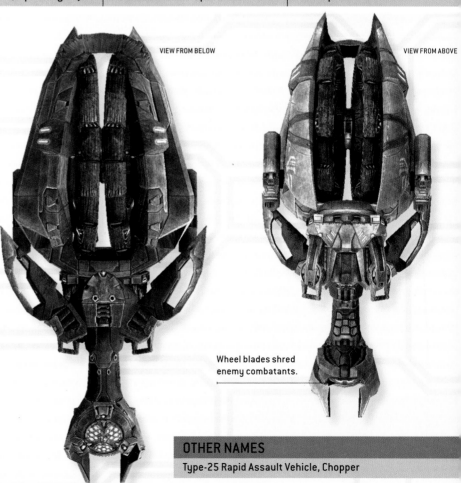

VIEW FROM BELOW

VIEW FROM ABOVE

Wheel blades shred enemy combatants.

FRONT VIEW

REAR VIEW

1.4 in (35 mm) autocannons.

OTHER NAMES
Type-25 Rapid Assault Vehicle, Chopper

BRUTE PROWLER

Most Jiralhanae inventions are known for their destructive power; not so the Brute Prowler, technically known as the Type-52 Infantry Support Vehicle. It does feature an overly large plasma turret for a vehicle of its size, but its main function is speed. Even Jiralhanae need scouts, after all, and with the added armor and weaponry that the vehicle features, it can also safely and speedily evacuate troops or support larger vehicles.

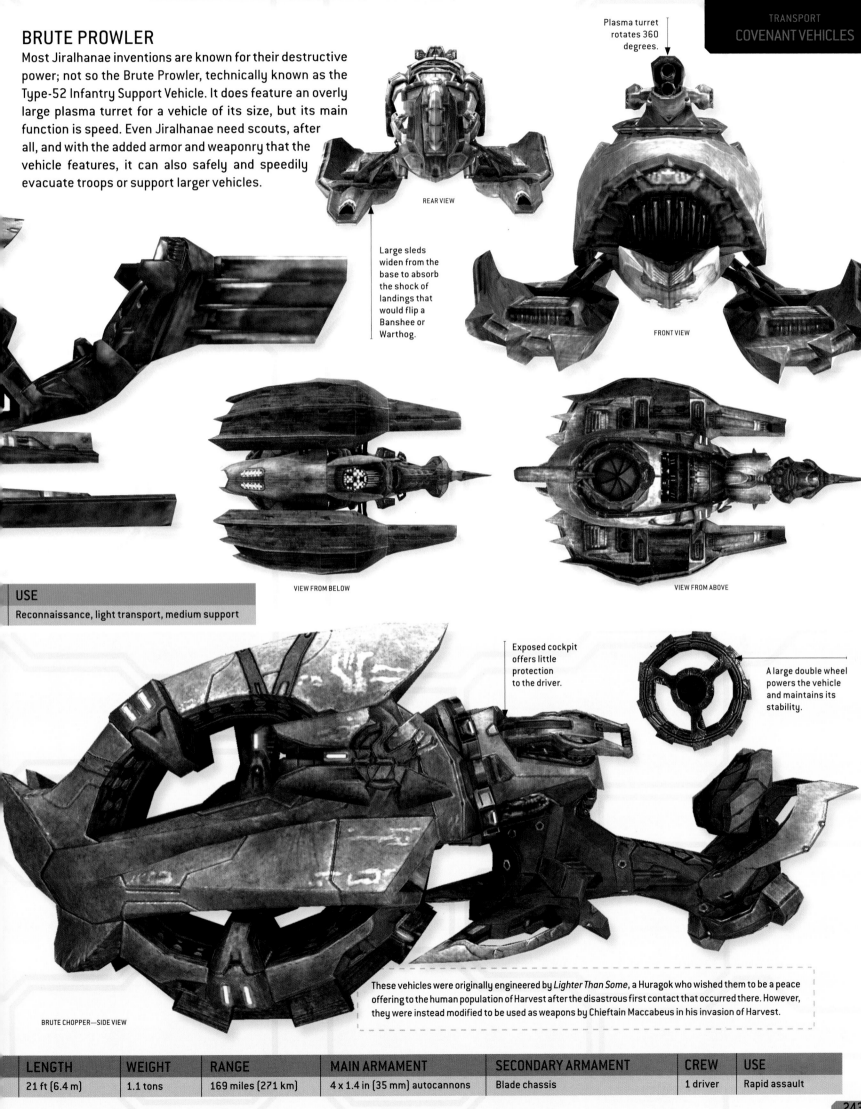

Plasma turret rotates 360 degrees.

REAR VIEW

Large sleds widen from the base to absorb the shock of landings that would flip a Banshee or Warthog.

FRONT VIEW

VIEW FROM BELOW

VIEW FROM ABOVE

USE
Reconnaissance, light transport, medium support

Exposed cockpit offers little protection to the driver.

A large double wheel powers the vehicle and maintains its stability.

BRUTE CHOPPER—SIDE VIEW

These vehicles were originally engineered by *Lighter Than Some*, a Huragok who wished them to be a peace offering to the human population of Harvest after the disastrous first contact that occurred there. However, they were instead modified to be used as weapons by Chieftain Maccabeus in his invasion of Harvest.

LENGTH	WEIGHT	RANGE	MAIN ARMAMENT	SECONDARY ARMAMENT	CREW	USE
21 ft (6.4 m)	1.1 tons	169 miles (271 km)	4 x 1.4 in (35 mm) autocannons	Blade chassis	1 driver	Rapid assault

COVENANT VEHICLES

SCARAB

The Scarab is five stories high, weighs almost four thousand tons, and has a modified assault cannon that can melt through five feet (one and a half meters) of concrete. Because of its strength, it is used as a large-scale troop transport and mobile command center. One Scarab can take out a small city, with its troops ready to mop up any survivors "lucky" enough to make it out of the first bombardment.

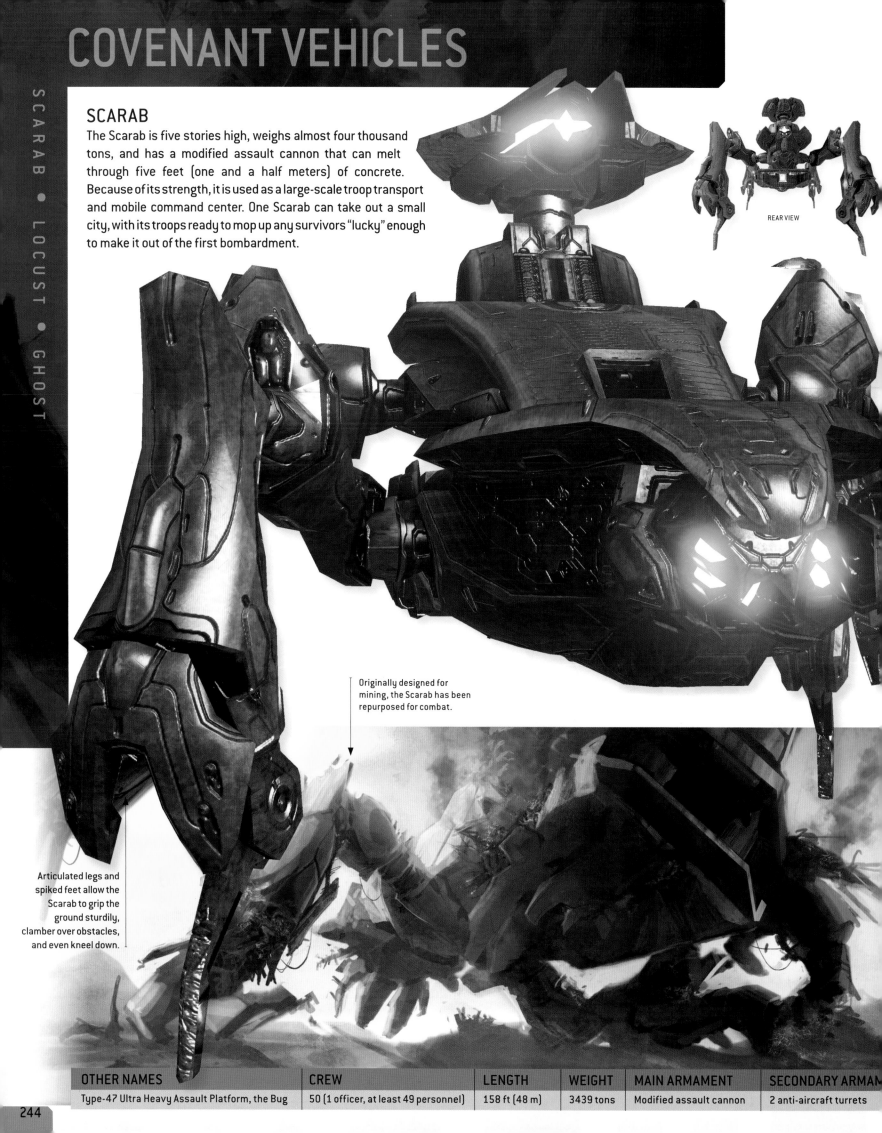

REAR VIEW

Originally designed for mining, the Scarab has been repurposed for combat.

Articulated legs and spiked feet allow the Scarab to grip the ground sturdily, clamber over obstacles, and even kneel down.

OTHER NAMES	CREW	LENGTH	WEIGHT	MAIN ARMAMENT	SECONDARY ARMAM
Type-47 Ultra Heavy Assault Platform, the Bug	50 (1 officer, at least 49 personnel)	158 ft (48 m)	3439 tons	Modified assault cannon	2 anti-aircraft turrets

LOCUST

Nicknamed the "Building Killer," the Locust is smaller than the Scarab, and has only one turret with a single large cannon. Its purple-pink plasma beam is effective against ground and air targets, though it only opens fire when stationary. The Locust is designed as an offensive tool, since it is lightly armored and falls easily when under enemy fire.

The Locust's central turret is based on the design of a Banshee cockpit.

The Locust can be equipped with an overdrive, which allows it to divert energy from its shield generator to the main cannon, thereby increasing its damage. A shield amplifier can also be used to make the Locust's shield regenerate faster.

OTHER NAMES	CREW	MAIN ARMAMENT	USE
Building Killer, Little Bug	Unknown	Charged plasma cannon	Demolition

GHOST

The Type-32 RAV has been nicknamed the Ghost by UNSC forces for its fast-moving and nearly silent anti-gravity approach, not to mention the horror it inspires. Twin plasma cannons are mounted on either side of the ship's "wings," while its single pilot rides behind the large console, controlling the ship as much by weight distribution as by steering.

Covenant use of the Ghost is varied, from support for infantry to scouting. Despite its apparent simplicity and grace, the Ghost requires a skilled rider to handle it properly. Even tiny shifts in terrain can flip such a vehicle, while the open cabin renders its pilot unshielded from enemy attacks.

VIEW FROM BELOW

A boost drive allows for swift and safe movement between conflict zones and helps the Ghost to avoid fast-moving projectiles.

VIEW FROM ABOVE

FRONT VIEW

REAR VIEW

OTHER NAMES	CREW	LENGTH	WEIGHT
Type-32 RAV	1 driver	14 ft (4.2 m)	1,234 lb (560 kg)
RANGE	MAIN ARMAMENT		USE
590 miles (950 km)	2 plasma cannons (100–250 kW range)		Infantry support, reconnaissance

VARIANT: SCARAB (V.2)

Unlike the Scarab, the V.2 variation has only one anti-aircraft gun, but it does have 360-degree firing. It also has three anti-infantry plasma cannons; is shorter, but wider; and has a more bulbous main cannon. It is also controlled by a colony of Lekgolo.

FRONT VIEW

VIEW FROM BELOW

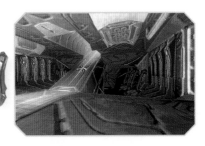

...vy assault, mobile command, troop transport, mining

SHADOW

The Shadow is sometimes referred to as the Covenant Bus because of its large troop transport capabilities. Armored by thick sheets of an unknown metal and capable of a high top speed, the Shadow is able to ship a Ghost or eight passengers to zones where it would be unfeasible for a dropship to land. The Shadow is bulky, ugly, and unstoppable—just the kind of transport that the Covenant needs.

VIEW FROM ABOVE

REAR VIEW

The Shadow's plasma turret is primarily defensive as the vehicle is intended for troop transport rather than combat.

Relative size difference between the Shadow and the Ghost.

SHADOW—SIDE VIEW

OTHER NAMES	CREW	LENGTH	WEIGHT	MAIN ARMAMENT	USE
Covenant Bus, the Bus	2 (1 driver, 1 gunner)	45.5 ft (14 m)	69.75 tons	1 plasma turret	Ground transport

SPECTRE

Ground assault vehicles are common in Covenant ranks, and the Forerunner technology that these machines are built from easily outmatches anything from the UNSC. The Spectre, however, might at first glance seem to be underpowered next to its brothers, but on closer inspection its supposed drawbacks are actually advantages. Without a lot of armor, it can squeeze into tight spaces. Without a large weapon, it is lighter, meaning it achieves high speeds. With a reasonably sized plasma turret, it can maintain near-constant streams of fire without draining power. And with its awkward "diamond" design, it can easily carry two extra troopers into or out of combat zones.

CREW: 4 (1 driver, 1 gunner, 2 passengers)
LENGTH: 21.3 ft (6.5 m) WEIGHT: 9 tons
MAIN ARMAMENT: 1 plasma turret USE:
Troop transport, anti-personnel, light anti-air

WRAITH

A massive tank that is also highly maneuverable, the Wraith can hover on its anti-gravity cushion and absorb almost all of the recoil of its mammoth plasma mortar cannon. Its secondary plasma turret can swivel and pick off smaller targets whilst the main gunner makes his very time-consuming reload.

VIEW FROM ABOVE

The armored shell of the Wraith is nearly two feet (sixty-one centimeters) thick and is made of a polymer that human physicists had previously thought impossible.

VIEW FROM BELOW

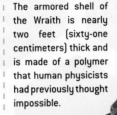

WRAITH—FRONT
SIDE VIEW

OTHER NAMES	CREW	LENGTH	WEIGHT	MAIN ARMAMENT
Type-25 Assault Gun Carriage, Covenant Tank	2 (1 driver, 1 gunner)	28.5 ft (8.6 m)	47 tons	1 plasma mortar cannon

SECONDARY ARMAMENTS	USE
2 plasma cannons, 1 plasma turret (variants)	Heavy armor, infantry support, anti-vehicle, anti-armor, siege warfare

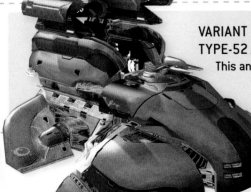

VARIANT
TYPE-52 ANTI-AIRCRAFT ARTILLERY:
This anti-aircraft variant of the Wraith is equipped with twin rapid-fire fuel rod cannons.

REAR VIEW

The fixed mounting of the Wraith's plasma emitter requires the vehicle to face targets directly.

FRONT VIEW

THE UNSC'S SHIPS come in varying sizes, depending on their role. One of the largest, most powerful warships is the carrier, which has a full complement of deadly Longsword and Shortsword attack craft. The UNSC also utilizes smaller ships, such as the Frigate, which are cheaper to produce, but excel at high-speed maneuvers and ship-to-ship combat.

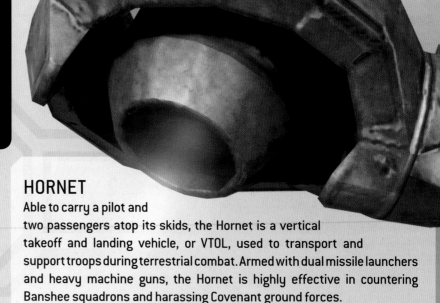

UNSC DESTROYER

Easily one of the fastest and most nimble classes of UNSC vessels, Destroyers are typically used as escorts for larger capital ships. Heavily armored and armed, a group of Destroyers can give even the largest Covenant vessels a run for their money. With dual MAC Guns, three Shiva missiles, over eight hundred Archer missiles, and eight 50mm point defense guns, Destroyers are protected by two meters of Titanium-A plate.

LENGTH: 1,590 ft (485 m) USE: Escort and defense of larger vessels FAMOUS SHIPS OF THIS TYPE: UNSC *Glasgow Kiss*, UNSC *Brasidas*, UNSC *Heracles*, UNSC *Iroquois*, UNSC *Iwo Jima*, UNSC *Resolute*, UNSC *Tharsis*

BLACK CAT-CLASS SUBPROWLER

Black Cats operate in high-risk missions, which demand subterfuge over armament. Like other ships within the Prowler class, they often serve in a reconnaissance capacity, deploying and collecting troops behind enemy lines. These vessels were used effectively during the highly covert SPARTAN-III mission known as Operation: TORPEDO.

LENGTH: Over 164 ft (50 m) USE: Troop exfiltration, reconnaissance

CORVETTE

Within the UNSC, Corvettes come in two classes: Mako and Prowler. The Mako-class, although now decommissioned due to maintenance issues, once found popularity thanks to its small size. The Prowler-class, facilitated by a significant volume of monitoring software, can infiltrate enemy-controlled space undetected and monitor enemy transmissions. One Prowler is assigned to every UNSC battle group to gather intelligence and perform stealth missions. Prowlers are normally equipped with stealth nuclear mines, which have proven surprisingly effective against unsuspecting Covenant vessels. Some have suggested that such vessels in the Human-Covenant War serve little purpose due to the heavy encoding of enemy transmissions and the naturally existing communication gap between species, but the Office of Naval Intelligence prefers to keep the ships in the field to watch over both Covenant and human forces.

LENGTH: 532 ft (162 m) USE: Intelligence gathering, mine-laying FAMOUS SHIPS OF THIS TYPE: UNSC *Lark*, UNSC *Dusk*, UNSC *Applebee*, UNSC *Razor's Edge*, UNSC *Bum Rush*, UNSC *Circumference*, UNSC *Apocalypso*, UNSC *Coral Sea*, UNSC *Pony Express*

HORNET

Able to carry a pilot and two passengers atop its skids, the Hornet is a vertical takeoff and landing vehicle, or VTOL, used to transport and support troops during terrestrial combat. Armed with dual missile launchers and heavy machine guns, the Hornet is highly effective in countering Banshee squadrons and harassing Covenant ground forces.

It has existed since at least 2424 CE, when it was used during the UNSC's campaign against the Insurrectionists, and was still in service nearly three decades later, during the final days of the Human-Covenant War.

The Hornet is a valuable anti-infantry and anti-vehicle weapon, but its lack of shielding makes it susceptible to anything larger than small-arms fire.

OTHER NAMES	USE
AV-14 Attack VTOL	Close air support, light troop transport, ship-to-ship combat

UNSC FRIGATE

One of the smallest UNSC starships, the Frigate's weak armor and armaments make it a poor choice against most Covenant vessels. They are primarily used to ferry supplies and personnel. Their status as the largest UNSC ship able to hover in an atmosphere makes them ideal for air support in terrestrial warfare, as well as inserting and extracting supplies and troops. Their armaments consist of a single MAC Gun, one to three Shiva missiles, 480 Archer missiles, and eight 50mm point defense guns. Combined with twenty-four inches (sixty centimeters) of Titanium-A plate, they fall far short of Destroyers and Cruisers in their offensive and defensive capabilities.

LENGTH	SPAN	USE
1,568 ft (478 m)	499 ft (152 m)	Ferrying equipment and troops

FAMOUS SHIPS OF THIS TYPE

UNSC *Commonwealth*, UNSC *Aegis Fate*, UNSC *Forward Unto Dawn*, UNSC *Arabia*, UNSC *Fair Weather*, UNSC *Tannenberg*, UNSC *Gettysburg*, UNSC *In Amber Clad*, UNSC *Midsummer Night*, UNSC *Redoubtable*, UNSC *Vostok*, UNSC *Meriwether Lewis*

HAWK

The Sparrowhawk, more commonly known as the Hawk, is an air-to-ground anti-tank aerodyne. Its speed and maneuverability make it ideal for use in a support and anti-armor role to eliminate tanks and heavy-armor advances. Hawks employ wing-mounted GUA-23 Autocannons and a variant of the M6 nonlinear rifle used by infantry. The Hawk was in wide production during the first decade of the war, but several propulsion-related malfunctions limited its deployment later in the war.

USE
Close air support, air escort

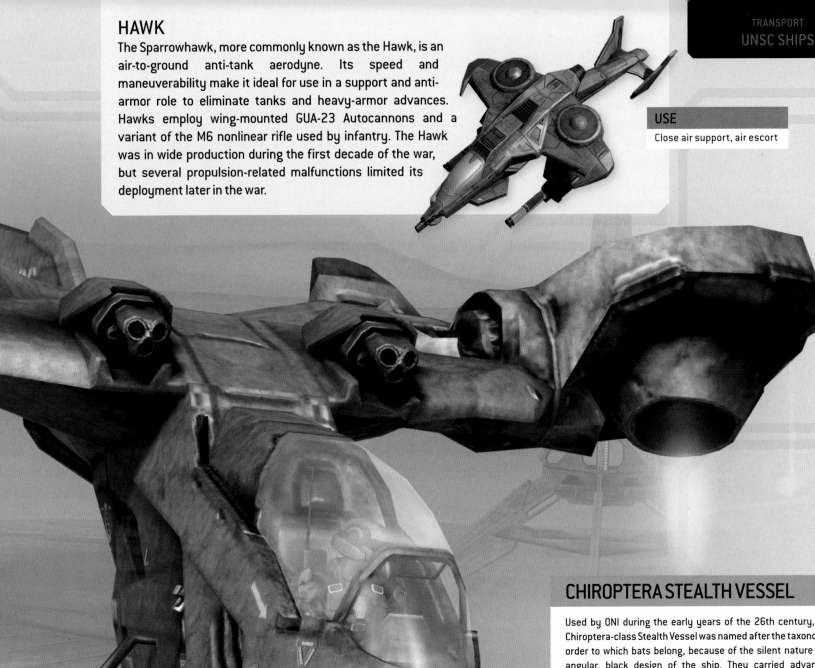

CHIROPTERA STEALTH VESSEL

Used by ONI during the early years of the 26th century, the Chiroptera-class Stealth Vessel was named after the taxonomic order to which bats belong, because of the silent nature and angular, black design of the ship. They carried advanced counter-intrusion software and the smallest Slipspace engines ever produced by the UNSC. Unfortunately, without an onboard controlling AI, the sensitive components of the ship were prone to failure and the entire class was discontinued in 2512 CE. At least one, the *Beatrice*, still existed during the Human-Covenant War. It belonged to an Eridanus Rebel leader named Jacob Jiles and was appropriated by Dr. Catherine Halsey and Kelly-058 for their mission to Onyx.

LENGTH: 164 ft (50 m) **USE:** Infiltration and reconnaissance
FAMOUS SHIPS OF THIS TYPE: *Beatrice*

UNSC CARRIER

The UNSC Carrier is a classification of UNSC warship. They are armed with three hundred Archer missiles, a pair of fusion rockets, and a MAC gun and can also deploy Longsword fighters and Pelican dropships. Their standard crew complement is 2,100. Although they are equipped with fourteen inches (thirty-six centimeters) of Titanium-A plating, Carriers are slow and must rely on Fighters and other support ships for defense.

LENGTH: 1.8 miles (3 km) **SPAN:** 394 ft (120 m) **USE:** Deployment of fighter ships and ground troops **FAMOUS SHIPS OF THIS TYPE:** UNSC *Magellan*, UNSC *All Under Heaven*, UNSC *Musashi*, UNSC *Atlas*, UNSC *Stalingrad*

ALBATROSS

The Albatross is a class of heavy-lift Dropship that is used to transport cargo such as vehicles and weapons. It possesses no offensive capabilities, but is sufficiently armored to serve as a makeshift base or command center.

LENGTH: 121 ft (37 m) **USE:** Heavy-lift Dropship

CALYPSO EXFILTRATION CRAFT

The Calypso has no armaments and only limited Slipspace capabilities. Although it operated similarly to other covert exfiltration crafts, it was eventually decommissioned when more effective vessels made the Calypso obsolete.

LENGTH: Over 164 ft (50 m) **USE:** Troop exfiltration

USE

Ground attack, air attack

Directed-thrust jets
on the underside
of the Vulture
enable it to hover.

VULTURE—SIDE VIEW

Impressive armaments include
massive Autocannons for defense
against individual ground units.

VULTURE

One of the UNSC's most powerful units, the Vulture is a formidable vehicle in any battle. It is the UNSC's largest aircraft, able to carry an impressive amount of weapons. Armed with Argent V missiles and GUA-23 autocannons, the Vulture can fire off large barrages of missiles, causing devastation over a wide area.

Due to its weapon configuration, the ship can fight against both air and ground units. The Vulture's large size makes it slow, increasing its vulnerability to attack, but it is resilient and can withstand huge amounts of damage before its destruction.

The Vulture requires highly trained UNSC pilots and gunners, which makes it very costly to use. This, and the amount of time it takes to build one, means that the Vulture is usually only reserved for difficult and lengthy battles.

CRADLE

Simple in its construction, a Cradle is a refitting station of Titanium-A capable of refitting and repairing up to six Destroyers in space, three on the upper surface, and three more on the lower. Their finest hour occurred in the battles of Sigma Octanus IV and Reach, when Cradles manned by skeleton crews were sacrificed in order to block orbital guns and other ships from Covenant plasma fire.

USE: Refitting station

WELCOME WAGON

A general name for cargo transports designed to traverse space elevator strands, Welcome Wagons were used for the mass evacuation of civilians from Harvest after the planet fell to the Covenant. Of 237 Welcome Wagons used to evacuate the planet, only one in six survived.

SHIP TYPE: Civilian transport

BUMBLEBEE

Able to transport eight passengers and a pilot, Bumblebees are placed on cruisers and other large ships to act as escape pods. They lack any substantial maneuverability and their thrusters are not powerful enough to escape a planet's atmosphere. Additionally, they can only be used once, as their air brakes disengage upon descent. Despite harnesses designed to stabilize passengers, Bumblebee landings are extremely dangerous and fatalities are common.

LENGTH: 34.5 ft (10.5 m) SPAN: 17 ft (5.2 m); With air brakes deployed: 30.5 ft (9.3 m) USE: Escape pod

LENGTH	SPAN	RANGE	USE	FAMOUS SHIPS OF THIS TYPE
210 ft (64 m)	246 ft (75 m)	Varies	Fighter, interceptor, bomber	7-89, Knife 26

C709 LONGSWORD-CLASS INTERCEPTOR

The C709 Longsword is the primary fighter craft of the UNSC fleet. It fills numerous roles during battle, from defending its parent ship to bombing major Covenant vessels or engaging Covenant Seraph Fighters.

Despite filling a niche similar to 21st-century fighter jets, Longswords are actually similar in size and shape to 21st-century stealth bombers or passenger aircraft. They can carry a crew of up to four, but generally fly with two, and can be piloted by an AI. Their stock armaments are 110mm rotary cannons and 120mm ventral guns, but they can be outfitted with any number of larger weapons, including Scorpion and ASGM-10 missiles, Moray mines, and even Shiva warheads. Their versatile nature makes Longswords a valuable weapon against the Covenant during deep-space battles.

Twin fusion reactor engines create enough force to reach the escape velocities for Earth and Installation 04.

Longsword aerodynamics allow the craft to operate in atmosphere as well as in the vacuum of space.

C709 LONGSWORD-CLASS INTERCEPTOR —FRONT SIDE VIEW

The Longsword-class Interceptor is relatively inexpensive to produce and yet is one of the most versatile UNSC crafts: It can be a fighter, a bomber, or an escort, all with equal effectiveness.

REAR SIDE VIEW

ARGUS DRONE

ARGUS Drones are aerial drones used by the UNSC to remotely detect explosive devices commonly used by the Insurrectionists. They are equipped with targeting systems and single Lancet Micro-Missiles for the neutralization of enemy targets.

Despite their widespread use, ARGUS Drones are not infallible, having wrongly identified explosives on an innocent civilian on at least one occasion. They share a name with Argus Panoptes, the hundred-eyed giant of Greek mythology.

SPAN: 3.3 ft (1 m) USE: Bomb detection, destruction of small targets

UNSC CRUISER

Cruisers are the backbone of the UNSC fleet. Eschewing small fighters for heavy offensive weapons and thick armor, cruisers are equipped with five fusion rockets, 1,800 Archer missiles, a pair of MAC guns, 24 Longsword fighters, and 75-inch (191-cm) Titanium-A plating. They carry a standard complement of one thousand and are generally commanded by a captain or a rear admiral.

Although cruisers are the largest and most formidable ships in the UNSC fleet, they are dwarfed by their Covenant counterparts and suffered heavy losses during the Human-Covenant War. As a result, many were pulled back to defend the Inner Colonies and Earth. There are two classes of UNSC cruiser: The newer Marathon-class and the older Halcyon-class.

LENGTH: Varies based on class SPAN: Varies based on class USE: Heavy offensive firepower

MARATHON-CLASS CRUISER

Replacing the Halcyon-class cruisers some time prior to the Human-Covenant War, the Marathon-class is twice the size of UNSC Frigates and is known for its ability to take and dish out massive amounts of damage. Due to their durable and fierce nature, Marathon-class cruisers are often reserved for admirals to use as command ships. Despite their ability to withstand numerous plasma blasts and their oversized weaponry, all but several Marathon-class cruisers were destroyed during the early years of the Human-Covenant War. This led to the surviving ships being pulled back and used as a last line of defense for the Inner Colonies and Earth.

LENGTH: 3,910 ft (972 m) USE: Capital engagements, planetary invasion FAMOUS SHIPS OF THIS TYPE: UNSC Leviathan, UNSC Hannibal

HALCYON-CLASS CRUISER

Designed in 2510 CE by Dr. Robert McLees, the Halcyon only saw a brief era of service due to costly construction and maintenance, a lack of speed, and concerns regarding its tactical viability. Composed of five hexagonal and octagonal sections fitted together, the Halcyon is the smallest UNSC vessel to be designated a cruiser. Armed with a sole MAC gun, 180 Archer missiles, and four Shiva missiles, the Halcyon was outclassed in every way by the Marathon-class cruisers that replaced it.

When the Human-Covenant War required every ship available to fight, many Halcyon-class ships were refitted with thousands of extra Archer missiles and a three hundred percent engine capacity increase.

OTHER NAME: Human Attack Ship class C-II LENGTH: 3,840 ft (1,170 m) SPAN: 1,155 ft (352 m) USE: All-purpose attack and defense, troop and supply transport FAMOUS SHIPS OF THIS TYPE: UNSC Pillar of Autumn, UNSC Dawn Under Heaven

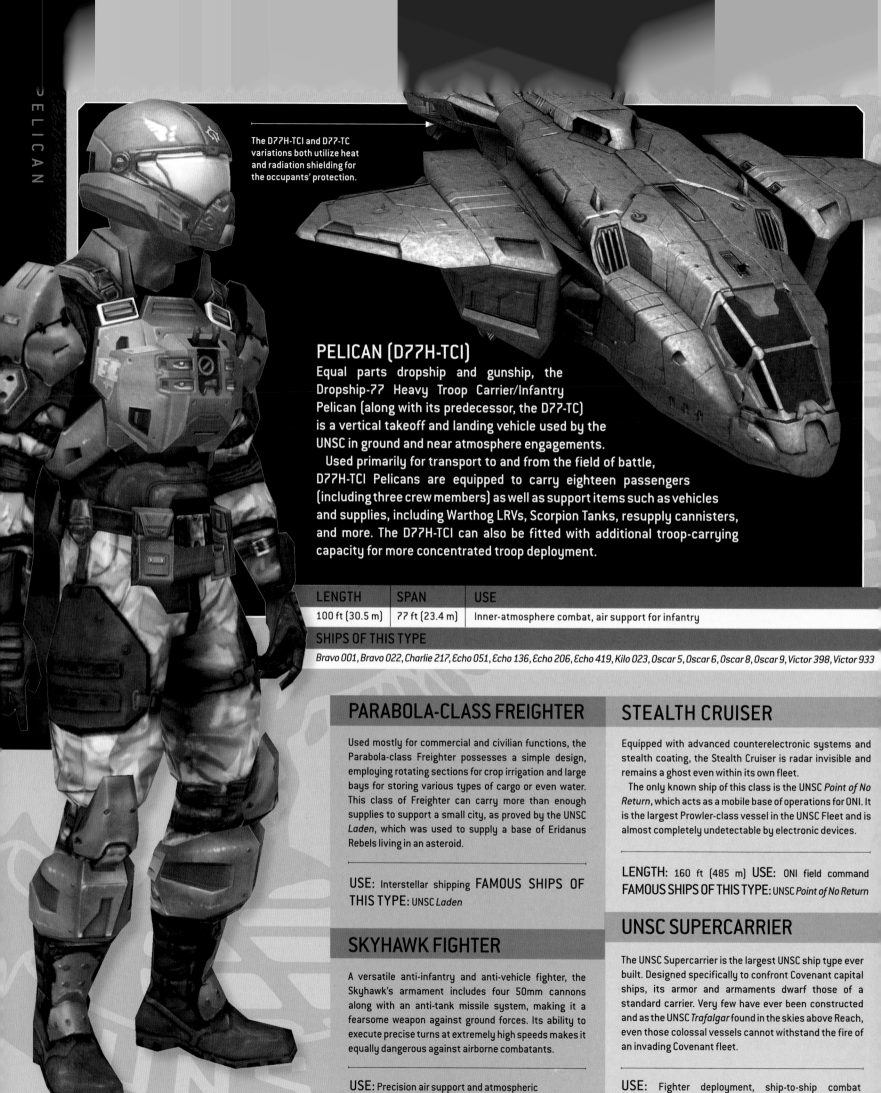

The D77H-TCI and D77-TC variations both utilize heat and radiation shielding for the occupants' protection.

PELICAN (D77H-TCI)

Equal parts dropship and gunship, the Dropship-77 Heavy Troop Carrier/Infantry Pelican (along with its predecessor, the D77-TC) is a vertical takeoff and landing vehicle used by the UNSC in ground and near atmosphere engagements.

Used primarily for transport to and from the field of battle, D77H-TCI Pelicans are equipped to carry eighteen passengers (including three crew members) as well as support items such as vehicles and supplies, including Warthog LRVs, Scorpion Tanks, resupply cannisters, and more. The D77H-TCI can also be fitted with additional troop-carrying capacity for more concentrated troop deployment.

LENGTH	SPAN	USE
100 ft (30.5 m)	77 ft (23.4 m)	Inner-atmosphere combat, air support for infantry

SHIPS OF THIS TYPE

Bravo 001, Bravo 022, Charlie 217, Echo 051, Echo 136, Echo 206, Echo 419, Kilo 023, Oscar 5, Oscar 6, Oscar 8, Oscar 9, Victor 398, Victor 933

PARABOLA-CLASS FREIGHTER

Used mostly for commercial and civilian functions, the Parabola-class Freighter possesses a simple design, employing rotating sections for crop irrigation and large bays for storing various types of cargo or even water. This class of Freighter can carry more than enough supplies to support a small city, as proved by the UNSC *Laden*, which was used to supply a base of Eridanus Rebels living in an asteroid.

USE: Interstellar shipping FAMOUS SHIPS OF THIS TYPE: UNSC *Laden*

SKYHAWK FIGHTER

A versatile anti-infantry and anti-vehicle fighter, the Skyhawk's armament includes four 50mm cannons along with an anti-tank missile system, making it a fearsome weapon against ground forces. Its ability to execute precise turns at extremely high speeds makes it equally dangerous against airborne combatants.

USE: Precision air support and atmospheric interception

STEALTH CRUISER

Equipped with advanced counterelectronic systems and stealth coating, the Stealth Cruiser is radar invisible and remains a ghost even within its own fleet.

The only known ship of this class is the UNSC *Point of No Return*, which acts as a mobile base of operations for ONI. It is the largest Prowler-class vessel in the UNSC Fleet and is almost completely undetectable by electronic devices.

LENGTH: 160 ft (485 m) USE: ONI field command FAMOUS SHIPS OF THIS TYPE: UNSC *Point of No Return*

UNSC SUPERCARRIER

The UNSC Supercarrier is the largest UNSC ship type ever built. Designed specifically to confront Covenant capital ships, its armor and armaments dwarf those of a standard carrier. Very few have ever been constructed and as the UNSC *Trafalgar* found in the skies above Reach, even those colossal vessels cannot withstand the fire of an invading Covenant fleet.

USE: Fighter deployment, ship-to-ship combat FAMOUS SHIPS OF THIS TYPE: UNSC *Trafalgar*

Pelicans are armed with heavy machine guns and small missile pods, the configuration of which varies slightly depending on the model. The newer model D77H-TCI is slightly more angular, with its machine guns mounted on its wings rather than its chin and a different seating configuration for the pilot and co-pilot. The new model also features external magnetic clamps on its rear, allowing it to carry extra loads.

PROWLER

Prowlers are Corvette-class stealth ships equipped with active camouflage, counter-electronic systems, and a minimal amount of weapons and armor. The ship's primary function is the undetected gathering of intelligence. This limited mission scope generally only requires a crew of forty to ninety people. One Prowler is assigned to every UNSC battlegroup. For combat purposes, Prowlers are equipped with stealth-enabled Hornet mines, used to create undetectable minefields in the hopes of destroying unsuspecting enemy vessels. It is notable that Prowlers are also sometimes armed with pulse lasers, though it is unknown whether these were reverse-engineered from Covenant technology or whether they were created independently by UNSC scientists.

LENGTH: 531 ft (162 m) USE: Intelligence gathering, mine-laying
FAMOUS SHIPS OF THIS TYPE: UNSC *Apocalypso*, UNSC *Applebee*, UNSC *Bum Rush*, UNSC *Circumference*, UNSC *Coral Sea*, UNSC *Dusk*, UNSC *Lark*, UNSC *Point of No Return*, UNSC *Pony Express*, UNSC *Razor's Edge*

SKT-13 SHUTTLECRAFT

Essentially a military taxi, the Shuttlecraft is used to transport small numbers of personnel and supplies between larger craft.

USE: Ferrying supplies and personnel

YACHT

Yachts are personal luxury spacecraft used for vacationing and transport by wealthy civilians. Not unlike their 21st-century ocean-going counterparts, Yachts are often seen as status symbols. Several ONI Prowlers, including the UNSC *Apocalypso* and the UNSC *Circumference* were outfitted to look like Yachts to avoid suspicion while on classified missions.

USE: Civilian leisure vessel

> THE SIGHT OF AN APPROACHING PELICAN IS A RELIEF TO ALL UNSC GROUND TROOPS.

FAMOUS UNSC SHIPS

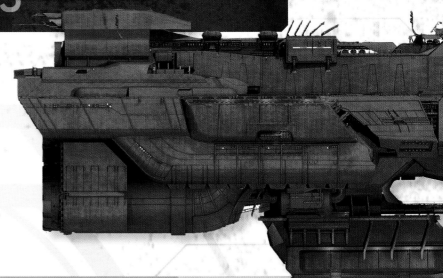

EACH INDIVIDUAL ship in the UNSC fleet, no matter what type of craft it is, has its own name, and many of these ships, crewed by exceptional soldiers and AIs, have gone down in history for the role they played in the campaign against the Covenant. Here are some of the most signigicant.

UNSC *CIRCUMFERENCE*

The UNSC *Circumference* has had an interesting history. It participated in the SPARTAN-II deployment at Delphi Station and Operation: HYPODERMIC, but the moment the *Circumference* will most likely be remembered for was its security breach.

Docked in an orbiting station high above the planet Reach, the *Circumference* posed a major security violation because when it was evacuated its NAV Computers had not been wiped according to the Cole Protocol. SPARTAN-IIs were able to assault the vessel and destroy its NAV data prior to the Covenant apprehending it, but the Spartans and the UNSC Marines tasked with securing the ship suffered heavy casualties in the process.

SHIP TYPE: Prowler FAMOUS EVENTS: The battle of Reach, Operation: HYPODERMIC

UNSC *MIDSUMMER NIGHT*

Midsummer Night fought in the Rubble in the 23 Librae System. Its stealth ability allowed it to penetrate deep into Covenant territory for special operations. Jacob Keyes served aboard the UNSC *Midsummer Night* before being transferred to the UNSC *Iroquois*.

SHIP TYPE: Frigate

UNSC *HANNIBAL*

The UNSC *Hannibal* fought in the battle of Reach in 2552 CE. Its MAC gun was destroyed during the battle, leaving the ship helpless. Its final fate is unknown, but it was most likely destroyed.

SHIP TYPE: Marathon-class Cruiser FAMOUS EVENTS: The battle of Reach

UNSC *BUM RUSH*

The UNSC *Bum Rush* participated in Operation: TREBUCHET in 2524 CE, providing a tactical operations center for a battalion of Marines fighting on Harvest.

SHIP TYPES: Corvette FAMOUS EVENTS: Operation: TREBUCHET

HAN

A small Slipspace-capable diplomatic shuttle, the *Han* transported Jacob Keyes and Dr. Catherine Halsey in 2517 CE on their mission to investigate children for the SPARTAN-II Program. It was equipped with cryo tubes and lacked artificial gravity on the bridge. It was manned by an AI named Toran.

SHIP TYPE: Diplomatic shuttle

ODYSSEY

The Odyssey was the first Human ship to attempt to colonize territory outside the Sol System. It was launched on January 1, 2362 CE, a day which will forever be remembered as the moment humanity took its first few steps into the unknown.

SHIP TYPE: Colony Ship

UNSC *APPLEBEE*

The UNSC *Applebee* was an ONI Prowler docked above Reach in August 2552 CE. Cortana broke into its database and discovered that its true nature was a stealth vessel. The *Applebee* was likely destroyed during the battle of Reach.

SHIP TYPE: Prowler FAMOUS EVENTS: Operation: HYPODERMIC, the battle of Reach

UNSC *LARK*

The UNSC *Lark* was an ONI Prowler, which was involved in Operation HYPODERMIC and the battle for Reach. Its fate remains unknown.

SHIP TYPE: Prowler FAMOUS EVENTS: Operation: HYPODERMIC, the battle of Reach

UNSC *CHALONS*

A Corvette that saw action at the second battle of Earth, the UNSC *Chalons* was used as a diversion, allowing a team of SPARTAN-IIs to stop the Covenant from stealing a cache of nuclear weapons.

SHIP TYPE: Corvette FAMOUS EVENTS: The second battle of Earth

UNSC *ARGO*

The UNSC *Argo* was a scout ship dispatched to Harvest not long after the UNSC lost contact with the colony. After exiting Slipspace near Harvest, it encountered a Covenant Cruiser, which was in the process of glassing the planet. Despite warnings from Mack, Harvest's agricultural AI, the scout ship strayed too close and was destroyed by the Covenant Cruiser.

SHIP TYPE: Scout ship FAMOUS EVENTS: The battle of Harvest

UNSC *GLASGOW KISS*

The UNSC *Glasgow Kiss* was part of the battlegroup Stalingrad sent to rescue Dr. Catherine Halsey and a team of Spartans from Onyx. During a battle with Covenant forces, the *Glasgow Kiss* moved in front of its flagship to shield it from plasma fire. Although the *Glasgow Kiss* was destroyed in the process, most of the crew managed to escape.

SHIP TYPE: Destroyer FAMOUS EVENTS: The battle Sigma Octanus IV

UNSC *ALLEGIANCE*

During the battle of Sigma Octanus IV, the UNSC *Allegiance* responded to a signal sent from the UNSC *Iroquois* and intercepted a retreating Covenant carrier.

SHIP TYPE: Destroyer FAMOUS EVENTS: The battle of Onyx

CLASS	LENGTH	COMMANDING OFFICER
Modified Phoenix-class Colony Ship	1.5 miles (2.5 km)	Captain James Gregory Cutter

UNSC *SPIRIT OF FIRE*

The *Spirit of Fire* was originally commissioned as a colony ship in 2473 CE. As Outer Colony tensions increased, however, a Magnetic Accelerator Cannon (MAC) Gun was added, capable of accelerating low-mass or depleted uranium slugs to a fraction of light speed. When the Human-Covenant War started, the *Spirit of Fire* was further repurposed. Vessel bays that once housed prefabricated schools and atmosphere processors now store mobile armories, self-assembling fusion reactors, and other groundside facilities that can be dropped into combat directly from orbit.

The *Spirit of Fire* and its crew are currently considered "lost with all hands," having dropped out of communication after investigating Covenant activity on the planet Arcadia.

UNSC *CORAL SEA*

The UNSC *Coral Sea* was involved in the conflicts above Earth when the High Prophet of Regret's fleet first arrived. It is believed that the *Coral Sea* followed *In Amber Clad* as it entered Slipspace behind the Prophet's Carrier, but there is no record of it afterward.

SHIP TYPE: Corvette FAMOUS EVENTS: The first battle of Earth, the first battle of New Mombasa

UNSC *BASRA*

The UNSC *Basra* was severely damaged during the conflict that took place above the planet Reach. After the battle, it was moved by the Covenant into an enormous ship graveyard over Reach's northern pole.

FAMOUS EVENTS: The battle of Reach

UNSC *MINOTAUR*

The UNSC *Minotaur* fought in the battle of Reach, where it was completely destroyed when a Covenant flagship scored a direct hit on its reactor. This ship shares a name with a monster from Greek mythology.

SHIP TYPE: Destroyer FAMOUS EVENTS: The battle of Reach

UNSC *AGINCOURT*

The UNSC *Agincourt* was a transport vessel tasked with offloading supplies at Camp Currahee on the planet Onyx in October 2552 CE. The ship was most likely named after the famous battle that occurred during the Hundred Years' War. Two hundred newly awakened Onyx Sentinels subsequently destroyed the *Agincourt*.

SHIP TYPE: Frigate

UNSC *MAGELLAN*

Jacob Keyes was assigned to the UNSC *Magellan* in 2517 CE, upon his graduation from Luna OCS Academy. These orders were rescinded when he was ordered to assist Dr. Catherine Halsey with her search for candidates for the SPARTAN Project.

SHIP TYPE: Carrier

UNSC *MUSASHI*

The UNSC *Musashi* fought alongside many other vessels during the Covenant's assault on Reach, where it was destroyed by a Covenant vessel.

SHIP TYPE: Carrier
FAMOUS EVENTS: The battle of Reach

UNSC *COMMONWEALTH*

In 2525 CE, the UNSC *Commonwealth* was used to transport Dr. Catherine Halsey and the SPARTAN-IIs to the Damascus Testing Facility on Chi Ceti IV. Upon arriving, the ship engaged a Covenant vessel, and was able to destroy the ship with the assistance of the SPARTAN-IIs. Despite nearly being crippled during the engagement, the *Commonwealth* survived and was able to return to Reach for repairs.

SHIP TYPE: Frigate KNOWN COMMANDERS: Captain Wallace FAMOUS EVENTS: The battle of Chi Ceti

UNSC *LANCELOT*

One of the many vessels which responded to the distress call from Sigma Octanus IV, the UNSC *Lancelot* was last seen by Jacob Keyes as it charged straight into the Covenant fleet.

It was most likely destroyed, although no physical evidence of this has ever been recovered.

SHIP TYPE: Destroyer FAMOUS EVENTS: The battle of Sigma Octanus IV

UNSC *ALL UNDER HEAVEN*

In 2545 CE, the UNSC *All Under Heaven* was assigned to the 51 Pegasi-B System as the staging ground for Operation: TORPEDO. While still in Slipspace, the ship launched three hundred SPARTAN-IIIs via long range stealth orbit insertion pods.

SHIP TYPE: Carrier FAMOUS EVENTS: Operation: TORPEDO

UNSC *BRASIDAS*

The UNSC *Brasidas* was part of the battlegroup *Stalingrad*, which was sent to retrieve Dr. Catherine Halsey and the Spartan team trapped on Onyx. It was damaged extensively by Covenant fire during the initial skirmish. It managed to transfer its load of Hornet mines to the *Prowler Dusk*, before being destroyed by Covenant reinforcements.

SHIP TYPE: Destroyer FAMOUS EVENTS: The battle of Onyx

UNSC *BUNKER HILL*

The UNSC Destroyer *Bunker Hill* served as a staging area for the SPARTAN-II team led by John-117, which attacked a Rebel base called Camp New Hope on Victoria in the 111 Tauri System.

SHIP TYPE: Destroyer

UNSC *MERIWETHER LEWIS*

Jacob Keyes received a Medal of Honor for his exploits on the UNSC *Meriwether Lewis*, where he defended the vessel against an overwhelming Covenant boarding party.

SHIP TYPE: Frigate

UNSC *GORGON*

Ensign William Lovell served aboard the UNSC *Gorgon* before he was assigned to the Sigma Octanus monitoring post. The ship was previously part of Vice Admiral Preston Cole's fleet in 2525 CE.

SHIP TYPE: Frigate FAMOUS PERSONALITIES: Ensign William Lovell

UNSC *LEVIATHAN*

The UNSC *Leviathan* took part in the battle of Sigma Octanus IV. It was damaged in that engagement and was destroyed later at the battle of Reach.

SHIP TYPE: Marathon-class Cruiser KNOWN COMMANDERS: Michael Stanforth FAMOUS EVENTS: The battle of Sigma Octanus IV, the Battle of Reach

UNSC *HERODOTUS*

The UNSC *Herodotus* is notable for being the first human vessel destroyed by a Covenant energy projector. The use of this weapon at the battle of Sigma Octanus IV marked the first time it was seen by UNSC forces.

SHIP TYPE: Destroyer FAMOUS EVENTS: The battle of Sigma Octanus IV

CONSTRUCTION PLATFORM 966A

Construction Platform 966A, also known as Station Delphi, was a deep space shipyard and construction platform located in a remote sector of space. It was comonly used to refit UNSC ships. The platform was equipped with cranes and docking pods, but was later decommissioned. The platform was later used by ONI when they staged an operation in which SPARTAN-051 was captured for the SPARTAN-III Program.

OTHER NAME: Station Delphi SHIP TYPE: Construction platform

UNSC *ATHENS*

Stationed in the Epsilon Eridani System in 2525 CE, the UNSC *Athens* was tasked with alerting the UNSC *Pioneer* should anything go wrong with the SPARTAN-IIs on their mission to capture the leader of a Rebel base.

SHIP TYPE: Prowler

BEATRICE

The *Beatrice* was an ONI Chiroptera-class Prowler that was decommissioned in 2512 CE and later became the personal flagship of the Insurrectionist leader Governor Jacob Jiles.

The *Beatrice* was later stolen by Dr. Catherine Halsey and taken to Onyx, where it crash-landed after being attacked by Onyx Sentinels.

SHIP TYPE: Chiroptera-class Prowler KNOWN COMMANDERS: Governor Jacob Jiles FAMOUS EVENTS: The battle of Onyx

UNSC *HERACLES*

In October 2525 CE, the UNSC *Heracles* arrived in the Harvest system with the remainder of battlegroup 4 to investigate why contact had been lost with the colony. After a brief battle with Covenant forces stationed there, every UNSC ship except the *Heracles* was destroyed, forcing it to retreat to Reach.

SHIP TYPE: Destroyer FAMOUS EVENTS: The first battle of Harvest KNOWN COMMANDERS: Captain Veredi

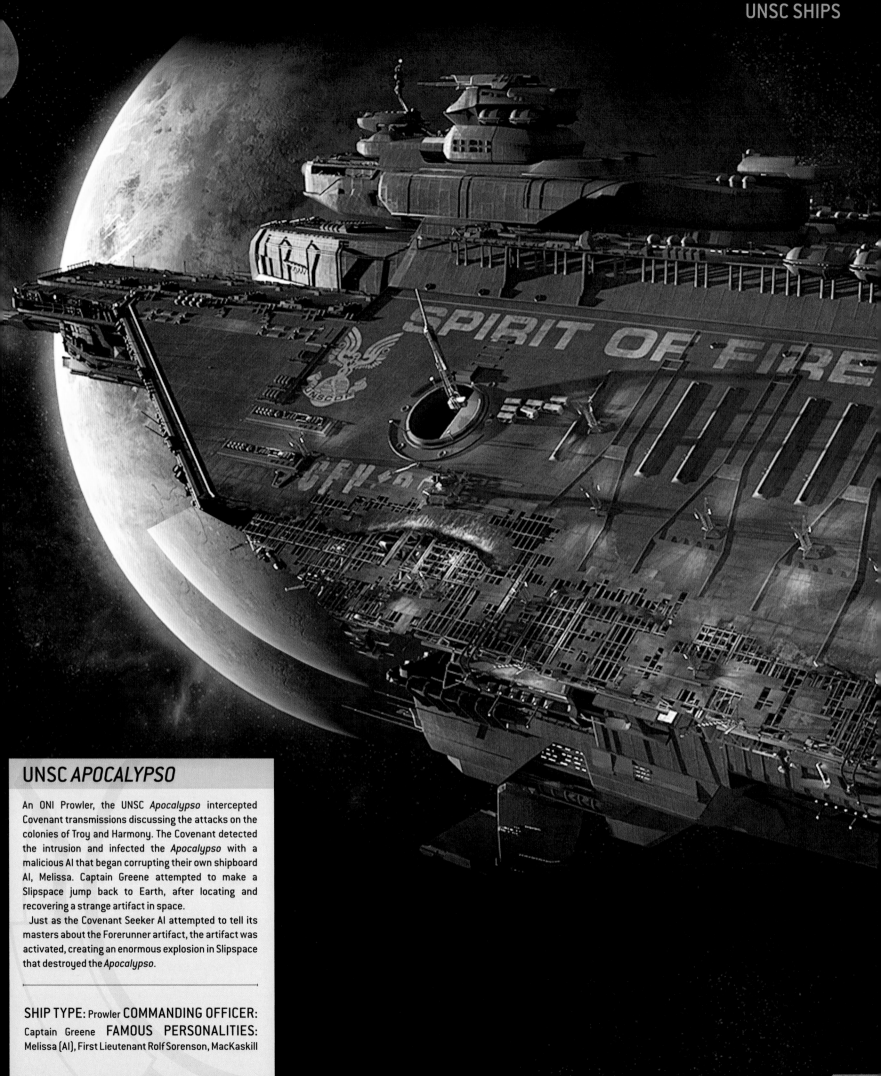

UNSC *APOCALYPSO*

An ONI Prowler, the UNSC *Apocalypso* intercepted Covenant transmissions discussing the attacks on the colonies of Troy and Harmony. The Covenant detected the intrusion and infected the *Apocalypso* with a malicious AI that began corrupting their own shipboard AI, Melissa. Captain Greene attempted to make a Slipspace jump back to Earth, after locating and recovering a strange artifact in space.

  Just as the Covenant Seeker AI attempted to tell its masters about the Forerunner artifact, the artifact was activated, creating an enormous explosion in Slipspace that destroyed the *Apocalypso*.

SHIP TYPE: Prowler COMMANDING OFFICER: Captain Greene FAMOUS PERSONALITIES: Melissa (AI), First Lieutenant Rolf Sorenson, MacKaskill

UNSC *PILLAR OF AUTUMN*

The *Pillar of Autumn* was scheduled to be scrapped along with the other Halcyon-class Cruisers, but was refitted for a special mission during the final days of the Human-Covenant War. It was placed under the command of Captain Jacob Keyes, who, along with Master Chief, his Spartans, and Cortana, was ordered to capture a Covenant Prophet. This mission was waylaid, however, by the UNSC defeat at the Battle of Reach. The *Pillar of Autumn* escaped the carnage when Cortana initiated a Slipspace jump using coordinates gleaned from the Sigma Octanus IV artifact. The *Autumn* exited Slipspace near the gas giant Threshold and discovered Installation 04 (also known as Alpha Halo), a mysterious ringworld that would alter the course of the Human-Covenant War and threaten the entire Galaxy with destruction.

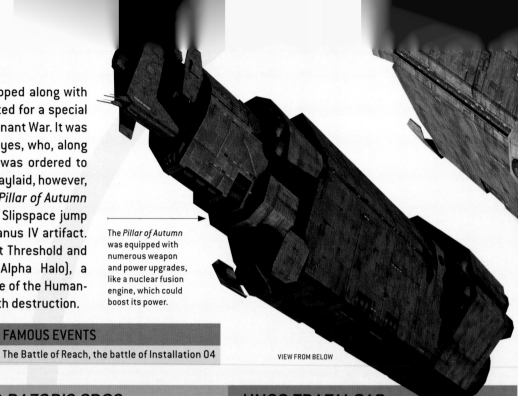

The *Pillar of Autumn* was equipped with numerous weapon and power upgrades, like a nuclear fusion engine, which could boost its power.

VIEW FROM BELOW

OTHER NAMES	KNOWN COMMANDERS	FAMOUS EVENTS
The *Autumn*, the *POA*	Captain Jacob Keyes	The Battle of Reach, the battle of Installation 04

WHOLESALE PRICE

The *Wholesale Price* was a freighter used by the AI constructs Sif and Mack to send transmissions from Harvest to Reach.

SHIP TYPE: Freighter

UNSC *VOSTOK*

The *Vostok* was one of three ships that made up UNSC battlegroup 4, led by Captain Maribeau Veredi aboard the UNSC Destroyer *Heracles*, and was tasked with investigating the loss of communications with Harvest in 2525 CE. The *Vostok* was destroyed on arrival at Harvest by the Covenant.

SHIP TYPE: Frigate

THARSIS

Tharsis sustained significant damage during the [R]each. Covenant forces established a scrapyard of [a]nd destroyed ships over Reach's northern pole, [the] remains of the *Tharsis* among the debris. Cortana [after] fusing the crippled *Tharsis* to the *Ascendant* [chose] the UNSC *Gettysburg,* due to its better [con]dition and functioning MAC gun.

[SHIP TY]PE: Destroyer
[FAMOUS] EVENTS: The Battle of Reach

PIONEER

[The P]ioneer acted as a staging vessel for the launch of [a m]ission against Rebel forces in the Eridanus [system. For] this mission, a team of SPARTAN-II soldiers led by [Master Chi]ef infiltrated a Rebel base and captured Rebel [colo]nel Robert Watts.

[SHIP TY]PE: Destroyer

UNSC *RAZOR'S EDGE*

The UNSC *Razor's Edge* is a Prowler that fought in the battle of New Harmony in 2537 CE. During that conflict, the *Razor's Edge* was able to secure a telemetry probe to the hull of a fleeing Covenant frigate. The probe led to the discovery of K7-49, a Covenant shipyard that was subsequently destroyed by SPARTAN-III soldiers during Operation: PROMETHEUS.

SHIP TYPE: Prowler
FAMOUS EVENTS: The battle of New Harmony

UNSC *REDOUBTABLE*

The UNSC *Redoubtable* participated in the first battle of Earth, as well as the first battle of New Mombasa. It was one of the few ships quick enough to follow the UNSC *In Amber Clad* into Slipspace in pursuit of the High Prophet of Regret's assault carrier. Its fate following the discovery of Halo Installation 05 is unknown.

SHIP TYPE: Frigate FAMOUS EVENTS: The first battle of Earth, the first battle of New Mombasa

UNSC *SILBERG*

During the Battle of Reach, the UNSC *Silberg* was off-world conducting a deep space reconnaissance mission. The *Silberg* is a stealth craft, though its make, model, and mission are classified.

SHIP TYPE: Stealth

TWO DRINK MINIMUM

The *Two Drink Minimum* is a human luxury liner that served a non-stop route from Earth to Arcadia for many years. Henry "Hank" Gibson, the first human to come in contact with a member of the Covenant, served on the *Two Drink Minimum* for over fifteen years, including five years as the ship's first mate.

SHIP TYPE: Luxury liner
FAMOUS PERSONALITIES: Henry Gibson

UNSC *TRAFALGAR*

The UNSC *Trafalgar* was one of the most revered ships in the UNSC fleet. At the Battle of Reach in 2552 CE, the first Covenant flagship ever seen by humanity destroyed the *Trafalgar*.

This ship shared a name with the Battle of Trafalgar, a decisive naval engagement during the Napoleonic Wars.

SHIP TYPE: Supercarrier
FAMOUS EVENTS: The Battle of Reach

UNSC *WALK OF SHAME*

The UNSC *Walk of Shame* was an ONI Sloop used by Jilan al-Cygni when investigating the initial Covenant presence near Harvest. It had a delta-wing-shaped hull and was equipped with stealth technology and a single Archer ship-to-ship missile. Al-Cygni sent the ship to Reach bearing initial information on the first contact with the Covenant.

SHIP TYPE: Sloop KNOWN COMMANDERS: Jilan al-Cygni

UNSC *WITCH BUCKET*

The UNSC *Witch Bucket* is an ONI ship used to take surveillance imagery of Corporal Avery Johnson's assassination of the Secessionist Union leader Jerald Mulkey Ander on Harvest.

THIS END UP

This End Up, piloted by Henry "Hank" Gibson, was a freighter traveling from Harvest when it came in contact with the Covenant vessel *Minor Transgression*, making Hank Gibson the first human to encounter the Covenant, as well as the first fatality in what would become the Human-Covenat War.

SHIP TYPE: Civilian freighter
KNOWN COMMANDERS: Henry Gibson

FRONT VIEW

REAR VIEW

After a frenzied naval engagement with a dozen Covenant ships, the crippled *Pillar of Autumn* made a crash-landing on Installation 04. Most of its crew were able to survive and utilize the ship as a headquarters for a guerilla war against against landing Covenant troops. The ship was eventually overrun by the Covenant and later, the Flood, at which point Master Chief detonated the ship's fusion cores, destroying the ship and Installation 04 along with it.

UNSC *PILLAR OF AUTUMN*

UNSC *STALINGRAD*

The UNSC *Stalingrad* served as the flagship for a small battle group tasked with rescuing Dr. Catherine Halsey and the few surviving Spartans from Onyx in 2552 CE. During this rescue attempt, overwhelming Covenant forces destroyed the *Stalingrad*.

This ship shares its name with the Battle of Stalingrad, one of the bloodiest battles of Earth's Second World War.

SHIP TYPE: Carrier KNOWN COMMANDERS: Admiral Carl "Buster" Patterson
FAMOUS EVENTS: The battle of Onyx

UNSC *PONY EXPRESS*

The *Pony Express*, a UNSC corvette, was originally selected to carry a team of SPARTAN-II soldiers to Onyx following Lord Hood's reception of an urgent communiqué from Dr. Catherine Halsey. The Spartans eventually hijacked a faster Covenant destroyer to reach their destination.

SHIP TYPE: Corvette
FAMOUS EVENTS: The second battle of Earth

UNSC *PARIS*

The UNSC *Paris* participated in the first battle of Earth, including the conflict in New Mombasa. It was one of the few ships able to follow the UNSC *In Amber Clad* into Slipspace in pursuit of the High Prophet of Regret's assault cruiser. Its fate following the discovery of Halo Installation 05 is unknown.

SHIP TYPE: Frigate FAMOUS EVENTS: The first battle of Earth, the first battle of New Mombasa

UNSC *SKIDBLADNIR*

The UNSC *Skidbladnir* was used to transport colonists to the planet Harvest. It was equipped with an AI called Loki who, once Harvest had been colonized, used the *Skidbladnir* to assist in the construction of the orbiting space station, the Tiara. Following that, the ship landed on the planet's surface and was scrapped for materials such as its power plant, which was used to power the capital city of Utgard. The ship shared its name with a ship built for the God Loki from Norse mythology.

SHIP TYPE: Phoenix-class Colony Ship
USE: Civilian/cargo transport

UNSC *TANNENBERG*

The UNSC *Tannenberg* assisted the ONI Prowler *Circumference* in the unsuccessful search for SPARTAN-051 near the Groombridge 34 System in 2531 CE. It was called away shortly afterward in response to nearby Covenant activity.

SHIP TYPE: Frigate

UNSC *POINT OF NO RETURN*

One of the most advanced ships ever built by the UNSC, the *Point of No Return* acts as a field command ship for ONI. Oversized for a Prowler, the *Point of No Return* is equipped with stealth ablative coating, advanced counter-electronics, and a Faraday Cage, which protects the occupants of its conference room, code named "Odin's Eye." It was inside this room that the SPARTAN-III Project was approved in 2531 CE. The ship as a whole is highly classified and ONI and the UNSC deny its existence entirely.

SHIP TYPE: Prowler/Stealth Cruiser

UNSC *ONAN*

The UNSC *Onan* is a symmetrical cargo ship with limited Slipspace capabilities. During the events of the first battle of Earth it assisted the war effort by ferrying supplies to military and civilian installations around the globe. Its current status is unknown.

SHIP TYPE: Freighter
FAMOUS EVENTS: The first battle of Earth

URF *ORIGAMI*

The URF *Origami* was a ship belonging to the United Rebel Front. A team of Spartans destroyed the ship in early 2531 CE.

SHIP TYPE: Destroyer

UNSC *TWO FOR FLINCHING*

The UNSC *Two For Flinching* is a fast-attack Corvette. In late 2524 CE it served as a transport for Staff Sgt. Avery Johnson and Petty Officer First Class Healy on their journey from Earth to Harvest.

SHIP TYPE: Corvette

UNSC *RESOLUTE*

The UNSC *Resolute* was serving in the Lambda Serpentis System at the time of the SPARTAN-II victory on Jericho VII. The ship retrieved the Spartan team following the battle but was forced to retreat when the Covenant fleet glassed the planet.

SHIP TYPE: Destroyer
KNOWN COMMANDER: Captain De Blanc
FAMOUS EVENTS: The battle of Jericho VII

➤ ON THE GROUND, THE SPARTANS ALWAYS WON. THE PROBLEM WAS, THEY COULDN'T TAKE THEIR SUCCESSES INTO SPACE.

COVENANT SHIPS are hugely versatile. Larger ships are used as fleet flagships and are heavily armed for combat. Thanks to their size, they are also used to dispatch troops. Smaller ships, like the Cruiser, are used to support and defend larger ships.

COVENANT ASSAULT CARRIER

The main flagships of the Covenant fleet, assault carriers are designed for planetary attacks, utilizing their extensive weaponry to break through orbital defenses before deploying a wide array of ground troops and artillery. Equally deadly during ship-to-ship encounters, the assault carrier's combat versatility is the main reason it was chosen to lead Covenant fleets into battle.

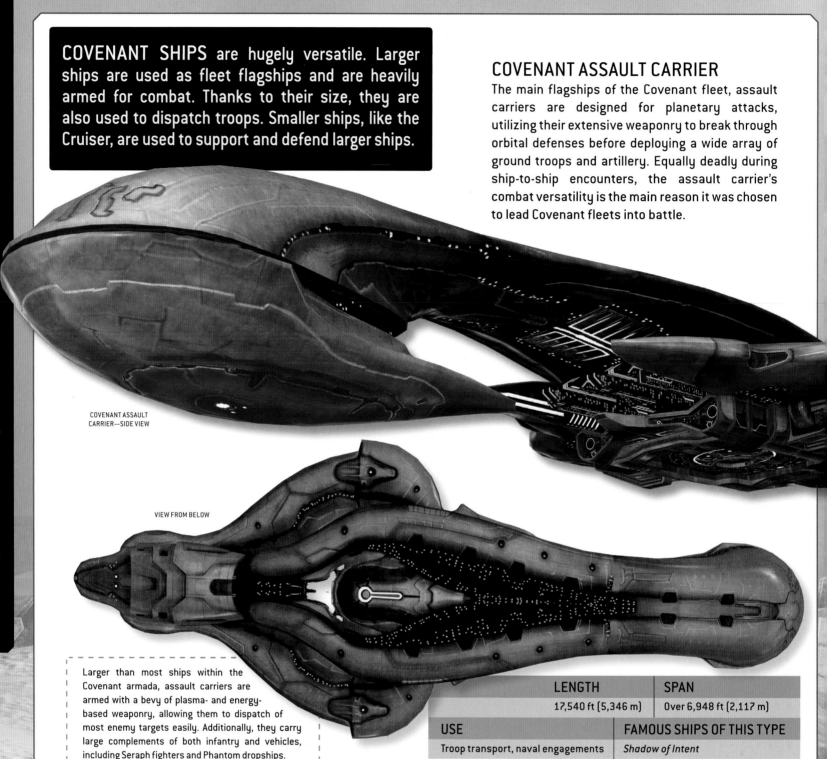

COVENANT ASSAULT CARRIER—SIDE VIEW

VIEW FROM BELOW

Larger than most ships within the Covenant armada, assault carriers are armed with a bevy of plasma- and energy-based weaponry, allowing them to dispatch of most enemy targets easily. Additionally, they carry large complements of both infantry and vehicles, including Seraph fighters and Phantom dropships.

LENGTH	SPAN
17,540 ft (5,346 m)	Over 6,948 ft (2,117 m)

USE	FAMOUS SHIPS OF THIS TYPE
Troop transport, naval engagements	*Shadow of Intent*

FLAGSHIP

"Flagship" is not a class of ship, but rather a title designated to the commanding vessel in a given fleet. In the Covenant fleet, they tend to be supercarriers, assault carriers, or Reverence-class cruisers.

FAMOUS SHIPS OF THIS TYPE: *Incorruptible Seeker of Truth, Shadow of Intent, Sublime Transcendence*

REVERENCE-CLASS CRUISER

Nearly two miles from stem to stern, the Reverence-class cruiser is a massive vessel capable of bringing large amounts of infantry for planetary deployment. Only one of these ships is said to have survived the Covenant Civil War, but it was destroyed soon after in a conflict that erupted near the world of Onyx.

FAMOUS SHIPS OF THIS TYPE: *Incorruptible*

COVENANT BATTLESHIP

Covenant battleships are equipped with a dozen energy projectors, making them among the best-armed ships in the Covenant fleet. They are capable of decimating entire UNSC fleets from long range. The massive amount of firepower they possess also makes them ideal for defending key locations and ships.

LENGTH: 656 ft (200 m) **USE:** Naval engagements

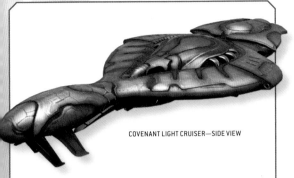

COVENANT LIGHT CRUISER—SIDE VIEW

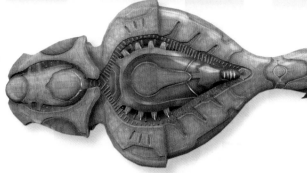

VIEW FROM ABOVE

LENGTH	USE
3,280–4,775 ft (1,000–1,455 m)	Capital ship support

COVENANT CRUISER

Cruisers are mid-sized ships that pack plenty of offensive punch by way of their impressive plasma torpedo array. They often serve in a supporting role for Covenant flagships.

COVENANT LIGHT CRUISER

The light cruiser is a smaller version of the Covenant cruiser. Utilized during the occupation of Reach, light cruisers have been described by UNSC forces as looking like "luminous manta rays."

LENGTH	USE
984 ft (300 m)	Support

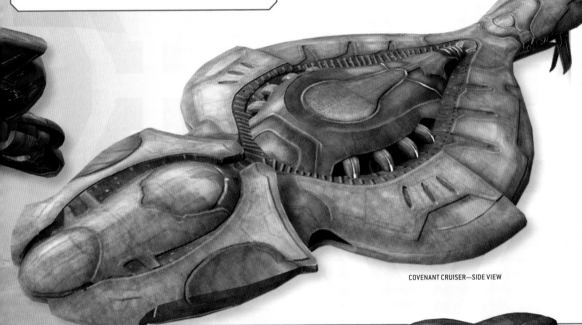

COVENANT CRUISER—SIDE VIEW

CCS-CLASS BATTLECRUISER

The CCS-class battlecruiser is the Covenant ship best known to UNSC forces, due to the extensive amount of time spent aboard the *Truth and Reconciliation* by Master Chief and numerous Marines during the battle of Alpha Halo.

They are a mid-sized capital ship in the Covenant fleet, and their offensive and defensive abilities, combined with a large personnel and equipment capacity, make them ideal for troop and vehicle deployment during ground engagements, as well as participating in ship-to-ship naval combat.

The CCS is shaped to allow for mobility in atmosphere during the deployment of infantry, as well as for a significant level of agility when battling in space. The interior is well documented by UNSC forces and its various features include a network of service corridors, a centrally located CIC (Combat Information Center) and bridge, a single gravity lift, and an extensive hanger bay. This information has given significant insight into the interiors of other Covenant vessels.

LENGTH: 5,847 ft (1,782 m) SPAN: 2,827 ft (862 m) USE: Troop transport, ground support FAMOUS SHIPS OF THIS TYPE: *Purity of Spirit, Sacred Promise, Triumphant Declaration, Truth and Reconciliation*

COVENANT SUPERCARRIER

One of the largest known vessels in the Covenant fleet, only a few supercarriers have ever been observed by UNSC forces. Extremely large and extremely powerful, Supercarriers are often used as flagships for Covenant fleets, such as the Second Fleet of Homogeneous Clarity, which defends the Covenant Holy City of High Charity, and the Combined Fleet of Righteous Purpose. The Prophets also use them as their personal flagships.

LENGTH: 17,552 (5,354 m) USE: Defense of strategic locations, naval engagements FAMOUS SHIPS OF THIS TYPE: *Sublime Transcendence*

COVENANT CARRIER

Despite being heavy warships in their own right, the primary role of the Covenant carrier is to launch fighters during naval engagements. It boasts thirteen launch bays containing a total of three hundred Seraph fighters, two hundred Banshees, and thirty-four dropships. It is crewed by upwards of four thousand Covenant troops. Additionally, it is armed with multiple plasma torpedo launchers and pulse laser turrets. The carrier is a less common and more powerful ship than the Covenant cruiser and is most likely meant to act as a command ship and a source of fighter support.

LENGTH: 4,790 ft (1,455 m) USE: Troop and single-pilot fighter transport, firing support FAMOUS SHIPS OF THIS TYPE: *Lawgiver*

BANSHEE

A single-man vehicle, the Banshee is mainly used by the Covenant as an aerial assault craft during ground engagements. Resembling a tiny jet, the Banshee pilot lays prone to access the vehicle's control panels and is protected by a bulbous nose section, which angles upward and back. Capable of reaching speeds of over sixty-two miles (one hundred kilometers) per hour it is extremely maneuverable, performing loops and barrel rolls with ease.

Heavy weapons and explosives are required to destroy the Banshee despite its lack of shielding. Small arms fire is only useful for dispatching the pilot. One of the most effective tactics for countering a Banshee is to stick it with a plasma grenade as it passes.

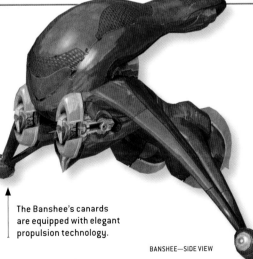

The Banshee's canards are equipped with elegant propulsion technology.

BANSHEE—SIDE VIEW

OTHER NAMES	LENGTH
Type-26 Ground Support Aircraft	18 ft (5.5 m)

USE	
Anti-infantry, bomber, reconnaissance	

➤ BANSHEES OF LEGEND WARNED OF DEATH, AND TODAY ALL UNSC VETERANS KNOW THE CRY OF THIS GLITTERING ALIEN TERROR.

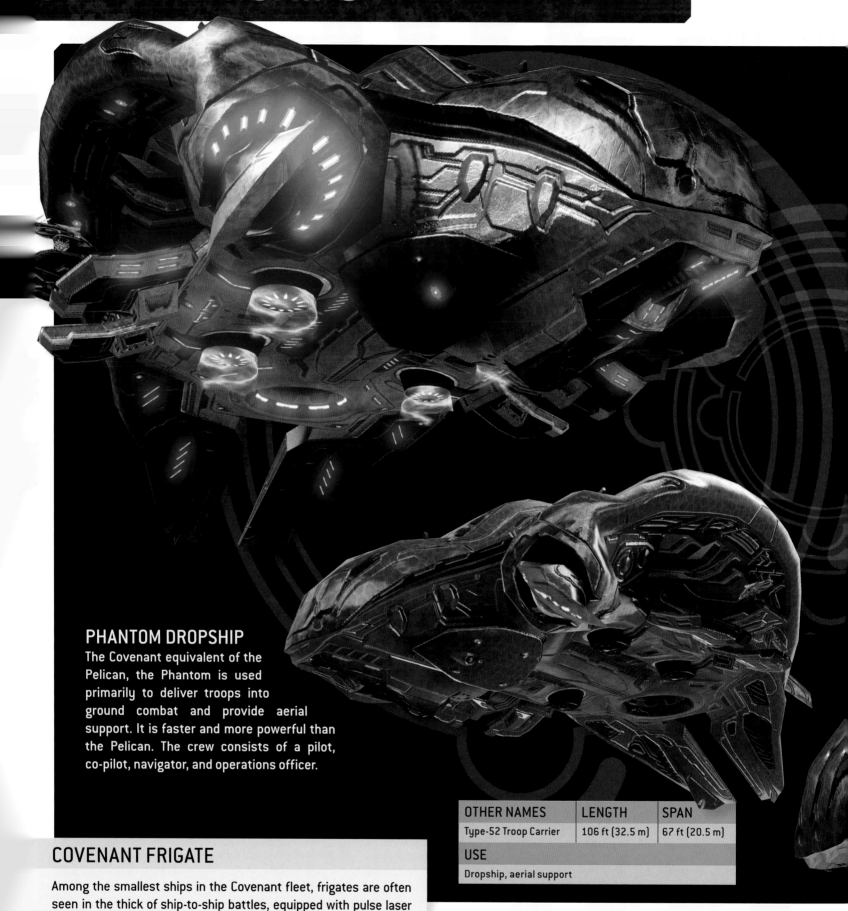

PHANTOM DROPSHIP

The Covenant equivalent of the Pelican, the Phantom is used primarily to deliver troops into ground combat and provide aerial support. It is faster and more powerful than the Pelican. The crew consists of a pilot, co-pilot, navigator, and operations officer.

OTHER NAMES	LENGTH	SPAN
Type-52 Troop Carrier	106 ft (32.5 m)	67 ft (20.5 m)
USE		
Dropship, aerial support		

COVENANT FRIGATE

Among the smallest ships in the Covenant fleet, frigates are often seen in the thick of ship-to-ship battles, equipped with pulse laser turrets, plasma torpedo launchers, and a variety of tertiary weapons systems depending on the commanding officer and crew. During the opening conflicts of the Covenant's civil war over High Charity, Brutes primarily used frigates against the outlying Elite forces.

LENGTH: 3,280 ft (1,000 m) USE: Support and escort FAMOUS SHIPS OF THIS TYPE: *Revenant, Tenebrous, Twilight Compunction*

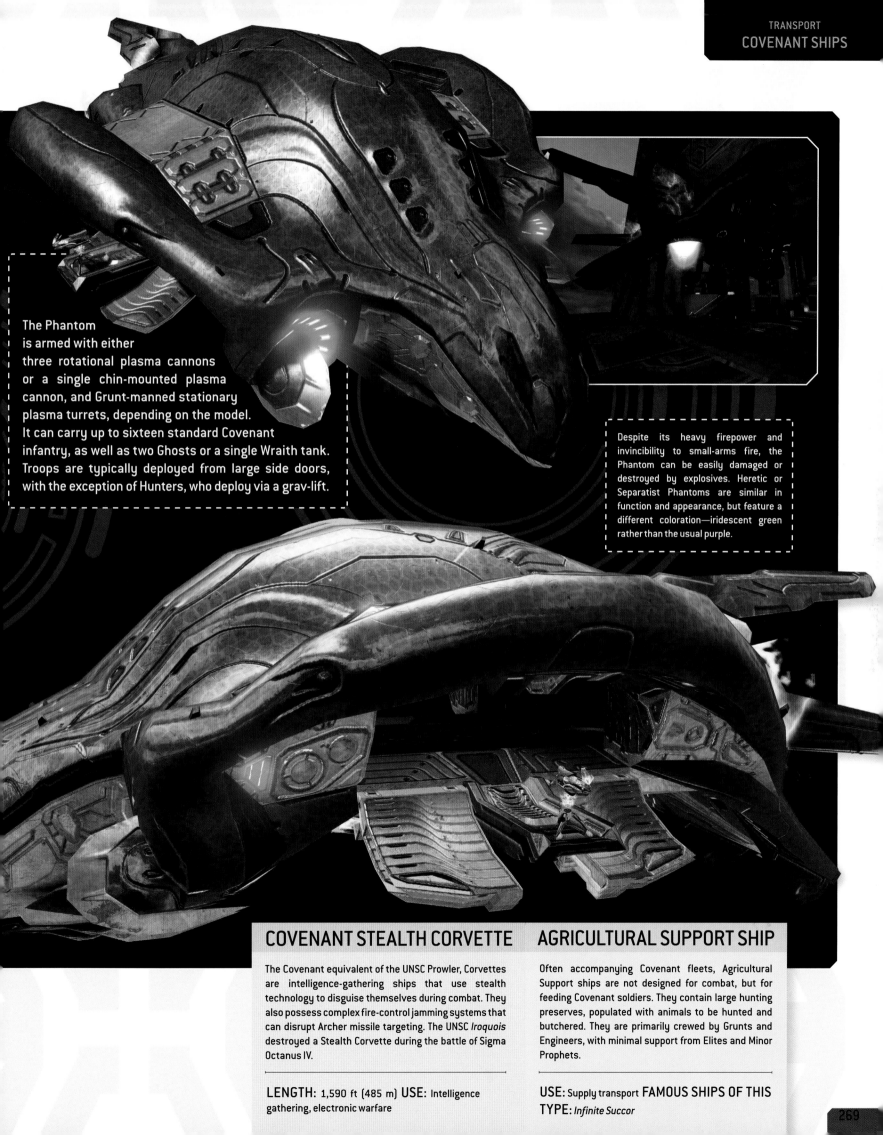

The Phantom
is armed with either
three rotational plasma cannons
or a single chin-mounted plasma
cannon, and Grunt-manned stationary
plasma turrets, depending on the model.
It can carry up to sixteen standard Covenant
infantry, as well as two Ghosts or a single Wraith tank.
Troops are typically deployed from large side doors,
with the exception of Hunters, who deploy via a grav-lift.

Despite its heavy firepower and
invincibility to small-arms fire, the
Phantom can be easily damaged or
destroyed by explosives. Heretic or
Separatist Phantoms are similar in
function and appearance, but feature a
different coloration—iridescent green
rather than the usual purple.

COVENANT STEALTH CORVETTE

The Covenant equivalent of the UNSC Prowler, Corvettes
are intelligence-gathering ships that use stealth
technology to disguise themselves during combat. They
also possess complex fire-control jamming systems that
can disrupt Archer missile targeting. The UNSC *Iroquois*
destroyed a Stealth Corvette during the battle of Sigma
Octanus IV.

LENGTH: 1,590 ft (485 m) USE: Intelligence
gathering, electronic warfare

AGRICULTURAL SUPPORT SHIP

Often accompanying Covenant fleets, Agricultural
Support ships are not designed for combat, but for
feeding Covenant soldiers. They contain large hunting
preserves, populated with animals to be hunted and
butchered. They are primarily crewed by Grunts and
Engineers, with minimal support from Elites and Minor
Prophets.

USE: Supply transport FAMOUS SHIPS OF THIS
TYPE: *Infinite Succor*

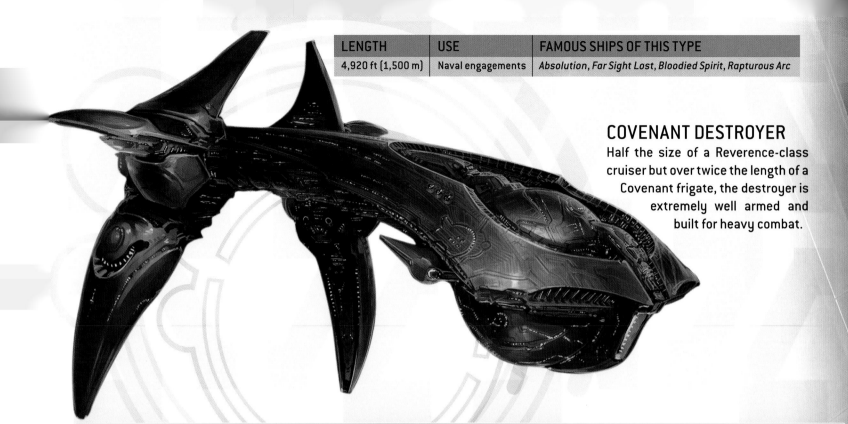

LENGTH	USE	FAMOUS SHIPS OF THIS TYPE
4,920 ft (1,500 m)	Naval engagements	*Absolution, Far Sight Lost, Bloodied Spirit, Rapturous Arc*

COVENANT DESTROYER

Half the size of a Reverence-class cruiser but over twice the length of a Covenant frigate, the destroyer is extremely well armed and built for heavy combat.

COVENANT NAME	LENGTH	SPAN
DX-class Dropship	91 ft (28 m)	59 ft (18 m)

SPIRIT

Shaped like a tuning fork, the Spirit dropship features two parallel troop bays extending forward from a rear cockpit, each able to hold fifteen Covenant warriors. Its lack of substantial offensive or defensive weapons suggests that it was intended for supply transport rather than troop transport.

The Spirit is armed with a singular rotating plasma cannon that is just below the cockpit. Despite appearing cumbersome in battle, the Spirit is a fast vessel, capable of reaching speeds in excess of 680 miles (1,094 kilometers) per hour.

COMBINED FLEET OF RIGHTEOUS PURPOSE

A massive Covenant fleet consisting of a composite of other fleets, Righteous Purpose was designated as vanguard for Covenant-occupied regions. Imperial Admiral Xytan 'Jar Wattinree led Righteous Purpose and its collection of over two hundred vessels. At the start of the civil war between members of the Covenant, Brutes had intended on laying siege to the fleet's anchor outpost, a planet called Joyous Exultation, but by the time they arrived, the world had been obliterated by a UNSC NOVA bomb.

NOTABLE SHIPS: *Sublime Transcendence, Far Sight Lost, Absolution*

FLEET OF PARTICULAR JUSTICE

Prior to its destruction, the Fleet of Particular Justice was led by Supreme Commander Thel 'Vadam. After destroying the planet of Reach, the fleet gave chase to the UNSC *Pillar of Autumn*, eventually arriving at Installation 04. There, the vast majority of the fleet was destroyed when the UNSC warship's fusion reactors went critical and set off a chain reaction that destroyed the *Autumn*, the installation, and most of the surrounding Covenant ships.

NOTABLE SHIPS: *Ascendant Justice, Infinite Succor, Seeker of Truth, Truth and Reconciliation*

COVENANT BOARDING CRAFT

Despite greatly outclassing the UNSC in naval engagements, the Covenant has shown a desire to capture human ships and technology. This behaviour may stem from the Covenant's longstanding approach to technological advancement through the replication of captured Forerunner artifacts. Two models of boarding craft have been observed, one carrying less than a dozen troops, the other carrying approximately seventy-five.

LENGTH: Varies SPAN: Varies
USE: Boarding

SERAPH FIGHTER

The Covenant equivalent of the Longsword Fighter, Seraphs are teardrop-shaped single-man ships, piloted by either Elites or Brutes.

Attacking in formations of ten and patrolling in pairs, Seraphs are used for everything from dogfighting to bombing runs. Despite their speed and power in space, they are awkward and sluggish in atmospheric conditions due to their odd shape.

LENGTH	USE
91 ft (28 m)	Attack

Armed with heavy plasma cannons, pulse lasers, and plasma charges, Seraphs are more than a match for even the most hardened Longsword pilots. They are also equipped with standard energy shields.

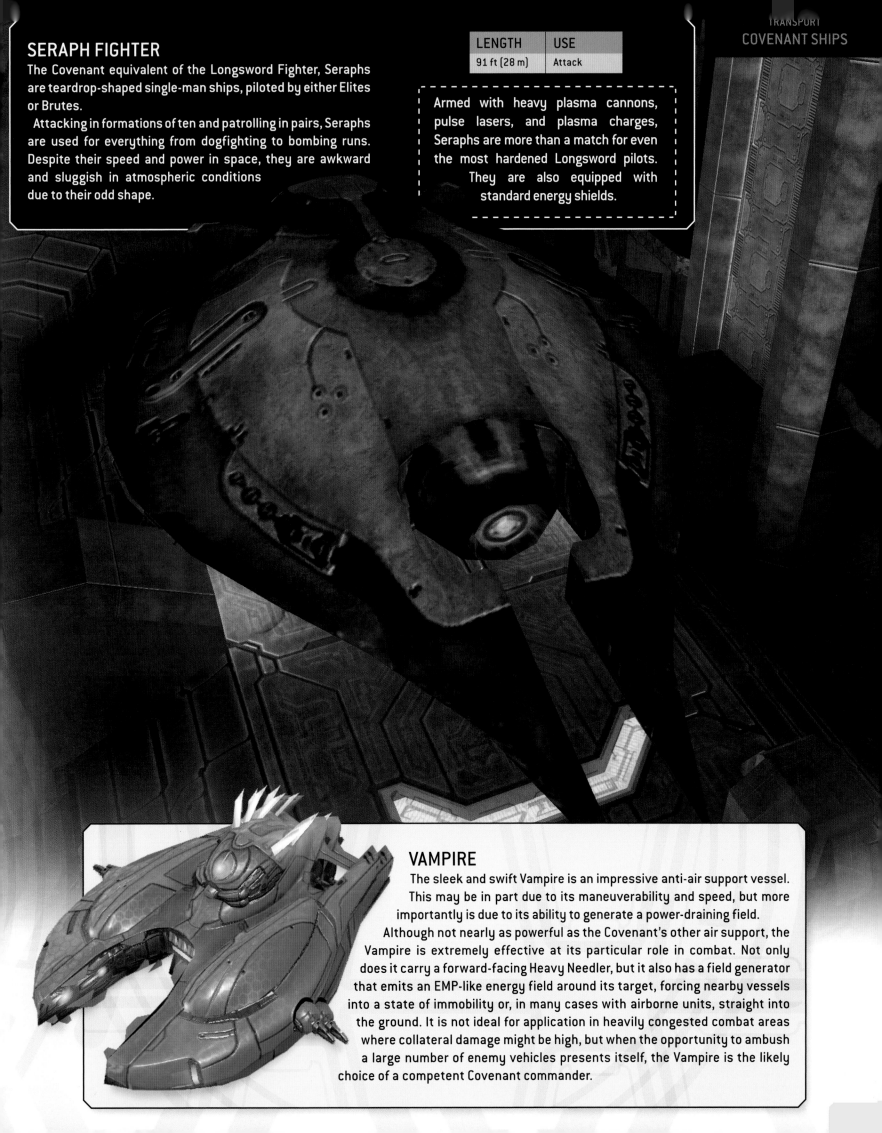

VAMPIRE

The sleek and swift Vampire is an impressive anti-air support vessel. This may be in part due to its maneuverability and speed, but more importantly is due to its ability to generate a power-draining field.

Although not nearly as powerful as the Covenant's other air support, the Vampire is extremely effective at its particular role in combat. Not only does it carry a forward-facing Heavy Needler, but it also has a field generator that emits an EMP-like energy field around its target, forcing nearby vessels into a state of immobility or, in many cases with airborne units, straight into the ground. It is not ideal for application in heavily congested combat areas where collateral damage might be high, but when the opportunity to ambush a large number of enemy vehicles presents itself, the Vampire is the likely choice of a competent Covenant commander.

COVENANT SHIPS TYPICALLY carry a bevy of both offensive and defensive weapons in addition to the expected amounts of infantry, equipment, vehicles, and other material. These are named Covenant ships that have played significant roles in the Covenant's campaigns.

SHIP TYPE	KNOWN COMMANDERS
Assault carrier	Rtas 'Vadumee, the Arbiter
FAMOUS EVENTS	

The battle of Delta Halo, the second battle of Earth, the battle of Installation 00

ASCENDANT JUSTICE

Though it is believed that the *Ascendant Justice* was a leading ship within the Fleet of Particular Justice, no hard evidence apart from its appearance in the debris field of Installation 04 substantiates this.

When the ship did arrive in this sector, a band of human survivors, including the Master Chief, boarded the vessel and killed the rather shallow number of Covenant forces aboard. Using the alien ship, they returned to Reach and were able to exfiltrate with the remnants of Spartan Red Team and Dr. Catherine Halsey, among others.

Using the UNSC *Gettysburg* to generate more power, *Ascendant Justice* eventually carried the Spartans to the Unyielding Hierophant (a Covenant battle station) where, after a strategic ground operation, the ship was used to draw a majority of the local Covenant forces in before its reactors overloaded and destroyed everything within range. The Spartans managed to narrowly escape aboard the UNSC *Gettysburg*.

SHIP TYPE: Flagship (unconfirmed) FAMOUS EVENTS: The battle of Delta Halo

INFINITE SUCCOR

Attached to the Fleet of Particular Justice, the *Infinite Succor* was responsible for providing the fleet with food via its massive hunting preserve. Following the battle of Installation 04, the Flood-infected Spirit dropship *Brilliant Gift* was able to dock on the *Infinite Succor*. Crewed only by Grunts and Engineers, the *Infinite Succor* was powerless to halt the infestation.

A strike team, led by Rtas 'Vadumee, was dispatched to rescue a minor Prophet aboard the *Infinite Succor* and destroy the Flood infestation. Finding the Prophet and the entire crew infected, Rtas 'Vadumee managed to set the *Infinite Succor* on a Slipspace vector for the nearest star. Although he managed to survive, the remainder of his team was lost with the ship.

SHIP TYPE: Agricultural support ship

REVERENCE

The *Reverence* was a CPV-class Destroyer that took uncharacteristic opportunity to communicate with the crew of the UNSC *Pillar of Autumn*.

SHIP TYPE:
CPV-class destroyer

BRILLIANT GIFT

The *Brilliant Gift* was a Covenant Spirit dropship that crash-landed in a swamp on Halo Installation 04. Master Chief battled with its crew during the battle of Installation 04. Later, the ship was repaired by Flood Combat Forms, which used it to escape the destruction of the installation. The *Brilliant Gift* later boarded the *Infinite Succor*, which was also infected by the Flood. When a team of Covenant Elites destroyed the *Infinite Succor*, the *Brilliant Gift* was presumed destroyed.

SHIP TYPE: Spirit dropship

RAPTUROUS ARC

Attached to the Second Fleet of Homogenous Clarity, the *Rapturous Arc* arrived at Halo Installation 05 as one of the vanguard ships of High Charity. During the battle of Delta Halo, it was one of the four Destroyers that attempted to destroy all Flood-infected vessels escaping from the Halo. The *Rapturous Arc* was eventually overtaken by the Flood and crashed into another ship in an attempt to spread the infection.

SHIP TYPE: Destroyer

TENEBROUS

Attached to the Second Fleet of Homogenous Clarity, the Brute-controlled *Tenebrous* assisted the *Twilight Compunction* in attacking the Elite-controlled *Incorruptible*. The *Tenebrous* was destroyed by an attack from the *Incorruptible's* energy projector.

SHIP TYPE: Missionary ship
KNOWN COMMANDERS:
Chur'R-Yar (Jackal)

SHADOW OF INTENT

During the events following the Covenant civil war high above High Charity and Delta Halo, *Shadow of Intent* and its corresponding Fleet of Retribution gave chase to a single Covenant cruiser entering Slipspace, a cruiser infected by the Flood.

Upon exiting, they realized they had reached the Sol System and the planet Earth. It was here that the Arbiter led Shipmaster Rtas 'Vadum into an uneasy alliance with the UNSC, an alliance which ultimately won the war.

Following the Covenant to the Ark, the *Shadow of Intent* directed Elite and UNSC forces, resulting in the obliteration of the local Covenant contingency and the assassination of the Prophet of Truth.

SHADOW OF INTENT

TRUTH AND RECONCILIATION

As a part of the Fleet of Particular Justice, the *Truth and Reconciliation* was one of the hundreds of Covenant vessels that participated in the battle of Reach. It is a CCS-class battlecruiser.

When the *Pillar of Autumn* escaped into Slipspace, *Truth and Reconciliation* led the pursuit party. After the *Pillar of Autumn* crashed on Installation 04, the *Truth and Reconciliation* became the Covenant command center during the ensuing battle. Despite being unable to destroy the *Pillar of Autumn* for fear of damaging the Halo, the ship was eventually able to capture Captain Jacob Keyes. A UNSC force led by the Master Chief, which managed to eliminate most of the Covenant forces aboard and take the ship, retrieved Keyes from the *Truth and Reconciliation*.

When Major Antonio Silva was left in command of the vessel it was decided to take the ship back to Earth. First Lieutenant Melissa McKay realized that the potential for Flood infection of Earth made this a dangerous gamble and she destroyed the navigation controls on the ship, causing it to crash into the surface of Halo Installation 04.

SHIP TYPE: CCS-class battlecruiser **FAMOUS PERSONALITIES:** Zuka 'Zamamee, Bako 'Ikaporamee (Elites) **FAMOUS EVENTS:** The Battle of Reach, the battle of Installation 04

COMMITMENT AND PATIENCE

Little is known of *Commitment and Patience* or the vessels *Sacred Promise* and *Devotion*, which were in its company during their fateful engagement with UNSC forces. A black box recovered by ONI from *Sacred Promise*'s wreckage, however, has opened a brief window into the stratagem of Covenant warfare.

SHIP TYPE: (Redacted)

FAMOUS COVENANT SHIPS

ABSOLUTION

A vessel in the Combined Fleet of Righteous Purpose, the *Absolution* found itself ambushed by Onyx's expansive network of Sentinels during a brief skirmish near the planet. Attempting to gain a strategic advantage, the *Absolution* was destroyed by Sentinels.

SHIP TYPE: Destroyer FAMOUS EVENTS: The battle of Onyx

CONTRITION

Little is known about the Covenant Frigate *Contrition* apart from its crew's attempts at psychological warfare during space combat, most notably with the UNSC *Hermes II*.

SHIP TYPE: CAR-class frigate

BLOODIED SPIRIT

Part of the Covenant's assault on Earth, *Bloodied Spirit*'s crew was intent on securing a portion of the UNSC's nuclear arsenal. When a team of Spartans covertly stormed their vessel, the Covenant aboard were quickly killed.

Under new orders, the Spartans then used the ship to travel to Onyx, where they were forced to escape before the vessel was destroyed by the planet's hostile Sentinels.

SHIP TYPE: Destroyer

RAPID CONVERSION

Considered unfit for Sangheili use, the *Rapid Conversion* was relegated to the Jiralhanae, who made do with its numerous disabled mechanical systems and generally poor condition. Led by Chieftain Maccabeus, the ship was crewed by a pack of ten Jiralhanae and also consisted of approximately sixty Grunts and a hive of Drones. After rescuing Dadab and *Lighter Than Some* following the destruction of *Minor Transgression*, the *Rapid Conversion* became the first Covenant warship to directly assault a human world when initial contact with the colony of Harvest went horribly awry.

SHIP TYPE: Cruiser KNOWN COMMANDERS: Maccabeus (Brute) FAMOUS PERSONALITIES: Tartarus, Vorenus, Grattius, Licinus, Strab, Ritul, Druss

FAR SIGHT LOST

A part of the Combined Fleet of Righteous Purpose, the *Far Sight Lost* journeyed to Onyx as a member of the *Incorruptible*'s battlegroup. Upon arrival, the *Far Sight Lost* was sent ahead to make contact with the Onyx Sentinels, believing them to be emissaries of the Forerunners. The Sentinels quickly destroyed the ship during this attempt.

SHIP TYPE: Destroyer FAMOUS EVENTS: The battle of Onyx KNOWN COMMANDERS: Qunu (Elite)

REVERENCE

Lost in a series of transmissions captured during battle, the *Reverence* was one of a group of ships that threatened the *Pillar of Autumn* during a space engagement.

SHIP TYPE: CPV-class destroyer

SACRED PROMISE

Heavily damaged during a battle with UNSC forces, the *Sacred Promise* had originally requested support from the *Devotion* and the *Commitment and Patience*. Its engine control disabled by a heavy UNSC weapon, the vessel began accelerating uncontrollably toward a nearby moon. The crew abandoned ship and the *Sacred Promise* was presumably destroyed upon impact.

SHIP TYPE: CCS-class battlecruiser

SUBLIME TRANSCENDENCE

As the flagship of the Fleet of Righteous Purpose, the *Sublime Transcendence* retrieved a NOVA bomb from Reach for further examination. Several months later, the ship had returned to the world of Joyous Exultation, its crew discussing the ramifications of the Covenant Civil War. However, the ship, its fleet, and the planet were all destroyed when Engineers accidentally activated the NOVA bomb.

SHIP TYPE: Supercarrier KNOWN COMMANDERS: Imperial Admiral Xytan 'Jar Wattinree (Elite)

REVENANT

Attached to the Second Fleet of Homogenous Clarity, the *Revenant* was a Brute-controlled vessel that was heavily engaged with Elite ships during the battle of Delta Halo. It assisted the *Twilight Compunction* in tracking the *Incorruptible*, but was destroyed by an energy projector in the confusion following the arrival of the human-controlled *Bloodied Spirit*.

SHIP TYPE: Frigate FAMOUS EVENTS: The battle of Delta Halo

TWILIGHT COMPUNCTION

The *Twilight Compunction* was a Frigate within the Second Fleet of Homogenous Clarity which was seized by the Brutes at the start of the Covenant Civil War. Heavily damaged during an engagement with the Elite-occupied *Lawgiver*, the vessel joined with *Revenant*, another Brute-controlled frigate, to attack the Separatist cruiser *Incorruptible*. They would have seen success, had it not been for the *Bloodied Spirit*, which emerged from Slipspace during the battle, effectively blocking their pursuit. *Twilight Compunction* turned its attention to this new Covenant ship, which, to its crew's surprise, was being operated by humans.

SHIP TYPE: Frigate **FAMOUS EVENTS:** The battle of Delta Halo

TRIUMPHANT DECLARATION

A part of the Fleet of Furious Redemption, the *Triumphant Declaration* captured Colonel James Ackerson during the second battle of Earth. After his interrogation, the ship led an attack on the city of Cleveland in an attempt to locate the Key of Osanalan.

SHIP TYPE: CCS-class battlecruiser **FAMOUS EVENTS:** The second battle of Earth **KNOWN COMMANDERS:** Lepidus (Brute)

PIOUS INQUISITOR

Considered one of the fastest ships at the Covenant's disposal, the *Pious Inquisitor* saw action at the first battle of Earth when the High Prophet of Regret assaulted the city of New Mombasa. It later returned for the second battle of Earth and as part of the Fleet of Retribution, operated by Covenant Separatists who were pursuing a Flood-controlled cruiser to Earth. Given the luxurious nature of its interior, it is speculated that it may have been the flagship of the High Prophet of Regret.

FAMOUS EVENTS: The first battle of Earth, the second battle of Earth

PURITY OF SPIRIT

The *Purity of Spirit* was involved in an engagement with UNSC's forces near Reach, where it taunted the *Pillar of Autumn*, among other ships.

SHIP TYPE: CCS-class battlecruiser

ESTEEM

The *Esteem* was one of several Covenant vessels which engaged in psychological warfare when battling with UNSC forces near the planet of Reach.

SHIP TYPE: CPV-class destroyer

INCORRUPTIBLE

During the battles which broke out near High Charity and Delta Halo, the Cruiser known as *Incorruptible* was almost destroyed by its own commander when Tano 'Inararee, belonging to the Governors of Contrition who believed the Flood to be part of the Forerunners' divinity, moved the vessel toward the parasite's exposure on Installation 05.

When Voro 'Mantakree led a mutiny against his Shipmaster, they averted this fate and after a series of engagements with Brute-controlled ships, returned back to the outpost world of *Joyous Exultation*. There, the crew received a new mission to the planet of Onyx in search of Forerunner artifacts. After reaching the human world, the *Incorruptible* met its fate when it collided with UNSC Hornet mines during a brief battle above the planet's surface.

SHIP TYPE: Reverence-class cruiser **FAMOUS EVENTS:** The battle of Onyx; also involved in battles over High Charity and Delta Halo **COMMANDERS:** Tano 'Inanraree, Voro Nar 'Mantakree (Elites)

LAWGIVER

Attached to the Second Fleet of Homogeneous Clarity, the *Lawgiver* found itself embroiled in a battle between Elite- and Brute-controlled ships when war broke out near High Charity and Delta Halo. The *Lawgiver* was crewed by Elites and rushed to defend the *Incorruptible*, which was being attacked by the Brute-controlled *Twilight Compunction*.

The *Lawgiver* damaged *Twilight Compunction* while simultaneously taking several missiles meant for the *Incorruptible*. Its final fate is not known.

SHIP TYPE: Carrier

PENANCE

The *Penance* was part of a contingency of Covenant ships engaged near Reach. These ships were best known for their taunting transmissions to the UNSC outposts and vessels during battle.

SHIP TYPE: CAR-class

MINOR TRANSGRESSION

Operating for the Ministry of Tranquility, *Minor Transgression* was a missionary vessel which made first contact with humanity when stumbling upon a UNSC freighter. Under the impression that the vessel housed Forerunner artifacts, the Jackal crew saw this as a financial opportunity and continued to raid human ships in search of valuable relics. They eventually ran afoul of a trap set by the UNSC, who initially believed *Transgression* to be a ship of human Insurrectionist pirates. When it looked as though the UNSC would take the ship, the commander of the *Minor Transgression* destroyed it.

SHIP TYPE: Missionary ship **KNOWN COMMANDERS:** Chur'R-Yar (a Jackal)

WITH ITS DISTINCTIVE geometric and angular appearance, the Forerunner Dreadnought was an important vessel used in the Forerunner-Flood war. As the only ship able to activate the portal that allowed access to the Ark, the Forerunner Dreadnought was also a vital part of the Forerunner strategy against the Flood. It was thought that all the Forerunner Dreadnought ships had been destroyed during the battle of the Maginot Sphere, however the San 'Shyuum discovered one ship that had survived the destruction. This ship, which was simply known as the Dreadnought, was worshipped by the San 'Shyuum who used it to explore the Galaxy.

THE LAST FORERUNNER SHIP

When the San 'Shyuum discovered the last surviving Forerunner Dreadnought they used it in a devastating war against Sanghelli. After the two races signed the Writ of Union—the treaty that led to the creation of the Covenant—the Dreadnought was decommissioned, stripped of its weapons and used to power the city of High Charity, which was built around it.

Later, just prior to the Human-Covenant War, the dormant Oracle inhabiting the Dreadnought awoke and informed several Prophets that the humans, not the Covenant, were the chosen race of the Forerunners. The Prophets subverted this information, thus setting the stage for the Human-Covenant War.

Several decades later, following the battle of Installation 05, the Flood attacked High Charity and the High Prophet of Truth escaped by detaching the Dreadnought from the city and jumping into Slipspace. Master Chief managed to stow away aboard the ship and escaped before the High Prophet landed atop an ancient Forerunner machine, activating the portal to the Ark. UNSC forces then assaulted the ship, but they were unable to prevent the opening of the portal, which transported the ship to the Ark. The Dreadnought was most likely inoperable by the time it arrived on the Ark, and was presumably destroyed along with it.

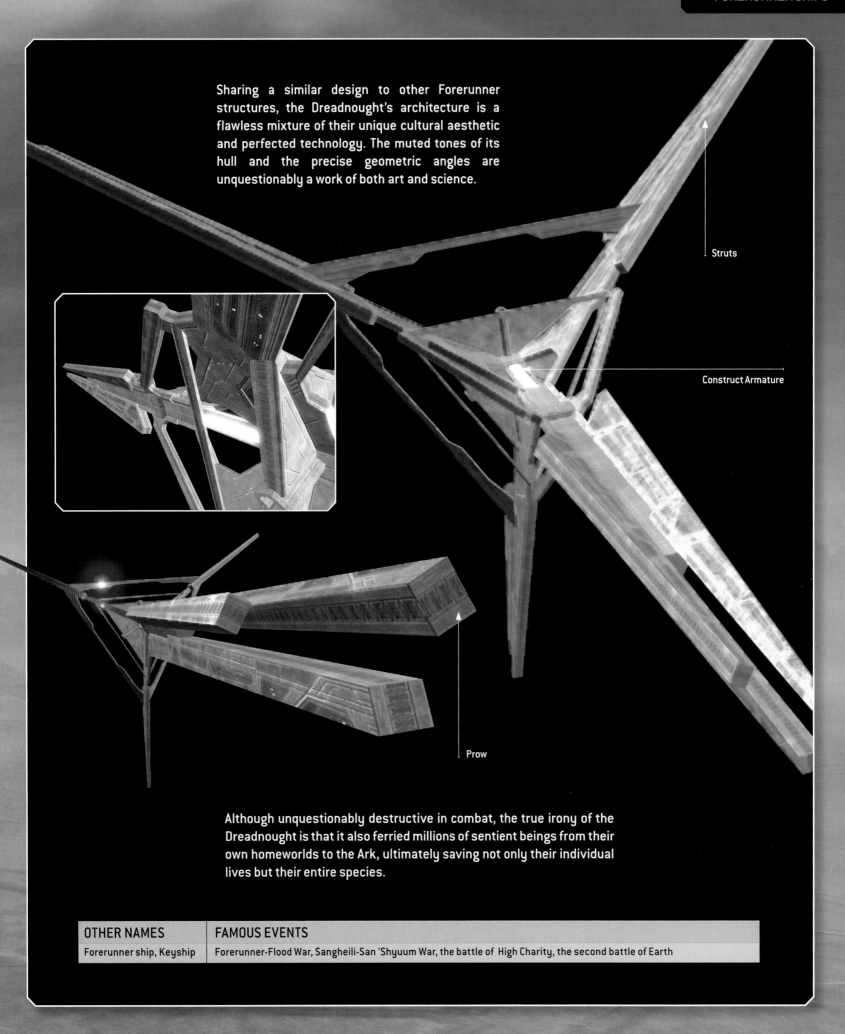

Sharing a similar design to other Forerunner structures, the Dreadnought's architecture is a flawless mixture of their unique cultural aesthetic and perfected technology. The muted tones of its hull and the precise geometric angles are unquestionably a work of both art and science.

Struts

Construct Armature

Prow

Although unquestionably destructive in combat, the true irony of the Dreadnought is that it also ferried millions of sentient beings from their own homeworlds to the Ark, ultimately saving not only their individual lives but their entire species.

OTHER NAMES	FAMOUS EVENTS
Forerunner ship, Keyship	Forerunner-Flood War, Sangheili-San 'Shyuum War, the battle of High Charity, the second battle of Earth

LOCATIONS

SEMI-PERMANENT AND transportable, UNSC bases can be dropped from orbit into hostile territory. They can comprise a command center, barracks, production facilities, and tactical communications, all in one compact outpost.

BASE TURRETS

UNSC bases are defended by turrets. Standard-issue turrets use M202 XP machine guns but other types can be armed with flame mortars, rail guns, and anti-aircraft missile launchers.

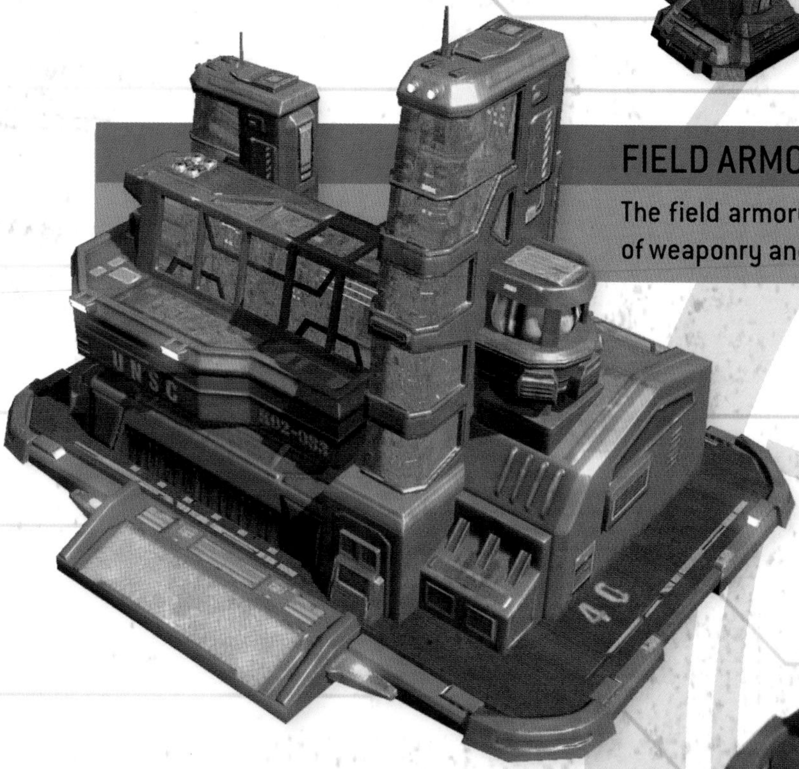

FIELD ARMORY

The field armory is a base's source of weaponry and ammunition.

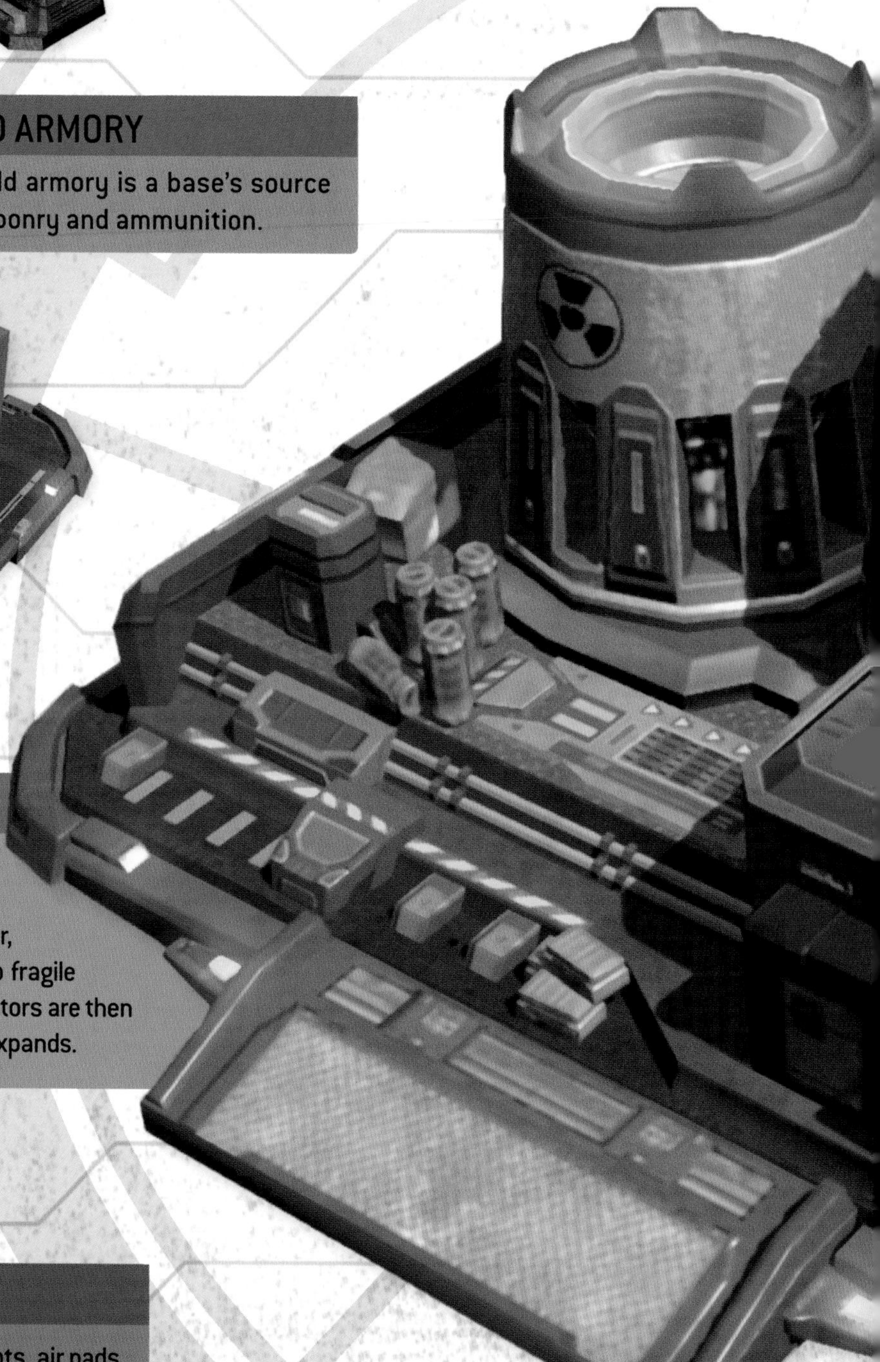

REACTOR

Every base is powered by a hydrogen reactor. Bases are initially equipped with a relatively small reactor, since larger power generators are too fragile to be dropped reliably from orbit. Reactors are then enhanced on the ground as the base expands.

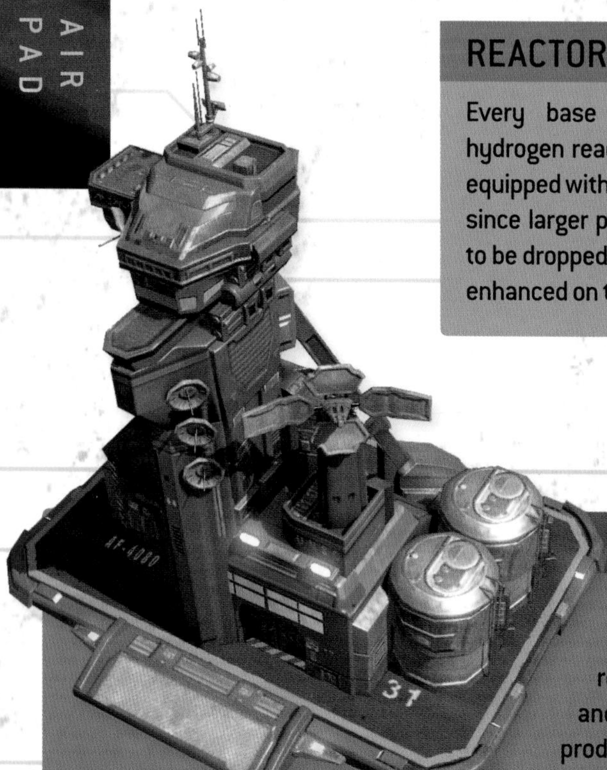

AIR PAD

Similar to vehicle depots, air pads are sites for constructing and repairing aircraft such as the Hornet and Vulture. As well as being a production facility, air pads also contain ready rooms and simulators for pilots.

BARRACKS

Far from having any creature comforts, the barracks is nevertheless home for UNSC soldiers. This is where the infantry units—Marines, Flamethrowers, and Spartans—enjoy the long waits between battles.

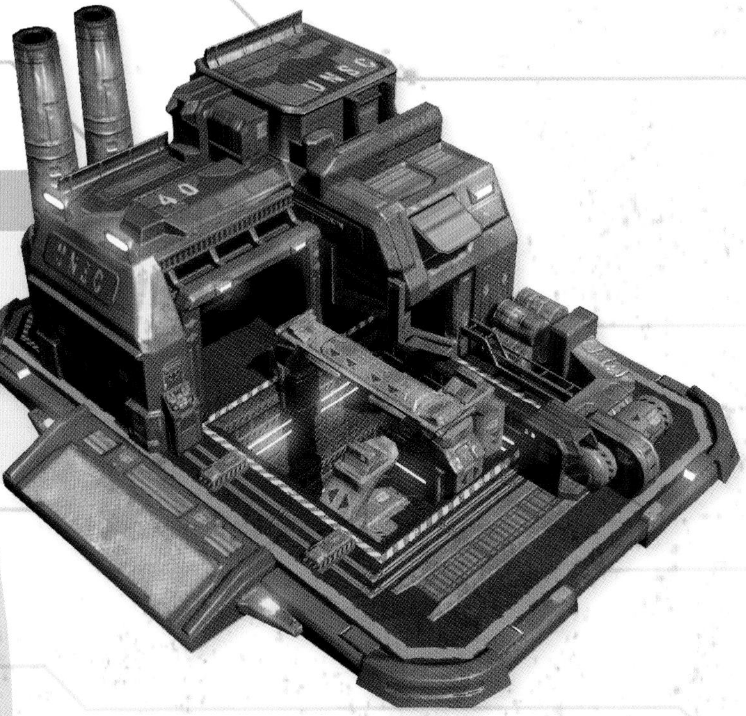

VEHICLE DEPOT

The vehicle depot is the center of vehicle production on UNSC bases. Facilitated by heavy equipment and hydraulic cranes, specially trained troops assemble and repair Scorpions, Cobras, and Wolverines from kits transported in via supply pads.

SUPPLY PAD

Supply pads are used to receive resources from orbiting space craft. The lifeblood of any base, they are the conduit for everything from medical kits and food to fully assembled tank engines.

THE SOL SYSTEM

LOCATED IN ORION'S ARM, the Sol System is the heart of the UNSC. Its third planet, Earth, is the birthplace of humanity and remains one of its largest production areas. When humankind encountered the Covenant, the UNSC developed the Cole Protcol to keep the Sol System hidden, but the Covenant did eventually find Earth. Two major battles were fought there, and now that the conflict is essentially over, rebuilding must begin.

EARTH

LOCATION: Third planet of the Sol System
DESCRIPTION: Mostly water, humanity's home planet, polluted, overcrowded

Home. No matter how far away a Marine may go, his heart always returns to Earth. It is haven, mother, father, and everything every human is fighting for. Billions still live there despite the ongoing colonization of the stars, and for good reason. Despite its sometimes polluted shores, it is where humanity was born and where it will eventually die. The Covenant, of course, hoped to speed up that process and spent many, many years and much of their efforts trying to locate this planet. To prevent this, the UNSC developed the Cole Protocol, which called for the dumping of any information prior to a Covenant capture, and forced fleeing ships to jump to random points away from Earth.

Eventually however, humanity's enemy did find the Sol System. For over a hundred thousand years, humans had been the dominant species, but within a matter of hours, the entire population of Earth was cut in half as the first battle of Earth began.

UNSC forces did manage to fight back, thanks in part to the efforts of Master Chief, but the Covenant later returned to lead the second battle of Earth. Even with all of the bases, forces, and defenses of the planet, the UNSC could only hold out for so long. The Covenant was on a religious quest, not simply the cause of extermination.

Deep below the surface of the planet lay the Forerunner portal. For an unknown reason, the Forerunners had placed that link to their Ark installation on Earth. Is this linked to why the Forerunner language refers to humans as "Reclaimers?" What will become of Earth—and humanity—now that the Human-Covenant War has ended?

LUNA

LOCATION: Orbiting Earth
DESCRIPTION: Barren surface, tidal influencer, atmospherically devoid
MAJOR LOCATIONS: Luna OCS Academy

Earth's moon and closest neighbor has inspired humanity since the dawn of time. It has no atmosphere to speak of, while its surface is covered by pockmarked meteor collisions. Now, thanks to advances in technology, Luna is home to several stations and domes, most notably the Luna OCS Academy. Large-scale terraforming has not taken place there, largely due to the moon's low gravity.

CAIRO STATION

LOCATION: Orbiting Earth

Cairo Station is one of many Orbital Defense Platforms (ODPs) in geosynchronous orbit above Earth. Like other platforms, Cairo belongs to a battle cluster and its primary function is the maintenance and use of its massive MAC gun. It is named for the Egyptian city of Cairo, which it orbits above.

The legendary Master Chief was aboard Cairo Station during the first battle of Earth. There, he staved off Covenant invaders intent on bombing the station and punching a hole through its battle cluster. Although other platforms fell, Cairo remained intact. Fleet Admiral Hood commanded Earth's defensive systems from the station as well. When it became clear that the battle was shifting from orbital defense to a ground battle, he ordered Master Chief and Avery Johnson to take the fight planetside.

ATHENS AND MALTA STATIONS

LOCATION: Orbiting Earth

Of the same type and construction as Cairo Station, Athens and Malta Stations were defensive command posts for Earth, but they were destroyed nearly simultaneously by a pair of Covenant bombs. Prior to its destruction, Athens held in geosynchronous orbit over the city of the same name.

The destruction of Athens Station, combined with that of Malta Station, allowed the High Prophet of Regret's assault carrier to slip into Earth's atmosphere to assault the African city of New Mombasa.

STATION WAYWARD REST

LOCATION: Orbiting Earth

Station Wayward Rest served as the terminus facility of the Centennial Orbital Elevator which was tethered to the city of Havana as an immense structure that ferried large loads of materials from Earth into orbit. During an operation involving Spartan Blue Team, Station Wayward Rest was destroyed alongside the COE when the super-soldiers vaporized a nearby Covenant vessel by arming and detonating six FENRIS nuclear warheads within it.

MARS

LOCATION: Fourth planet of the Sol System
DESCRIPTION: Iron-rich, fully terraformed, first human-colonized planet
MAJOR LOCATIONS: New Manila, New Legaspi, Chiron Testing Station, Chiron TL-34, Misriah Armory, Reyes-McLees Shipyards, Argyre Planitia, Mare Erythraeum, Phobos Penal Colony

Mars was one of the first planets known to the ancients, and so it is perhaps fitting that it became the first planet that humanity colonized. After centuries of terraforming, the "Red" planet is now as green and blue as Earth, but with less population. Its features may seem bizarre to those who have never ventured beyond humanity's homeworld, but to those who live there, it is nothing but their home.

This world also has the dubious distinction of being the first planet to rebel from UNSC control. In the events leading up to the Interplanetary War, Mars harbored many activists and Rebels who would later take part in the conflict. When the first shots were fired, many Martians joined the neo-communist Koslovics. These revolutionaries were eventually put down in the harsh blitzes that eventually purged the Sol System of such idealists.

After many centuries of tranquility, Mars once again saw war when the Covenant's fleets arrived in the Sol System. Colonel James Ackerson participated in the engagements on the surface of Mars but was captured in the fields of Mare Erythraeum. These actions ultimately assisted the UNSC in delaying the Covenant forces in their protracted assault on Earth.

MERCURY

LOCATION: First planet of the Sol System
DESCRIPTION: Tiny, barren, atmospherically void, hot

Mercury is the planet closest to Sol. The heat and its small size have contributed to its atmosphere (if there ever was one) being boiled from the surface.

Because of this harsh nature, it is of little use to UNSC forces.

JUPITER

LOCATION: Fifth planet of the Sol System
DESCRIPTION: Gas giant, several habitable moons, radiation-emitter

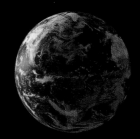

As humanity does not yet have the technology to mine on gas giants, Jupiter remains in its original capacity—a scientific curiosity. Its swirling winds give information on the formation of storms, while many other features (its intense radiation, ring system, and orbital path) also allow scientists to analyze mysteries of the universe.

Mainly, however, Jupiter is the planet around which many habitable moons have been colonized. Humans have been there since the first days of colonization and Jupiter was the starting point of the Interplanetary War when the Colonists bucked against the control of Earth.

CALLISTO

LOCATION: Orbiting Jupiter
DESCRIPTION: Rock and ice ball, atmospherically devoid, UNSC-controlled, minimally colonized

Discovered by Galileo, Callisto has long been a source of fascination for humans. Even colonized, it remains a source of mystery. Why, even though it is ninety-nine percent the size of Mercury, does it have a third less of the mass? How did ice manage to form there without the aid of an atmosphere? Is there an ocean beneath the surface of the moon?

These questions are now secondary to Callisto's actual purpose, which is primarily militaristic in nature. The UNSC has several bases there, all of which are capable of launching their units and ships within an hour's notice.

IO

LOCATION: Orbiting Jupiter
DESCRIPTION: Massively volcanic, atmospherically volatile, unstable, populated

Io is a volcanic moon of Jupiter that, while volatile, nonetheless supports a large colony of humans. It was one of the first planets settled by humanity during the infancy of interstellar travel.

When Jovian Secessionists attacked the United Nations Colonial Advisors on Io, it led to three months of bloodshed between Earth's military and the localized forces. This initial conflict sparked a series of battles which came to collectively be known as the Interplanetary War.

The UNSC base on Io later discovered the Slipspace wake of a Covenant fleet as it traveled to Earth. This was the force that led the first battle of Earth. Io's reconnaissance allowed Earth's forces to deploy in time to confront the Covenant fleet.

EUROPA

LOCATION: Orbiting Jupiter
DESCRIPTION: Terraformed, atmospherically frosty, militaristically uninteresting

Europa was once thought to be the location with the highest likelihood of life within the Sol System—other than Earth. Its icy surface hid an ocean deep beneath, where scientists theorized ocean vents could create amino acids and the building blocks of life.

When the first interstellar Colonists landed there, however, they discovered that this was not the case. Colonization occurred without the discovery of any new life forms and culminated in a thriving outpost that survives to this day.

For all of its qualities, Europa does not figure much militarily. The Spartans completed a mission there before the Fall of Reach, but that was the liveliest incursion since the Jovian Moons Campaign. Even when the Covenant attacked the Sol System, Europa went unmolested.

GANYMEDE

LOCATION: Orbiting Jupiter
DESCRIPTION: Partially terraformed, well populated

Ganymede is the largest moon of Jupiter and is controlled by the UNSC. It has been terraformed, though it supposedly retains a harsh climate. The country of Aigburth is located on Ganymede. Aigburth is home to the Low/Zero Gravity Testing Facility, where the EVA Armor was developed.

SATURN

LOCATION: Sixth planet of the Sol System
DESCRIPTION: Gas giant, massive rings, former tourist destination

The planet Saturn is the third largest body in the Sol System (behind Sol and Jupiter), but is one of the most visually arresting due to its system of rings. Unlike the other gas giants in that system (all of which feature pale hoops of stardust), Saturn's rings are astonishingly bright and large. It was because of this that Saturn became a tourist destination of sorts, although its practical applications have always been limited. Saturn's moons are less explored than Jupiter's, the planet is much further from the sun, and Jupiter is already well established. Thus, Saturn remains a curiosity and little else.

URANUS

LOCATION: Seventh planet of the Sol System
DESCRIPTION: Gas giant, anomalous, mostly unexplored, unpopulated

Named for the mythical creator of the universe, Uranus is an oddity among planets for several reasons. First and foremost, its axial tilt has its poles turned past a ninety-degree angle. Secondly, while still freezing and unmapped, it features a number of alarming radiation spikes that have yet to be addressed.

Much like Saturn, Uranus is much further out from the sun than would be cost-effective to investigate. Its moons are also less understood than Jupiter's, while its anomalies are worrying.

NEPTUNE

LOCATION: Eighth planet of the Sol System
DESCRIPTION: Gas giant, most distant planet in system, mostly unexplored

Neptune lay undiscovered by humanity until well into the second millennium, and only revealed its position with the coming of sophisticated telescopes. Its gaseous form shows off as a brilliant blue, so it was named for the Roman God of the Sea. Like its brothers Uranus and Saturn, Neptune has been overlooked in favor of the much larger Jupiter. Unlike those other planets, however, Neptune is in a unique position to slingshot ships coming in from Pluto deep into the system with its gravity well. This only works when the two planets are relatively aligned (and when Slipspace travel would be deemed unreasonable), so it is still a rather rare occurrence. But compared to the barren wastes that are its closest two planets, Neptune is relatively bustling.

PLUTO

LOCATION: Kuiper Belt
DESCRIPTION: Diminutive planetoid, atmospherically void

Pluto was once classified as a planet, having been discovered in the early 20th century and thought to be the reason for anomalies in Neptune's orbit. In fact, Pluto was ill-suited to create these disturbances and was later downgraded to a dwarf planet. Its gravity makes it too non-robust to maintain an atmosphere of any kind, but it does have several stations orbiting it for scientific and militaristic purposes.

> ➤ JUPITER'S MOONS WERE THE LOCATION OF SOME OF HUMANITY'S EARLIEST COLONIES AND CONFLICTS IN SPACE.

EVEN AS HUMANITY spread throughout the Milky Way colonizing new planets, Earth remained its spiritual home and the center of the UNSC, the administrators of the Galaxy. "Planetside" Earth still encompasses seven continents, but geopolitically it has changed significantly since the beginning of the 21st century. "Orbital Earth" includes stations built to defend Earth.

AFRICA

DESCRIPTION: Verdant and desert, war-torn
MAJOR LOCATIONS: Cairo, New Mombasa, Arab Republic of Egypt, Republic of Kenya, Voi, the Forerunner Portal, United Republic of Tanzania, Arusha
MAJOR EVENTS: The first battle of Earth, the battle of New Mombasa

Africa is the second-largest continent on Earth. Taking up almost twenty percent of the planet's land area, it features a multitude of cultures, peoples, and languages. Due to its wealth, it has also been the center of innumerable wars since the dawn of time. Most recently, Africa took center stage during the Covenant's invasion of Earth. During the first battle of Earth, most of the fighting took place in Cairo and New Mombasa, while later, in the events of the second battle of Earth, the Sangheili glassed part of the southern region to prevent the newly-invaded Flood from spreading.

ARAB REPUBLIC OF EGYPT

LOCATION: Africa, Earth
DESCRIPTION: Desert/tropical, bisected by Nile River
MAJOR LOCATIONS: Cairo

The Arab Republic of Egypt is a technological, economic, and military dynamo. Sitting on the Nile, it has capitalized on this strategic location for over six thousand years, which is why it is so integral to UNSC defenses of Earth. Its capital is Cairo.

REPUBLIC OF KENYA

LOCATION: Africa, Earth
DESCRIPTION: Industrialized, war-torn
MAJOR LOCATIONS: New Mombasa, Old Mombasa, the New Mombasa Orbital Elevator, Voi

The Republic of Kenya is a country in Eastern Africa. After the events of 2552 CE, Kenya became most renowned for the historic standoff between UNSC forces and the Covenant in the city of New Mombasa, as well as the unearthing of the Forerunner machine buried below the town of Voi. It was there that humanity finally defeated the Covenant, bringing an end to over a quarter of a century of war.

UNITED REPUBLIC OF TANZANIA

LOCATION: Africa, Earth
DESCRIPTION: Industrialized, UNSC-controlled
MAJOR LOCATIONS: Zanzibar Islands, Wind Power Station 7, Arusha

The United Republic of Tanzania is a country in East Africa where the UNSC has established many bases throughout its history. Tanzania is bordered by Kenya and is connected to that country by way of the Tsavo Highway, which links Arusha in Tanzania and Voi in Kenya.

THE EUROPEAN UNION

LOCATION: Earth
MAJOR LOCATIONS: London, Edinburgh, Paris, Barcelona, Madrid, Brussels, Berlin, Florence, Rome, Essen

A democratic confederation of nations on a subcontinent of Eurasia, the EU is economically and politically powerful and proudly multicultural.

BEWEGLICHR STUNGSYSTEME TESTING FACILITY

LOCATION: Essen, Germany

A UNSC research and development facility that has created mobile armament and MJOLNIR Mark VI armor systems.

ASIA

LOCATION: Earth
DESCRIPTION: Largest continent, but also the most-populated and most-polluted

Asia is the largest and most populous of Earth's seven traditional continents. The UNSC has long taken an interest in Asia, for no better reason than its vast size. Chinese, Japanese, Korean, Indian, and Pakistani interests have long held sway over humanity's decision-making processes, and yet now, with the UNSC in control, it is no different.

CHINA

LOCATION: East Asia, Earth
DESCRIPTION: Overcrowded, ancient foundations, international superpower

China is one of Earth's oldest civilizations, dating back thousands of years before humanity broke the bonds of Earth and began to colonize the stars. When that colonization began, China was one of the most enthusiastic and effective colonizing forces and many of the vital resource colonies that supplied the UNSC war effort were initiated by Chinese efforts.

In 2004 CE, Dana Awbrey, creator of the website ilovebees.com, fled to China after an AI called the Operator attempted to kill her. The Operator was actually a damaged fragment of the AI known as Melissa, thrown back in time from the 26th century.

DIEGO GARCIA

LOCATION: Indian Ocean, Earth
DESCRIPTION: UNSC military base
MAJOR LOCATIONS: Diego Garcia UNSC Base

Diego Garcia is the largest known atoll on Earth and is found within the Indian Ocean. Because of its proximity to India, Hong Kong, Pakistan, and Africa, the British installed a military base there for both training and refueling. It has been used as such ever since. During the first battle of Earth, the UNSC staged its first counterattacks from Diego Garcia. These proved to be pivotal, and later, as the second battle of Earth unfolded, the Covenant sent in a capital ship to destroy it.

JAPAN

LOCATION: Pacific Ocean, Earth
DESCRIPTION: Crowded, technologically advanced, economically volatile

Japan is an island-nation in the Pacific Ocean, off the coast of mainland Asia. It remained in political and cultural isolation for several centuries, but in the 1800's the nation underwent a massive renewal of technology and economic activity. Now, seven hundred years later, Japan is as well endowed with scientists, economists, and global culturalism as any other nation on Earth.

KOREA

LOCATION: Korean Peninsula, Asia, Earth
DESCRIPTION: Formerly divided (now unified), technological powerhouse
MAJOR LOCATIONS: Kyonggi Province, Songnam, Special Warfare Center

Korea, as a nation, had only existed in its unified form for a few hundred years prior to the events of the Human-Covenant War. Before then, it had been separated into two countries; North and South. After the long-anticipated treaty which united Korea and due to its strong emphasis on education, Korea has become a technological powerhouse. For this reason, the UNSC has established many bases—military and otherwise—there for officer training and weapons testing. The best known of these bases is the Special Warfare Center, where the MJOLNIR Mark VI armor was tested.

PAKISTAN

LOCATION: Middle East/South Asia, Earth
DESCRIPTION: Islamic Republic, overcrowded

Pakistan is one of the last Islamic Republics remaining on Earth in the 26th century. It has radically modernized itself, however, and is not as harsh a region as it once was. During the second battle of Earth, the UNSC managed to defeat a large force of Covenant Loyalists at the Pakistani-Afghani border.

UNITED REPUBLIC OF NORTH AMERICA (URNA)

LOCATION: Earth
DESCRIPTION: Desert to tundra, verdant
MAJOR LOCATIONS: United States, Cleveland, Commonwealth of Kentucky, Mexico, Canada, UNSC Supreme Headquarters, Greater Chicago Industrial Zone, Fueder Construction Headquarters, Base Segundo Terra

The United Republic of North America is a loose association of the nations of Canada and Mexico and the political remnants of the United States. The UNSC has many military bases and other facilities spread across the URNA, as the association with the former United Nations and its headquarters in New York City still ties the organization closely to this part of the world.

REPUBLIC OF CUBA

MAJOR LOCATIONS: Havana, Centennial Orbital Elevator

Its equatorial proximity made the Republic of Cuba ideal for the Orbital Space Elevator of "Tallo Negro de Maiz." Its ability to ferry cargo to orbit made Cuba a powerful and prosperous nation in a way never before seen in its history. It is, however, a small island, and with a brisk tourist trade has become a partner with all countries of Earth.

ANTARCTICA

LOCATION: Earth
DESCRIPTION: Polar, tundra and desert, ice-ridden
MAJOR LOCATIONS: Mount Erebus, Ross Island

Antarctica sits on the southern pole of Earth. It is almost entirely covered in ice, and was the last continent to be fully explored. Other than a few bases and points of interest—most notably Ross Island's Mount Erebus—it is uninhabited by Humans. During the second battle of Earth, Covenant forces tried to excavate a Forerunner artifact they believed to be below Mount Erebus, but were stopped by Spartan Blue Team.

COMMONWEALTH OF AUSTRALIA

LOCATION: Pacific and Indian Oceans, Earth
DESCRIPTION: Tropical to desert environment, densely populated
MAJOR LOCATIONS: Sydney, Perth, HIGHCOM Facility Bravo-6, Sydney Synthetic Intellect Institute

The Commonwealth of Australia has long been an economic powerhouse. Situated in the Southern Hemisphere between the Indian and Pacific Oceans, it is a country of many divergences: Deserts next to paradise, beauty mixed with danger, kindness mixed with cruelty. It is a place of paradoxes and mystery, and remains so through the 26th century.

Australia, due to its stability, became the seat of many technological and militaristic locations. Because of this, it was heavily bombarded by the Covenant during the Human-Covenant War.

HIGHCOM FACILITY BRAVO-6

LOCATION: Sydney, Australia, Earth
DESCRIPTION: UNSC High Command, High Security Area, High Risk Strike Area
MAJOR LOCATIONS: The Hive

After the Fall of Reach, the UNSC High Command relocated to its next-most secured position: The HighCom Facility in Sydney. Actually, the facility is located below Sydney, as such a significant target needs to be protected from possible orbital bombardment. All major UNSC decisions must pass through these walls at some point, particularly experimental or high-cost projects.

Even farther beneath Bravo-6 is another location, known as the Hive. It is here that many ONI projects began. So many secrets and scandals of the UNSC are located here that only those members with the highest possible security clearance are allowed past the first security checkpoint.

SYDNEY SYNTHETIC INTELLECT INSTITUTE

LOCATION: Sydney, Commonwealth of Australia, Earth
DESCRIPTION: Advanced AI-Development Laboratory, Classified Military Applications

Almost all major Artificial Intelligence advances in the last half-century have occurred at Double SI: The differentiation between "smart" and "dumb" AIs, calculation refinement, and (among much else for the military) marrying AI components to Naval Computational Navigation Software.

It was here that the first micro AI, Jerrod, became operational. Jerrod was only supposed to have survived for a few days, but he surpassed all expectations and eventually became quite close with Dr. Halsey.

> ► THE UNSC ESTABLISHED MANY BASES IN TANZANIA THROUGHOUT ITS HISTORY. TO CAPITALIZE ON ITS EXCELLENT DEFENSIVE OPPORTUNITIES, MANY BASES WERE BUILT INTO THE SLOPES OF MOUNT KILIMANJARO.

HUMAN COLONIES

THE UNITED NATIONS Space Command had acquired many colonies by the end of the 24th century. The Inner Colonies were the first to be terraformed. The Outer Colonies are those farthest from Earth and Reach. Many were eventually overrun and glassed by the Covenant.

CHI CETI SYSTEM

DESCRIPTION: Yellow Star, 77 light years from Earth
MAJOR LOCATIONS: Chi Ceti IV

Other than the UNSC training and production facility on Chi Ceti IV, there was little of note in the Chi Ceti System, located in the outer bands of human-populated systems. Its distance made transport there prohibitively difficult. When the Covenant vessel *Unrelenting* arrived, it quickly engaged the nearby UNSC *Commonwealth*.

During the skirmish, three Spartans boarded the Covenant ship and detonated an ASM near its reactor, ultimately destroying the ship. This operation claimed the life of the Spartan Samuel-034 and left an indelible memory with the team leader, Master Chief.

CHI CETI IV

SYSTEM: Chi Ceti
DESCRIPTION: Underpopulated

Chi Ceti IV sits on the outskirts of the Outer Colonies. A top-secret installation, the Damascus Testing Facility, is situated on its surface and is where the SPARTAN-IIs were upgraded with their refined MJOLNIR Mark IV armor during the battle of Chi Ceti. This facility was abandoned and, because it was the only known human installation on the planet, was most likely destroyed by the Covenant. Above this planet lies the location of Samuel-034's death. He died after his suit ruptured while inside a Covenant ship, thus forcing him to stay behind and defend his fleeing comrades while they escaped the Covenant ship's destruction.

EPSILON ERIDANI SYSTEM

LOCATION: 10.5 light years from Sol
DESCRIPTION: Sol-Proximate, high traffic, formerly UNSC center of production
MAJOR LOCATIONS: Reach, Beta Gabriel, Circumstance, Tantalus, Tribute

This system is most notable as being the home of the planet Reach. It was one of the first systems explored and then later colonized by humans. This is due to its proximity to Earth; at just over 10.5 light years away, it is a relatively quick jaunt home. It was also one of the most important systems in all of the UNSC until it fell to the Covenant in 2552 CE.

REACH

SYSTEM: Epsilon Eridani
DESCRIPTION: Earthlike, forested, temperate atmosphere, mineral-rich
MAJOR LOCATIONS: Highland Mountains, Menachite Mountain, CASTLE Base, Camp Hathcock, Camp Independence, Reach Naval Academy, ONI Medical Facility, Orbital Defense Platforms, Reach Station Gamma

Aside from Earth, there is—or rather, there was—no planet more important to the UNSC than Reach. The Covenant glassed it in the battle now known as the Fall of Reach. Before that, however, Reach was the site of many military projects. Rich in minerals and metals (particularly titanium), the planet soon became a major production and testing facility. ONI forces had a major base there, while Marines prepared many operations on its forested surface. Even the SPARTAN-IIs trained here; Master Chief admitted that, with no memories of his real homeworld, Reach was the closest he would get. Unknown to the UNSC, however, there was a large Forerunner installation buried beneath the Highland Mountains. Perhaps it was this that drew the Covenant here in such large numbers, bypassing many Outer Colonies. In any case, the Covenant attacked in numbers previously unseen. The Orbital Defense Platforms, state-of-the-art and ready-made to destroy Covenant ships, fell swiftly. On the ground, human forces were soon wiped out, despite some heroics staged by a group of SPARTAN-IIs. In the end, the Covenant glassed almost the entire surface of the planet, save for the Highland Mountains. They attempted to retrieve an artifact beneath it, but Dr. Catherine Halsey, aided by a recently returned Master Chief and several other Spartans, took the object with them and out into the "safety" of Slipspace.

Reach is a cautionary tale for all UNSC brass. Much like the "unsinkable" Titanic, the planet fell despite its defenses and distance from the front lines. Earth and the rest of the Inner Colonies beefed up their defenses in response, which may have saved them when the Covenant invaded again only a few weeks afterward.

TITANIUM MINES

LOCATION: Menachite Mountain, Reach
SYSTEM: Epsilon Eridani
DESCRIPTION: Abandoned, partially explored, Forerunner-Proximate

Deep beneath the hills of Reach there lay thick veins of elements that, when properly smelted, created titanium. It was this source that originally made Reach such a valuable asset for the UNSC. Though many of the original mines dried out over the centuries, some continued until the planet fell. One such mine housed part of ONI's CASTLE Base, deep within Menachite Mountain. When Dr. Halsey and the surviving Spartans were forced to flee the base, they traveled through these abandoned mines, eventually finding themselves in a large, artificial cavern. There, controlling the whole complex, sat a crystalline stone that the Forerunners had left behind when they vanished. Its radiation signature had drawn Covenant forces there and saved that part of Reach from being glassed, though that also meant that the Spartans were able to find and retrieve it too. The stone's exact properties and uses are unknown, but it allowed advanced (although more dangerous) Slipspace travel from Reach when Dr. Halsey and the Spartans escaped from the planet.

CASTLE BASE

LOCATION: Menachite Mountain, Reach
SYSTEM: Epsilon Eridani
MAJOR LOCATIONS: Level Aqua, Level Scarlet, Level Lavender

Deep within Menachite Mountain, protected by a structure that could withstand an eighty-megaton blast, lies CASTLE Base, ONI's biggest secret on Reach. It was here that many of the details of the SPARTAN-II Program were hammered out, including specifications for MJOLNIR, the energy shields stolen from the Covenant, and refinements of every kind of weapon that the UNSC employed. CASTLE Base fell with the rest of Reach after the Covenant attacked. However, Dr. Halsey—who had managed to survive by hiding deep within the bowels of the base—initiated Operation: WHITE GLOVE, which wiped out all of the sensitive material (including the base's AI), thus preventing the Covenant from learning any human secrets.

ARCADIA

LOCATION: Inner Colonies
SYSTEM: Procyon System
DESCRIPTION: Tourist drawing, atmospherically tropical
MAJOR LOCATIONS: Deep Space Research Array

Described as a "tropical paradise," Arcadia is a popular destination for tourists, famed for its safaris, and cruise ships are in constant transit between it and Earth. It was once a heavily populated Forerunner world. Today, the Forerunner ruins are now mostly destroyed by erosion or are hidden deep beneath the surface of the planet. Limited settlement or even exploration of the planet's surface beyond the tourist zones prevented the discovery of local Forerunner remnants for a surprisingly long time.

The location of Arcadia makes it a perfect spot for the Deep Space Research Array, which orbits the planet searching for heavy gravity events in the universe.

BETA GABRIEL

DESCRIPTION: Uninhabited
SYSTEM: Epsilon Eridani

With no permanent human residents prior to the Fall of Reach, Beta Gabriel most likely fell to Covenant hands—if it was not glassed like its neighbor, the planet Reach itself.

CIRCUMSTANCE

SYSTEM: Epsilon Eridani
DESCRIPTION: Center of justice and education

Circumstance was formerly a UNSC colony world in the Epsilon Eridani System, along with Tribute, Beta Gabriel, and Reach. It was apparently famous for its universities and courts of justice.

Although the planet's status is unknown, contact with the Epsilon Eridani system was lost after the Fall of Reach so it is thought unlikely that Circumstance survived the inevitable onslaught.

TANTALUS
SYSTEM: Epsilon Eridani

Tantalus is yet another UNSC colony world located in the system of Epsilon Eridani. It had a small contingent of UNSC ships orbiting overhead, all of which were called into service by Admiral Roland Freemont during the Fall of Reach.

TRIBUTE
SYSTEM: Epsilon Eridani

Tribute was once a major UNSC colony, though it paled in comparison to the nearby Reach. Still, it had a good population, centered in the city of Casbah, as well as a strong economy and thriving spaceport traffic. Unfortunately, with all of the ships coming and going, Insurrectionists soon left their mark. Many people on Tribute bristled at tight UNSC control already, being so close to Reach. When riots broke out, the UNSC enacted elements of Operation: TREBUCHET to subdue the Insurrectionists. The Covenant took control of the Epsilon Eridani System soon after the Fall of Reach. With a sizable colonist population, it is unlikely that Tribute survived.

EPSILON INDI SYSTEM
LOCATION: 11.83 light years from Sol
DESCRIPTION: Lightly trafficked, tranquil, life-producing
MAJOR LOCATIONS: Harvest

The Epsilon Indi System (centered around the star of the same name) was relatively quiet under the UNSC for some time. Aside from its hub on the planet of Harvest, very little of the system was actively explored. In the depths of this system, however, came first contact between humans and the Covenant, when a Kig-Yar vessel attacked and pirated a transport ship. Sergeant Avery Johnson and others were sent to investigate, eventually culminating in the Human-Covenant War.

HARVEST
SYSTEM: Epsilon Indi
DESCRIPTION: Mineral-abundant, fecund and lush, since glassed
MAJOR LOCATIONS: Tiara, Vigrond, Utgard, Hugin, Munin, Gladsheim, Bifrost, Tigard, Harvest Long Range Orbital Platform, Utgard Space Elevators

Harvest was, by all accounts, a wonderful place to live. Many people noted the planet for its rolling plains, lush fields, beautiful skyscapes, and astonishing bounty. Though sparsely populated, the planet produced much of the food that supplied UNSC space, from livestock to mineral water to vegetable and fruit goods. Settled mainly by Lutheran Americans of Germanic ancestry, Harvest became synonymous with backwater productivity.

Harvest, being on the fringe of the Outer Colonies, had little hope of receiving reinforcements or a major evacuation. Even though citizens outnumbered Covenant soldiers one hundred to one, the scope of the Covenant weaponry made much of the planet a charred wasteland within days of the first firefight. It might have been worse were it not for Avery Johnson and his militia. Stationed on Harvest after going AWOL on Earth, Johnson thought it to be the perfect place to clear his head from the horrors of his past. Instead, the Covenant attacked, and he had to lead the farm boys under his command into battle.

There was no hope of victory, but aided by the AIs Sif and Mack (known as Loki in his more destructive form), Johnson and his crew were able to evacuate many of Harvest's citizens before major Covenant forces united overhead and glassed the planet. In fighting the Covenant, Johnson found his purpose in life and he saved thousands of civilians, but the first shot in the Human-Covenant War had been fired.

Harvest later saw the largest UNSC fleet ever assembled investigate the planet's demise and try to win it back at all costs. It was eventually retaken, but two-thirds of all UNSC ships in the fleet were destroyed in the battle.

ERIDANUS SYSTEM
DESCRIPTION: Pirate-ridden, Insurrectionist base
MAJOR LOCATIONS: Eridanus II, Eridanus Asteroid Belt

Rebellions and insurrections have plagued the UNSC from its foundation. The Eridanus System has been a particular thorn in its side, due to the well-organized Rebel base on the asteroid Eridanus Secundus. Eridanus II was one of the major population centers of the system before the Covenant glassed many of the planets there in 2530 CE. Much more importantly, at least from the perspective of hindsight, is the fact that one of the children plucked from its folds in the early part of the 26th century grew up to become the hero known as Master Chief.

ERIDANUS II
SYSTEM: Eridanus
DESCRIPTION: Temperate wonder, piratical nature, since glassed, birthplace of Master Chief
MAJOR LOCATIONS: Elysium City

ERIDANUS ASTEROID BELT
LOCATION: The "Belt" of Eridanus
SYSTEM: Eridanus
DESCRIPTION: Devoid of natural life, asteroid shards in make-up

MAJOR LOCATIONS: Eridanus Secundus

The Eridanus Asteroid Belt—primarily the asteroid Eridanus Secundus—has long been a hideout for pirates and Rebels. Even when the UNSC was free of external conflict, these brigands were hard to locate. Master Chief and the Spartans managed to infiltrate Eridanus Secundus and extract Colonel Robert Watts, but that was an exception. Even after the Covenant entered the system and glassed Eridanus II, the Rebels kept quiet and remained hidden. It was not until the *Ascendant Justice-Gettysburg*, under the control of Admiral Whitcomb and Cortana, entered the system on their way back to Earth that the Rebels finally gave up. Master Chief had proposed refitting at the asteroid hideout, which he had thought was destroyed during his first mission, but found it still quite active, albeit running silent. In exchange for pardons, the leader of the Rebels, Governor Jacob Jiles, allowed the ship to dock for repairs. Covenant forces were not far behind, however. The Rebels made a valiant effort to stop their advance, but were eventually all killed. Their sacrifice allowed Master Chief and the *Ascendant Justice-Gettysburg* to escape once more.

MINISTER
LOCATION: Inner Colonies
DESCRIPTION: UNSC colony world

Minister remains one of the few UNSC worlds not known to the Covenant. Its obscurity, even within the UNSC, seems to have saved it.

MIRIDEM
DESCRIPTION: UNSC Colony World

One of the many UNSC colony worlds that got in the way of the Covenant's path of destruction, the SPARTAN-IIs were sent in to protect its citizens. The Spartan Sheila died there during this mission.

NEW HARMONY
DESCRIPTION: UNSC Colony World
MAJOR EVENTS: The battle of New Harmony

New Harmony is a UNSC colony world and the site of one of the few UNSC naval victories in the Human-Covenant War. Vice Admiral Danforth Whitcomb participated in this battle, in which a telemetry probe was launched onto a Covenant frigate. This led to the eventual discovery and destruction of K7-49.

➤ REACH IS A CAUTIONARY TALE FOR ALL UNSC BRASS. MUCH LIKE THE "UNSINKABLE" TITANIC, THE PLANET FELL DESPITE ITS DEFENSES AND DISTANCE FROM THE FRONT LINES.

BALLAST
LOCATION: Inner Colonies
DESCRIPTION: UNSC colony world
MAJOR EVENTS: The battle of Ballast

Located within the Inner Colonies, Ballast became infamous as one of the first worlds in that zone to come under Covenant attack. Rumor holds that the UNSC Defense Force stopped that invasion, but it is unknown whether this is the truth or propaganda spread by ONI forces to combat low morale.

CHARYBDIS IX
SYSTEM: Charybdis System
DESCRIPTION: UNSC colony world, insurrectionist planet
MAJOR EVENTS: Insurrectionist riots

Charybdis IX was a promising colony world until Insurrectionists caused mass unrest in its populace. Large riots ensued, during which Jacob Keyes was forced to kill in self-defense. Keyes used this memory to stall the mind that infected him when he became host to a Flood intelligence on Halo Installation 04. Charybdis IX was later glassed by the Covenant.

DRACO III
DESCRIPTION: UNSC colony world, now uninhabited
MAJOR EVENTS: Invasion of Draco III

Draco III had been a standard colony world for some time when the Covenant invaded it. The SPARTAN-IIs were sent to rescue the few humans who survived the initial attack, but the Covenant left no prisoners. Instead, they left the survivors to suffer ravenous Unggoy and Kig-Yar. The Spartans watched this via satellite link-up; the images spurred them to kill every Covenant soldier on the planet. The planet remains in UNSC control, but is now uninhabited.

FAR ISLE
DESCRIPTION: Former UNSC colony world, nuked surface

Far Isle was a human colony world and the site of one of the major atrocities committed by the UNSC. A rebellion broke out on the planet and, unable to contain the populace, the UNSC declared a Code: BANDERSNATCH and nuked the entire colony. None survived, while the memory of this planet later led to larger rebellions, including, possibly, the Insurrectionist movement.

GILGAMESH
DESCRIPTION: Mob-controlled, colony world
MAJOR LOCATIONS: Gilgamesh Brothel

Gilgamesh is a relatively obscure planet due to its mob connections. However, it does have one feature that most UNSC Marines know of: A large, refined, and famous brothel. Cortana used this brothel in a scheme to repay Colonel James Ackerson for his attempts at destroying her, the Master Chief, and the MJOLNIR project. Laundering money through several locations, she made it seem as if Ackerson had spent a large amount of money at the brothel, which proved to be awkward when Ackerson's wife received the confirmation for the "purchase."

GROOMBRIDGE 34 SYSTEM
LOCATION: Inner Colonies
DESCRIPTION: Binary star system, cold, prohibitively uninhabitable

In 2531 CE, when a group of Spartans was sent to the Groombridge 34 System to investigate reports of insurrectionist operations, Kurt-051 went missing near a decommissioned construction platform. Unlike most Spartans who had perished but were reported as MIA, Kurt-051 was, in fact, still alive, operating as a training officer for the classified SPARTAN-III Project.

HAWKING SYSTEM
The Hawking System, though within UNSC space, has never been fully explored and so is technically a "neutral" system. In 2552 CE, three dozen Covenant carriers gathered in the Hawking System to transfer Seraph fighters in preparation for their attack of Earth.

HELLESPONT SYSTEM
LOCATION: Inner Colonies
DESCRIPTION: Earth-Proximate, loosely controlled, evacuated
MAJOR LOCATIONS: Troy

The UNSC once controlled the system known as Hellespont, principally for its colony world, Troy. Shortly before the battle of Earth, however, Troy was glassed by the Covenant but not before part of its population managed to escape.

TROY
SYSTEM: Hellespont
DESCRIPTION: Former UNSC colony world, now glassed

Once a neighbor to Earth, the colonial world of Troy was glassed by the Covenant shortly before their arrival at the human homeworld. Along with Harmony, its imminent destruction was discovered through the code-breaking procedures headed by Colonel Herzog at ONI. However, to ensure that the Covenant did not realize that their code had been breached, ONI allowed both planets to be glassed.

HYDRA SYSTEM
LOCATION: UNSC-controlled space
DESCRIPTION: Frequently attacked, piratical, rebellious

Located within the constellation Hydra, this system of the same name is mostly known for the series of massacres that have occurred periodically throughout the history of the UNSC. With pirates and Insurrectionists being common in this near-lawless system, military forces occasionally descend and mete out justice with the long arm of nuclear missiles.

SIGMA OCTANUS SYSTEM
LOCATION: FLEETCOM Sector Three
DESCRIPTION: UNSC victory site, sparsely populated, UNSC-controlled
MAJOR LOCATIONS: Sigma Octanus IV

Many things have occurred within the Sigma Octanus system, but none of them is so famous as the battle of Sigma Octanus IV. During this battle, a large group of UNSC warships defeated a smaller but much more heavily armored Covenant armada, thanks in part to the quick thinking of Captain Jacob Keyes. Keyes employed what came to be known as the "Keyes Loop" during his assault on a Covenant ship. This broke the lines of the Covenant and allowed the UNSC to destroy or drive off the rest of the fleet.

The battle was a Pyrrhic victory at best, as every surviving UNSC ship needed at least some major repairs, while most were destroyed. The boost in morale cannot be quantified, though, as this was the largest UNSC victory since the beginning of the war.

SIGMA OCTANUS IV
LOCATION: UNSC-controlled space
SYSTEM: Sigma Octanus
DESCRIPTION: Archipelagic
MAJOR LOCATIONS: Côte d'Azur

Sigma Octanus IV was known for its white-sand beaches, small continents, and lush landscapes, as well as its fishing and great beauty. Its capital, Côte d'Azur, functioned as the base of UNSC activity for much of the system. Because of this, Sigma Octanus IV was chosen as a major offensive site by the Covenant. They arrived without warning and immediately began bombardment. Sigma Octanus IV might have suffered the same fate as Troy and Eridanus II, and been glassed, had Commander Keyes and the SPARTANS-IIs not intervened. It was a battle on two fronts, with the Spartans on the ground and a collection of UNSC vessels in space. The Spartans won by obliterating Côte d'Azur with a nuclear weapon, while Keyes performed what became known as the "Keyes Loop," returning Covenant fire back on itself.

It was a Pyrrhic victory, but a major morale coup. Though Côte d'Azur and much of the UNSC fleet had been destroyed, the Covenant had been defeated. Sigma Octanus IV, though absent of any human population, remains an inhabitable world.

NEW JERUSALEM
SYSTEM: Cygnus
DESCRIPTION: Colony world
New Jerusalem is a major UNSC colony planet in the Cygnus System. Although it has never been confirmed, ONI operative Lieutenant Commander Jilan al-Cygni is said to have been born there.

PARIS IV
SYSTEM: Paris
DESCRIPTION: Colony world, battle site
The fourth world in the Paris System, this planet was the site and namesake of the Siege of Paris IV. A major conflict in the Human-Covenant War, it was here that Sergeant Avery Johnson received the major dose of radiation that led to his case of Boren's Syndrome.

111 TAURI
LOCATION: UNSC-controlled space
SYSTEM: Taurus
DESCRIPTION: Serene setting, contact inhibited, Rebel presence
MAJOR LOCATIONS: Victoria
Located within the Taurus System, 111 Tauri is known primarily for its colony world, Victoria, which fell to the revolutionary group, the United Rebel Front, under the command of General Howard Graves. Contact with the system was lost soon afterwards. Its fate is unknown.

VICTORIA
LOCATION: 111 Tauri
SYSTEM: Taurus

DESCRIPTION: Forested, briefly Rebel-controlled
Victoria was a sparsely populated forest world on the edge of UNSC-controlled space. It fell to the revolutionary group, the United Rebel Front, under the command of General Howard Graves. Five SPARTAN-IIs, including John-117 and Kurt-051, were assigned to take down Graves and his camp at New Hope. Contact with the system was lost soon afterwards. Its fate is unknown.

ZETA DORADUS SYSTEM
LOCATION: Dorado Constellation
DESCRIPTION: Limited habitability, relatively unknown
MAJOR LOCATIONS: Onyx
The Zeta Doradus system is home to several icy planets and gas giants. Its "goldilocks" zone of habitability is very small, and thus, only its planet Onyx was colonized by the UNSC, although "colonized" would not be the correct word. It was chosen as a secret military base, perfect for use far from the prying eyes of the population.

ONYX
LOCATION: UNSC-controlled space
SYSTEM: Zeta Doradus
DESCRIPTION: Atmospherically habitable, formerly Forerunner-controlled, construct
MAJOR LOCATIONS: The Sharpened Shield, SPARTAN-III Training Facility, Forerunner Ruins, Zone 67
When Onyx was discovered in 2491 CE, it was thought to be an unusual but habitable planet. It featured a nitrogen-oxygen atmosphere, alarmingly prolific flora and fauna, and a temperate atmosphere, despite being in a system otherwise known for its lifelessness.

It was only later, after the discovery of a massive Forerunner site that the truth came out: Onyx was not a planet at all, but an enormous construct, left over from the Forerunners' exodus one hundred thousand years earlier. The SPARTAN-III Program continued on with this knowledge, even as more antiquities popped up and teams went missing. The UNSC even added extra

manpower to help unwrap some of the mysteries.

After Installation 04 was destroyed, however, the Sentinels hidden within the construct's walls awoke and began the battle of Onyx, the first Forerunner-Human battle. During this conflict, the Sentinels attacked all UNSC forces and eventually caused a meltdown of the planet's surface, though saving the Forerunner artifacts hidden within. Endless Summer, the UNSC's AI, helped Kurt-051 and CPO Mendez led the survivors into the center of the planet, where a Slipspace rift allowed them to enter a micro-Dyson sphere known as "The Sharpened Shield."

THE SHARPENED SHIELD
LOCATION: Beneath the surface of Onyx, Slipspace
SYSTEM: Zeta Doradus
DESCRIPTION: Shield-shaped, Forerunner-constructed, located in Slipspace
Although the entranceway to the Sharpened Shield could be found in the Core Room in the Forerunner Installation on Onyx, the structure itself actually existed in Slipspace. Dr. Halsey theorized that it was constructed by the Forerunners to hide and ride out the destruction brought upon by the activation of the Halos. This would seem plausible, in that the structure could only be entered when Installation 04 went active. Within the structure were many habitats suitable for sentient life from around the Galaxy. Halsey and the others who fled into the shield during the battle of Onyx found it deserted.

23 LIBRAE
LOCATION: Outer Colonies
CONSTELLATION: Libra
MAJOR LOCATIONS: Madrigal, Hesiod, the Rubble
23 Librae's lone planet of Madrigal was destroyed by the Covenant in 2528 CE. Those who escaped joined Insurrectionists in the "Rubble," a band of asteroids near the gas giant, Hesiod. When it surfaced that Kig-Yar were operating a black-market weapon ring with humans, the Insurrectionists engaged with the UNSC and the Covenant.

> ➤ ONYX WAS NOT A PLANET AT ALL, BUT AN ENORMOUS CONSTRUCT, CREATED BY THE FORERUNNERS BEFORE THEIR EXODUS ONE HUNDRED THOUSAND YEARS AGO.

➤ THE COVENANT FORCES THEN ATTACKED AND DESTROYED THE HUMAN COLONY ON HARVEST.

COVENANT BASES

THERE ARE THREE main types of Covenant advance bases: Keeps, which have a command center, enough room for five combat support structures, and four turret foundations; Outposts, which have a command center, three building sites, and no turret foundations; and Citadels, as seen here.

CITADELS

The largest type of Covenant advance base, Citadels contain a command center, up to seven troop/armory/worship structures, four turret foundations, and a gravity lift to transport resources.

These kinds of forward outposts are used by the Covenant as moveable sites from which to command invasions and defensive operations, assemble vehicles and aircraft, and train and house troops.

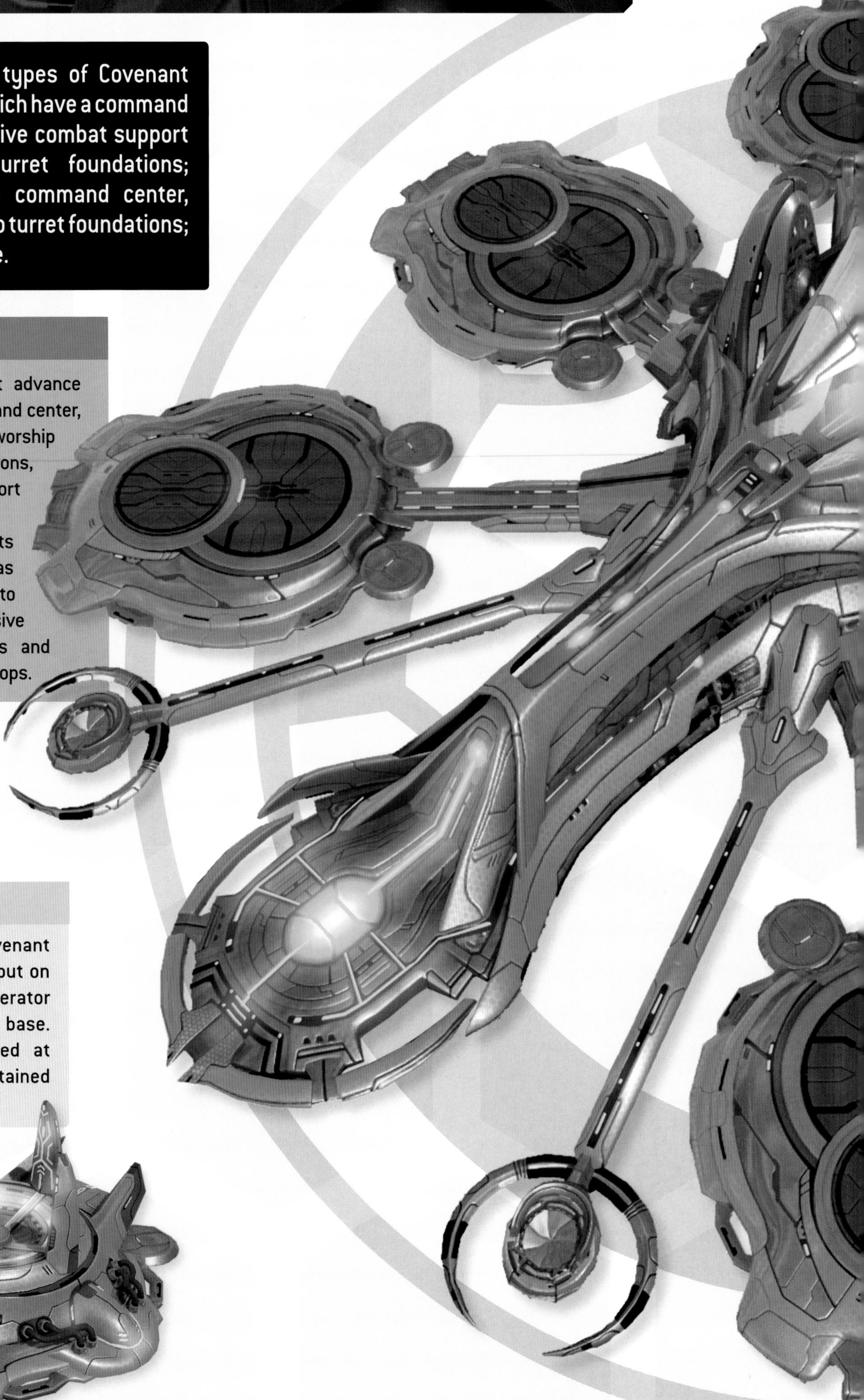

SHIELD GENERATOR

Similar in function to other Covenant energy shielding technology but on a much larger scale, this generator protects all buildings on the base. Multiple shields can be used at once to protect from sustained bombardment.

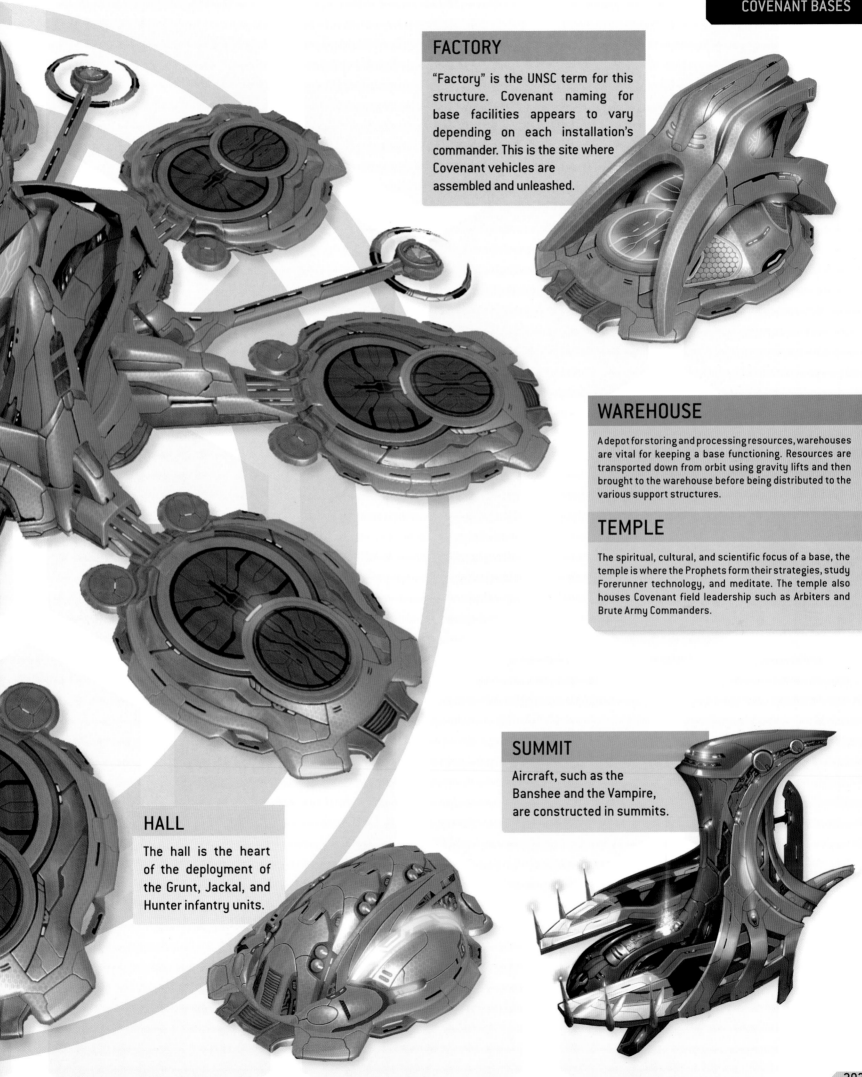

FACTORY

"Factory" is the UNSC term for this structure. Covenant naming for base facilities appears to vary depending on each installation's commander. This is the site where Covenant vehicles are assembled and unleashed.

WAREHOUSE

A depot for storing and processing resources, warehouses are vital for keeping a base functioning. Resources are transported down from orbit using gravity lifts and then brought to the warehouse before being distributed to the various support structures.

TEMPLE

The spiritual, cultural, and scientific focus of a base, the temple is where the Prophets form their strategies, study Forerunner technology, and meditate. The temple also houses Covenant field leadership such as Arbiters and Brute Army Commanders.

SUMMIT

Aircraft, such as the Banshee and the Vampire, are constructed in summits.

HALL

The hall is the heart of the deployment of the Grunt, Jackal, and Hunter infantry units.

COVENANT WORLDS

THE COVENANT'S HOMEWORLDS are numerous and varied because of the different species that make up the alliance. For a long time, the common base of the Covenant was High Charity.

OTHER NAMES: The Prophet's Holy City, The Holy City of the Covenant
SIZE: Variable/Expanding
LOCATION: Mobile (destroyed)
DESCRIPTION: Holiest Covenant location, mobile space station, Forerunner-technology reliant, San 'Shyuum homeworld (after destruction of original homeworld)

HIGH CHARITY

Nothing is quite as holy to the Covenant as the space station known as High Charity. An immense mobile planetoid, High Charity was constructed following the Sangheili-San 'Shyuum War as a physical representation of the Covenant itself and to act as the ultimate command center, a central city, and a place of spiritual and cultural unification. Created at the culmination of the War, it marked the beginning of what later became known as the Covenant. Atop it sat the Forerunner Dreadnought, the ever-lasting symbol of the gods of the Covenant, and below it teemed millions of different alien species. High Charity was, in essence, a microcosm of the Covenant itself.

High Charity was capable of Slipspace jumps and possessed its own artificial star, which regulated a typical solar night and day. A giant dome-shaped structure, High Charity featured typical Covenant architecture, with numerous towers floating above a methane-rich field inhabited by the Grunts. An immense combined fleet of ships protected the city.

Deep within its recesses, the High Prophets governed these functions of the station (and the Covenant as a whole) from their chambers, the Sanctum of the Hierarchs, and many other places both secret and sacred. Such a powerful statement did not go unnoticed by enemy forces, however, and though the station had seen its fair share of battles, it was not infallible. The soldier known as the Master Chief infiltrated the station as it became overrun with the Flood. He followed the High Prophet of Truth as he launched the Dreadnought from its resting place, leaving millions of Covenant citizens and soldiers to their fates. The Gravemind then took over High Charity and piloted it to the Ark. It hoped to spread the Flood's influence across the entire Galaxy, but it was not to be. The Master Chief once again took it upon himself to wrest control of the space station from the Flood's grasp. He overloaded the station's reactor core, causing its destruction—along with its many relics and the Gravemind.

Nothing remains of what was once the Covenant's cultural and political center, save for the traditions and memories left in its wake.

High Charity was more than just a center of pilgrimage. It could refit and house thousands of warships, from personal fliers to cruisers. The station also boasted firepower unknown to even the largest Covenant battleship.

HIGH CHARITY DEFENSE FLEET

The High Charity Defense Fleet was an enormous fleet of ships that protected the Covenant city of High Charity. The Second Fleet of Homogeneous Clarity was either a part of this fleet or a synonym for it.

SECOND FLEET OF HOMOGENEOUS CLARITY

One of many fleets which were tasked with the responsibility of High Charity's safety, the Second Fleet of Homogeneous Clarity took part in the civil war. As the Covenant shattered into pieces, the solidarity of the fleet splintered apart and ships battled each other along the lines of Brute or Elite control.

NOTABLE SHIPS: *Twilight Compunction, Lawgiver, Incorruptible, Revenant, Tenebrous, Rapturous Arc*

UNYIELDING HIEROPHANT

Sergeant Avery Johnson once described the Unyielding Hierophant's design as akin to a pair of squids kissing. Although he was likely being facetious, his description was not far from accurate. Similar to the architecture of High Charity, the Unyielding Hierophant consists of a pair of elongated, tear-drop structures with a narrow port and docks extending from each end. The interior was constructed to resemble a terrestrial setting, complete with animals, foliage, and slender corridors for internal transportation. At over eleven miles (eighteen kilometers) in length, it could field more than five hundred Covenant ships, hundreds of thousands of troops, and enough firepower to destroy any ship within the UNSC.

It could not, however, stop the SPARTAN-IIs. Led by Master Chief, these warriors assaulted the Unyielding Hierophant using a Covenant dropship. The Spartans soon learned that the Covenant intended to invade Earth and would be using this fleet to do so.

Using a ruse to draw the outlying Covenant vessels toward the center of the station, the Spartans overloaded Unyielding Hierophant's reactor. Although they suffered losses during the operation, the Spartans managed to escape the destruction of the station and nearly all five hundred surrounding ships.

LOCATION: Mobile, Tau Ceti (when destroyed) **LENGTH:** 11 miles (18 km) **DESCRIPTION:** Massive construct, engineering marvel, Covenant-built space station **MAJOR EVENTS:** The battle of Unyielding Hierophant

CHU'OT

Chu'ot is the only Covenant planet of which humans were aware prior to first contact. Even though its presence was only known through radio waves, much that was inferred from these transmissions turned out to be correct. The planet is a gas giant, cold, and about the size of Neptune. It is also completely devoid of life. That being said, its moon, Eayn, is of particular note. It is, after all, the Kig-Yar homeworld. Chu'ot thus has a religious significance to many of the old-time religions of the Kig-Yar. Since the coming of the Covenant, it is just another gas planet that happens to be orbited by a planetoid that is diminishing in value with every Kig-Yar that jumps ship.

SYSTEM: Y'Deio **DESCRIPTION:** Gas giant, Neptune-sized **MAJOR LOCATIONS:** Eayn (moon)

COVENANT WORLDS

BALAHO

The Unggoy are known as unpredictable but tenacious creatures, willing to live with thousands of their kind packed tightly together in inhospitable conditions that would kill most other species. The Covenant uses Unggoy as cannon fodder, relying on their sheer numbers to make up for the forces that are routinely lost during the natural course of battle. Yet, the Unggoy persist and endure. Why? Because their world, Balaho, is perhaps worse than anything the Covenant can throw upon these diminutive creatures.

For the most part, Balaho is toxic, frozen, and dangerous. Ice covers much of the surface, while a methane atmosphere sustains unusually hardy forms of life. Its chilling temperatures, ranging from forty-one degrees Fahrenheit (five degrees Centigrade) at its balmiest, and far down into the negative degrees, allow brackish flats to exist only at the most equatorial latitudes. There, large pillars of fire erupt when the methane condenses, making even those relatively temperate regions exceedingly dangerous.

So, when the Covenant landed on Balaho, most Unggoy leapt at the chance to join them. Much later, a revolution of these creatures (known today as the Grunt Rebellion) nearly forced the Covenant to glass the entire planet. The Grunts cared little for their planet, but the prospect of losing so many breeding partners (the key to their rebellion's success) forced their capitulation.

Today, Balaho is a backwater in the Covenant's empire. It is avoided by most shipping routes, while enough Unggoy breed on other planets so as to make its population unnecessary. Still, each Unggoy thinks fondly of its homeworld. It may be ugly, foul, and frozen, but it's home.

SYSTEM: Tala **DESCRIPTION:** Frozen, methane atmosphere, backwater location, Unggoy homeworld
MAJOR EVENTS: The Grunt Rebellion

EMERALD COVE

Emerald Cove was known through the UNSC as a colony world of sublime beauty. Thousands of miles of white sands, azure oceans, and beautiful colonists made any trip there a happy one. Even the Spartans enjoyed their time there during a training mission; after CPO Mendez sabotaged half of their air-tanks, the Spartans stole his and hid out on a deserted island. There, they spent a week with nothing but bonfires, baked clams, surfing, and relaxation.

Emerald Cove was abandoned by the UNSC in 2542 CE because of the danger of nearby Covenant forces. Its current status—glassed? unharmed? invaded?—remains unknown.

LOCATION: Covenant-controlled space **DESCRIPTION:** Former UNSC colony world, archipelagic environment, tourist and military destination

G 167 G

Not much is known about this planet, save that one hundred thousand years ago, this is where the Forerunners came into contact with the beings that would later be known as the Flood. It was therefore able to sustain some kind of population.

LOCATION: Forerunner-controlled space, bordering Halo Installation 04 **SYSTEM:** G617 System
DESCRIPTION: Life-sustainable **MAJOR EVENTS:** Forerunner-Flood first contact

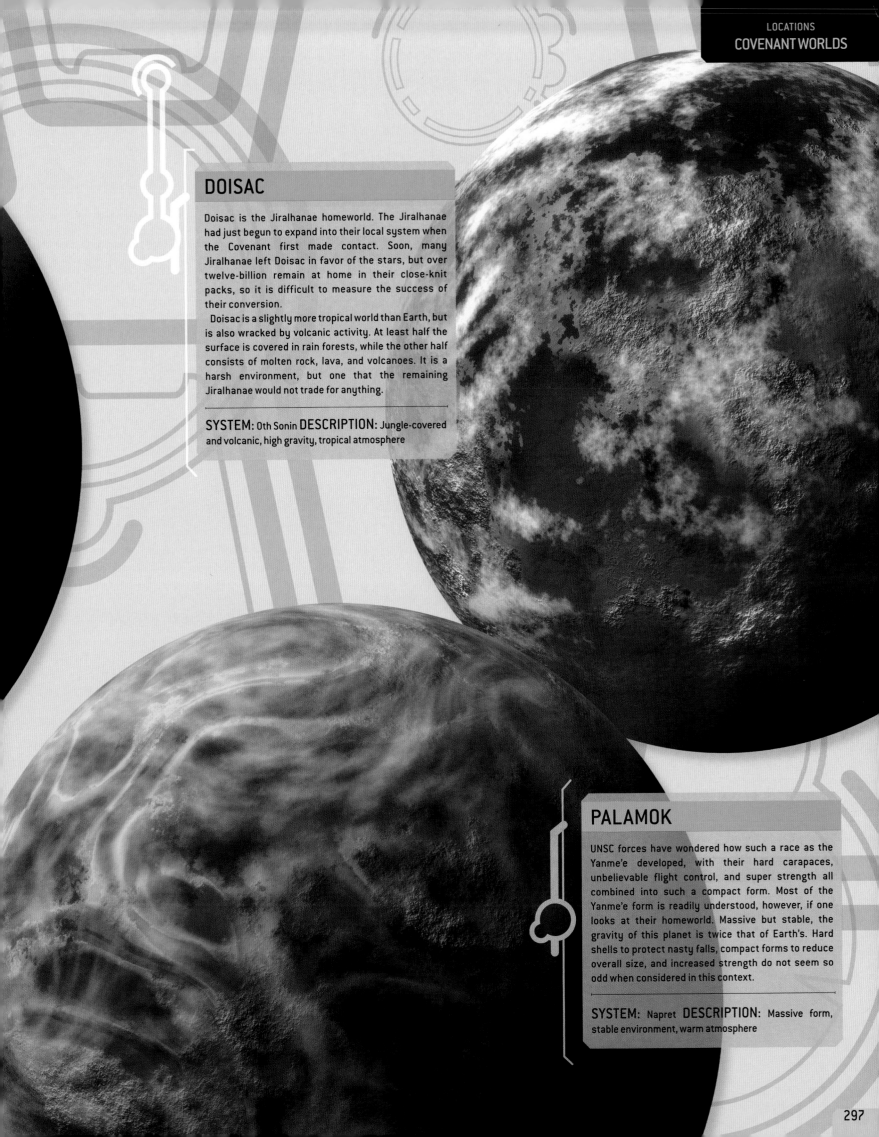

DOISAC

Doisac is the Jiralhanae homeworld. The Jiralhanae had just begun to expand into their local system when the Covenant first made contact. Soon, many Jiralhanae left Doisac in favor of the stars, but over twelve-billion remain at home in their close-knit packs, so it is difficult to measure the success of their conversion.

Doisac is a slightly more tropical world than Earth, but is also wracked by volcanic activity. At least half the surface is covered in rain forests, while the other half consists of molten rock, lava, and volcanoes. It is a harsh environment, but one that the remaining Jiralhanae would not trade for anything.

SYSTEM: Oth Sonin DESCRIPTION: Jungle-covered and volcanic, high gravity, tropical atmosphere

PALAMOK

UNSC forces have wondered how such a race as the Yanme'e developed, with their hard carapaces, unbelievable flight control, and super strength all combined into such a compact form. Most of the Yanme'e form is readily understood, however, if one looks at their homeworld. Massive but stable, the gravity of this planet is twice that of Earth's. Hard shells to protect nasty falls, compact forms to reduce overall size, and increased strength do not seem so odd when considered in this context.

SYSTEM: Napret DESCRIPTION: Massive form, stable environment, warm atmosphere

COVENANT WORLDS

THRESHOLD

Gas giants contain a wealth of rare and valuable gases, and Threshold is no different. The Forerunners established one of many mines there, which may have been later refitted to study the Flood within a relatively safe gravity well.

However, Threshold is important for several other reasons, chief among them is Installation 04. It was there that the Master Chief struck the first major blow to the Covenant's forces by destroying the Halo and obliterating a Covenant armada in the process.

After the destruction of Installation 04, Elites were stranded at the gas mine and there discovered the truth about Halo. When this message was broadcasted at large, the Prophet of Truth sent an Arbiter there to eliminate the now heretical Elites. He was successful and the gas mine was sent plummeting into the depths of Threshold.

LOCATION: Covenant-controlled space
DESCRIPTION: Gas giant, mining colony
MAJOR LOCATIONS: Halo Installation 04 (was in orbit of the Halo prior its to destruction)
MAJOR EVENTS: The battle of the Gas Mine, the battle of Installation 04

MADRIGAL

A UNSC colony world, Madrigal sat the closest of any UNSC world to Harvest. It is unlikely that it survived the early days of the war, and no transmissions have been received from the planet.

LOCATION: Covenant-controlled space
DESCRIPTION: Former UNSC colony world, probably glassed

SUBSTANCE

Substance is a gas giant which provides the orbital home to Delta Halo (Installation 05), and may define a "safety" pattern of locating Halo facilities near dense gas giants. During a series of conflicts on its surface, the ring world was subsumed by the Flood parasite along with High Charity and large portions of the Covenant's local fleet. Several Elite-controlled fleets destroyed a significant portion of the Flood threat as well as cauterizing the installation's surface, but they were unable to address the sudden departure of High Charity or determine its level of infection.

LOCATION: Covenant-controlled space
DESCRIPTION: Gas giant
MAJOR LOCATIONS: Halo Installation 05 (orbiting)
MAJOR EVENTS: The assault of Installation 05

SAN 'SHYUUM HOMEWORLD

Not much is known about the San 'Shyuum homeworld because the Prophets are secretive when discussing matters of their race with other cultures. It has to have been a Forerunner colony in the distant past, as it is well-known that the San 'Shyuum developed their culture alongside ancient Forerunner relics.

However, other vital information, such as the planet's size and location, remains hidden. What is known is that some thirty-two centuries before the Human-Covenant War, the San 'Shyuum split into two factions: The Stoics and the Reformers. The Stoics were the hardliners of their Forerunner-worshipping religion and did not wish to enter the Forerunner Dreadnought that sat on their homeworld, for fear of offending their gods. The Reformers, meanwhile, were technologically obsessed and hoped to learn more about the universe through their investigations of it.

From this schism, a civil war erupted. The Reformers locked themselves away within the Dreadnought and launched it into space, leaving their world forever. The Stoics dared not destroy such a sacred vessel, and so they let the Reformers go but banished them from ever returning.

Whether or not the San 'Shyuum physically returned to their orginal homeworld is unknown, but it is clear that they recognized that their planet faced obliteration when the star it orbited collapsed on itself. It was around this time that those same Reformers used the Forerunner Dreadnought to build the homeworld and vast structure they would call High Charity.

DESCRIPTION: Low gravity, former Forerunner colony **MAJOR EVENTS:** The San 'Shyuum Schism

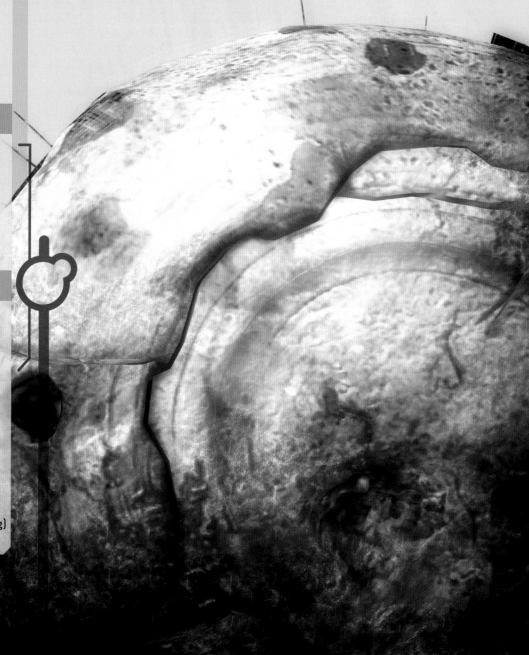

HARMONY

Harmony is yet another UNSC colony world that is now in Covenant-controlled space, having been glassed and forgotten. Along with the planet Troy, its imminent destruction was revealed through the code-breaking procedures headed by Colonel Herzog at ONI. However, to ensure that the Covenant didn't realize that their code had been breached, ONI allowed both planets to be glassed. A terrible but necessary sacrifice.

LOCATION: Covenant-controlled space
DESCRIPTION: Former UNSC colony world, glassed
MAJOR EVENTS: The battle of Harmony

K7-49

K7-49 was a Covenant shipyard located within an asteroid field extremely close to UNSC-controlled space. It was also the site of one of the largest battles ever fought by the SPARTAN-IIIs. After its discovery by a telemetry probe, ONI learned that a major Covenant shipyard had been built on the asteroid. Three hundred Spartans were sent to disable the shipyard as part of Operation: PROMETHEUS. They succeeded, but all died in the process.

LOCATION: Covenant-controlled space
DESCRIPTION: Asteroid-based shipyard, production zone MAJOR EVENTS: Operation: PROMETHEUS

Sanghelios is very similar to Earth in many respects. It features a saline ocean and multiple continents, and shares a similar size, gravity, atmosphere, as well as a wide variation in temperature and vegetation. If one were to step out onto the surface, the only thing that would be immediately different would be the sky: It varies in hue, from bright yellow to blood red, due to the large amounts of suspended particles in the upper atmosphere.

Possibly due to the harsh and capricious environmental conditions created by its three suns, Sanghelios has always been a breeding ground for martial societies. The Elites are the very pinnacle of that forced evolution.

SANGHELIOS

Sanghelios—orbiting the triple suns of Urs, Fied, and Joori—is the homeworld of the Sangheili. Almost nine billion of them now inhabit the varied surface of the world, and most will never venture to the stars. But those who show promise—either physically or intellectually—can join the forces of the Covenant, travel to distant places, and kill for the glory and honor inherent in the act. Sanghelios was one of the major sites of the war between the Sangheili and the San 'Shyuum races. Most, if not all, Sangheili warriors have come from the planet, including the latest Arbiter.

SYSTEM: Urs-Fied-Joori System
MAJOR EVENTS: Sangheili-San 'Shyuum War

TE

Beneath the clouds of this seemingly gaseous planet lies a population of nearly two trillion Lekgolo. One hundred thousand years ago, these worm-like creatures were ignored by the Forerunners who controlled Te, but when those ancient beings disappeared, the Lekgolo evolved into consciousness. They ate the remains of the Forerunners' technology, forming the rings that surrounded the planet and emitting the gas that would later cover it. When the Sangheili eventually discovered Te, they thought the worms to be an abomination for this act. Starting the war that came to be known as "the Taming of the Hunters," the Sangheili found their match in the Lekgolo. The Covenant, newly formed, was handed its first defeat, and the Sangheili were forced to resort to diplomatic methods of control, namely, the threat of the nuclear destruction of the planet. The Lekgolo surrendered and joined the Covenant cause.

Now, so many years later, the Lekgolo continue to live on Te, fed by metals sent to them by the Hierarchs of the Covenant. Few other members of the Covenant journey to Te; the planet's atmosphere and gravity are dangerous to most non-native creatures, while almost all of the Forerunner artifacts that survived have since been removed. The planet continues to revolve without much care from outside forces. The Lekgolo eat, breed, and continue on in their existence, with only those large colonies known as the Mgalekgolo being pressed into military service.

SYSTEM: Svir
DESCRIPTION: Homeworld of the Lekgolo, massive, ringed, mineral-rich
MAJOR LOCATIONS: Uhtua, Rantu (moons)
MAJOR EVENTS: The Taming of the Hunters

WEAPONS

UNSC WEAPONRY

➤ HUMAN WEAPONS—FOR SPACE, AIR, AND GROUND FORCES—ARE MOSTLY BASED ON BALLISTIC CAPABILITIES AND EXPLOSIVE MUNITIONS, WHEREAS THE COVENANT USES ENERGY-BASED WEAPONS.

FUSION ROCKETS

Fusion rockets are linear-path munitions that use a scaled-down version of the FDS for thrust. Because of the weapon's low mass, it can reach tremendous velocity in seconds, making the rocket difficult to avoid. However, due to its straight-line trajectory, it is possible to dodge. Fusion rockets are fairly large, so they are not carried aboard fighters. They are also ideal for strikes on stationary targets such as space stations or Orbital Defense Platforms. Only one-third of human vessels carry a fusion rocket and their count is never higher than three. The cost of building the drive system is prohibitive, and thus far they have proved largely ineffective against Covenant energy shields.

MASS WEAPONS

The equivalent of modern-day artillery, mass weapons fire super-dense projectiles, typically depleted uranium or other heavy metals, at extremely high velocity. Larger mass weapons use magnetic rail gun systems to propel projectiles at a target. In the event of shipboard power loss, such weapons can use a vehicle's own inertia to launch munitions. Smaller mass weapons are little more than high-powered computer-assisted Magnetic Linear Accelerators (MLA), autocannons and miniguns, which can fire thousands of rounds a minute.

MISSILES

Missiles are composed of guided munitions of varying sizes and payloads. Most are computer controlled and can lock onto energy sources, such as an enemy vessel's weapons emplacements or engines, heat signatures, or targets marked by laser designators.

Missile payloads range from massive chemical explosives to low-yield nuclear warheads. Tactical missiles are also common, including decoys, which broadcast a false radar image of a ship to lure away pursuit. Communication jamming equipment and sensor scramblers are also part of the human missile arsenal.

ARMOR

Ships of the line are plated with heavy Titanium-A armor, a form of titanium that has been specially strengthened on a molecular level. As much as one-third of a standard military ship's mass is armor. In general, the armor limits conventional damage, but Covenant weaponry has proven quite capable of boiling through even meters-thick plates of armor.

ARMORED SHIPS

All human ships under military control are equipped with armor and weapons. Fighters and capital ships are kitted with fusion rockets, mass weapons, missiles, and Titanium-A armor plating.

THE UNSC's arsenal is extensive but primarily contains projectile-based weaponry, both hand-held and vehicle-mounted. Each weapon has strengths and weaknesses and comes into its own in different situations.

magnification.

VARIANTS

XBR55: A 60-round variant. This version was the prototype, which was later remodeled to suppress "walking."

BR55HB: A heavy-barrel variant, also known as the "Mammoth Stopper."

MA5 ASSAULT RIFLE

The inaccuracy of the MA5 has rendered it obsolete on most battlefields, and its weakened attack against energy shields makes it a liability against the Covenant. However, due to its large magazine and high rate of fire, it is ideal for expeditionary forces, where accuracy is often secondary to firepower.

REAR SIDE VIEW

MA5 MAGAZINE

SIDE VIEW

SPARTAN-IIs regularly used the MA5B in the Human-Covenant war.

VARIANTS

MA5B: This version of the MA5 served reliably through the majority of the Human Covenant War. Its sixty-round clip provided many Marines with comfort on the battlefield.

MA5C: A more balanced form with an increase in barrel length, slight technical changes throughout, and is more accurate than the MA5B. The magazine size is reduced to thirty-two rounds.

MA5K: A stripped down, skeletal, Carbine-like version that is less accurate, but much lighter.

BR55 BATTLE RIFLE

When nothing else gets the job done, the BR55 battle rifle will do. As the standard gun for all UNSC forces, the BR55 is the easiest gun to pick up and use. Almost all soldiers have trained with it, making its slight defects less noticeable, while accentuating its high rate of fire and accuracy. With both semi-automatic and burst-fire modes, the BR55 is the backbone of the UNSC armed forces.

REAR SIDE VIEW

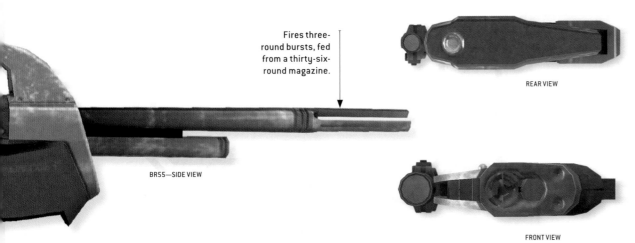

Fires three-round bursts, fed from a thirty-six-round magazine.

BR55—SIDE VIEW

REAR VIEW

FRONT VIEW

OTHER NAMES	LENGTH	WEIGHT	CARTRIDGE	
Monkey Wrench, BR, the Big Boy	35.4 in (89.9 cm)	8.38 lb (3.8 kg)	0.37 in (9.5 mm) x 40 FMJ (Full Metal Jacket)	
MAGAZINE CAPACITY	RANGE		USE	
36 rounds	Max. effective range: 656 ft (200 m)		Standard-use, all forms of combat	

VULCAN

Primarily mounted onto the backs of Warthogs, the Vulcan is capable of releasing up to 550 rounds per minute in a frenzy of not-so-accurate firepower. Combined with the natural protection of its vehicle's frame, a soldier holding "Old Faithful" can feel fairly intimidating and invincible, especially because of the armor-piercing strength of the gun's kick.

OTHER NAMES: M41 Vulcan Light Anti-Aircraft Gun, M41, Buggy Gun, Old Faithful, Widow Maker, Old Reliable, the Big'un, the Mule LENGTH: 34.6 in (88.14 cm) WEIGHT: 160.9 lb (72.98 kg) CARTRIDGE: 0.5 in (12.7 mm) x 99 FMJ/L (Full Metal Jacket/linkless) RANGE: 328 ft (100 m) USE: Mounted, crowd clearing, light anti-aircraft

HOG ROCKET

Generally seen mounted on the Warthog, the 102mm SC-HE rocket turret, more commonly known as the Hog Rocket, is essentially a triple-barreled rocket launcher that provides more anti-armor capacity than the traditional mounted machine gun. With a relatively short reload time of four seconds, a rocket turret's strength and speed is limited only by the Warthog it is mounted on.

OTHER NAMES: 102mm SC-HE Rocket Turret CARTRIDGE: 4-in (102-mm) HEAT rockets MAGAZINE CAPACITY: 3 rockets USE: Anti-vehicle

VIEW FROM BELOW

Display shows how many rounds are left in the magazine.

OTHER NAMES	LENGTH	WEIGHT	CARTRIDGE	
AR, Pop-gun, Harvey, the Gun, the Unit, the Lover	34.6 in (87.9 cm)	11.5 lb (5.22 kg)	0.37 in (9.5 mm) x 40 FMJ (Full Metal Jacket)	
MAGAZINE CAPACITY	RANGE	USE		
60 rounds	984 ft (300 m)	Suppression fire, non-shielded foes		

VIEW FROM ABOVE

REAR VIEW

M7 SUBMACHINE GUN

The M7 is a gas-operated, magazine-fed, noisy, and jam-prone automatic submachine gun. Despite its many failings, the control and recoil features are second-to-none on automatic weapons. This, added to its psychological effect on combatants, makes it good for close combat and suppressing fire tactics, meaning that not a lot of skill is needed for it to be deadly. Submachine guns, while not accurate over long distances, are particularly effective in close quarters. The M7 is primarily issued to vehicle crews and is also a favorite of commando teams in its sound suppressed version—the M7S.

M7 SUBMACHINE GUN–SIDE VIEW

OTHER NAMES		
SMG, Bullet Hose, Black Box, Chum, Popcorn, Jumper, Submash		
LENGTH		**WEIGHT**
Stock extended: 24.68 in (62.69 cm); stock retracted: 18.66 in (47.39 cm)		2.86 lb (1.29 kg)
CARTRIDGE	**MAGAZINE CAPACITY**	
0.2 in (5 mm) x 23 cased/caseless	60 rounds	
RANGE	**USE**	
Max. effective: 164 ft (50 m)	Suppression fire, crowd control, shoot-and-cover tactics	

110MM ROTARY CANNON

The 110mm rotary cannon is a ship-to-ship projectile weapon mounted on Longswords. Its shells are made of depleted uranium, but compared to the weaponry of a Covenant Seraph, the rotary cannon is hopelessly archaic.

OTHER NAMES: The Rotary
USE: Spaceship warfare

M301 40MM GRENADE LAUNCHER

The M301, known throughout the UNSC as the "Forty Mike Mike," is a dependable add-on to any MA5. When correctly utilized, it can lob 40mm grenades at targets within a 99-foot (30-meter) zone and up to 164 feet (50 meters) depending on wind, trajectory, and skill. These kinds of weapons have been with Marines since the 20th century, but their annoying tendency to detonate in the hands of unskilled soldiers has made them of limited use. The M301 has also been found on other weapons as well, most notably the 6334 DS. It is this versatility that has seen its use increase in the last hundred years.

OTHER NAMES: Forty Mike Mike **USE:** Secondary fire, suppression-fire, anti-armor, anti-vehicle

70MM CHAIN GUN

Mounted onto the noses of Pelicans, the 70mm chain gun can lay down a blanket of fire to protect both the Pelican and the troops it carries. It is a powerful weapon, but not very accurate, relying on its fully automatic firing to make cover; in outer space and at other significant distances, a Pelican must rely on its speed and maneuverability rather than the nose gun.

OTHER NAMES: Pelican Gun, Nose Gun
CARTRIDGE: 70mm rounds **USE:** Anti-personnel, suppression fire, infantry support

M6 MAGNUM SIDEARM

The M6 personal defense weapon system is the standard sidearm family of the UNSC, designed primarily for ruggedness and reliability. Certain models have been modified for use with technology yielded from Project MJOLNIR.

REAR VIEW

M6 MAGNUM SIDEARM —FRONT VIEW

The M6 series guns are recoil-operated and magazine-fed. They fire 12.7mm x 30 semi-armor-piercing high-explosive ammunition (standard issue). M6 series handguns are issued in three different finishes: Hard chrome, black polymer, and electroless nickel. Though not as powerful as most other weapons issued by the armed forces, the M6 makes up for that in its weight, size, and power-to-effectiveness ratio, making it a well-loved addition to any soldier's arsenal.

OTHER NAMES

M6 Personnel Defense Weapon System, Go-mag, Cannon, Hand Cannon, Power Drill, HE Pistol, Heavy Pistol

LENGTH	WEIGHT
Standard: 9 in (22.86 cm); "Up-sized": 26.7 cm (10.5 in)	Standard: 1.8 kg (4.09 lb); "Up-sized": 2.7 kg (5.95 lb)
CARTRIDGE	**MAGAZINE CAPACITY**
0.5 SAPHE (Semi-armor piercing high-explosive)	12 rounds
RANGE	**USE**
328–492 ft (100–150 m), depending on user	Secondary arms, light combat, tight-quarter combat

VARIANTS

M6A: Standard issue with black polymer finish.

M6B: "Officer's model" with a smart-linked scope [KFA-2] and hard chrome finish.

M6C: "Up-sized" standard issue with black polymer finish.

M6C/SOCOM: Accurized, with a smart-linked scope [VnSLS/V 6E] and black polymer finish.

M6D: "Up-sized," "officer's model," with a hard chrome finish and a smart-linked scope [KFA-2].

M6E: Standard issue with electroless nickel finish.

M6F: "Officer's model" with electroless nickel finish and a smart-linked scope [KFA-2].

M6G: "Up-sized" standard issue with electroless nickel finish.

M6H: "Up-sized," "officer's model" with a smart-linked scope [KFA-2] and electroless nickel finish.

M6I: Select-fire variant with detachable shoulder-stock and black polymer finish.

M6J/C: Carbine variant with a 35mm barrel, detachable shoulder-stock, and electroless nickel finish.

M6K: Police "undercover" variant with a six-round magazine and black polymer finish.

M6C/SOCOM

M68 GAUSS CANNON

The gauss cannon is a powerful anti-vehicle addition to the back of a Warthog.

Similar to (but distinct from) the M41 Vulcan in that both are mounted on Warthogs and other vehicles, the M68 is, due to its size and capabilities, more of an anti-vehicle gun than an anti-personnel weapon. Powered by asynchronous LIMs (Linear Induction Motors), the cannon is able to shoot its projectiles at hypersonic speeds, tearing almost any armor to shreds. Unprotected infantry within sixty-six feet (twenty meters) of the muzzle may suffer permanent hearing damage or loss when the weapon is fired.

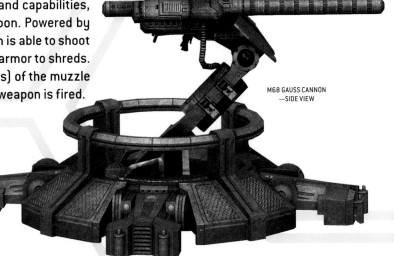

M68 GAUSS CANNON —SIDE VIEW

OTHER NAMES	LENGTH	WEIGHT
68, Rail Gun, Tent Pole, the Gas Gun	114.7 in (291 cm)	243 lb (110 kg)

CARTRIDGE

0.98 in (25 mm) x 130 APLP/F (Armor-piercing, limited-penetration/frangible)

MAGAZINE CAPACITY	RANGE	USE
750 rounds	5 miles (8 km) with good sight range	Anti-armor, anti-aircraft

M90A Shotgun

M6 Magnum
Sidearm

AIE-486H Heavy
Machine Gun

➤ SPARTANS ARE MASTERS OF ALL WEAPONS

Spartan Laser

Covenant Energy Sword

BR55 Battle Rifle

M7 Submachine Gun

SNIPER RIFLE—SIDE VIEW

REAR VIEW   FRONT VIEW

SHOTGUN (M90 CLOSE ASSAULT WEAPON SYSTEM)

The M90 CAWS (Close Assault Weapon System) shotgun is a devastating close-quarters weapon. While heavy and featuring tremendous recoil, the M90's stopping power at close-range is second-to-none, making it a favorite amongst seasoned UNSC troopers. Compatible with dozens of ammunition types (flechette, rifled slugs, incendiary, etc.), the M90 makes up for its few minor setbacks with unparalleled firepower.

SHOTGUN—SIDE VIEW

OTHER NAMES

The Hammer, Deck Clearer, Mop, Broom, Universal Translator, Boomstick, Hick Stick, Thunderer, Betsy, Equalizer, Waster, the Okay-47, and many, many others

LENGTH	CARTRIDGE	MAGAZINE CAPACITY	RANGE	USE
45.3 in (115 cm)	8 Gauge (.91 caliber)	12 shells	Max. effective: 131 ft (40 m)	Close quarters, crowd control, hit-and-run

HARD SOUND RIFLE (HSR)

A corpse found without burns, powder residue, or entry wounds is becoming an all-too-common sight on planets with significant mob ties, thanks to the Hard Sound Rifle, also known as the Buzzer. Developed by the Navy as a nearly silent weapon for political assassinations, it has been (illegally) co-opted by criminal forces, due to the lack of evidence associated with the gun's blast. Using compressed sound waves, the HSR delivers a resonance cascade that can cause a cerebral hemorrhage with a well-placed shot. UNSC forces are hard at work trying to control the flow of these weapons in non-military hands, but with the Covenant threat, it is slow going.

OTHER NAMES: Hard Sound Rifle, HSR, the Buzzer, the Skull-Splitter, Soundwave
RANGE: 3,000 ft (915 m) USE: Sniping, espionage, political assassination

STANCHION

Using the same technology as MAC guns but on a smaller scale, the M99 special application scoped rifle, otherwise known as the Stanchion, is the most powerful sniper rifle ever developed by human forces. Using linear magnets, the M99 can launch its undersized rounds at up to 49,212 ft (15,000 m) per second, ripping through anything not as strong as a foot (thirty centimeters) of titanium. Its recoil and size means a trained sniper must handle it.

OTHER NAMES: M99 Special Application Scoped Rifle, M99 Stanchion Gauss Rifle, the M99, 99
LENGTH: 67 in (170 cm) WEIGHT: 44 lb (20 kg) CARTRIDGE: .21 caliber rounds MAGAZINE CAPACITY: 10 rounds RANGE: 4.66 miles (7,500 m) USE: Sniping

SNIPER RIFLE (SRS 99D-S2 AM)

The standard long-range gun of the UNSC, the S2AM is a powerful sniping tool, effective at almost a mile (1.6 kilometers) in range, and capable of eliminating targets with a single shot. Recoil is a non-issue and its high rate of fire and reload speed counter the limited (four-round) ammo clip.

VIEW FROM ABOVE

OTHER NAMES		LENGTH	WEIGHT
99D-S2 Sniper Rifle, Flagpole, Eye of God, Cherry Picker, Mister, Trunk		66.38 in (168.6 cm)	44 lb (19.96 kg)
CARTRIDGE	MAGAZINE CAPACITY	RANGE	USE
14.5 x 114mm APFSDS (armor-piercing fin-stabilized discarding-sabot)	4 rounds	4,920 ft (1,500 m)	Long-range sniping

FLAMETHROWER—SIDE VIEW

FLAMETHROWER

Meant for non-combat use, the Flamethrower's, or M7057 Defoliant Projector's, use by the UNSC is tactical; the psychological aspect of a wall of fire is a strong deterrent to many of the Covenant. Despite being practically obsolete; its weight and difficulty in use are nothing compared to the emotional impact it can have on both allies and enemies.

OTHER NAMES		LENGTH	WEIGHT
M7057 Defoliant Projector, DP, Toaster, Dragon, Torch, Flamer		46 in (117 cm)	87 lb (39.5 kg)
CARTRIDGE	MAGAZINE CAPACITY	RANGE	USE
N/A (Pyroxene-V semi-liquid fuel)	9 x 3 second bursts	44 ft (13.4 m)	Special ops, jungle and urban warfare

FRONT SIDE VIEW

HMG-38 RIFLE

An older-model rifle, the HMG-38, or heavy machine gun-38, was originally used by UNSC Marines before being replaced in 2525 CE by a newer class of rifle. Though considered obsolete by the UNSC, the HMG-38 has entered the black market weapons trade, becoming common amongst the Eridanus Rebels.

OTHER NAMES: Heavy Machine Gun-38, the 38
CARTRIDGE: Large-caliber cartridges **USE:** Anti-personnel, infantry support

JILAN AL-CYGNI'S PISTOL

This small handgun was developed by ONI to have the ability to shoot a large selection of ammunition despite its size. Jilan al-Cygni incapacitated the governor of Harvest, the Honorable Nils Thune, with TTR (Tactical Training Rounds) when Thune refused to step down during the crisis that occurred there.

USE: Stealth, assassination

VIEW FROM ABOVE

> "IT TAKES A REAL LUNATIC TO USE A FLAMETHROWER..."
—UNSC E2-BAG/1/7 SERVICEMAN

UNSC WEAPONS

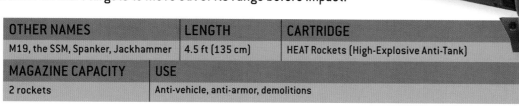

M19 SSM ROCKET LAUNCHER

The shoulder-mounted, computer-guided M19 is capable of anti-personnel destruction, demolitions, and many other uses besides its primary function as an anti-vehicular rocket launcher. When detonated, the M19's munitions create a large, but concentrated, spread of damage, though its slow velocity over large distances can allow for alert targets to move out of its range before impact.

OTHER NAMES	LENGTH	CARTRIDGE
M19, the SSM, Spanker, Jackhammer	4.5 ft (135 cm)	HEAT Rockets (High-Explosive Anti-Tank)
MAGAZINE CAPACITY	USE	
2 rockets	Anti-vehicle, anti-armor, demolitions	

M41 SSR MAV/AW ROCKET LAUNCHER

With the M41, the UNSC standard rocket launcher has morphed from its previous role in anti-vehicular warfare to an all-around anti-personnel weapon. Most targets cannot withstand a direct hit, while the fifteen-foot (four-and-a-half-meter) blast radius can also clear the area of additional targets.

Care must be taken in loading, unloading, and firing the M41; an unsteady hand can mean death not just for the person firing it but also for any nearby comrades.

M41 SSR MAV/AW—SIDE VIEW

102MM HIGH-EXPLOSIVE ANTI-TANK (HEAT) MISSILE

OTHER NAMES		
Spanker, Jackhammer, Pain, Launcher, Breath of God, Can Opener		
LENGTH	WEIGHT	CARTRIDGE
53.5 in (136 cm)	33.9 lb (15.38 kg)	102mm High-Explosive Shaped-Charge
MAGAZINE CAPACITY	RANGE	USE
2 rockets	1,300 ft (400 m)	Anti-armor, anti-aircraft, demolitions

.308 CALIBER MACHINE GUN

The .308 caliber machine gun (known more grotesquely, but commonly as the Confetti Maker) is an outdated machine gun from a bygone era, as evidenced by the SPARTAN-II's attack on the United Rebel Front's encampment Camp New Hope, on the planet Victoria. There, the Rebels who used the gun found that it proved ineffective against a well-trained foe who recognized the weapon's limited range, and quickly neutralized the Rebel forces to accomplish their mission. Due to its low cost and acceptable effectiveness at close-range, the Confetti Maker remains a popular choice for various revolutionary and criminal forces.

OTHER NAME: Confetti Maker LENGTH: approx. 30 in (76.cm) WEIGHT: approx. 12 lb (5.44 kg) CARTRIDGE: 0.308 in (7.6 mm) RANGE: 98.4 ft (30 m) USE: Close-quarters combat, guard duty

NARQ-DART PISTOL

A non-lethal sidearm, the Narq-dart pistol can stop a rhino at sixty feet (eighteen meters) and is deployed during training exercises. The SPARTAN-IIs practiced with this ammunition during their time on Reach. The rounds have been known to be lethal when they impact an eye or the temple of a target's head, so although they are used in training exercises, a significant level of safety must be maintained.

OTHER NAMES: Narqs, Nyquil, or Nyqs, Reds LENGTH: 10 in (25.40 cm) WEIGHT: 5 lb (2.27 kg) loaded CARTRIDGE: Narq-tipped 5mm handgun ammo MAGAZINE CAPACITY: 12 rounds RANGE: 65.62 ft (20 m) USE: Training

PAINT PELLET GUN

Paint pellet guns are used by UNSC forces training to mark targets without the risks associated with live-fire ammunition. They were commonly used by CPO Mendez and his drill instructors in the SPARTAN-II training program to introduce the trainees to the unpredictability of front-line combat zones.

OTHER NAMES: Painter, Graffiti Gun, Gumball Gun, Gummer LENGTH: 24.45 in (62.10 cm) WEIGHT: 8 lb (3.63 kg) CARTRIDGE: .68 caliber paint pellets MAGAZINE CAPACITY: 60 rounds RANGE: 98.43 ft (30 m) USE: Training

Two rockets can be fired in quick succession before launcher has to be reloaded.

M19 SSM—SIDE VIEW

FRONT VIEW

FRONT VIEW

SIDE VIEW

VIEW FROM ABOVE

SPARTAN LASER—SIDE VIEW

FRONT VIEW

OTHER NAMES			LENGTH
Weapon/Anti-Vehicle Model 6 Grindell/Galileian Nonlinear Rifle, the Grindel			38.9 in (98.81 cm)
WEIGHT	**CARTRIDGE**	**MAGAZINE CAPACITY**	**USE**
42 lb (19 kg)	Red chemical laser	100 battery units (five shots)	Heavy anti-personnel, anti-armor

Due to its size and recoil, the Spartan Laser was designed to be shoulder-fired.

INTERCONTINENTAL BALLISTIC MISSILE

Intercontinental Ballistic Missiles (ICBMs) have not changed much since their invention during the Cold War. More accurate than their primitive ancestors, the 26th-century version (the 11-B1) was thought obsolete, thanks to relative stability within the UNSC (that is, to say, no inter-state warfare) and the large-scale destruction and radiation that follow a blast. Those thoughts were discarded with the arrival of the Covenant. Now, ICBMs are used as a last-resort weapon against enemy forces who have dodged planetary MAC gun defenses. With their megatons of nuclear damage, ICBMs are a catastrophic but effective means of slowing down or stopping invaders...at the cost of fallout later. But when the choices are a damaged ecosphere or a glassed planet, the decision becomes simple.

OTHER NAMES: ICBMs, Yardsticks, Bulldogs RANGE: 3,500 miles (5,632 km) USE: Nuclear warfare

SPARTAN LASER

The Weapon/Anti-Vehicle Model 6 Grindell/Galileian Nonlinear Rifle, or Spartan Laser as it is more commonly known, is the only UNSC laser-powered weapon, making it the most powerful tool of destruction used by ground troops. While it shares several notable disadvantages with other heavy weapons, such as a delayed charge cycle between shots, a limited power cell that allows only five discharges per fully charged battery, and its cumbersome size, its brute strength more than makes up for any ungainliness—even a Wraith cannot withstand a fully charged shot.

OTHER NAMES	CARTRIDGE
The Noisemaker	Heat-seeking armor-piercing missiles
MAGAZINE CAPACITY	USE
8 missiles	Anti-aircraft, anti-vehicle, anti-armor

LAU-65D/SGM-151/ MISSILE POD

Mounted upon defensive walls, emplacements, or vehicles, the LAU-65D is a missile launcher capable of bringing a load of destruction down on any unsuspecting target.

Although the missile pod is massive and cumbersome, it can nevertheless be wielded by Spartans and particularly strong Sangheili.

Marines have reported that the Master Chief wielded this weapon while defending Voi during the Covenant's invasion of Earth.

MISSILE POD—FRONT SIDE VIEW

The MAC Gun is mounted on all UNSC spaceships large enough to hold it.

MAC GUN

The Magnetic Accelerator Cannon (MAC) gun is one of the largest (and best) weapons that the UNSC has in its fleet. Utilizing thousands of magnetic relays, it can ram a 600-ton projectile at nearly forty percent the speed of light. Able to pulverize most Covenant ships in one to three blasts, these weapons are mounted on all UNSC spaceships large enough to hold them. Unfortunately, MACs are slow to fire and, due to their size, require the entire ship on which they are built to maneuver in order to align fire. During the Fall of Reach, MAC gun barrages were able to destroy whole swaths of Covenant destroyers, but in the time it took for them to reload, faster alien ships had already penetrated the human defenses. Work is constantly underway in hopes of upgrading these weapons into faster, stronger, and more maneuverable models.

OTHER NAMES	LENGTH	
Magnetic Accelerator Cannon, the Big Stick	1,200 ft (366 m)	
WEIGHT	CARTRIDGE	MAGAZINE CAPACITY
Variable by ship	600-ton Ferric-Tungsten slugs	1 round
RANGE	USE	
10,000 miles (16,093 km)	Ship-to-ship warfare, defense, anti-siege warfare	

VARIANTS

STABILIZED VARIANT: The "Super" Mac or "Big" Mac is five-hundred percent larger than the ship-based original and is capable of firing a 3,000-ton slug at nearly half the speed of light. Due to its size, a Super MAC can only be stationed on planets or orbital weapons platforms.

AIE-486H HEAVY MACHINE GUN

The HMG's large capacity, fast rate, and quick reloading time do not deviate from the usual pattern of typical stationary guns, but its strength definitely sets it apart. Coupled with armor-piercing rounds, the HMG can take down even the toughest Sangheili with only a few rounds. When used by a Spartan, it can even be carried into battle like any other heavy weapon.

OTHER NAMES			
Heavy Machine Gun Turret, HMG, the Yeller			
CARTRIDGE	MAGAZINE CAPACITY	RANGE	USE
0.38 x 2 in (7.62 x 51 mm) Armor-piercing rounds	200 rounds	328 ft (100 m)	Defense

M202 XP MACHINE GUN

The M202 XP machine gun is a type of automated stationary gun turret. It was no longer in use as of 2541 CE. It fires stun rounds for training and can fire bullets if needed. The gun has a minimum angle of fire; a person can stay out of the cone of fire to avoid getting shot.

OTHER NAMES: The Trainer, the Simpleton
USE: Training

M247 GENERAL PURPOSE MACHINE GUN TURRET

The M247 machine gun can punch through almost anything, living or inanimate. Mounted on its stationary base, it functions superbly as both an offensive and defensive support weapon, mowing down crowds of enemy combatants and giving friendlies time to move.

OTHER NAMES: M247 GPMGT, Meat Chopper, Chainsaw, MG, Butcher, (incorrectly but colloquially) Uzi, the Pig, Pork, Porky **LENGTH:** 59 in (149.86 cm) **WEIGHT:** 23 lb (10.43); With tripod: 42.5 lb (19.28 kg) **CARTRIDGE:** 0.3 in (7.62 mm) x 51 Full Metal Jacket (linkless) **MAGAZINE CAPACITY:** 100 rounds **RANGE:** 1,203 yards (1,100 m) **USE:** Support (offensive and defensive) **VARIANTS:** M247 GPMG, M247T

GRENADES

FRAG GRENADE

Grenades have been used since the invention of gunpowder as an all-around crowd clearer, powered by nothing more than the human arm and a fuse. The Frag—capable of bouncing, rolling, and ricocheting several times before detonation—is a more powerful version of those ancient weapons, but still remarkably simple. Pull the pin, toss, and duck.

FRAG GRENADE—SIDE VIEWS

OTHER NAMES		
M9 HE-DP, Damage, Firecracker, Pineapple, Blast Beetle, Hopper, Croaker		
DIAMETER	WEIGHT	DAMAGE RADIUS
3.7 in (93.98 mm)	14 oz (397 g)	50 ft (15 m)

Armor-piercing
fin-stabilized
discarding-sabot

Full Metal
Jacket (FMJ)

Semi-armor piercing
high-explosive

M68 GAUSS CANNON

25 x 130 mm

M41 LIGHT
ANTI-AIRCRAFT GUN

12.7 x 99 mm

SRS99C S2 AM RIFLE

14.5 x 114 mm

M7 SUBMACHINE GUN

5 x 23 mm
FMJ CASELESS

M90 SHOTGUN

8-GAUGE SHELL

BR55 RIFLE

9.5 x 40 mm

MA5B RIFLE

7.62 x 51 mm FMJ

M6 PISTOL

12.7 x 40 mm

> ➤ "I NEED A WEAPON."
> —MASTER CHIEF TO SGT. MAJOR AVERY JOHNSON

COVENANT WEAPONS

MOST OF THE Covenant's arsenal is plasma-based, so is effective against energy shielding and body armor and fires a high number of shots. However, the UNSC has not discovered how to recharge Covenant weapons. Once the plasma reserves are used up, the weapon is useless, except as a melee weapon.

BACK VIEW

Firing rate allows for quick, precise shots.

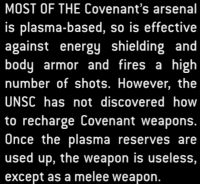

PARTICLE BEAM RIFLE — SIDE VIEW

OTHER NAMES

Type-50 Sniper Rifle System, Beam Rifle, Covenant Sniper, PBR

Master Chief used this pistol to his advantage throughout his mission on Installation 04, taking down Sangheili shields and then mopping up soldiers his discretion. However, the inability to charge it (like all plasma-based weapons) has generally limited the use of the Plasma Pistol by other UNSC forces.

VIEW FROM ABOVE

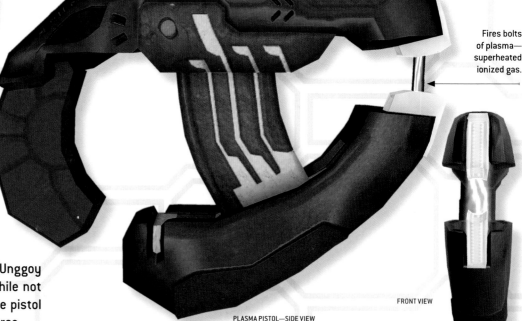

Fires bolts of plasma— superheated ionized gas.

PLASMA PISTOL

The Plasma Pistol is one of the most popular and versatile weapons for Covenant forces, although smaller units (Unggoy and Kig-Yar, specifically) tend to wield it most often. While not overwhelmingly powerful, a super-charged shot from the pistol is able to drain the whole of an energy shield's power source.

FRONT VIEW

PLASMA PISTOL—SIDE VIEW

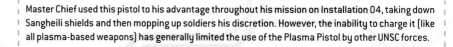

OTHER NAMES	LENGTH	WEIGHT	RANGE	USE	MAGAZINE CAPACITY
The Little C, Green, Greenboy, Greenie, P-Pistol, PP	13.5 in (34.3 cm)	7.75 lb (3.5 kg)	155 ft (50 m)	General use, energy-shield depletion	200 regular shots

PARTICLE BEAM RIFLE

The Particle Beam Rifle is capable of causing the instantaneous death of almost any being unlucky enough to be hit by its blast. The weapon is very much a counterpart to a UNSC sniper rifle; it is heavy, bulky, and not suited for close-range combat. However, at a distance, marksmen can even any odds by picking through troops like they were ducks on a range.

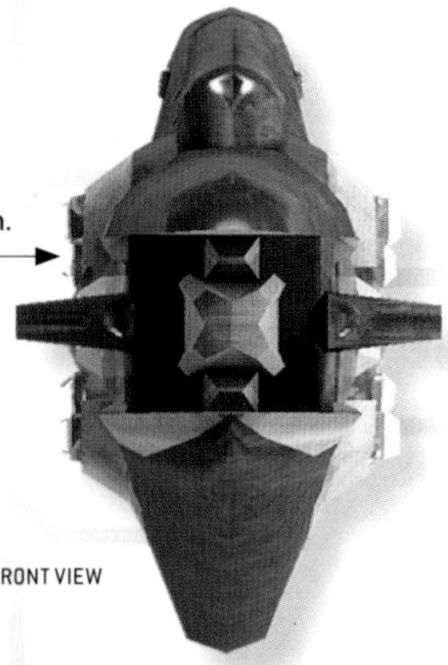

When battling Tartarus, the last appointed Chieftan of the Jiralhanae, Sergeant Avery Johnson used a Beam Rifle to lower his shield. Tartarus was then able to be killed by the Arbiter.

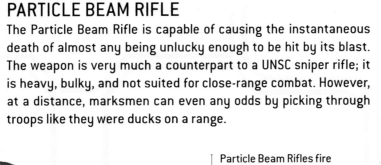

Fires a purple beam.

FRONT VIEW

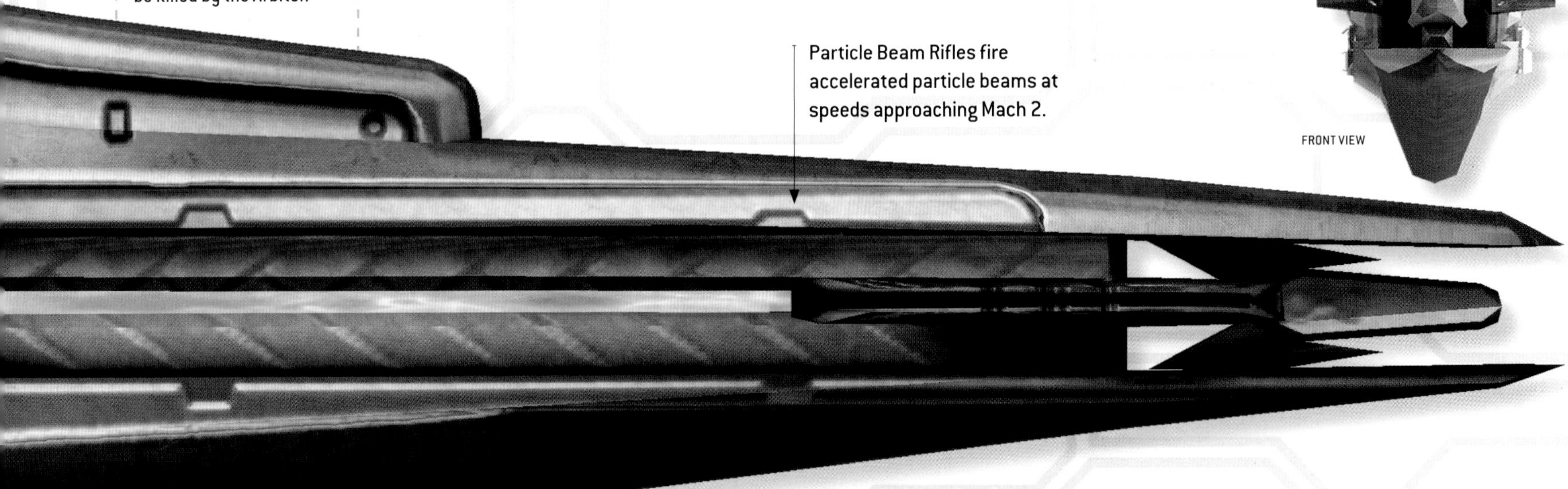

Particle Beam Rifles fire accelerated particle beams at speeds approaching Mach 2.

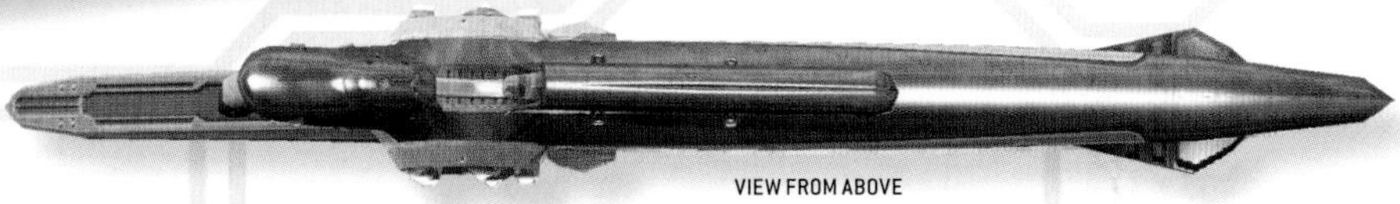

VIEW FROM ABOVE

LENGTH	WEIGHT	CARTRIDGE	MAGAZINE CAPACITY	RANGE	USE
63.2 in (160.4 cm)	39.6 lb (17.96 kg)	Accelerated particle beams	100 battery units (18–20 shots)	4,900 ft (1,500 m)	Sniping

PLASMA RIFLE

The Type-25 Plasma Rifle is the go-to gun for Sangheili forces in the Covenant. For the UNSC, its strength is somewhat limited by the inability to recharge the weapon, but a good soldier can counter that by keeping bursts short and on target.

BACK VIEW    FRONT VIEW

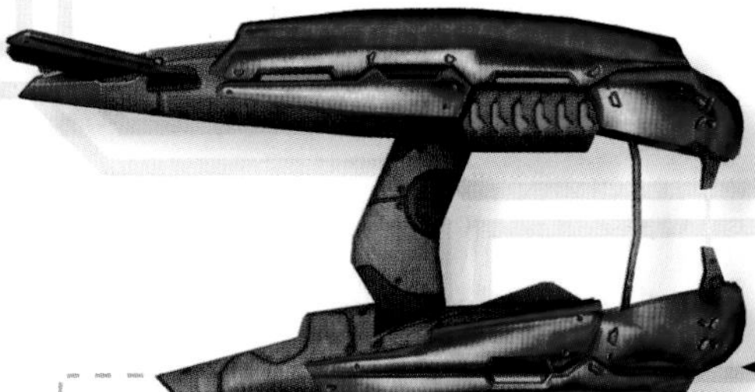

Fires 360 to 540 rounds per minute.

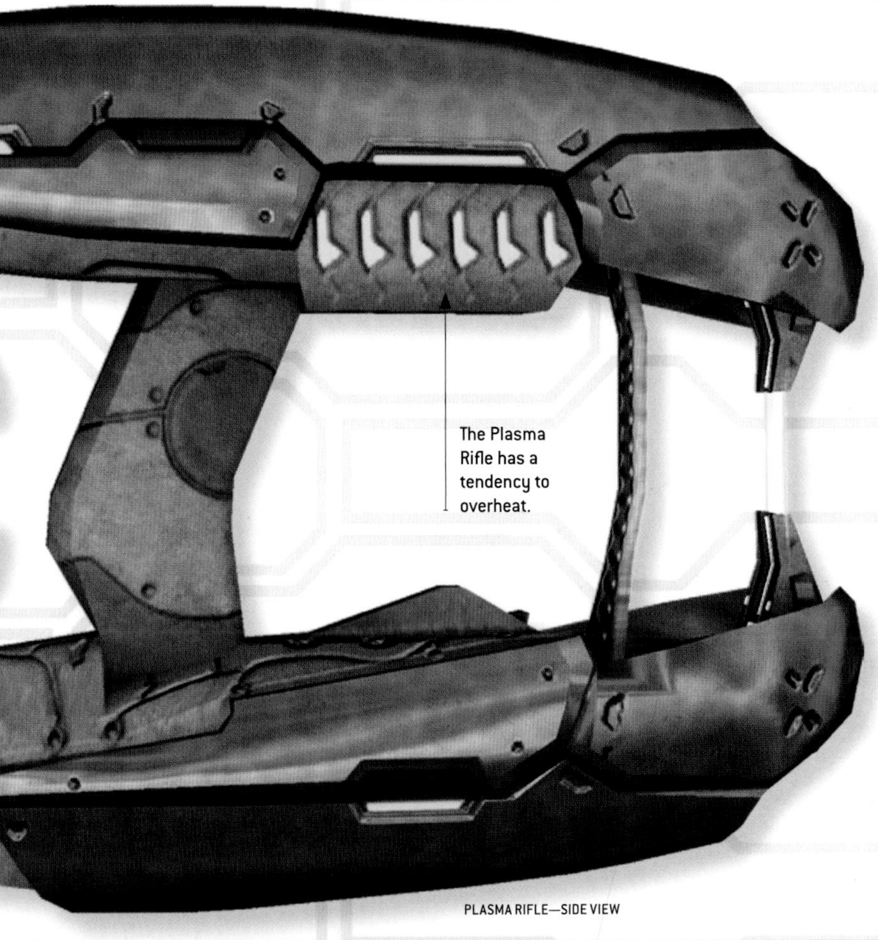

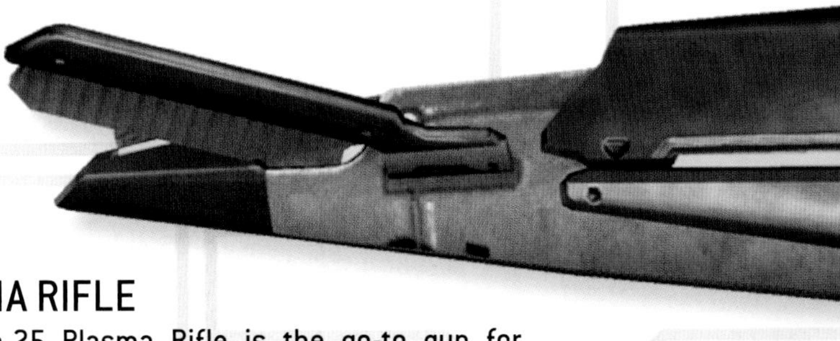

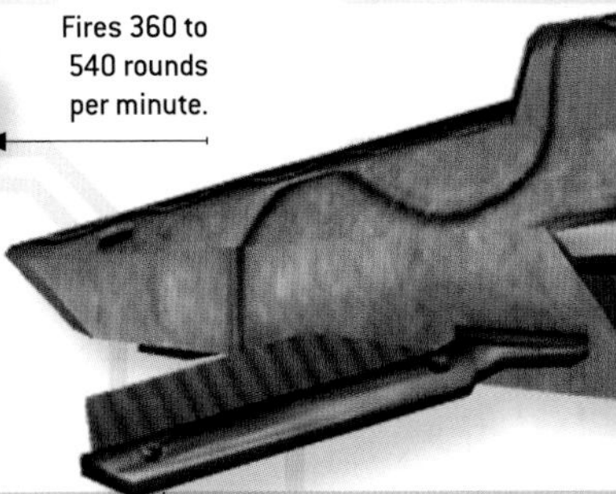

The Plasma Rifle has a tendency to overheat.

PLASMA RIFLE—SIDE VIEW

VARIANTS
BRUTE PLASMA RIFLE:
A faster, red version.

OTHER NAMES	LENGTH	WEIGHT	CARTRIDGE	MAGAZINE CAPACITY	RANGE	USE
The Big C, P-Rifle, PR	26 in (66 cm)	13 lb (5.90 kg)	Unknown (pending negotiations with the Sangheili)	400 shots	155 ft (50 m)	General use, energy-shield depletion

COVENANT WEAPONS

CARBINE RIFLE

The Type-51 Carbine Rifle can be used in a multitude of ways. Kig-Yar marksmen are known to pick off unsuspecting officers with the weapon's long-range capabilities, while Sangheili and Jiralhanae sometimes carry it into battle as a mid-range weapon.

CARBINE RIFLE—SIDE VIEW

VIEW FROM ABOVE

OTHER NAMES	LENGTH	WEIGHT		
Type-51 Carbine, CR, CC	48.3 in (122.8 cm)	Unloaded: 15.5 lb (7 kg); Loaded: 19.5 lb (8.8 kg)		
CARTRIDGE		MAGAZINE CAPACITY	RANGE	USE
8mm x 60 caseless radioactive projectiles		18 rounds	1,968 ft (600 m)	Sniping, general combat

The Carbine marks itself as different by its ammunition. Rather than use plasma bursts (which are inaccurate, noisy, and slow at long range), this weapon utilizes caseless radioactive projectiles, shot out at supersonic speeds. It is unknown how or when the Covenant developed this weapon, but it is theorized that it was based on technology similar to the larger fuel rod weapons.

NEEDLER

The Needler, is a unique weapon utilized by Covenant forces. Using charged slender energy shards, called needles, as ammunition, the barrel propels homing, but relatively slow-moving, projectiles at enemies. The rounds themselves bounce off oblique angles and bury into flesh, exploding after a time-delay.

Several needles are usually more than enough to take out any normal-sized combatant, but the small clip and slow rate of fire (along with the explosion time-delay) makes this an ineffective weapon against properly trained forces.

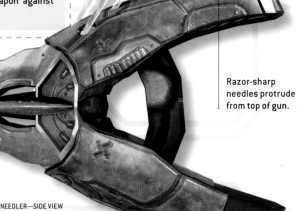

Razor-sharp needles protrude from top of gun.

NEEDLER—SIDE VIEW

NEEDLES

The needle is a crystalline latticework of unknown origin. When placed into a Needler, however, its full purpose can be readily seen. The weapon breaks and fires off pieces of the ammunition, which can home in on targets, digging into flesh or bouncing off hard surfaces. These shots are slow-moving but are more dangerous than they appear; the combined explosion from multiple simultaneous needles is more than enough to kill any Marine, while a single needle at a bad angle can disable a soldier.

OTHER NAMES: Pinkies, Crystal Shards WEIGHT: Varies

ASSAULT CANNON

Similar to the Fuel Rod Gun used by Covenant ground forces, the assault cannon is a larger, heavier version that can only be carried by Mgalekgolo. It is capable of firing large bursts or in a continuous stream, and while its blasts are slow and easily dodged, the blast radius from the weapon's impact can knock over objects as large as a Warthog from up to thirty feet (nine meters) away.

OTHER NAMES: Hunter Fuel Rod
CARTRIDGE: Incendiary Gel Tubes (Fuel Rod Cells) USE: Heavy weaponry, troop support

VIEW FROM BELOW

VIEW FROM ABOVE

OTHER NAMES		LENGTH	
Type-33 Guided Munitions Launcher, Pinkies, Shrimp Shooter		22.75 in (57.80 cm)	
WEIGHT		CARTRIDGE	
Unloaded: 8.25 lb (3.74 kg); Loaded 9.5 lb (4.3 kg)		Unknown (pending negotiations with the Sangheili)	
MAGAZINE CAPACITY	RANGE	USE	
19 rounds	210 ft (64 m)	Close-quarters combat, squad-based attacks	

FRONT VIEW

323

MAULER—SIDE VIEW

MAULER

The Type-52 Pistol, more commonly known as the Mauler, combines the dexterity of a revolver with the power of a shotgun and can do a surprising amount of damage with its five rounds despite its limited range and weight drawbacks. Jiralhanae primarily use it as a close-quarters sidearm to support their more traditional Spikers or Plasma Rifles.

VIEW FROM ABOVE

VIEW FROM BELOW

OTHER NAMES	OPERATION	MAGAZINE CAPACITY	
Type-52 Pistol	Gas-operated	5 rounds	
ACCURACY	**RANGE**		**USE**
Low to medium	Unknown (short range)		Anti-personnel

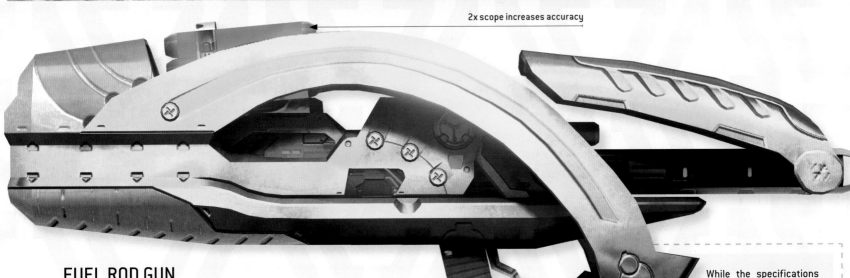

2x scope increases accuracy

FUEL ROD GUN

Heavy and powerful, the Fuel Rod Gun can be handled by any Covenant soldier, but due to the weapon's instability, it is almost always carried by the Unggoy. It is in this use that the "Thud Gun" has entered into the nightmares of the UNSC: A dim outline of green in the night, a sudden blast, and death for anything within a ten-foot (three-meter) radius.

While the specifications and technology behind the Fuel Rod Gun remain unknown, the power of the weapon is enough to make any Marine forget the beast that is usually attached to it—almost. Early variants of the weapon utilized an automated self-destruct system. Most extant models lack this component.

FUEL ROD GUN—SIDE VIEW

A lethal ballistic projectile explodes on impact with targets.

VIEW FROM ABOVE

OTHER NAMES

Type-33 Light Anti-Armor Weapon, Farg, the Thud Gun, the Shine Box

LENGTH	WEIGHT	
51.26 in (103.2 cm)	Unloaded: 46 lb (20.8 kg); Loaded: 52 lb (23.3 kg)	
CARTRIDGE	RANGE	USE
0.32 in (8.2mm)	541 ft (165 m)	Anti-armor, anti-personnel

FUEL ROD CANNON

The Fuel Rod Cannon is a powerful anti-vehicle (ground and air) weapon utilized by Covenant forces, most notably on Banshees, anti-aircraft Wraiths, and some types of defensive turret. When triggered, the cannon will fire an intense burst of green plasma that is marginally weaker than a plasma mortar but much faster and more accurate.

OTHER NAMES: Big Green Death, Green Death LENGTH: 51.26 in (130 cm) WEIGHT: 51 lb (23 kg) CARTRIDGE: 1.5-in (3.8-cm) Fuel Rods RANGE: 550 ft (168 m) USE: Anti-vehicle, anti-aircraft, anti-personnel, anti-armor

CLASS-2 PROJECTILE

Class-2 projectiles are emitted from a modified version of the Fuel Rod Gun and are mounted onto certain classes of Banshee and other Covenant aircraft. Although not as powerful as the Mgalekgolo's weapons, the Class-2 projectiles recharge somewhat faster. Little else is known about their ballistics, save for their impressive destructive power.

USE: Infantry support, anti-vehicle, anti-armor, suppression fire, ship-to-ship combat

REAR VIEW   FRONT VIEW

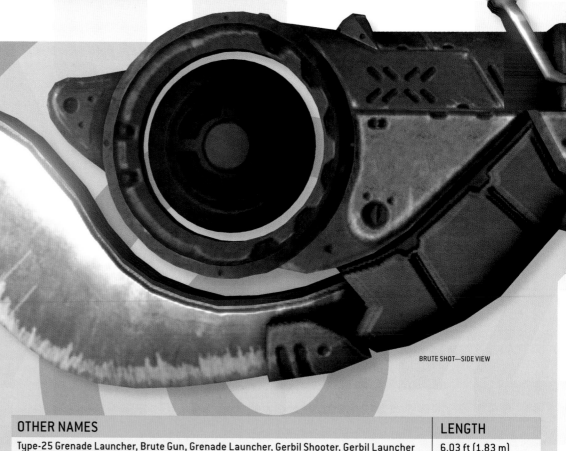

BRUTE SHOT

The Jiralhanae are not known for their subtlety, but what they lack in grace they make up for in sheer power. Take the Brute Shot: It can launch up to six grenades in a time span of three seconds, taking out large groups of opposing infantry and knocking out most vehicles. When the dust settles, Covenant ground forces can go in and mop up the survivors (if there are any). And, like most Jiralhanae-devised weaponry, the Brute Shot carries a large bayonet for close-quarters combat.

BRUTE SHOT—SIDE VIEW

OTHER NAMES			LENGTH
Type-25 Grenade Launcher, Brute Gun, Grenade Launcher, Gerbil Shooter, Gerbil Launcher			6.03 ft (1.83 m)
CARTRIDGE	MAGAZINE CAPACITY	USE	
Grenades	4 or 6 grenades	Infantry support, suppressive fire	

VIEW FROM BELOW

VIEW FROM ABOVE

SPIKER—FRONT SIDE VIEW

Fires super-hot, razor-sharp metal spikes that are one foot (thirty centimeters) long.

PIKER

e Spiker was first seen during the battle of arvest, but did not come into widespread use til the waning days of the Human-Covenant nflict. It is an automatic weapon, firing perheated metal spikes at a rate of eight unds per second. These projectiles cut rough flesh and armor like butter, and, like the yonet pair on the end of this weapon, they ould not be dealt with lightly.

ER NAMES	LENGTH	WEIGHT		
25 Carbine, Spike Rifle	32.17 in (81.7 cm)	Unloaded: 14.2 lb (6.44 kg); Loaded: 15.5 lb (7.03 kg)		
TRIDGE	MAGAZINE CAPACITY	RANGE	USE	
rheated metal spikes	40 spikes	131 ft (40 m)	Close-combat, melee combat, general use	

SIDE VIEW

Fired beams
flash a brilliant
purple-white.

SHADE

Covenant ground forces often employ stationary
energy turrets to strengthen defensive positions.
Shades are made of three primary components:
The energy emitter (the "gun barrel"), the gunnery
seat, and the mounting base unit. Shades fire
a series of rapid-fire plasma "pulses" from the
energy emitter, which inflict tremendous
damage. The gunner sits in the "ball" section,
directly behind the energy emitter. The
"ball" in turn floats on an anti-grav
cushion located in the wide, claw-footed
mounting structure. The turret rotates
a full 360 degrees, and can be
employed against aerial and ground
targets.

Anti-gravity cushion
supports guns

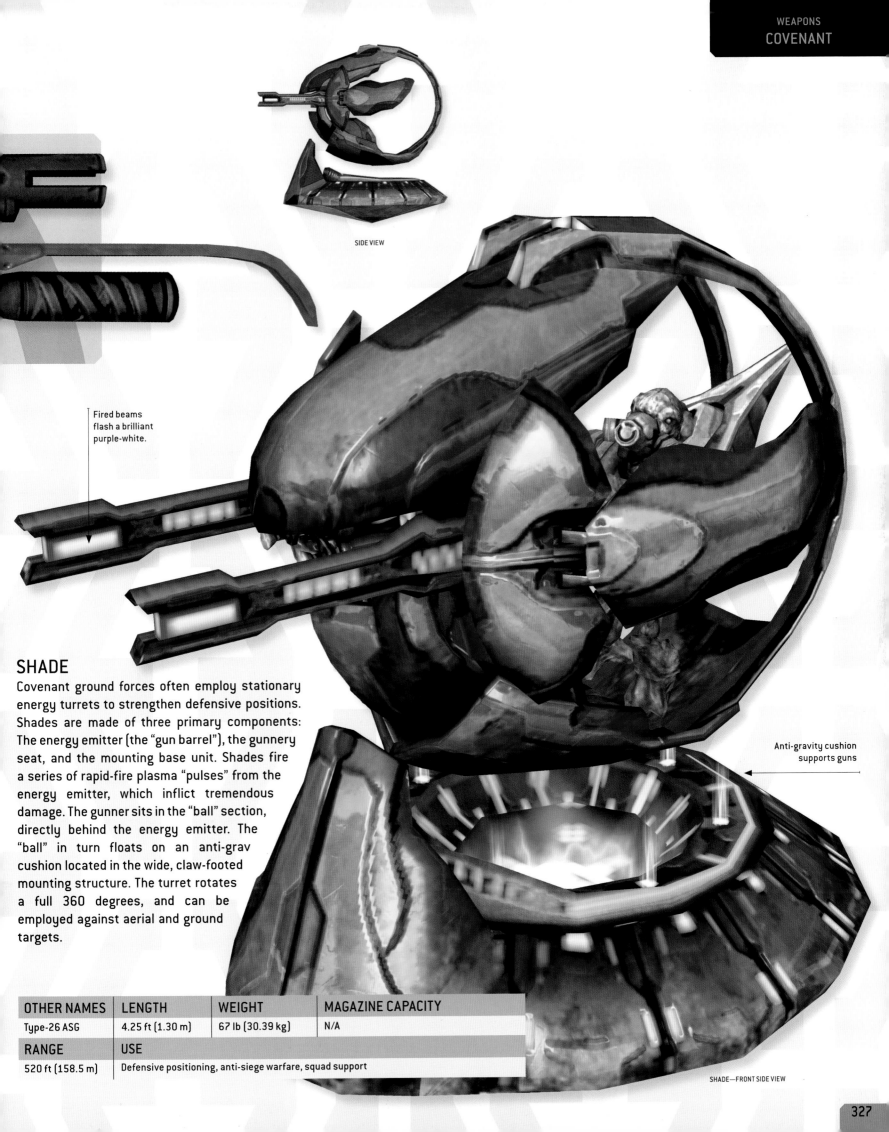

OTHER NAMES	LENGTH	WEIGHT	MAGAZINE CAPACITY
Type-26 ASG	4.25 ft (1.30 m)	67 lb (30.39 kg)	N/A
RANGE	**USE**		
520 ft (158.5 m)	Defensive positioning, anti-siege warfare, squad support		

SHADE—FRONT SIDE VIEW

TESTIMONIAL: MAJOR ROLAND HUFFMAN; UNSC (RET.) ACTIVE DUTY 2548–2573 CE

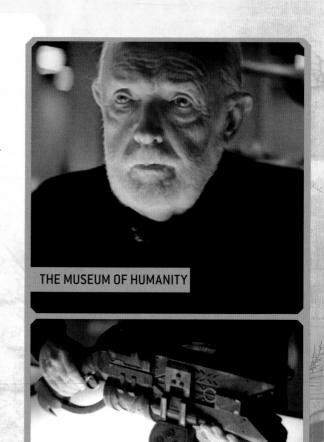

THE MUSEUM OF HUMANITY

"CAN YOU TELL US A BIT ABOUT THIS ONE?"

"WE SAW A LOT OF THESE. THIS IS AN OLD COVENANT WEAPON. IT'S A SPIKE RIFLE, WE CALLED IT A SPIKER."

"AND WHO USED IT?"

"WELL, THE BRUTES MOSTLY."

"AND CAN YOU SHOW US HOW IT WORKED?"

"SURE. THEY USED IT AS A HAND-HELD. THAT'S HEAVY. HOLDING AN ENEMY WEAPON LIKE THIS...IS...ER...FEELS... I DON'T LIKE IT. IF YOU'D HAVE TOLD ME A FEW YEARS AGO THAT WE'D BE HERE IN, IN THIS PLACE LIKE THIS, TALKING ABOUT THIS, I'D HAVE SAID 'NO WAY. IT'S NOT GOING TO HAPPEN.' IF THERE'S ONE REASON WHY WE'RE HERE, I WOULD SAY, IT'S BECAUSE OF THE CHIEF."

REAR SIDE VIEW

PLASMA CANNON WITH
ANTI-GRAVITY BASE

Without an anti-gravity base, the hand-held plasma cannon is limited to two hundred units of power.

Motion trackers detect approaching enemies.

PLASMA CANNON

Covenant ground forces often employ stationary energy weapon turrets to strengthen defensive positions. Plasma turrets are carried, deployed, and crewed by Grunts, in addition to being wielded portably by some Brute Chieftains. Plasma cannons fire bolts of energy similar to those of the Plasma Rifle, with a rate of fire of just over three-hundred rounds per minute. A battery or plasma core is built into the stationary base of the weapon, which offers the weapon unlimited fire power when it remains attached. When removed from the base, however, the gun can only use the firepower remaining within the weapon.

AUTOMATED PLASMA
TURRET—SIDE VIEW

OTHER NAMES	LENGTH	WEIGHT		
Type-52 Directed Energy Support Weapon	51.85 in (131.7 cm)	67 lb (30.39 kg)		
MAGAZINE CAPACITY	RANGE	USE		
N/A (200 shot charge when dismounted)	520 ft (158.5 m)	Defensive positioning, anti-siege warfare, squad support		

PLASMA CANNON—SIDE VIEW

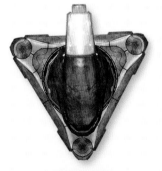

VIEW FROM ABOVE

CLASS-2 ENERGY GUN

Class-2 energy guns are a newer plasma-based projectile weapon mounted onto small Covenant craft, most notably the Banshee and dropships. From just a small power source, these weapons are able to produce considerable firepower, bringing down Marines in a few well-placed shots.

CARTRIDGE: Concentrated plasma USE: Infantry support, anti-vehicle, anti-armor, suppressive fire, ship-to-ship combat

PULSE LASER TURRET

The Pulse Laser Turret (PLT) is a light ship-to-ship weapon used on smaller Covenant vessels as a primary weapon and on larger ships as a secondary weapon. It is able to gut most UNSC fighters with one direct burst. Captured weapons of this sort have allowed ONI to develop their own version, which has been deployed on Prowlers.

OTHER NAMES: PLT, Pulser, Heartbeat CARTRIDGE: Concentrated plasma USE: Ship-to-ship combat

SCARAB GUN

Able to destroy a bunker in one blast (not to mention infantry and most vehicles), this gun makes any Scarab more than capable of decimating an entire city by itself. The Scarab gun can also be fired on its own in a portable form when removed.

OTHER NAMES: Beetle Gun USE: Anti-personnel, anti-armor, anti-vehicle, anti-fortification

AUTOMATED PLASMA TURRET

The APT is a seventy-eight-inch (two-meter) high, motion-tracking turret used to watch over perimeters and bases. It is found only in places where other forms of protection would lack sufficient lethality. It is one of the few weapons that can fire through Bubble Shields, Invincibility, and Overshields.

VIEW FROM ABOVE

OTHER NAMES	CARTRIDGE
Plasma Wall, APT	Unknown (pending treaty negotiations with the Sangheili)
USE	
Defensive positioning, anti-siege warfare	

35MM AUTOCANNON

The Covenant Loyalists, led by Jiralhanae on the ground, required a weapon that would equal those developed (and retained) by the Sangheili. So they took existing Jiralhanae technology and constructed a variant for their newly-developed Chopper vehicle. The cannons are similar to the Spiker weapon, although they fire more slowly and require more overall control.

OTHER NAMES: Kong Cannon, Bike Cannon, Bike Blaster CARTRIDGE: Superheated metal spikes USE: Anti-vehicle, anti-personnel

COVENANT GRENADES AND BOMBS

COVENANT GRENADES and bombs, like other Covenant weaponry, utilize batteries rather than ballistics, and so while they are very effective, once the plasma reserves are depleted, they become largely useless.

SPIKE GRENADE

A Jiralhanae invention, the Spike Grenade works on roughly the same principles as the Plasma Grenade: Lob, stick, and duck. The difference is that the Spike Grenade attaches itself to objects via its spikes, rather than bonding with the contacted surface. When the fuse detonates, the super-heated shrapnel extrudes violently away from the initial point of impact, in a similar way to a claymore mine.

Shrapnel from the Spike Grenade reaches a temperature of about 270–315 degrees Centigrade (518–599 degrees Fahrenheit).

The Plasma Grenade emits a blue plasma gas when activated.

PLASMA GRENADE

PLASMA GRENADE

The Type-1 Antipersonnel Grenade, more commonly known as a Plasma Grenade or Sticky Grenade, is a dangerous hand-thrown grenade utilized by Covenant forces, typically Unggoy. Using technology that is barely understood, even by the Covenant, a primed Plasma Grenade will "bond" with any organic material it touches, making removal impossible. The resulting explosion will most certainly kill the target and wreak havoc up to forty feet (twelve meters) away. One frightening tactic which has been seen on the battlefield is one in which mortally wounded or psychologically unstable Unggoy attach primed grenades to their bodies before hurling themselves at their enemies.

Scientists theorize that prolonged exposure to the radiation emitted by Plasma Grenades can cause a deviation in the neural pathways of the user, a rare disorder called Boren's Syndrome. Currently, Sergeant Avery Johnson of the UNSC is the only known human to have suffered from this disease and survived.

OTHER NAMES

Type-1 Antipersonnel Grenade, Stickies, Demon Flare, Blue Ball

DIAMETER	WEIGHT	DAMAGE RADIUS	USE
5.75 in (14.6 cm)	2 lb (907 g)	Kill radius: 13 ft (3.96 m); Damage radius: 40 ft (12.19 m)	General use

ANTIMATTER CHARGE

While humans use nuclear power (fission and fusion), antimatter is the energy of choice for the Covenant. In lay terms, antimatter is the "opposite" of normal matter, and when the two collide, they produce an amount of energy that shames even the largest UNSC reactors—for example, an H-Bomb only utilizes seven percent of its total potential energy, while all antimatter explosions utilize one hundred percent. Through this, the Covenant has developed engines that "never" need recharging and weapons that can glass entire planets. Humanity, meanwhile, can only produce less than a gram of antimatter a year, even with its most advanced laboratories.

OTHER NAMES	USE
No-matter, Zero-stuff	Nuclear warfare, energy

Lethal spikes can stick to almost anything

SIDE VIEW

Upon impact, the outer casing converts into liquid form.

While troopers have been known to capture these weapons from fallen Jiralhanae, they are loath to use it; the sight of so many charred skeletons has put a dark cloud over them.

INCENDIARY GRENADE

Developed by the Covenant for its psychological aspect as much as for its damage potential, the "Firebomb," as it is commonly known, is a little bit of hell wrapped in a package the size of a football. When detonated, the incendiary gel within the grenade can burn at up to 2200 degrees Centigrade (3992 degrees Fahrenheit) for four and a half seconds, gutting metal and vaporizing all flesh within its explosive range.

INCENDIARY GRENADE

OTHER NAMES			LENGTH
Type-3 Antipersonnel/Antimateriel Incendiary Grenade, Firebomb, Flame Grenade			12 in (30.48 cm)
WEIGHT	**CARTRIDGE**	**BLAST RADIUS**	**USE**
8 lb (3.63 kg)	Incendiary gel	12 ft (3.66 m)	Anti-personnel

PLASMA MORTAR

Built as the main ammunition for Covenant Wraith tanks, the Plasma Mortar (PM) is the most powerful ground-based application of Covenant energy weapon technology. The barrel of the Wraith hurls a voluminous charge of plasma through the air, much like a human artillery shell. This packet detonates upon impact, creating a burst of heavy damage on targets within its blast radius. Unlike human mortar, however, the Plasma Mortar is fairly effective at close range, though its main use remains in shelling and vehicle warfare.

OTHER NAMES: PM, Comet, Brimstone **DIAMETER:** 3 ft (0.91 m) **WEIGHT:** Unknown (pending treaty negotiations with the Sangheili) **DAMAGE RADIUS:** Kill radius: 20 ft (6.09 m); Damage radius: 50 ft (15.24 m) **USE:** Anti-vehicle, anti-personnel, shelling

SPIKE GRENADE—
FRONT VIEW FROM ABOVE

OTHER NAMES	LENGTH	WEIGHT
Type-2 Antipersonnel Fragmentation Grenade, Key	36 in (91.44 cm)	4.2 lb (1.9 kg)
DAMAGE RADIUS	**USE**	
Kill radius: 10 ft (3.05 m); Casualty radius: 36 ft (10.97 m)	Anti-personnel, demolitions	

COVENANT MELEE WEAPONS

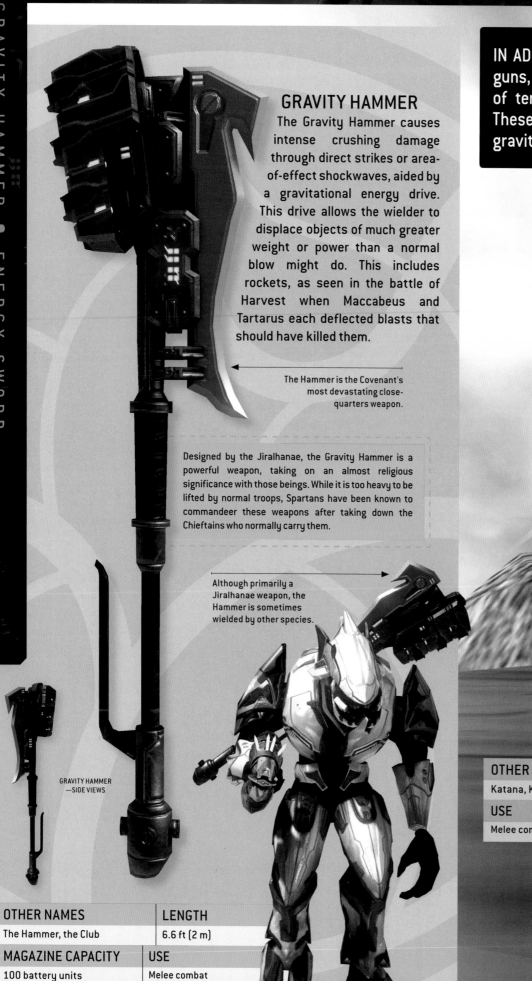

GRAVITY HAMMER

The Gravity Hammer causes intense crushing damage through direct strikes or area-of-effect shockwaves, aided by a gravitational energy drive. This drive allows the wielder to displace objects of much greater weight or power than a normal blow might do. This includes rockets, as seen in the battle of Harvest when Maccabeus and Tartarus each deflected blasts that should have killed them.

The Hammer is the Covenant's most devastating close-quarters weapon.

Designed by the Jiralhanae, the Gravity Hammer is a powerful weapon, taking on an almost religious significance with those beings. While it is too heavy to be lifted by normal troops, Spartans have been known to commandeer these weapons after taking down the Chieftains who normally carry them.

Although primarily a Jiralhanae weapon, the Hammer is sometimes wielded by other species.

GRAVITY HAMMER —SIDE VIEWS

IN ADDITION TO their impressive arsenal of guns, the Covenant also has a variety of terrifying melee weapons to draw on. These deadly arms harness power from both gravitational energy and plasma energy.

The energy blade coalesces when the hilt is activated.

OTHER NAMES	LENGTH	WEIGHT
Katana, Kill Beam	52 in (1.32 m)	5.2 lb (2.36 kg)
USE		
Melee combat, assassination		

OTHER NAMES	LENGTH
The Hammer, the Club	6.6 ft (2 m)
MAGAZINE CAPACITY	USE
100 battery units	Melee combat

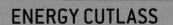

ENERGY CUTLASS

The Energy Cutlass is a Kig-Yar weapon, designed for light fighting in close quarters. As the Kig-Yar remain a largely piratical species, these blades serve them well in the confines of their victims' ships.

Composed of a complex lattice of chemicals, plasma, and alloys, the Cutlass can be made to shatter in a low-level explosion when embedded in soft flesh, like a Needler round.

LENGTH: 2 ft (61 cm)
USE: Close-quarters combat

ENERGY GARROTE

When a mission requires a quick and quiet kill, a handful of Covenant SpecOps Elites have been known to bring an Energy Garrote. The weapon itself is simple. It is comprised of a split cylinder with focused plasma at the center. This plasma, while not powerful enough to cut through flesh, can choke and burn an enemy from behind, ending his or her life silently and in a matter of seconds.

USE: Stealth, assassination

ENERGY STAVE

Nothing so seemingly ordinary could be as honorific as an Energy Stave. These staves, wielded by Honor Guards and the Light of Sanghelios, are not actual weapons but more symbols of office. In actual combat, an Honor Guard is more likely to use an Energy Sword. However, the Stave is not without its uses; it can eviscerate a stray Unggoy or Kig-Yar if they wander too close to—or too impertinently near—a High Prophet.

OTHER NAMES: Honor Guard Pike **LENGTH:** 14.03 ft (4.28 m)
USE: Symbolic, close combat, melee combat

ENERGY SWORD

An Energy Sword on an approaching Sangheili warrior is enough to make any human flee in terror. That is because the plasma sheet that makes up the blade of the weapon does not hack or carve, but boils away anything it comes into contact with. Anyone unlucky enough to be in the path of its slice is assured a most painful and messy death. The only saving grace (for human attackers, at least) is that any Sangheili brave enough to wield such a weapon will be temporarily helpless against long-range attacks.

➤ THE GRAVITY HAMMER EMITS DEADLY GRAVITY SHOCKWAVES UPON IMPACT, BUT THOSE IT STRIKES DIRECTLY ARE USUALLY TOO BUSY BEING CRUSHED TO NOTICE.

MOST OF THE defensive weaponry constructed by the Forerunners consisted of high-powered energy beams, but they also used some plasma-based weaponry. Both forms are effective at containment, but their use is limited.

Non-rechargeable battery runs out quickly

SIDE VIEW

SIDE VIEW

SENTINEL BEAM—FRONT SIDE VIEW

SENTINEL BEAM

Constructed by the Forerunners toward the end of their era, Sentinels are able to produce a directed energy beam that has the ability to slice through flesh, bone, and even metal. While the technology was reworked into some Covenant weapons, even the Prophets themselves are not entirely certain how the weapon works. Except for the artificial constructs which inhabit the Halo installations, no one has much information regarding the weapon's operational details.

OTHER NAMES		MAGAZINE CAPACITY
Slicer, Beam, Laser Gun, Phaser, Ray Gun		100 battery units
RANGE	USE	
300 ft (91 m)	Protection against the Flood	

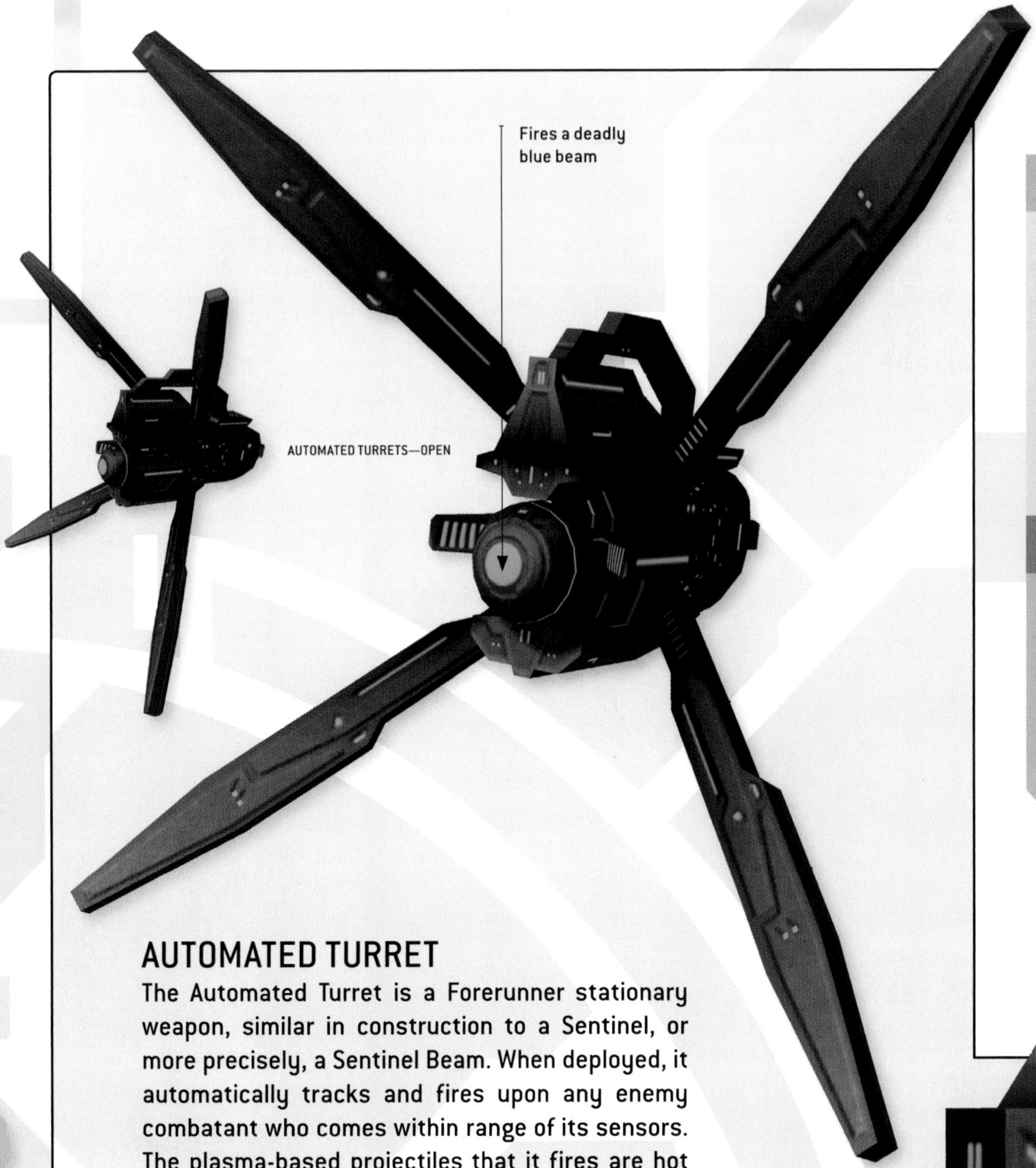

Fires a deadly
blue beam

AUTOMATED TURRETS—OPEN

COMBAT SKIN

Not much is known about Combat Skin, the referenced armor worn by the Forerunners. While dealing with the Flood on Installation 04, 343 Guilty Spark admonishes Master Chief for wearing what is, in essence, "Class 2 Combat Skin." With a range of Skins going up to Class 18, and possibly beyond, it can be assumed that, like the rest of Forerunner technology, this armor is beyond the capacity of understanding for any of the extant contemporary cultures.

USE: Armor, protection against the Flood

PULSE BEAMS

Utilized by Forerunner Enforcers, Pulse Beams fire fast-moving projectiles capable of devastating a target by inflicting maximum damage in a short period of time.

OTHER NAMES: Red Death, the Reds RANGE: 150 ft (45.72 m) USE: Protection against the Flood

AUTOMATED TURRET

The Automated Turret is a Forerunner stationary weapon, similar in construction to a Sentinel, or more precisely, a Sentinel Beam. When deployed, it automatically tracks and fires upon any enemy combatant who comes within range of its sensors. The plasma-based projectiles that it fires are hot enough to melt steel.

AUTOMATED TURRET—CLOSED

OTHER NAMES	USE
Turret	Defense

BATTLEFIELD EQUIPMENT

ALTHOUGH WEAPONS AND vehicles play an extensive role within combat, a role of almost equal importance is filled by battlefield equipment.

After about twenty seconds the anti-projectile dome collapses and the generator explodes.

BUBBLE SHIELD

When activated, the Bubble Shield's generator creates an anti-projectile dome around the focal point, up to twenty feet (six meters) in diameter. This only lasts for a brief period of time, during which a unit is nearly invulnerable, albeit with limited mobility.

OTHER NAMES	USE
The BS, the Bull Suit, the Golf Ball	Defense

BUBBLE SHIELD—UNACTIVATED

Invisibilty lasts for only a short period of time

ACTIVE CAMOUFLAGE
—ACTIVATED

ACTIVE CAMOUFLAGE

Reverse-engineered by the Huragok from Forerunner technology, Active Camouflage is the ultimate stealth weapon, rendering anyone that touches it temporarily invisible. Although the specifics are not well understood, what the device does is refract light around a target, blending him or her into the background as long as the wearer limits his or her movement.

OTHER NAMES	USE
Invisibility, Active Camo, Camo	Stealth

BUBBLE SHIELD
—ACTIVATED

Bright bands protect the user for ten seconds

With Invincibility shielding, any warrior can become a ten-second tower of terror.

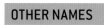

INVINCIBILTY—CLOSED

USE
Shock tactics

INVINCIBILITY

Invincibility equipment is unique and was developed by the Covenant for its obvious battleground potential. It is carried by Brutes and when utilized allows the wielder invincibility for a total of ten seconds.

Although the UNSC has determined that the source of protection stems from a latent energy field, their ability to reverse-engineer the technology has led to largely inconclusive results.

INVINCIBILITY
—ACTIVATED

FLARE—ACTIVATED

REAR VIEW

FRONT VIEW

FLARE

The Flare is a piece of equipment used to blind opponents temporarily. Similar to a stun or flash grenade, the Flare is a non-lethal combat tool used for distraction and misdirection, before forces move in to eliminate an enemy target. Developed by the Jiralhanae, the Flare appears to be based on the same technology as the Radar Jammer and Power Drainer.

WEIGHT	USE
6.82 lb (3 kg)	Infantry support

CLOAKING

Much like Active Camouflage, the Cloaking device is a single-use piece of equipment with a limited power supply. Developed by the Jiralhanae to aid in their battles against the UNSC and heretic factions within the Covenant, when activated, the device renders its user nearly invisible for twelve seconds by bending light rays around his or her position.

OTHER NAMES: Invisibility Cloak
USE: Stealth, reconnaissance, assassination, general use

OVERSHIELD

The Overshield is a Covenant invention that renders an extra layer of shielding to its wielder. When worn, the Overshield can withstand blasts from even heavy weaponry.

OTHER NAMES: Extra Energy, Shield
USE: General use, melee combat

The shield turns a reddish-orange color when it is damaged.

DEPLOYABLE COVER

Much like the Stationary Shield Generators (SSG) developed by the Covenant, the Deployable Cover (DC) is a near-perfect shield that can withstand all projectile weaponry and has a limited ability to absorb plasma-based explosives. The main advantage of the Deployable Cover is its portability, which allows for an as-needed combat defense system. Though only large enough to offer protection from one angle, even this shortcoming has its advantages as it allows its user the option to strategically return fire, unlike the Bubble Shield.

DEPLOYABLE COVER—TOP SIDE

DEPLOYABLE COVER—UNDER SIDE

OTHER NAMES
DC, One-Way Wall, One-Way Mirror, One-Way Sign, Walking Shield

WEIGHT	USE
30.8 lb (14 kg)	Infantry support, shock tactics

BATTLEFIELD EQUIPMENT

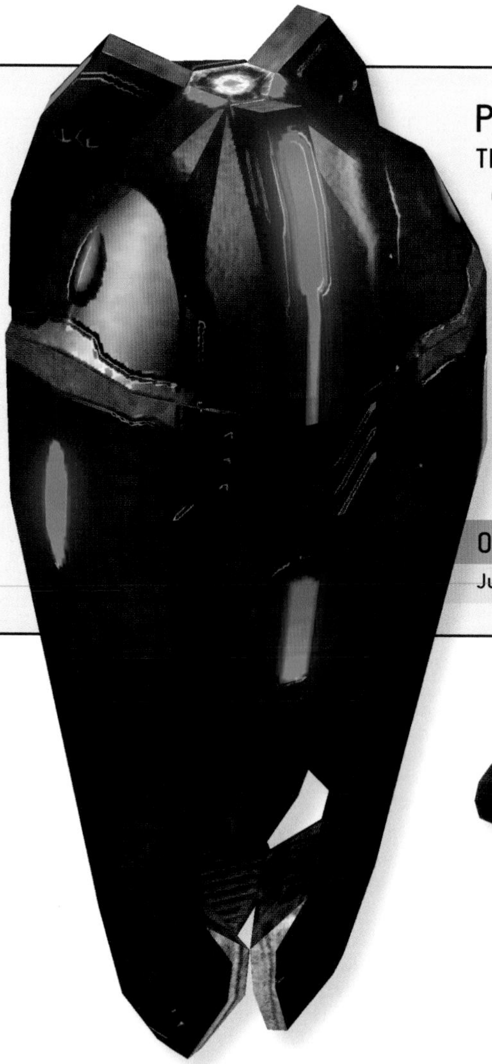

Bluish-purple gravity beam lifts objects

PORTABLE GRAVITY LIFT

The portable gravity lift, or grav lift, is a personal elevation device that emits a concentrated gravity beam capable of lifting objects up to several tons in weight, making it a useful combat tool for both battlefield maneuvering and defensive purposes. Ideal for scaling large obstacles with ease and speed, the grav lift can change the momentum of a firefight or aid troopers in need of a tactical retreat.

GRAVITY LIFT—OPEN

OTHER NAMES	WEIGHT	DIAMETER
Jumper, Grav Lift, Booster	43.2 lb (19.6 kg)	33 ft (10 m)

TRIP MINE—DORMANT

SIDE VIEW—DORMANT

SIDE VIEW—ACTIVATED

TRIP MINE

Trip mines are used mainly in the defense of perimeters or along enemy paths. Trip wires or beams are used to trigger the detonator whenever something large enough comes within range.

Though deadly to anyone close to the explosion, the mine's damage rapidly decreases outward. Trip mines are designed to serve more as warning devices with an extra punch than as actual weapons.

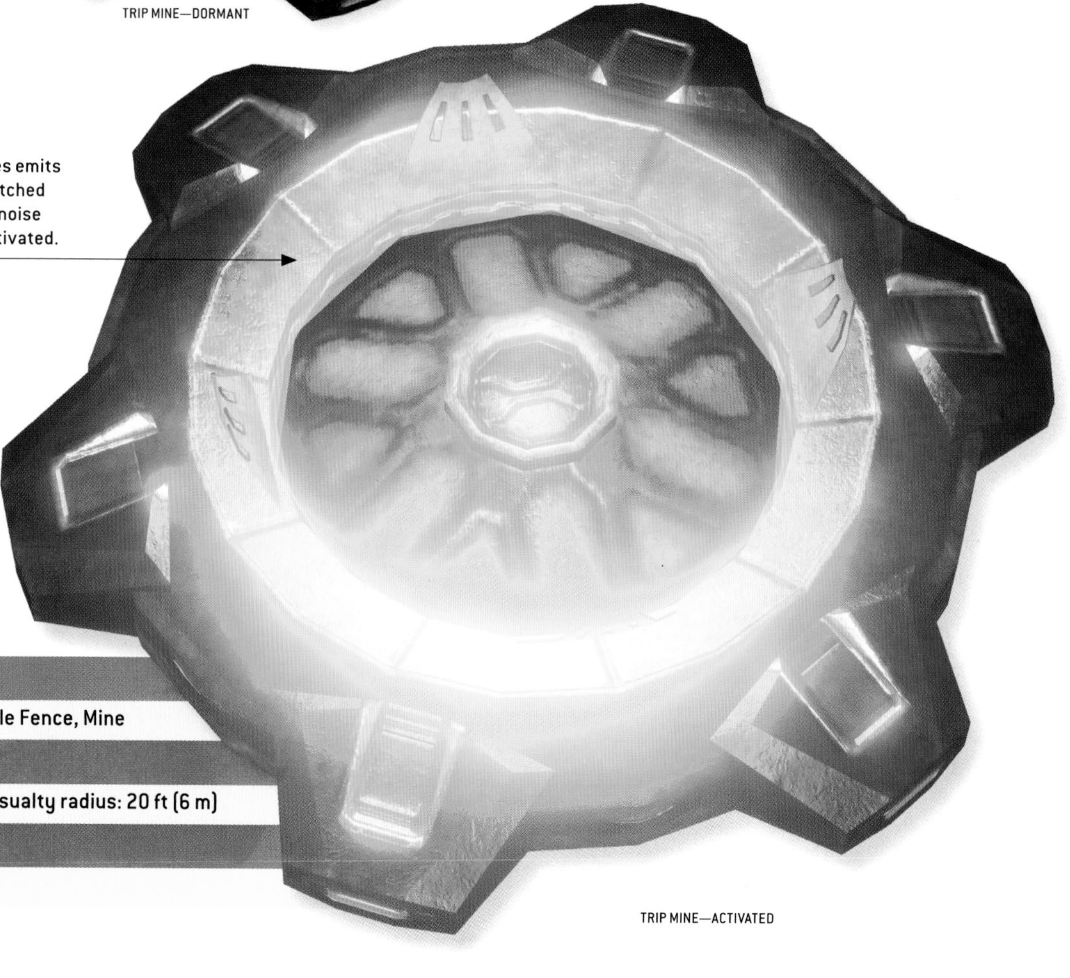

Trip mines emits a high-pitched beeping noise when activated.

OTHER NAMES

TR/9 Antipersonnel Mine, Tripper, Skippy, Automatic Guard, Invisible Fence, Mine

DIMENSIONS	WEIGHT	DAMAGE RADIUS
1.3 ft (40 cm) cube	21.7 lb (9.8 kg)	Kill radius: 10 ft (3 m); Casualty radius: 20 ft (6 m)

USE

Defense, siege warfare, guerilla tactics

TRIP MINE—ACTIVATED

RADAR JAMMER—ACTIVATED

ACTIVATED

DORMANT

POINT DEFENSE GAUNTLET

The Point Defense Gauntlet (PDG) is a purely defensive device carried only by the Kig-Yar during battle. Developed by the Covenant from Forerunner technology, the shield is activated by a gauntlet worn on the user's wrist. Once activated, a four-foot (1.2-meter) wide shield blinks into existence. It is able to withstand most projectile-based attacks, including those of a needle-shot, and though plasma-based weapons can take a PDG down, the shields are regenerative.

OTHER NAMES: Lizard Shield, Lizard Screen, Chicken Screen
LENGTH: 4 ft (1.22 m) diameter USE: Personal defense

OTHER NAMES	WEIGHT
Scrambler, Jammer	20.5 lb (9.3 kg)
USE	
Infantry support	

RADAR JAMMER

The Radar Jammer is a simple device, used by Covenant forces to confuse an enemy's radar screens. When activated, the Jammer emits radio waves that trick nearby combatants' motion sensors into thinking that there are many more combatants than there actually are. These phantoms show up as false dots on the screen, covering an escape or shielding real soldiers as they move in for the kill.

Once activated the top of the Regenerator spins around 360 degrees

REGENERATOR—ACTIVATED

REGENERATOR

Much like the Bubble Shield, the Regenerator "protects" shielded combatants within its range of effect for a short period of time, typically around fifteen seconds. It does this by recharging energy shields, even if they belong to an enemy combatant. Users should not grow over-reliant on this piece of equipment, as it takes some time for the Regenerator to activate and it must be recharged after use.

WEIGHT	RANGE	USE
44.3 lbs (20.09 kg)	20 ft (6.10 m)	Infantry support

OTHER NAMES	WEIGHT	USE
Draino, Drainer	11.2 lb (5.08 kg)	Infantry support

DORMANT   SEMI-ACTIVATED

POWER DRAINER

The Power Drainer is a short-range energy-disrupter device used by the Covenant to lower the electrical systems of any combatant within range. By emitting a short-range EMP, it short-circuits all electronics within its emission radius, effectively lowering personal energy shields and halting vehicles in their tracks.

POWER DRAINER—ACTIVATED

The electromagnetic pulse emitted by the Power Drainer lasts for about six -and-a-half seconds.

REGENERATOR—DORMANT

ADMIRALTY, THE see HIGHCOM

AGES
The cycles of time into which the Covenant divide their history and define their present. There are seven Ages, but more than one of each and they do not necessarily follow in the same order. They are the Ages of Abandonment, Conflict, Discovery, Reconciliation, Conversion, Doubt, and Reclamation.

AI (ARTIFICIAL INTELLIGENCE)
An intelligence created by replicating the neural pathways of a human brain that has been subjected to bursts of electrical energy. AIs may be either "dumb" or "smart." Dumb AIs can only function within their original programming, whereas Smart AIs are able to learn new information but they are susceptible to rampancy.

ALPHA PRIME
The leader of a clan of Brutes.

ARK, THE
A secure installation outside the range of the Halo Array, created by the Forerunners. On it, they stored samples of all sentient races of the Milky Way before they activated the Halo rings and wiped all life from the Galaxy. It is also known as Halo Installation 00.

ARBITER, THE
A Covenant commander who has been responsible for a defeat is sometimes given a chance to regain his honor by becoming the Arbiter. In this role, he will be sent on a suicidal mission and thus die as a Covenant martyr.

ARTIFICIAL GRAVITY
A system to create gravity in a place where it would not normally exist, such as a space craft. It can make conditions aboard much easier, but consumes large amounts of energy.

AUGMENTATION
The process of adding artificial enhancements to Spartan soldiers. These included ceramic bone grafts, catalytic thyroid implants, occipital capillary reversals, superconductive fabrication of neural dendrites, and certain muscular enhancements.

AVATAR
The unique appearance taken on by an AI. Most AIs choose their own avatar, usually in line with whatever function they perform.

BANSHEE
A Covenant vehicle used for recon and making attacks from the air during ground combat. A small, single-pilot craft with stubby wings, it is highly maneuverable and can reach speeds of 62 mph (100 kph).

BATTALION
Within the UNSC, four companies along with another group known as "Battalion Headquarters Section," totaling 800 men.

BETA-5 DIVISION
The arm of ONI responsible for research and development.

BLOODING
A term used by the Elites, meaning to gain first experience of battle.

BONDED PAIR
Two Hunters who have formed a permanent tandem battle unit. Hunters always operate as bonded pairs.

BRAIN FORM see PROTO-GRAVEMIND

BRUTES
A violent, savage species whose homeworld is Doisac. They are about 8 ft 5 in (2.59 m) tall, bulky, and covered in shaggy fur. The Brutes joined the Covenant in 2492 CE. The Elites have always considered the Brutes dangerous and kept them under tight control.

CARVER FINDINGS
A theory published by human political sociologist Dr. Elias Carver in 2491 CE. It argued that the rebellions in the Colonies must be crushed, otherwise civil war would be inevitable.

CALLISTO TREATY
The treaty by which the Koslovic and Friedan forces surrendered to the UNSC in 2170 CE.

CASTLE BASE
A high-security underground complex in the planet Reach from which Dr. Catherine Halsey operated.

CHIEFTAIN
The highest military rank in the Brute hierarchy.

CLONE
The scientific product of replication of cells donated by a living subject, with the aim of creating new tissue, functioning organs, or even entire beings. See FLASH CLONING

COLE PROTOCOL
A ruling by the UNSC that human craft, when retreating, must use random coordinates and must not move on a path toward Earth or any other human planet because of the risk of giving away its location to the Covenant. If capture is inevitable, they should destroy their navigational data and self destruct.

COLONIAL ADMINISTRATION AUTHORITY
A group that once governed the Colonies. It had its own separate military fleet, but ultimately was absorbed by the UEG.

COLONIES
Permanent human settlements on worlds other than Earth. Those closer to the home planet are known as the Inner Colonies, while those in more remote areas of space are known as the Outer Colonies.

COMPANY
Within the UNSC, four platoons along with another group known as a "Company Headquarters Section." Each company in a battalion is named alphabetically: Alpha, Beta, Gamma, and so on.

CONFEDERATION
A league, alliance, or union.

COVENANT, THE
A confederation of various alien races who all share one religion. Its central belief is that through the holy rings (the Halos) they will transcend the world and reach a higher plane of existence.

COVENANT CIVIL WAR see GREAT SCHISM

COVENANT WAR
A major series of conflicts between humans and the Covenant, beginning in 2525 CE.

CRYO-SLEEP
A sleep state induced by placing the subject in low temperature conditions in order to lower their metabolic rate. The UNSC uses cryonic sleep, or cryo-sleep, to reduce the demand on resources on longer flights.

CRYO-ITCH
Dry, itchy skin affecting those who have recently

woken from cryo-sleep.

CYTOPRETHALINE
A chemical that protects cell membranes against ice damage during cryo-sleep.

DIDACT, THE
A Forerunner military commander responsible for firing the Halo Array. He was the lover of the Librarian.

DIVISION
Within the UNSC, three regiments along with a group known as "Division Headquarters Section." It totals 14,000 men.

DREADNOUGHT
A type of warship used by the Forerunners in their conflict with the Flood. The only surviving Dreadnought is the keyship around which High Charity was built and which opened Earth's portal to the Ark.

DRONES
An alien species with a practical nature and a hive mentality. They joined the Covenant in 1112 CE, and their role is to perform maintenance and simple combat roles. Drones are insect-like in appearance and their home system is Palamok.

ELITES
The first race to join with the San 'Shyuum (Prophets) to form the Covenant. For a long time the Elites were the second highest caste, with only the Prophets above them. Elites are about 7 ft 4 in (2.25 m) tall with an appearance that is partly reptilian, partly mammalian.

ENGINEERS
Engineers are thinking machines rather than true life forms. Their duties are excavating and gathering Forerunner artifacts. Engineers are purplish-pink in color and move about by floating on lighter-than-air gases.

EPSILON ERIDANI
A star system that contains the planet Reach. It is 10.5 light years from the Sol System.

FDS (FUSION DRIVE SYSTEM)
A system that uses fusion reactors to generate power. The power provides thrust for human vessels. A scaled down version provides thrust for fusion rockets

FLASH CLONING
A method of creating a clone at a vastly accelerated speed. Flash-grown clones have many weaknesses and the procedure is officially banned.

FLASH THAWING
Awaking subjects from cryo-sleep in a very short time frame. It has a twenty percent mortality rate and is only done in emergency situations.

FLEETCOM (UNSC FLEET COMMAND)
The main operational group of the UNSC Naval Forces. It controls all naval vessels in the UNSC.

FLOOD, THE
A parasitic alien species which relies on other sentient species for its nourishment and growth. There are several Flood forms: The Infection Form, Combat Form, Carrier Form, Pure Form, Juggernaut Form, Prophet Form, Brain Form or Proto-Gravemind, and Gravemind.

FORTRESS WORLD see SHIELD WORLD

FORERUNNERS
An ancient race who dominated the Milky Way 100,000 years before the Common Era. The Forerunners considered themselves benevolent stewards of the Galaxy, and protected all other species within it.

FRIEDEN MOVEMENT
A neo-fascist political movement arising on Earth in 2160 CE. It began as a reaction to the Koslovic movement.

FSC (FLOOD SUPER CELL)
The cell type which forms the biomass of the Flood alien race. FSCs are similar to neurons, and can be arranged to mimic bodily organs.

GALAXY
A large group of stars, gases, and dust.

GLASSING
When Covenant ships bombard the surface of a human planet with powerful plasma weapons, the surface of the planet often vitrifies. The glass-like appearance of such devastated worlds gave rise to the UNSC slang term "glassing."

GLYPHS
The "letters" that make up the written Forerunner language.

GRAVEMIND
The collective consciousness of the Flood, which became powerful enough to take on a physical form.

GRAY TEAM SPARTANS
A squad of SPARTAN-IIs specially trained to perform covert espionage.

GREAT JOURNEY
A term used by the Covenant to describe the process of transformation into godlike beings that they believe will be set in motion when they find and activate all the holy rings (the Halos).

GREAT SCHISM
The conflict between Covenant Loyalists and Separatists, who split apart in 2552 CE. It is also known as the Covenant Civil War.

GRUNTS
A small, squat species from the world of Balaho. They joined the Covenant in 2142 CE. At first they were used as lowly laborers, but after a rebellion in 2462 CE they were given an increase in status to infantry.

HALO ARRAY
Seven ring installations that, when fired in unison, bring about the destruction of all sentient life in the Galaxy.

HARVEST
A planet in the Epsilon Indi system, once an important producer of food crops for humanity. It was the first human planet to be attacked by the Covenant, who "glassed" it.

HERETICS
A splinter group formed by members of the Covenant. Heretics believed that the High Prophets had lied to their people about the Halo rings being instruments of salvation. The High Prophets attempted to stamp them out.

HIERARCHS see HIGH PROPHETS

HIGH CHARITY
The capital and holy city of the Covenant. It is built around a Forerunner Dreadnought, and is the place of residence of the three High Prophets.

HIGHCOM (HIGH COMMAND)
The highest echelon of the UNSC. Composed of fewer than twenty of the highest-ranking officers, HighCom controls planning, personnel, resources, and equipment. It is also known as "the Admiralty."

HIGH COUNCIL
The highest echelon of the Covenant, who are responsible for making all important decisions. It is made up of about 200 Prophets and Elites. The High Council is headed by the three High Prophets.

HIGH PROPHETS
The three highest leaders of the Covenant, also known as the Hierarchs. The most recent High Prophets are the High Prophet of Mercy, the High Prophet of Truth, and the High Prophet of Regret.

HOLY RINGS
Covenant term for the Halo rings, which they believe have deep religious significance.

HUMAN-COVENANT WAR see COVENANT WAR

HUNTERS
Gigantic warriors formed by colonies of Lekgolo worms operating as one. Each colony shapes itself into a single entity with the appearance of a giant bipedal armored figure.

HURAGOK see ENGINEERS

INSURRECTIONISTS
Humans who seek to break away from the UNSC and the United Earth Government and form their own governments.

INTERPLANETARY WAR
Series of conflicts between the UNSC, the Koslovics, and the Friedans beginning in 2164 CE and ending in 2170 CE.

JACKALS
A spiny, sharp-toothed species who are part of the Covenant. Jackals demonstrate less religious conviction than other members and view their membership as an opportunity to siphon off resources. Their rank is just above the Grunts. They were accepted into the Covenant in 1342 CE.

JIRALHANAE see BRUTES

KEYSHIP
A Forerunner spacecraft with the ability to open portals to the Ark. Keyships are the only ships able to do this.

KIG-YAR see JACKALS

KOSLOVIC MOVEMENT
A political movement arising on Earth in 2160 CE which held as its ideal the Soviet Communist system of the 20th century. It was strongest in the Outer Colonies.

LEKGOLO
A race of worms who became part of the Covenant in 784 BCE. The Covenant first destroyed those Lekgolo who were capable of harming Forerunner artifacts. Some Lekgolo form themselves into pairs of Hunters, the Mgalekgolo.

LIBRARIAN, THE
A Forerunner responsible for gathering samples of the Galaxy's species before the firing of the Halo Array. These samples were later used for reseeding the Galaxy.

"LIFE-OATH"
The pledge by a Hunter to commit itself to the causes of the Covenant.

LINE, THE see MAGINOT SPHERE

LONGSWORD INTERCEPTORS
UNSC fighter craft used to take out Covenant vessels traveling to or from their main ships, and also as an escort for larger UNSC ships such as cruisers and frigates.

LOYALISTS
Those Covenant members who remain faithful to their Prophets and fight against the Heretics.

LUMINARIES
Scanners used by the Covenant to locate other species. The Covenant scavenged them from Forerunner ships.

M12 WARTHOG LRV
UNSC ground vehicle that has been through more than ten incarnations. Speedy and highly maneuverable, it is often used to clear the way before advancing Scorpion tanks.

M808B SCORPION MAIN BATTLE TANK
The standard battle tank of the UNSC. It is virtually impervious to missiles and bullets and is able to negotiate almost any kind of terrain. There have been more than six different versions of the Scorpion Tank.

MAGINOT SPHERE
A defensive sphere of unknown construction that the Forerunners drew around themselves to prevent infection by the Flood.

MANTLE, THE
An ethical code followed by the Forerunners, under which all species in their domain were protected and allowed to evolve without interference.

MARK OF SHAME
A brand applied to the chest of those who are considered to have betrayed or brought shame upon the Covenant.

MASS WEAPONS
Weapons that fire super-dense projectiles at high velocity.

MENDICANT BIAS
The AI on the Forerunner Dreadnought of High Charity. Long before this, it had defected to the Gravemind, becoming rampant and turning against the Forerunners.

METABOLIC CASCADE FAILURE
Sudden physical degeneration of flash-grown clones, due to metabolic instability.

MGALEKGOLO see HUNTERS

MILKY WAY
The Galaxy that contains Earth and the Sol System.

MJOLNIR ARMOR
Advanced armor worn by SPARTAN-IIs in battle. In differing models and generations, it incorporated a fusion-powered exoskeleton, reverse-engineered Covenant energy shields, AI-interface, vacuum-capable coating, and automatic medications. MJOLNIR armor is sometimes referred to as "the Skin" or "the Shell."

MONITORS
Constructs left by the Forerunners on Halo installations to log daily events and ensure the Flood remained in containment. There is one monitor for each Halo. The Covenant call them Oracles.

NAVCOM (NAVIGATION COMMAND)
The UNSC organization responsible for human vessels in space. It is made up of Fleetcom (Fleet Operations Command), NavLogCom (Logistical Operations Command), and NavSpecWep (Naval Special Weapons Operations).

NAVSPECWEP (UNSC NAVAL SPECIAL WEAPONS OPERATIONS)
The branch of the UNSC with operational authority over the Spartans.

NEEDLER
A Covenant weapon frequently used in the Human-Covenant war. It fires pink shards of crystal that home in on an enemy and bury themselves in their flesh, exploding after a time delay.

OFFENSIVE BIAS
A Forerunner AI created to defend against the rampant Mendicant Bias. Ultimately defeated Mendicant Bias after the firing of the Halo Array.

ODST (ORBITAL DROP SHOCK TROOPERS)
UNSC troops who make their combat landings individually rather than by dropships. To do this they use pods known as a Single Occupant Exoatmospheric Insertion Vehicles (SOEIVs), or Human Entry Vehicles. The 105th ODSTs are also known as "Helljumpers."

ONI (OFFICE OF NAVAL INTELLIGENCE)
The arm of NavCom that is responsible for gathering and analyzing information. Many of the organization's orders are taken directly from HighCom.

ORACLE OF HIGH CHARITY, THE
An AI left by the Forerunners on the Dreadnought in the center of High Charity. See MENDICANT BIAS

ORACLES see MONITORS

ORION ARM
A part of the Milky Way Galaxy.

ORION PROJECT
A project created by the ONI to produce improved soldiers by means of bioengineering. It was later resurrected as the SPARTAN-I program.

PARASITE
A life form that draws nourishment from another organism.

PATH, THE
A term used by the Covenant to describe the struggle toward salvation from which no member must waver.

PELICAN
The D77-TC Pelican is a combined dropship and gunship used by the UNSC in operations at ground and near-atmosphere levels. It is also capable of taking off and landing vertically. Armed with machine guns and missiles, it is capable of carrying Scorpion and Warthog Tanks.

PERSONAL ENERGY SHIELD
A 4-foot (1.22-meter) wide shield that Jackals use to protect themselves against projectile attacks in battle. It is activated via a wrist gauntlet. The Covenant developed it using Forerunner technology.

PLASMA GRENADE
Also known as "stickies," these hand-thrown grenades bond with any organic target and explode, causing devastation over an area of up to 40 feet (12 meters). They are a Covenant weapon.

PLASMA PISTOL
A favorite weapon of the Covenant, the Plasma Pistol fires ionized gas bolts that are capable of instantly draining an energy shield.

PLATOON
Within the UNSC, three squads (totalling 36 men) led by a second lieutenant.

PORTABLE GRAVITY LIFT
A device that acts like an elevator but is able to lift and drop things at the same time. It is most used as a quick and discreet way of transferring troops.

PORTAL, THE
A collection of energy generated by a Forerunner artifact buried in Africa. When excavated, the machine opened up a Slipspace gateway to the Ark.

PROPHETS
The ruling caste of the Covenant, Prophets have absolute control in government and religious affairs. In appearance, Prophets are somewhat humanoid. Although more than 7 feet (2 meters) tall, physically they are relatively frail. Their skin is a grayish-pink color.

PROTO-GRAVEMIND
A Flood Form that results from a merging-together of many other forms. It is created when the Flood wants to combine the knowledge from many hosts into one individual. A Proto-Gravemind eventually evolves into a Gravemind.

RAINFOREST WARS
A series of conflicts between UN, Koslovic, and Frieden forces taking place in South America in the 2100s CE.

RAMPANCY
A state of information overload that may affect an AI and cause it to "think itself to death." A rampant AI goes unstable, which may result in madness, delusions of great power, and turning against its creators. Rampancy is dangerous and cannot be reversed, therefore any affected AI must be destroyed.

REACH
The second most populated planet in the UNSC, including several important military headquarters. It was also the UNSC's main naval base and home to many ONI bases, including CASTLE base.

"RECLAIMERS"
The real meaning of a sacred Forerunner glyph that described humans. It was mistranslated as "reclamation" by the Covenant, who thought it meant humans had artifacts to be collected.

REFLECTIVE ENERGY SHIELD
An invisible protective barrier around a vessel that repels most attacks by explosive, mass, and energy weapons.

REFORMERS
The group of San 'Shyuum who defied their people's tradition that it was heresy to enter the Dreadnought. After doing so, they were able to activate the craft and escape their homeworld.

REGIMENT
Within the UNSC, three battalions plus another group known as "Regimental Headquarters Section." It totals 3,000 men.

RESEEDING
Repopulating the Galaxy after it has been wiped of all sentient life by means of previously saved samples of species.

SANGHEILI *see* ELITES

SAN 'SHYUUM *see* PROPHETS

SCORPION TANK *see* M808B SCORPION MAIN BATTLE TANK

SECESSIONIST UNION
A rebel organization formed in 2461 CE by members of the Colonies who wanted to break away from the UNSC. It was also known as the People's Occupation Government.

SHIELD WORLD
An artificial planet with a Slipspace rift at its center. Within it, living beings could access a micro Dyson Sphere shelter while the Halo Array was fired.

SILENT CARTOGRAPHER
A map room on a Halo installation that shows the location of all its rooms, chambers, and passageways.

SOEIV (SINGLE OCCUPANT EXOATMOSPHERIC INSERTION VEHICLE)
The pod used by an ODST to make landings. It is about 18 feet (5.5 meters) tall and over 8 feet (2.4 meters) wide, but most of this space is taken up by equipment.

SLIPSPACE
An intertwining of several layers of dimensional space, giving the effect of a folded, scrunched, or rippled area. Slipspace can be traveled through at speeds faster than light, although at some significant risk.

SLIPSPACE PORTALS
Ruptures in space that allow faster-than-light travel between stars.

SOL SYSTEM
The home planetary system of humankind, made up of Mercury, Venus, Earth, Mars, Jupiter, Saturn, Uranus, and Neptune.

SPARTAN PROGRAMS
Three projects run by the UNSC with the aim of creating super-soldiers. SPARTAN-I was based on mental and physical augmentation of adult volunteers. In SPARTAN-II, genetically gifted children underwent years of intense training before being augmented with advanced technology. SPARTAN-III removed the emphasis on technology and concentrated on producing cheaper, expendable super-soldiers in greater numbers.

SQUAD
Within the UNSC, a group of twelve soldiers led by a corporal or lance corporal.

STOICS
The group of San 'Shyuum who refused to enter the Dreadnought, believing it too holy to set foot in. They were left behind on their homeworld by the Reformers, who departed on the ship after learning how to activate it.

TRANSFER AUTHORIZATION CODE
A code contained within a physical key (such as a chip) that enables an AI to move from one electronic system to another.

UEG (UNIFIED EARTH GOVERNMENT)
The global civilian government of Earth and its colonies that grew out of the UN at the conclusion of the Interplanetary War.

UNGGOY *see* GRUNTS

UNICOM (UNIFIED GROUND COMMAND)
The organization in control of human ground-based operations, such as infantry and recon operations.

UNSC (UNITED NATIONS SPACE COMMAND)
The organization in control of the combined military forces of the UEG in space.

UNSC CRUISER
The largest and most imposing ships in the UNSC fleet, cruisers are thickly armored and equipped with a heavy arsenal of weapons. They also carry twenty-four Longsword Interceptors.

UNYIELDING HIEROPHANT
An immense, 11-mile- (18-km) long Covenant space station. It could carry more than 500 ships and hundreds of thousands of troops. The Unyielding Hierophant was preparing to attack Earth when it was destroyed by Master Chief and his team.

WARTHOG *see* M12 WARTHOG LRV

"WASH OUT"
A hazard of the SPARTAN-II Program involving the physical breakdown of a soldier during the augmentation process. Nearly fifty percent of

SPARTAN-IIs "washed out," and most of these died.

WRIT OF UNION
The treaty by which a species formally joined the Covenant. The original Writ of Union was made between the San 'Shyuum and the Sangheili in 852 BCE.

YANME'E *see* DRONES

INDEX

LONDON, NEW YORK,
MELBOURNE, MUNICH, AND DELHI

ACKNOWLEDGMENTS

DK would like to thank Alicia Brattin, Frank O'Connor, Kevin Grace, Jonathan Goff, Jeremy
Patenaude, Rick Achberger, and Alicia Hatch at Microsoft. DK would also like to thank Tobias
Buckell for his Halo insight, Craig Mullins for his artwork, and his agent Melody Meisel Klein.
Thanks to Sarah Phillips and Patricia Hallam for editorial assistance and to James Stevenson
for his gaming expertise. Thanks also to Bungie Studios, who have created, informed and
defined the story of Halo since the very beginning. Lastly, thanks to Halo fans everywhere for
helping to fill this universe with your own stories, battles, and triumphs.

The publisher would like to thank the following for their kind
permission to reproduce their photographs:

(Key: a-above; b-below/bottom; c-center; l-left; r-right; t-top)

Corbis: E. M. Pasieka / Science Photo Library 214-215; Corbis: Bettmann
284-285; William Radcliffe /Science Faction 282-283, 283br;
Stocktrek Images 288-289; STScI / NASA /
ESA / J. Hester (ASU) / Hubble 286-287, 287br.

PROJECT EDITOR ELIZABETH DOWSETT

ADDITIONAL EDITORS:
JO CASEY, LUCY DOWLING, LAURA GILBERT, JULIA MARCH,
HEATHER SCOTT, VICKI TAYLOR

SENIOR DESIGNER LYNNE MOULDING

ADDITIONAL DESIGNERS:
OWEN BENNETT, DAN BUNYAN, JON HALL, GUY HARVEY, NATHAN MARTIN,
JOHNNY PAU, MARK RICHARDS, LISA SODEAU, JULIE THOMPSON

ART DIRECTOR LISA LANZARINI

MANAGING EDITOR CATHERINE SAUNDERS
PUBLISHING MANAGER SIMON BEECROFT
CATEGORY PUBLISHER ALEX ALLAN

PRODUCTION EDITOR SEAN DALY
PRODUCTION CONTROLLER NORMA WEIR

JACKET ILLUSTRATION BY CRAIG MULLINS

FIRST PUBLISHED IN THE UNITED STATES IN 2009 BY DK PUBLISHING
375 HUDSON STREET, NEW YORK, NEW YORK 10014
THIS EDITION PUBLISHED IN 2010

11 12 13 14 10 9 8 7 6 5 4
HD182—01/10

DK BOOKS ARE AVAILABLE AT SPECIAL DISCOUNTS WHEN PURCHASED IN BULK FOR SALES PROMOTIONS, PREMIUMS, FUND-RAISING, OR
EDUCATIONAL USE. FOR DETAILS, CONTACT: DK PUBLISHING SPECIAL MARKETS, 375 HUDSON STREET, NEW YORK, NEW YORK 100014,
SPECIALSALES@DK.COM.

A CATALOG RECORD FOR THIS BOOK IS AVAILABLE FROM THE LIBRARY OF CONGRESS.
ISBN: 978-0-7566-5549-5

REPRODUCED BY MDP IN THE UK
PRINTED AND BOUND IN CHINA BY LEO

DISCOVER MORE AT
WWW.DK.COM

➤ **"I THINK WE'RE JUST GETTING STARTED."**